THE IRAN-CONTRA CONNECTION

The Iran-Contra Connection

Secret Teams and Covert Operations in the Reagan Era

by

Jonathan Marshall
Peter Dale Scott
Jane Hunter

South End Press   Boston, MA

Design typeset and layout by the South End Press collective
Manufactured in the U.S.
Cover by Jeff Smith

Library of Congress Cataloging-in-Publication Data
Marshall, Jonathan.
    The Iran-Contra connection.

    Includes index.
      1. Iran-Contra Affair, 1985-   .   2. United States
—Foreign relations—1981-   .   3. Intelligence
service—United States—History—20th century.
4. United States. Central Intelligence Agency.
I. Scott, Peter Dale. II. Hunter, Jane .
III. Title.
E876.M36   1987   973.927   87-13059
ISBN 0-89608-292-x
ISBN 0-89708-291-1 (pbk.)

South End Press   116 St. Botolph St.   Boston, MA 02115

97 96 95 94 93 92 91 90 89 88 87   1 2 3 4 5 6 7 8 9

Table of Contents

Acknowledgements

Some of the material in this book appeared earlier, in different form, in the *Tribune* (Oakland, CA), Pacific News Service, *The Nation, Crime and Social Justice*, and *Israeli Foreign Affairs*.

The authors would like to gratefully acknowledge Eric Bentley, Pete Carey, the Data Center (Oakland, CA), Paul L. Hoch, Ted Rubinstein, and Peter Spagnuolo for their assistance in the preparation of this book. We dedicate this book to the victims of unjust U.S. policies, declared and undeclared—and to those who work to create a world in which there will be no more victims.

Preface

by Richard Falk

R.W. Apple, the *New York Times* correspondent with a sure feel for the sweet spot in the public mood, introduces the published text of *The Tower Commission Report* (Times Books, 1987, p. XV) with a focus on managerial ineptitude:

> [T]he report pictures a National Security Council led by reckless cowboys, off on their own on a wild ride, taking direct operational control of matters that are the customary province of more sober agencies such as the CIA, the State Department and the Defense Department.

As a summary this is not too misleading, but offered as it is, in praise of the aptness of the Tower Report, it contributes its bits to the rituals of mystification that have become part of the American experience whenever the integrity of the governmental process is called deeply into question. The Warren Commission Report after John F. Kennedy's assassination initiated this kind of exercise in the politics of reassurance that now seems indispensable at times of public crisis. And yet the reassurance rarely reassures. So it is with the Tower Report. Nothing essential about the Iran-contra disclosures is there resolved.

Contrary to the Tower presentation, the Iran-contra connections were not anomalous expressions of U.S. foreign policy, nor would the outcomes have necessarily been very different if the execution of the policy had been entrusted to professionals working for those supposedly more sober agencies. If we think back, the Bay of Pigs venture was pure CIA, exhibiting in 1961 at least as little respect for bureaucratic proprieties and simple dictates of prudence. Even without the benefit of recall, we need only consider the current CIA role in relation to the contras, which includes disseminating a manual advocating selective recourse to civilian assassination and arms supply arrangements that rely upon the darkest criminal and fascist elements to be found in the hemisphere.

The opportuneness of this book by Jonathan Marshall, Peter Dale Scott and Jane Hunter cannot be overstated. The authors provide a comprehensive account of what lies below the surface of mainstream perception, and as such, enable us to interpret these events in a coherent and clarifying fashion. Indeed, to be useful citizens these days we must be armed with such "subversive" texts. If we adhere to the customary decorum in the manner of Apple/Tower, we will find ourselves mesmerized by the investigative narrative of who did what when and who knew about it, especially in the White House. As Watergate showed us, such a drama can be exciting theater, but as politics it works out to be one more pacification program, closing down any tendency to ask questions about institutions, procedures, and prerogatives.

The Iran-Contra Connection is as disturbing as the Tower Report is consoling. This extraordinary book narrates a frightening, shocking story that shakes the foundations of the republic. Equally impressive, these crucial interpretations are accompanied by such substantial evidence and documentation as to be convincing for any reader with even a slightly open mind. It is quite remarkable that such a substantial book coincides with, or possibly precedes, the crest of the historical wave of public indignation and confusion occasioned by the original revelations of November 1986.

Briefly, let me mention some of the more dramatic aspects of the picture portrayed. There is, above all, the lucid exposure of the deep roots of what appears on the surface as bureaucratic malady. The policies embodied in both the arms sales and the diversion of funds for a variety of dirty purposes were carried out by powerful transnational networks of individuals and organizations long associated with rabid anti-communism, and centering on a mixture of former CIA officials and anti-Castro exiles, but stretching out to include military and civilian centers of reaction, as well as a mercenary cadre available for lethal undertakings of any sort. An extremely distressing element in the story is the incredibly durable half-life of former career participants in covert operations; only for plutonium is the disposal problem greater! For money, thrills, habit, and conviction these men find ways to regroup in the private sector and carry on with their efforts to destroy progressive and nationalist political possibilities in Third

World countries, as well as to sell arms and drugs, and carry out an unauthorized private sector foreign policy that is vicious and invisible and acknowledges no limits. An unappreciated cost of the Reagan years has been to introduce into the sinews of government the virus of fascist conspiratorial politics, especially in the Western Hemisphere. In this regard, the reliance on North and Poindexter is not a managerial glitch, but rather a decision to depend on those with such a passionate commitment to the radical right who happened to be positioned for action, and would be trusted to serve as faithful instruments of policy, uninhibited by either standard bureaucratic procedures or constitutional restraints.

It may be consoling, but it is wrongheaded to explain what went awry by reference to a rogue NSC or by the insistence that Reagan is indeed senile. It is now acknowledged that William Casey masterminded the whole undertaking, himself evidently seeking the more personalist control possible within the NSC setting than could be achieved within the reconstituted and still somewhat law-oriented CIA of the 1980s. Marshall, Scott, and Hunter explain the powerful circumstantial case that links large campaign contributions from and solicitation to the far right going back to the late 1970s, especially from sources prominently connected to the struggle to suppress democratic forces in Central America, with the Reagan resolve to stand and fight in El Salvador and Nicaragua. The immediate priority of the Reagan presidency to intervene in the region may well be an outgrowth of these pre-election relationships, and what is more, the subsequent tendency to adhere addictively to such policies despite their failure and unpopularity, and in the face of Congressional opposition, raises suspicions that some sort of illicit bargain had been struck. The adroit withdrawal from Lebanon after the 1983 incident killing 241 U.S. marines, exhibiting Reagan's skill in retrenchment, contrasts sharply with the compulsiveness of the contra commitment. All of Reagan's talent as a leader and command over the political process has been needed to keep the contra cause even vaguely viable during the years of his presidency, and at great cost to his leverage on other issues.

But what is more frightening than these indications of presidential gridlock is the extent to which the real center of power and decision making on these matters may not even have been in the White House. A significant degree of policy-forming leadership may have actually been "privatized," passing to an assortment of fringe forces represented by such notables as Singlaub, Secord, and Clines, who in this sense provided the basic framework within which Reagan, McFarlane and Casey have acted, with North and Poindexter featured as trustworthy handmaidens. In this regard, the deferred consequences of the long buildup within government during the 1950s and 1960s of a secret paramilitary capability entrusted with interventionary missions is beginning to be evident. The problem centers upon the CIA, and its large number of agents and ex-agents working around the globe in close collaboration with right-wing and criminal elements, including those that were operating death squads in El Salvador and Argentina, enlisting support from groups and individuals who were overtly fascist, even neo-Nazi. The laudable post-Vietnam move in Congress to cut back on the covert operations role of the CIA during the Nixon and Carter presidencies created an optical illusion that this secret government was being substantially destroyed, as indeed many hundred agents were prematurely retired or even fired. Thus CIA alumni were dumped into society or cynically relocated "off-shore," bitter, ambitious, and in contact with various anti-communist exile groups, as well as with a cohort of their colleagues continuing at work within the agency, themselves embittered by the adverse turn of the wheel of political fortune that deprecated their craft and scorned their politics. Such a subterranean presence brings terrorism home, as during the anti-Castro bombings of the 1970s carried out by exile extremists in the eastern part of the United States. At the same time, there is created the nucleus of a political conspiracy waiting to prey upon the very bureaucracy that seemed ungrateful, and lacks the convictions and capabilities needed to uphold American interests in a hostile world.

This drastic mind-set of the resentful paramilitary professional is receptive to any proposal for adventure, however sordid, so long as money, violence, and right-wing backing are assured. For Reagan to convict himself of terrorism by identifying as a contra is to suggest how close to power this kind of extremist politics apparently came. And what makes the whole dynamic so sinister is that the citizenry had become deluded enough to believe that by supporting Reagan they were affirming an archetypal embodiment of American values. At last, it seemed that most of us again had a president capable of making us feel good and proud to be Americans. True, this affirmation included a measured cruelty toward losers in the capitalist rumble, but this too struck the bulk of the middle-class white majority as the American way of sustaining a lean efficiency in an era of impending struggle over shares of the world market. Unlike the rosy picture accepted by most Americans, Reaganism has undermined constitutionalism in structural ways by implementing national security policy through a reliance on capabilities outside of government, entailing such violent and unprincipled action that it became disillusioning even for adherents of a neo-conservative political ethos. To embody this power shift in policy has made it necessary to circumvent Congressional will on the contra issue, which for rightist perspectives has become as symbolic as the Palestinian or South African issues are for the Third World. In effect, Iran is the tail wagging the contra dog. The dangerous temptation to wheel and deal in Tehran probably proved irresistible because it promised to shake loose some of the slush funds needed to pursue in earnest the forbidden agenda of the far right. The possible release of hostages from Lebanon was, from this angle, merely part of "the deep cover" for this kind of ideological cabal that takes added delight in defying Congress and public opinion, and overcoming the complacency and decadence of the American polity. At no time in American history have the basic forms of popular democracy been so jeopardized, rendered vulnerable to dangerous and destructive forces.

We find ourselves as a country in an extremely precarious situation. The Reagan presidency has rebuilt the formal legions of covert operations in the CIA and has, as well, given a taste of power to the shadow network of ex-CIA, ex-military, exile, and extremist forces in this country and abroad. Unless this structure is exposed and effectively discredited and dissolved, there is every prospect that it will continue to do severe damage. It is not just a matter of revitalizing constitutionalism at home, it is also a question of protecting innocent people overseas and here at home from cruelty, repression, and outright criminality. The dangers are societal, as well as statal. This paramilitary orientation ravages society by preying upon its capacities for law and morality, infusing drugs, corrupting police and local government, and convincing the citizenry that their lives are played out in a virtual cesspool of vice and menace, and that activism is futile and unpatriotic.

Reinforcing this drift toward contrapolitics has been the special relationship with Israel. This book devotes two chapters to documenting the degree to which Israel contrived the Iran-contra diplomacy and contributed to its implementation. Israel desperately needed customers for surplus arms, hard currency, and an involvement in Latin America that would enable some relief from its situation of diplomatic isolation. Pre-Khomeini Iran was a major outlet for Israeli surplus arms production. After the fall of the Shah, Israel became the only reliable base for United States strategic operations in the Middle East, long regarded as the most volatile war zone in the world. In light of public and Congressional opposition to support for the contras and the falling away of Argentina after the Falklands/Malvinas War, it was left to Israel to fill the void. In all, the Israeli role is part of the deviousness with which unpopular and unlawful foreign policy initiatives were sustained during the Reagan years.

Even before this book, it was evident that when it came to national security, our governmental system of checks and balances and electoral accountability was not working. The militarist consensus embodied in the state was too strong in relation to the formal checks of Congress and party rivalry and the informal checks of public opinion, media, and education. But now we find that even the modest limits set by these checks can be rendered inoperative by forces more extreme and corrupt than the governmental consensus, and that for these forces there are as yet no appropriate mechanisms of exposure and accountability. In this sense, North and Poindexter, like Rosencranz and Guildenstern, are quite expendable!

Richard Falk
Princeton, New Jersey
April 1987

I.
Introduction

The Iran-contra crisis has plunged President Reagan from his former Olympian popularity into the most serious political scandal since Watergate. In the process it has called into question not only the viability of his administration, but the future of U.S. intervention in the Third World and the ability of the public or Congress to redirect foreign policy along more humane and constructive lines.

"Iragua," "Iranscam," "Iranamuck"—the cute name for the latest crisis are as endless as the wags' imagination. But what they signify remains far from clear. In their narrowest and least useful meaning, the terms refer to the probable diversion of money paid into Swiss bank accounts by Iranian arms purchasers to the anti-Sandinistas known as the contras. In a broader and more urgent sense, they describe a usurpation of power by an imperial President bent on subverting democratic processes at home by covert means to satisfy the demands of ruthless policies abroad.

The intrigues that constitute that usurpation reach back long before the initiation of the Iran arms deals, back at least to the formulation of Reagan's anti-Nicaragua strategy in 1981. And to understand the people and institutions that made those intrigues possible requires an historical vision extending to the brutal covert wars in Cuba and Indochina in the 1960s, even to the founding of the CIA in 1947.

If the Iran and contra scandals have given the nation a chance to glimpse that vision, it is because they finally opened a crack in the

1

President's teflon political shield. On November 25, 1986 what had been a growing political controversy over revelations of US arms sales to Iran became a full-blown scandal. Reagan went before a nationally televised press conference to confess that he "was not fully informed on the nature of the activities undertaken in connection with this (Iran) initiative" and to announce that his national security adviser, Admiral John Poindexter, and his National Security Council aide, Lt. Col. Oliver North, had been relieved of their duties.

Then Attorney General Edwin Meese took the podium to deliver the bombshell: funds from the Iran arms sales had been diverted, possibly illegally, to the contras.[1] The issue was no longer one of judgment but of law.

What was revealed was nothing less than a conspiracy at the highest levels of government to break the law and contravene public policy on Iran, terrorism and military aid to the contras. Skeptics who deny the existence of conspiracies—after all, how many people can keep a secret?—miss the point. This conspiracy had never been a well-kept secret. The administration had a more effective defense than secrecy: a President whose personal popularity could deflect isolated charges and accusations and a political opposition whose disunity discredited it in the public's eye. Without Meese certifying before the nation the existence of a veritable scandal, prior press revelations never added up to an issue of political significance.

What made the difference, and what ultimately put Meese up on that podium, was a gradual and almost imperceptible weakening of the Reagan presidency in the fall of 1986. For the first time he had begun to lose the unquestioned support of his conservative constituency.

The broadest cause of the erosion of support was the administration's apparent inability to hit upon an agenda for the second half of its final term. The staggering federal deficit persisted despite Reagan's increasingly half-hearted attempts to command domestic budget cuts. The military buildup stalled in Congress. The President could not decide between arms control and Star Wars. Social legislation—on abortion, prayer in the schools and the like—was going nowhere. Tax reform inspired no great public enthusiasm. And forward movement was stalled by what one conservative commentator called the "internecine" warfare between Reagan's top aides.[2]

Then came a series of episodes that cast doubt on Reagan's leadership, judgment and political clout. His swap of a Soviet for the American journalist Nicholas Daniloff disappointed conservatives and foreshadowed future revelations of hostage bargaining with Tehran. Worse yet was for those conservatives Reagan's performance at Reykjavik; in impromptu arms talks with Soviet leaders, the President betrayed a hopelessly inadequate grasp of strategic issues. When Congress passed sanctions against South Africa, Reagan could not prevent a veto override in both Houses. Most important, on the first Tuesday in November Reagan lost his key political ally, the Republican Senate.

As the teflon chipped away, the press became bolder. It had always boasted a few fine investigative reporters whose early stories now seem remarkably prescient, like the CBS News account from 1984 of the CIA's use of Southern Air Transport, a private cargo line later tied to the Iran and contra affairs, to transport arms, airplane parts and soldiers to the contras via Honduras.[3] AP reporters Brian Barger and Robert Parry consistently broke stories throughout 1984 and 1985 about Oliver North, the private aid network, and the contras' involvement in arms and drug trafficking. Jack Anderson reported the administration's tilt toward Tehran, and its arms sales, in April 1986. In July 1986, the financial conduits used by North for his fund diversions began unravelling in public.[4] But few people listened: Reagan's popularity bolstered his aides' denials.

His weakness began to show—and the press in turn became more vigorous—following the crash of a contra supply plane in Nicaragua in early October 1986. Secretary of State George Shultz declared that the "private people" who hired the plane "had no connection with the U.S. government at all"[5]—otherwise the administration would be in violation of a law barring the provision of military aid to the contras.

But the pilot who survived, Eugene Hasenfus, made statements that top administration and CIA officials had their fingerprints all over the operation. Ample documentation that went down with the plane confirmed it. So did telephone records subsequently made available from the Salvadoran "safe house" where the whole supply operation was managed. The calls from that base to the White House clinched the case. In the following two weeks, a deluge of news stories painted a picture of mercenaries, terrorists and private "spooks" in the indirect employ of administration officials to evade the will of Congress.[6]

On October 8, the FBI announced that it was investigating the company linked to the two American pilots killed in the supply plane crash: Southern Air Transport. FBI officials were soon to learn, by way of worried NSC operators, that Southern Air was just then involved in top secret shipments of arms to Iran. A mini-coverup began—in fact, a 26-day delay in the FBI's investigation[7]—but the White House was fast losing control.

Behind the scenes, meanwhile, disgruntled Iranian political factions had lost faith in the arms-for-hostages deals with Washington. Leaflets distributed in Tehran in mid-October revealed some details of a secret US mission to Tehran. Then on November 3, the weekly Lebanese magazine *Al Shiraa*, quoting sources close to the Ayatollah Hussein Ali Montazeri, revealed that former National Security Adviser Robert McFarlane had personally visited Iran to trade military spare parts for American hostages held in Beirut. Not to be outflanked, the speaker of Iran's parliament who had been conducting the negotiations, Ali Akbar Hashemi Rafsanjani, moved preemptively to distance himself from the embarrassment of negotiating with representatives of the "Great Satan." His confirmation that McFarlane and four other Americans had traveled to Iran set the press loose on its next—and far more explosive—scandal.

What followed were a classic series of denials and half denials until the Reagan/Meese press conference blew the lid off the story. That press conference was the result of a complex correlation of forces: blackmail threats by investors in the Iran arms deals, complaints by Secretary of State Shultz over what he believed would be perjured testimony before Congress by CIA Director William Casey, and North's statement to Meese that funds had been diverted to Central America. Bureaucratic rivalries within the administration, in particular the bitter reaction of officials kept in the dark about the arms deals, ensured the quick disintegration of the administration's efforts at damage control.

Since then, the Senate Select Committee on Intelligence and the Tower Commission, appointed by President Reagan to report on the scandal, have issued initial findings on the Iran deals and certain related aspects of the contra supply operation. More investigations are underway by Congress, an independent counsel and armies of reporters.

We are indebted to all of these sources for the raw material of the book that follows. But as vital as the search for information is the contest to impose an interpretation. If the nation is to profit at all from its recent political trauma it must come to understand what went wrong and what is needed to cure the political pathologies that, in retrospect, were inadequately addressed after Watergate. But if the reporters and congressional investigators pose their questions too narrowly, the answers cannot supply that understanding.[8]

Was "Irangate" the Reagan-era equivalent of a third-rate burglary—an aberrational lapse by an inattentive president whose "compassion outstripped his competence," to quote Sen. Pete Wilson of California? Did it simply reflect the inadequacy of President Reagan's "management style," as members of the Tower Commission declared? Did it call merely for a housecleaning to rid the administration of a few bad "cowboys" among the NSC and CIA staff?

If the American public learns these lessons it will have learned nothing. New faces will inhabit the old slots. But the substance of policy and the potential for future abuses will remain intact.

We shall argue instead that the extraordinary breakdown in political judgment, the bizarre execution of policy and the outright violations of law were all part of a much broader aggrandizement of power by an administration committed to a militant program of foreign intervention and forced by domestic political opposition to use covert means to achieve it. Ronald Reagan's election in 1980 marked not only the personal triumph of a former conservative outcast, but the victory of individuals—many of them CIA or military special operations veterans—dedicated to regaining power at home and abroad through clandestine politics. Emboldened by Reagan's landslide victory, which they interpreted as a sweeping mandate for action, they turned the power of the presidency against Congress and the American people in the course of turning it against foreign enemies.

We shall argue further that the Iran and contra scandals were no aberration. They were a logical product of an administration that prized "covert" above "democratic" politics. In that spirit, former National Security Adviser Robert McFarlane wrote his long-time deputy Oliver North, "if only the world knew how many times you have kept a semblance of integrity and gumption to US policy, they would make you secretary of state. But they can't know and would complain if they did— such is the state of democracy in the late 20th century."[9]

Time and space constraints have necessarily limited the scope of this argument. We make no attempt to recount the full, sorry history of U.S. intervention in Latin America, nor the political and economic relationships underlying that history. A valuable and growing literature, including Noam Chomsky's *Turning the Tide*,[10] illuminates those essential topics. Nor, with our focus on the Reagan years, can we fully suggest the similar complicity of past administrations in foreign crimes and domestic coverups.

This is a book about Irangate and Contragate, not primarily about the contras or Iranians. There are relatively few Nicaraguan or Iranian names here, for this is emphatically a book about the United States. This analytical limitation imposes a narrower moral focus than the whole of the events in Central America and Middle East surely warrant. In the larger context, the murder of peasants and health workers in Nicaragua and the stoking of a war that has already claimed hundreds of thousands of lives in Iran and Iraq far outweigh the legal or constitutional implications of America's scandals.

But the millions of foreign victims have a stake in curbing the people and institutions in Washington that promote the destructive maintainance and expansion of American power abroad. To that end, an assertion of law and democratic control over foreign policy is at least a necessary, if not sufficient, condition. Our book is not written to promote a total politics of critical consciousness and understanding but to end the covert policies that have given Reagan—and prior presidents—the means to launch costly and often tragic interventions overseas. This is a subject to which we shall return in our conclusions. Suffice it to say for now that in Iran and Central America, as in the Vietnam War, those responsible for intervention were not the American people. Our book is an act of faith that ordinary citizens, if educated to the lies, law-breaking, drug-running and other scandals of the Iran-contra secret teams, can be roused to protest and force an end to such interventions, wherever their political sympathies lie.

II.
Contracting Out U.S. Foreign Policy

The imperial presidency, temporarily checked by the Vietnam defeat and Watergate scandal, has reemerged during the Reagan years. As always, the reason lies in excessive congressional deference to the executive branch. But since 1980, presidential power has been aggrandized by the Reagan administration's sophisticated strategies for circumventing Congress in the shaping and implementing of foreign policy.

President Reagan's secret weapon is "contracting out" such normal government functions as funding and executing policy to the "private" sector while keeping policy making itself in the hands of the state. But unlike typical commercial examples of the practice, the administration has contracted to agents who are themselves total creatures of government—in particular, of government intelligence agencies. In their "private" capacities, however, these agents nonetheless fall largely outside congressional purview.

This strategy involves much more than confining policy making and implementation to a tight circle within the National Security Council, however much a dismayed Secretary of State George Shultz has focused public attention on his personal exclusion from decisions. President Reagan's dependence on the NSC to the near exclusion of traditional bureaucracies is, after all, far from unique; Henry Kissinger mastered that art in the Nixon era and for it won the admiration of Congress and the American press.

7

Reagan's innovation was much more significant: while bypassing standard channels of government, his administration found foreign governments and rich individuals to contribute the money; CIA and military special operations veterans to contribute the manpower; and private firms to contribute the logistics for its operations. In effect, White House operatives set up a parallel Treasury, Army, Air Force and State Department to negotiate with terrorists, fight covert wars and subvert the law wherever they deemed appropriate. Farming such covert operations outside even the CIA served to insulate the president and his advisors from scrutiny and responsibility.[1]

As a result, major elements of White House policy escaped public notice or congressional review. This parallel private network functioned outside normal lines of oversight and accountability, and once set in motion, could operate effectively with minimal presidential guidance. But as distinguished from "privatization," a term often misapplied to the Iran and contra affairs, the contracting method always left essential policy direction in the White House.

The Reagan strategy had its roots in the classic intelligence practice of using proprietaries and "cut-outs" to effect policy while preserving deniability. Always useful against unwanted public scrutiny, these techniques were perfectly suited to the 1980s' political environment of presidential activism on behalf of the "Reagan Doctrine," the commitment to roll back pro-Soviet regimes in the Third World. Congressional doubts and public hostility made overt pursuit of that doctrine difficult or impossible. Even the CIA was a problematic tool of policy owing to legal requirements that it report covert operations to Congress.[2]

"Since the Vietnam War," one Reagan NSC member told a reporter, reflecting the widespread distrust of Congress by administration policymakers, "we have had this growing involvement by the legislative branch in the details of foreign policy that—you can make a constitutional argument—are properly left to the president. When you do that, you drive him in the direction of using other techniques to achieve objectives."[3]

Ironically, however, deep-cover contracting also appealed to administration activists frustrated by bureaucratic gridlock between warring departments and the tendency of rival policymakers to leak details of unpopular, unwise or illegal policies.

Such rivalries "made it impossible to function at all" except in secret, argued former Pentagon special operations planner Noel Koch. The lesson that individuals like Oliver North drew, according to Koch, was "If you're going to do anything bold or innovative, you're going to have to do things through irregular channels."[4]

Or as another "covert missions planner" said of North's decision to rely on former Pentagon special operations veterans for his secret missions, "the CIA and NSC have no capability to do things in a secure fashion. You want to do something quietly, then you can't tell the bureaucracies. Here's a guy who can go to key people in foreign countries and get things done. As a private citizen, he has no obligation to tell anyone."[5]

And quite apart from the matter of capabilities, many insiders doubted even the resolve of the CIA to implement tough policies abroad. Angelo Codevilla, a hawkish former staffer on the Senate Intelligence Committee, expressed the view of many "roll-back" conservatives in Washington:

> The Director of the Central Intelligence Agency, William Casey...personally seems to favor the victory of liberation movements. His Agency has the charter for dispensing the aid. But from among the CIA's senior personnel have come strong echoes of the State Department's view of the role of liberation movements in U.S.-Soviet relations. In their dealings with Congress and the NSC, CIA officials have often outdone even their colleagues in the State Department in reticence to provide aid to such movements quantitatively and qualitatively sufficient for victory, declaring that the Agency would rather be rid of the burden of supplying such aid at all.[6]

The White House decisionmaking center for covert operations and contracting-out strategy lay within a tiny team of select State, Defense, CIA and NSC officials known as the "208 Committee" or "Policy Development Group." Oliver North, the workaholic organizer of secret contra supply missions and Iran arms deals, was one of its most active members.[7] Meeting in the Crisis Management Center in Room 208 of the Old Executive Office Building, surrounded by secure computer data links to the National Security Agency, this group could plan secret operations free from the obligation to report to the intelligence committees of Congress. Its mission was to implement the Reagan doctrine of fighting Soviet influence throughout the Third World, wherever possible by supporting indigenous forces.[8] Its thorough overview of missions and logistics included such details as "which weapons will be shipped, which secret warehouse goods used, which middlemen will deliver them to clandestine airstrips."[9] For the most sensitive policies, as with the Iran arms shipments, only a few members of even this group took part in policy discussions.

For North and others in this select circle, the guiding principle was power and the task was to expand it without answering to other authorities. As one White House memo from 1982 outlined the mission of "Project Democracy"—the rubric under which the NSC began to undertake foreign policy initiatives of its own—"we need to examine how law and executive order can be made more liberal to permit covert action on a broader scale."[10] Contracting-out provided means to subvert the law and stretch the scope of executive orders.

Nicaragua: The Test Case

Nicaragua saw the first application of the strategy. The Reagan administration's policy toward the Sandinistas from the start was summed up by the title of a report prepared by then-State Department counselor Robert McFarlane in early 1981: "Taking the war to Nicaragua."[11] But owing to congressional reticence, the White House had to lie about its ultimate intentions, pledging that CIA assistance to the contras merely served to block Sandinista arms shipments to the Salvadoran rebels. "There were always two tracks," one CIA official explained, "the publicly stated CIA objective of interdicting weapons to Salvadoran guerrillas, and the overthrow of the Sandinista government."[12] On March 9, 1981, President Reagan took the first step to launching the covert war under that public goal by issuing an official "finding" that Nicaraguan arms smuggling was harming U.S. national security interests.

The need for continued deception and greater action prompted a November 16, 1981 presidential order to begin a full-scale campaign against Nicaragua. It authorized an initial $19.5 million for the guerrilla war, justified once again by the need for arms interdiction.[13] But as one contra source said of that rationale in 1982, "If that's what the CIA told Congress, they forgot to tell us."[14]

The November order specifically directed the CIA to wage its covert war "primarily through non-Americans" and "with foreign governments as appropriate."[15] In implementing that early version of the "contracting out" strategy, the CIA piggybacked on operations already underway by two other governments: Argentina and Israel.

The first of these "deniable" partners was Argentina, whose military rulers had, since the mid-1970s, unleashed an orgy of violence against their own civilian population in the course of stamping out a leftist guerrilla movement. Argentine agents had worked in Nicaragua even before Somoza's overthrow to help track down Argentine Montoneros guerrillas who had teamed up in exile with the Sandinistas; they also advised security forces and death squads in Guatemala and El Salvador. Now Argentina's military junta supplied as many as 100 veterans of its own dirty war against the left to train the first contras in urban terrorist tactics and guerrilla war. These were not just any contras: Argentina's proteges were all recruits from Somoza's brutal National Guard. Visits to Buenos Aires in 1981 by such Reagan administration emissaries as Joint Chiefs of Staff Chairman General Edwin Meyer, Ambassador-at-Large Vernon Walters and UN Ambassador Jeane Kirkpatrick helped establish the alliance of the CIA and Argentine military in Central America. A November 1 meeting of CIA director William Casey and the American-trained leader of Argentina's military junta, Gen. Leopold Galtieri, cemented it.[16]

At the same time, CIA paymasters—who had allocated $50 million to the training program[17]—prevailed on several key contra leaders to unify their anti-Sandinista groups behind the Argentine-trained veterans of Somoza's National Guard. Thus the Nicaraguan Democratic Front, or FDN, was formed on August 11, 1981, just when Gen. Galtieri was in Washington on an official visit.[18]

Foreign Money, Foreign Arms

Money for the contras that once flowed freely from CIA contingency accounts began to dry up in 1983 when Congress began setting limits on its funding of the burgeoning and ever-more-unpopular war. Legislators were finally awakening to the fact that the Argentine-trained Somocistas wanted not a democratic accommodation with the Sandinistas, but their ouster.

On December 8, 1982, the House of Representatives passed a bill sponsored by Rep. Edward Boland of Massachusetts barring U.S. covert actions "for the purpose of overthrowing the government of Nicaragua." That new law alone did not slow the administration down, but the demands of an enlarged war did. Later the next year, the CIA had to augment its budget by persuading the Pentagon to donate $12 million in "surplus" arms to the agency for delivery to the contras.[19] That December, however, Congress voted a $24 million ceiling on CIA spending for its covert war in the coming fiscal year.

In May 1984 that half-closed spigot was fully plugged in the wake of revelations that CIA agents, acting in the name of the contras, had seeded Nicaraguan harbors with mines. These agents included Salvadoran, Hondurans, Argentinians, Chileans and Ecuadorans—but ironically, no Nicaraguans. That provocative escalation had been conceived by the NSC's Oliver North and a top CIA officer in charge of anti-Sandinista operations to get more bang for limited bucks.[20] But it outraged Managua's

Western trading partners and chagrined Congress, whose intelligence oversight committees were taken by surprise. The fiction of "arms interdiction" held up no longer. Congress rejected a supplemental appropriation for the contras. Three months later, in August, it passed the Boland Amendment, prohibiting any administration agency involved in "intelligence activities" from "supporting, directly or indirectly, military or paramilitary operations in Nicaragua by any nation, group, organization or individual."[21]

The contras had some resources of their own to fall back on—most notably, as we shall see in Chapter VI, profits from drug trafficking. But without more substantial help from the United States, their cause still seemed doomed until North covered his own harbor-mining folly with an even greater one: the proposal (accepted by National Security Adviser Robert McFarlane) to subvert Congress' intent by building a "private" funding and supply network.[22] North claimed that the Boland Amendment's reference to any "agency or entity of the United States involved in intelligence activities" did not apply to the National Security Council.[23] He criss-crossed the globe in 1984 and 1985, raising as much as $1 million a month from private and foreign government sources to keep the administration's proxy war alive.[24] North's agents in turn carried cash from his office safe to Central America for disbursement to the rebels.[25]

One of North's allies in this project was Elliot Abrams, the Assistant Secretary of State for Inter-American Affairs and an enthusiast of the contra war against Nicaragua. Abrams solicited money from other countries, ostensibly for humanitarian purposes. But he consciously "decided to use the account opened by North without procedures for monitoring expenditures from the account," according to a Senate committee report.[26] This studied lack of interest closely paralleled the CIA's own official policy of asking no questions about the origin of large sums of money in the contras' bank accounts.

Together with Abrams and other officials and private agents, North raised money from a remarkable variety of sources outside the United States—and thus outside the jurisdiction of Congress. Amos Perlmutter, an American political scientist with close connections to the Israeli government, reports that, "All those who are clients of the United States have been told more or less, 'You've got to do something for the contras.'"[27]

According to contra fundraiser and presidential candidate Pat Robertson, one helping hand for the anti-Sandinista rebels came from South Africa.[28] For example, some of the planes that supplied the contras were made available by a South African air freight company,[29] apparently after the head of the CIA's Latin America division took a secret trip to

South Africa in early 1985 to solicit aid for the anti-Sandinista cause.[30] The South African aid may help explain Reagan's vigorous opposition to economic sanctions and CIA director William Casey's efforts to line up Saudi oil for the apartheid regime.[31]

Brunei: In the summer of 1985, during the dry spell in congressional aid, Secretary of State George Shultz and his chief assistant on Latin American affairs, Elliott Abrams, approached the Sultan of Brunei for a donation to the contra cause.[32] The sultan, fabulously wealthy from oil and gas revenues, reportedly deposited $10 million in a Swiss bank account controlled by Oliver North.[33] He was also a creditor to the key Irangate arms broker, Adnan Khashoggi.[34] Some U.S. officials suspect that the Sultan's money never reached the contras, but instead went to reimburse Khashoggi, who advanced millions of dollars to finance U.S. arms sales to Iran.[35]

Saudi Arabia: Casey also worked on Saudi Arabia—successfully— to support Washington's cause in Central America. The CIA director met with King Fahd in February 1984 to press his case. Working in tandem with Casey to persuade the royal family were two private individuals with tremendous experience in the field of Mideast arms sales: retired Air Force Gen. Richard Secord, who steered the sale of AWACS surveillance planes to Saudi Arabia through Congress in 1981, and Robert Lilac, former commander of the U.S. Air Force Logistics Command in Saudi Arabia, who left the NSC in 1983 and now works for the Saudi Ambassador in Washington, D.C.[36] The Saudi royal family reportedly turned over $32 million to the rebels in Honduras and Costa Rica in gratitude for the administration's success in overcoming the Israeli lobby's resistance to the $8.5 billion AWACS sale.[37] Saudi money also supported anti-communists in Angola and Afghanistan.[38] Most recently, evidence has come to light that Saudi Arabia financed arms purchases by its feared adversary Iran, in hopes of moderating the regime's revolutionary, messianic mission.[39] Some of these monies in turn were allegedly deposited by Israeli intermediaries in Switzerland for disbursement to the contras.[40]

South Korea: Less visibly, South Korea, too, has given generously to the contras,[41] and on at least one occasion shipped them arms paid for by Saudi Arabia.[42] It has also provided an important back channel for arms shipments to the Khomeini regime in Iran.[43] The arms and funding pipelines from South Korea were kept open by a combination of Washington lobbyists, ex-CIA officers and private organizations, many with ties to Saudi Arabia as well.[44]

No country, however, has played a more significant surrogate role in both Central America and Iran than Israel. As early as 1981, Israel's economic minister Ya'acov Meridor had declared, "Israel will be your proxy."[45] Although Israeli leaders have officially denied aiding the contras, the record of their involvement is clear and unequivocal.[46] As recently as September 1986, according to Assistant Secretary of State Elliot Abrams, Israel sent the contras by sea a large shipment of Soviet-made arms, presumably captured in Lebanon.[47]

Israel's proxy activities on behalf of the contras grew out of a long tradition of military support for authoritarian regimes in Central America, including that of Anastasio Somoza in Nicaragua. Israel was also in on the ground floor with the contras when Somoza finally fled the country. Haifa University professor Benjamin Beit-Hallahmi reports that "when the CIA was setting up the contra organization in 1981, the Mossad was also there, carrying out the training and support for the first units."[48]

Finally, Israel was a leading arms supplier to Argentina during the period of its military rule, despite anti-semitic violence and the Falklands War. Indirectly, therefore, Israel bolstered the contras by arming their direct military supporters in the first years of opposition.[49]

The first major Israeli arms deliveries to the contras appear to have begun shortly after the pull-out of Argentine trainers and suppliers from Central America in the aftermath of the Falklands War.[50] "As early as 1982," according to U.S. News and World Report, Gen. Richard Secord took charge of a Pentagon operation "in which Israel shipped tons of weapons captured during its invasion of Lebanon to a CIA arms depot in San Antonio. From Texas, the guns were shipped to the contras."[51]

More than arms seem to have been involved. Replacing the Argentine advisers were "retired or reserve Israeli army commanders...hired by shadowy private firms," according to Time magazine.[52] America's contractors had apparently subcontracted the job.

The point man for this cooperative strategy was David Kimche, a 30-year Mossad veteran who rose to direct Israel's Foreign Ministry until the fall of 1986. Known as Israel's "key contras specialist,"[53] he has been directly linked to surrogate funding of contras. And it was Kimche, by all accounts, who in 1985 persuaded the Reagan administration to sanction Israel's arms pipeline to Tehran in order to influence Iranian "moderates."[54] Kimche's Israeli patron Ariel Sharon was himself an architect not only of the contra supply operation but also of Israeli arms sales to Iran.[55] And Kimche's White House contacts on the Iran operation—Robert McFarlane and Oliver North—were in turn the masterminds of the contra aid network.

Nearly all of these foreign funding sources were either untraceable (AWACS kickbacks, Iran payments through Switzerland) or untouchable

(Israel, South Korea). A Congress united behind Israel was not (and still is not) inclined to ask too many questions about its arms deliveries in Central America or Iran.[56] Nor, after Jimmy Carter's abortive talk of a pullback from Korea, would Congress cut off the Seoul regime. Thus the White House could, for a time at least, safely flout the intent of Congress with help from these U.S. aid recipients.

Personnel and Logistics: Going Private

Just as Congress was loathe to touch these offshore suppliers, so was it reluctant to rein in the elaborate old-boy network of retired CIA and military covert operators who carried out Reagan's policies in the field. Their common experiences run the gamut from the CIA-sponsored war against Castro in the early 1960s, to the covert war in Laos later in that decade, to shady arms and intelligence operations in Iran by the mid-1970s. Out of these experiences came shared expertise, close-knit contacts and trusting friendships that would bring them together again as a covert network in the 1980s.

Among the most significant of these figures is retired Gen. John Singlaub, a veteran of the CIA and military "special operations" in Indochina who now implements the Reagan doctrine through his leadership of the World Anti-Communist League and his Pentagon advisory role. His special operations colleagues from the Vietnam era run similar aid groups, including the National Defense Council, Refugee Relief International, and Air Commandos Association. All these groups coordinated their efforts through Oliver North on the NSC.[57]

Working with North and Singlaub in Vietnam and Laos as an air supply specialist on CIA-connected covert missions was (then) Lieutenant Colonel Richard Secord. In 1981, as deputy assistant secretary of defense for the Near East, Africa and South Asia, he acted as the Pentagon's chief representative and lobbyist on the AWACS sale that set the terms for subsequent Saudi kickbacks to the contras. His job also put him in a position to follow Israel's covert arms shipments to Iran in the early 1980s. A career-long specialist in covert operations, Secord had what one congressional source called "incredible intelligence contacts."[58] After leaving the government in 1983, Secord and his Iranian-born business partner Albert Hakim managed the private supply network for the contras under North's supervision, using Saudi and Iranian money deposited in Switzerland to purchase planes and other supplies.[59] Secord was also a key logistics agent in the Iran arms deals of 1985-86.[60] One intelligence source called Secord "the 7-Eleven of this type of intelligence activity open 24 hours a day." North's own assessment was equally apt: "A man of many talents ol' Secord is."[61]

Another Laos-era associate of Singlaub and Secord was CIA officer Thomas Clines. As a private businessman by 1986, he helped Secord arrange clandestine arms deliveries to the contras out of Portugal, recruited ex-CIA pilots for the supply operation and helped Oliver North obtain a ship used in the attempt to rescue American hostages in Lebanon.[62]

Clines had begun putting together a private aid network even before Ronald Reagan entered the White House. In 1978, he and Ed Wilson, a former CIA agent and friend of Secord who has since been convicted of supplying explosive devices to Libya, reportedly began negotiating a $650,000 deal with Nicaraguan dictator Anastasio Somoza "to create a search and destroy apparatus against Somoza's enemies."[63] The negotiations commenced just as the Israelis were moving to supply essentially all of Somoza's arms. Both Israel's munitions representatives and Clines, who left the CIA on bad terms with the Carter administration, were operating directly against official policy toward Nicaragua. But their efforts foreshadowed perfectly Reagan's more militant strategy.

So, it would appear, did the work of another retired CIA officer, Felix Rodriguez, who had served under Clines in countless CIA operations in Cuba, the Congo and Vietnam.[64] In his "retirement," Rodriguez went to work for Clines in the late 1970s as a representative of his arms sales business in Latin America. Rodriguez also served as an arms broker for Gerard Latchinian in 1979-80. Latchinian, who would later be convicted of a drug-financed assassination plot in Honduras for the benefit of the CIA's favorite general, Gustavo Alvarez Martinez, was particularly close to Israeli arms merchants in Guatemala and Miami. Thus Rodriguez appears to have supplied a connection between Clines and the Israelis in Central America.[65] Rodriguez would later become the contras' logistics mastermind at Ilopango military airport in El Salvador.[66]

A host of lesser covert operators joined these private individuals in carrying out the aims of the Reagan White House. They included Cuban exile terrorist veterans of the secret war against Castro directed by Clines from the CIA station in Miami, former CIA contract pilots who flew supply missions to Central America, former Pentagon special operations officers skilled in covert missions, and a private aid network revolving around such organizations as the World Anti-Communist League, Sovereign Military Order of Malta and CAUSA, a political arms of Sun Myung Moon's Unification Church.

Serving this group was also a network of private companies long experienced at serving undercover operations of the government. The best known of these is Southern Air Transport, a CIA proprietary company since 1960 that was sold in 1973 to its president. Sales of other such proprietaries were conditioned on "an agreement that the proprietary would continue to provide goods or services to the CIA," according to a 1976 congressional report.[67] Southern Air Transport (SAT) was the airline of choice for both the private contra aid operation and the delivery of U.S. arms to Iran in 1985-86. The same aircraft that delivered U.S. weapons to Tehran via Israel picked up Soviet-made arms from Israeli-controlled stocks in Lisbon on their return trips to Central America.[68] One retired Air Force officer involved in supplying the contras warned crew members to protect SAT's cover: "We don't want to get SAT or ourselves burned with a leak or get money hung up where we would have to expose the op[eration] to get it back."[69]

In retrospect, the practice of contracting out foreign policy to such private agents, with all its dangers and abuses, was almost inevitable given the conditions of the Reagan presidency. A militant, sometimes radical group of policy makers confronted a much more cautious Congress and bureaucracy. A president flush with a tremendous election victory was frustrated by the unpopularity of so many of his specific foreign policies. The temptation under such circumstances was to skirt the law, even break the rules in the faith that deeply covered clandestine acts would go unnoticed and that the President's personal popularity would prevail in a showdown with political critics. The temptation, in short, was to use the contracting out strategy to achieve total presidential supremacy in foreign policy. Curbing the ability of future presidents to avoid public account-ability this way is an essential first step toward also curbing the domestic and foreign abuses that result.

III.
"Shadow Networks" and Their Stake in Covert Operations

Introduction

From their inception in 1979, the so-called contra anti-Sandinista forces have been involved in scandals, including the murder and torture of civilians, health workers, prominent clerics, and even members of their own forces.[1] These crimes, though they are not our subject, can hardly be subordinated to the more narrow Contragate scandal which has preoccupied the U.S. press since October 1986, and which, initially at least, focussed on the way bureaucratic backers of the contras in the Reagan White House National Security Council staff plotted to circumvent a cutoff of CIA aid dictated in 1984 by Congress.

The investigative reporting of Contragate, however, has revealed more clearly what to some was already obvious: that the scandals of the contras and of their bureaucratic backers are inter-related and indeed part of a much larger and older intrigue, which involved not just the contras and their NSC support team but also a larger "shadow network" of veteran intelligence operatives in and out of government, and their right-wing international allies. This well-organized and experienced cabal, working inside and outside the United States, with access to ruthless operatives and covert international funds, contributed both to Reagan's election in 1980 and to the self-damaging inflexibility of his commitment to the contra operation. The story of Contragate, seen from this perspective, is really a further chapter in the operation of the covert forces that the United States came to know through Watergate.

Looking back, it is clear that Watergate was in part a story of corruption and conspiracy involving the recycling of foreign-based funds into U.S. elections, and also a story of disputes between factions whose power depended on relations with the CIA and other intelligence agencies. It may be that, with so much free-floating money in the world today, U.S. democracy will never be wholly free of such influence: even the reform-minded Carter presidency was tainted by the "Billygate" and then the "Irangate" scandals of the 1970s, which were not unrelated (as we shall see) to the Iran-Contra connection of 1986. But in the Carter era there was also a concerted effort to cut back on illegal business payoffs, CIA political operations, and U.S. aid to foreign dictators (such as Anastasio Somoza of Nicaragua) who did not hesitate to invest some of the largesse back into the U.S. electoral process.[2]

Ironically, Carter's very reform movement, by forcing its opponents into defensive alliance, contributed to a more pervasive Iran-contra scandal of some seven years' standing: an on-going scheme (and in part an illegal conspiracy) to reverse the post-Watergate reforms of intelligence abuses, first by electing Ronald Reagan in 1980, and then by committing him, through the contra program, to a resurrection of abandoned CIA covert operations.

Contragate, in this larger sense, was not just a covert operation on behalf of a presidency; it can also be seen in part as an electoral conspiracy in support of a covert operation. And though the principal schemers were North American, they did not hesitate to invoke the aid of neofascist foreigners.

One principal foreign architect of this contra commitment appears to have been a former CIA Guatemalan protege called Mario Sandoval Alarcon, a leader of the reactionary World Anti-Communist League (WACL) and the so-called "Godfather" to all the death squads of Central America, including those of Major Roberto d'Aubuisson, his client in El Salvador. But Sandoval was not acting alone; his deals with the Reagan campaign in 1980 appear to have been part of a larger coordinated plan involving one of Washington's leading military-industrial lobbies, the American Security Council (ASC) at home, and ASC's WACL allies overseas—especially Guatemala, Argentina, and Taiwan.

In this chapter we shall see how the World Anti-Communist League has evolved since its origins in Taiwan in 1954, with the help of members of the U.S. "shadow network." This league was originally created by the ruling intelligence networks of Taiwan and South Korea to provide a platform to continue the militant cold war propaganda that Eisenhower had seemed to abandon when he negotiated an end to the Korean and Indochina Wars at the 1954 Geneva Conference. The groups attending these conferences from other countries and regions, and which eventually joined in 1967 to create WACL, all had one thing in common: their (often secret) links to U.S. intelligence and military experts in "political" or "psychological warfare." Through their annual conferences in different parts of the world, they have also played host to rising U.S. anti-Communist politicians, such as Richard Nixon in 1964.

Since their formation, the WACL chapters have also provided a platform and legitimacy for surviving fractions of the Nazi Anti-Komintern and Eastern European (Ostpolitik) coalitions put together under Hitler in the 1930s and 1940s, and partly taken over after 1948 by the CIA's Office of Policy Coordination.[3] In the late 1970s, as under Carter the United States pulled away from involvement with WACL countries and operations, the Nazi component of WACL became much more blatant as at least three European WACL chapters were taken over by former Nazi SS officers.

With such a background, WACL might seem like an odd choice for the Reagan White House, when in 1984 WACL Chairman John Singlaub began to report to NSC staffer Oliver North and CIA Director William Casey on his fund-raising activities for the contras.[4] We shall see, however, that Singlaub's and WACL's input into the generation of Reagan's Central American policies and political alliances went back to at least 1978. The activities of Singlaub and Sandoval chiefly involved three WACL countries, Guatemala, Argentina, and Taiwan, that would later emerge as prominent backers of the contras. In 1980 these three countries shared one lobbying firm, that of Deaver and Hannaford, which for six years had supervised the campaign to make a successful presidential candidate out of a former movie actor, Ronald Reagan.

Still unacknowledged and unexplained is the role which funds from Michael Deaver's Guatemalan clients played in the 1980 Reagan campaign. Although contributions from foreign nationals are not permitted under U.S. electoral law, many observers have reported that rich Guatemalans boasted openly of their illegal gifts. Half a million dollars was said to have been raised at one meeting of Guatemalan businessmen, at the home of their President, Romeo Lucas Garcia. The meeting took place at about the time of the November 1979 visit of Deaver's clients to Washington, when some of them met with Ronald Reagan.[5]

The Reagan campaign never admitted having received such illegal contributions. But observers of Latin America were struck by the presence at Reagan's first inauguration of several very controversial Guatemalans. Among these were Mario Sandoval Alarcon, the "Godfather" of the Central American Death squads.[6] On Inauguration Day, before dancing at the President's Ball, Sandoval "announced that he had met with Reagan defense and foreign policy advisers before the election, and indicated that the Guatemala rightists expect Reagan will honor 'verbal agreements' to resume military aid to Guatemala and put an end to criticism of the regime's human rights record."[7] The existence of these verbal agreements had been disclosed before the election by an American investigative journalist, Alan Nairn, who had learned of them from Guatemalan and U.S. businessmen. On October 30, 1980, Nairn reported that "perhaps most importantly, the Reagan supporters have agreed to cut back U.S. criticism of the death squads."[8]

One question to be answered by Michael Deaver is whether he knew of these "verbal agreements." Another is whether these agreements included aid and protection to Sandoval's Nicaraguan death squad on Guatemalan soil, one of the original components of today's contras. At this time members of this cadre had already gone for terrorist training to Argentina, another country represented by Deaver.[9] The cadre leaders were being put up at Sandoval's expense in an apartment house behind his home.[10]

A small group of these men, headed by Somozista Colonel Ricardo Lau, had arranged the murder of El Salvador's Archbishop Romero in 1980, under the direction of d'Aubuisson.[11]

Thanks to a captured notebook, some of these facts became known to Carter's State Department, so that Sandoval personally had good reason to fear "criticism" of his own human rights record.[12] Carter's Ambassador to El Salvador, Robert White, told Congress in April 1981 that the captured diary gave "the names of people living in the United States and in Guatemala City who are actively funding the death squads." Three years later he charged that "The Reagan Administration took on a great responsibility when it chose to conceal the identity of Archbishop Romero's murderer" and made d'Aubuisson "an honored guest at our Embassy."[13]

But Reagan in 1980 had promised a "housecleaning" of the State Department. Among the first to go were the members of Carter's Central America team, including Ambassador Robert White. Not only did the new administration issue d'Aubuisson the U.S. visa which Carter had denied him; it promptly used documents supplied by d'Aubuisson to create, in its so-called White Paper of February 1981, a pretext for supplying aid to

Sandoval's contras. All this was done with a speed which suggests the kind of pre-election verbal agreement Sandoval had referred to.[14]

One need not look only to financial payoffs to explain Reagan's initial enthusiasm for the contra forces in Nicaragua. Support for them was clearly indicated by his ideological anti-Communism and his strategic design for the hemisphere. But where Reagan's anti-communism elsewhere in the region has been at least pragmatically flexible (however ruthless)—in the case of the contras it has been unbending and geo-politically dangerous. For example, Reagan's initial support for the Garcia Meza regime in Bolivia waned as that regime was shown to be a mere front for local cocaine barons. But increasing reports of the contra involvement in the cocaine traffic seem only to have increased the administration's protectiveness and commitment (see Chapter VI).[15]

Contragate: A Hypothesis

The difference can be explained by the existence of a powerful coalition that wished to see the United States itself get back into the business of covert political and paramilitary operations. This coalition included the foreign beneficiaries of such operations: men like Sandoval in Guatemala (whose CIA connections went back to 1954), and, until his murder in September 1980, the Nicaraguan dictator Anastasio Somoza (who in 1954 had been his father's liaison with the CIA Guatemala operation).[16]

Other countries where the CIA had been active had an equal interest in seeing a restoration of CIA covert operations. South Africa wanted CIA assistance in supporting the UNITA rebels in Angola. Thailand wanted CIA help in Cambodia. Arab countries like Saudi Arabia wanted financial support for the tribal resistance in Afghanistan. Each got what it wanted from the new Reagan administration, which, in turn, used these nations to carry out its own ends as well. A global lobby for all of these covert operations, including the contras, existed in the form of the World Anti-Communist League, or WACL, of which Mario Sandoval Alarcon had been a long-time organizer and leader in Central America.

Before Reagan, the Taiwan-based WACL had been marginal to U.S. foreign policy, partly because of the involvement of some of its personnel in Nazi operations and the international drug traffic. Since 1984, however, WACL, under its American President retired General John Singlaub, has moved (with barely disguised White House connivance) into overt support for the contra operation, which its members (including Singlaub) apparently endeared to the Reagan campaign before the 1980 election.

WACL in Latin America had moved into a particularly extremist, conspiratorial, and drug-linked phase after 1975-76, with the establishment of the WACL-backed military dictatorship in Argentina. A new, overtly fascistic branch of WACL in Latin America (the Confederacion Anticomunista Latinoamericana, or CAL), coordinated international plotting for a chain of right-wing military plots: notably the Bolivian "cocaine coup" of 1980 (involving the Nazi war criminal turned drug trafficker, Klaus Barbie) and Sandoval's schemes for the contras and d'Aubuisson. Sandoval, "according to one right-wing Salvadoran admirer, was to be the 'on-site' manager who would put [CAL's] plans into action in Central America."[17]

The mechanics of this CAL network seem to have been masterminded primarily by the secret police of Argentina, Chile, and Paraguay; its political use seems to have been coordinated with other countries at CAL meetings. The conspiratorial Italo-Argentine Masonic lodge P-2, an outgrowth of old U.S. anti-Communist plotting with the Italian drug-trafficking Mafia, and later a political underpinning to the Argentine military junta, is alleged to have siphoned millions of dollars into Latin America in support of their anti-democratic politics. Through such right-wing schemes, one Italian veteran of P-2 fascist plotting in Italy, Stefano delle Chiaie, was able to take part in the Chilean murder network which killed Orlando Letelier in Washington, the Argentine-backed "cocaine coup" in Bolivia, and the training of the death squads headed by Sandoval and d'Aubuisson in El Salvador.[18] Thus it was all the more ominous that the invitees to Reagan's inaugural balls in 1981 should include not only Sandoval, the Central American "Godfather," but Licio Gelli, the Italian head of P-2.[19]

In addition to this foreign network, there was a strong domestic lobby for U.S. covert operations as well. At the heart of this lobby were the spokesmen and bankrollers of a "forward strategy" and "political warfare" or "psychological warfare," grouped mainly in the American Security Council, the most powerful lobby in Washington of the military-industrial complex. In the 1970s, with the increasing dependency of U.S. trade on arms exports and of U.S. industry on the defense budget, other U.S. business groups joined in the demand for a more aggressively anti-Communist foreign policy.[20] There was assuredly broad corporate support for "overcoming Watergate" and "ending the Vietnam syndrome" and this could only make it easier to overcome the disfavor into which covert operations had fallen.

But in 1980 the ASC was also supported by a more desperate, manipulative, and even conspiratorial group pushing for the restoration of U.S. covert operations. These were the CIA's veterans of the clandestine services, who (often in mid-career) had been eased or kicked out of the CIA in large numbers after the CIA began to retrench on such operations in the 1970s.[21]

Of the CIA's five most recent directors before 1980, four (beginning with Richard Helms) had faced the unpleasant task of creating dangerous enemies, by cutting back the CIA's Operations Division, especially after the scaling down of the Vietnam War. A thousand clandestine operators had been fired or forced to retire in 1973 by Nixon's Director of Central Intelligence (DCI), James Schlesinger. But the *coup de grace* to the clandestine services was delivered on October 31, 1977, by Carter's DCI, Admiral Stansfield Turner. By eliminating a further 820 positions, Turner is said to have reduced the clandestine services from 1200 to 400. John Ranelagh has written that "when Turner fired virtually all the [covert] operators in the DDO [Operations Directorate]—the whole clandestine service—in effect he eliminated the agency's special-project capability, forcing it to compete with specialized agencies in the burgeoning field of technical intelligence collection and analysis."[22]

These men, as we shall see, were on good terms with old CIA foreign contacts, such as Somoza and Sandoval, and in the Carter era they were increasingly forced to seek employment with them. As clandestine services fell more and more out of favor, their operators inside and outside the service resorted to more and more questionable activities. Revelations in the press about the work of rogue ex-CIA intelligence operative Edwin Wilson (for Libya's Khadafy) put several high-level CIA operators at risk: they faced possible prosecution unless (as happened) the election of Reagan and the restoration of CIA covert operations would result in the restoration of a *de facto* "CIA immunity" to prevent investigation of their past activities.

The story of the contras, and of Contragate, is involved with a number of such individuals: men such as Tom Clines, eased out by Turner because of his financial involvement in Ed Wilson's affairs, who then sought work with Nicaragua's Anastasio Somoza. We shall see how, after Reagan was elected, a Reagan appointee, Michael Ledeen, used allusions to a "covert operation" as part of a successful campaign to protect Clines and his suspected co-conspirators, two of whom were still working in the new Reagan administration. One of these, Richard Secord, was indeed already involved in the covert arms flow to the contras, and after his retirement in

1983 he became a "private" arms supplier to the contras, operating much as Wilson had.[23]

The Iran-Contra revelations of late 1986 revealed how heavily the Reagan administration, in defying a Congressional ban on support of the contras, had come to rely on a well-integrated network of military and intelligence veterans of covert operations, many of whom (like Secord) had come to have better relations with foreign groups than with their own government. Veteran CIA operatives and future contra backers, like Secord, John Singlaub, and Thomas Clines, came to be trusted by each other, and by the foreign backers of Contragate, more than by their superiors in Washington.

Contragate, the collusion to install and maintain a U.S. covert operation (despite the expressed will of Congress), can be traced back to the decisions of successive CIA directors to scale down and virtually eliminate clandestine services, and to the "offshore" intelligence operations that grew as the CIA's operational assets were dispersed. The major scandals of the Carter-Turner era involving the CIA's clandestine services—Edwin Wilson, the Sindona/P-2 affair in Italy, the drug-linked Nugan Hand Bank in Australia (see below), all strengthened the determination of former CIA operatives and their allies to restore their traditional immunity by reviving their former role in mounting covert operations.

The Covert Operations Lobby

Every historical change in modes of warfare has produced what is known as a disposal problem: what to do with no longer needed troops. This is one of the less apparent causes for America's current "contra" crisis. What is to be done, not just with the Nicaraguan mercenaries, who are now one of the major armies of Central America, but with their ex-CIA Cuban and American handlers, an increasingly powerful constituency inside the Reagan administration?

In the fifteenth century a problem much like this one—what to do with ravaging knights who lived off the land—was a powerful motive for England to prolong the Hundred Years' War and keep its knights in France. America's disposal problem with the contras is on the point of becoming acute, especially if the $100 million voted by Congress is actually used for its stated goal of turning the demoralized Nicaraguan contra forces into a well-disciplined army.

But the root disposal problem is the domestic one: what to do with a small but highly determined American army of covert operations specialists and their ex-CIA Cuban cohorts. This so-called "secret team"—old covert operations buddies like Generals Singlaub and Secord, and their CIA colleagues like Thomas Clines and Felix Rodriguez—are at the center of the Iran-contra conspiracy to keep U.S. funds flowing to the contras in defiance of a Congressional prohibition.

These men are not just fighting to preserve the contras; they are plotting above all to preserve their own style of clandestine warfare, despite a tentative consensus arrived at in the 1970s after Watergate and the ensuing Congressional investigations of the CIA—a consensus uniting the White House, Congress, CIA, and Pentagon—that such covert operations were counterproductive and ultimately injurious to larger U.S. interests.

We have seen that, after widespread agreement that the CIA's covert operations bureaucracy had become far too large, CIA directors under both Republican and Democratic presidents moved to cut back the clandestine services to a fraction of their former size with the two biggest steps taken by CIA directors James Schlesinger in 1973 under Nixon, who eliminated some 2000 CIA positions (1,000 people were fired), and Stansfield Turner in 1977 under Carter, who eliminated 820 more.[24]

And although Carter grew steadily less hostile to Pentagon paramilitary operations, especially after the fall of the Shah of Iran and particularly the seizure of the U.S. Embassy in Tehran, even here the rationale for the Pentagon effort was not covert warfare as such, but antiterrorism. To this end, the military formed two elite commando units ("Blue Light" and "Delta"), and later a joint task force for the rescue of the U.S. hostages, but all this was a far cry from the 15,000 troops which in 1984 the Reagan administration centralized under the Pentagon's Joint Special Operations Agency (see Chapter IX).[25]

In any case, the disposal problem of what to do with impatient Bay of Pigs troops, which confronted the newly-elected president John F. Kennedy (see Chapter VI), is a problem that has never gone away and has only contributed to a succession of much larger disasters. For a while Bay of Pigs veterans like Felix Rodriguez (later a supplier of the contras), when they could no longer be used with impunity against Cuba, were reassigned to CIA operations in the Congo and later the Vietnam War.

When that war ended in detente, the Cubans came home to Miami and a spate of domestic violence. This belligerence was only dispersed when the Cuban Bay of Pigs veterans were recruited for new secret wars: the Angolan fiasco of 1975-76; and then, since 1981, the training, supplying, and "advising" of the contras.

The key members of the "secret team" behind both the Cubans and the Contragate scandal were all working together by the time of the covert operations in Laos and Vietnam. General John Singlaub, the Reagan administration's chief liaison in the so-called "private" contra supply effort of 1984-86, was from 1966 to 1968 the chief of the SOG ("Studies and Operations Group") in Vietnam, which launched covert cross-border operations into Laos.

A number of men who were under Singlaub at SOG are now associated with him in the world-wide recruitment of mercenaries for the contras, through the branches of the World Anti-Communist League.[26] One of these associates is Singlaub's SOG Air Wing Commander, Harry ("Heinie") Aderholt, who now in retirement leads the Air Commando Association (uniting some 1500 U.S. special warfare veterans) in its "nonlethal" anti-Communist support operations in Central America, principally Guatemala.

Aderholt's successor as director of air support operations in Laos was Richard Secord, who after his retirement flew to Iran with Reagan's emissaries Robert McFarlane and Oliver North in the May 1986 Iran arms deal. Through one of his private companies, Secord also sold at least one airplane to the contras.[27] Secord's private company, Stanford Technology Trading Group International, was frequently phoned from the "safe house" in El Salvador housing the contra supply team of Eugene Hasenfus and his pilot, William Cooper. Hasenfus and Cooper, whom the *Los Angeles Times* called "one of the CIA's chief pilots in Southeast Asia," were both long-time veterans of Secord's covert air supply operations in Laos.[28]

In 1966-68, at the time of Singlaub's and Secord's Laotian operations, the CIA Chief of Station in Laos was Theodore Shackley, who from 1962-65 had been in charge of the CIA Miami station directing the Cuban Bay of Pigs veterans against Fidel Castro.[29] From 1969-72 Shackley was CIA Chief of Station in Saigon. Under him worked both Felix Rodriguez (whom he knew from Miami), and his colleague Donald Gregg, who today is Vice-President Bush's liaison with Rodriguez and the contras.[30] From 1980 to 1983, Shackley was a consultant with Stanford Technology, whose owner was Albert Hakim, Secord's business partner.

Oliver North, who has been depicted as the White House architect of the Iran-Contragate connection, was far junior to these men and, initially at least, guided by them. In 1968, when he graduated from Annapolis, he went out to counterinsurgency activities in Vietnam, where he is alleged by some sources to have served at least briefly with Singlaub and Secord in Laos.[31] His introduction to covert arms deals may have come in 1981, when under the guidance of Secord he lobbied for the Saudi AWACS deal that helped pay for the contra covert operation and others.

It is the collective bureaucratic clout of this well-coordinated team of U.S. secret war veterans, far more than that of the Cubans and Nicaraguans, that stiffens the Reagan administration's inflexibility, and drive towards escalation on the contra issue. They are fighting for the survival of special warfare itself.

All of these U.S. special warriors were on the outs at the end of the 1970s, unpopular not just with the Carter White House but with their own agencies. While it was President Carter who removed General Singlaub from his South Korea command for his political insubordination, the CIA itself sidetracked Theodore Shackley and his subordinate in Miami and Laos, Thomas Clines, thus provoking their resignations.

Shackley and Clines were suspected of possible involvement in an arms deal with Egypt, which allegedly "bilked the U.S. government out of $8 million."[32] The deal was said to have been put together by Shackley's former CIA contract employee Ed Wilson, who was later convicted for smuggling explosives to Libya.[33]

Richard Secord was also investigated in the same arms deal, even after Reagan was elected. He refused to take a lie detector test, was briefly suspended from his job, and after the case was settled out of court left the government in 1983. One of those who intervened with the prosecutor on this case was Michael Ledeen, who has since confirmed that as a National Security Council consultant he helped set up the first contacts between Teheran and Washington on the Irangate arms deals (see Chapter VIII).[34]

These men were at the heart of a larger "secret team," of what Administration officials later called a "board of directors of sorts," behind North's Iran-Contra arms dealings.[35] In plotting to preserve the contra operation against Congressional disapproval, this team was plotting for the survival of U.S. special warfare itself, since of all the U.S.-backed covert wars only the contra operation was being managed by large numbers of American covert war experts. Having allied themselves in the late 1970s with the incipient Reagan presidential campaign, this team played an important role in writing Reagan's foreign policy platform, and thus were well-positioned to implement covert warfare scenarios they themselves had helped devise.

More directly than this, all four men were fighting for personal vindication. Only by involving the White House in the once discredited notion of clandestine warfare could they redeem themselves from the personal disrepute into which they had all fallen. Their own fate was thus much like that of the ex-CIA Cubans who flocked to the contra cause, after having been arrested on charges ranging from drug trafficking to (in the case of Luis Posada, Felix Rodriguez' colleague in the contra supply operation) allegedly helping blow up a Cuban civilian airliner.

What is too little understood in the Contragate affair is the extent to which this secret team even more than their Cuban cohorts, helped engender the initial Reagan commitment to the contra cause. In the 1979-80 period General Singlaub, having linked his political future to that of presidential candidate Ronald Reagan, twice traveled to Central America to forge an alliance between the Reagan campaign and the local backers of what would later become the contra army.

A biography of Ed Wilson, *Manhunt* by Peter Maas, charges that Shackley's former assistant Tom Clines, "even before he left the CIA...was promoting a deal with the Nicaraguan tyrant, Anastasio Somoza, to create a search-and-destroy apparatus against Somoza's enemies."[36] (Ted Shackley has vigorously denied allegations that he sent Ed Wilson to offer assassination services to Somoza, who at that belated point had been abandoned politically by President Carter and was on the point of being ousted.)[37]

If Congress is to deal resolutely with the Contragate crisis, it must deal with more than the complex story of disappearing support funds in Swiss and Panamanian bank accounts. These are but the most recent symptoms of a much more serious disease: a self-serving bureaucratic determination to involve the United States in a covert war for which there is neither Congressional nor popular support. And, behind this, and beyond the scope of this volume, a decades long international policy geared not to enhance the well being of American or international citizens, but of American corporations and multinationals, a very different thing, indeed.

What is really at stake in the debate over what happened in the Iran events is the future of covert warfare itself. The difficulties of the "disposal problem" should not once again become an excuse for postponing a clear decision, when the consequences of postponement are so clearly a still greater disposal problem in the future.

The American "Secret Team" and Its Mafia-Drug Scandals

Though the recent Iran-contra scandal has raised political problems for President Reagan and his National Security Council Staff, it has also revived old concerns about what a Senate committee once called "allegations of substantial and even massive wrong-doing" within the CIA and the rest of the national intelligence system.[38]

The present crisis reopens these old controversies, for today's Contragate connection reunites elements of the alliance between the CIA, Cuban exiles, and Mafia to assassinate Fidel Castro in the early 1960s, one of the CIA's most notorious plots. More importantly, it also raises two old, and ongoing, institutional questions. The first is the extent to which the current controversy is centered on operations which were controversial in the past, and more particularly on the individuals responsible for them. The second is the more fundamental question whether covert operations are not, by their very nature, inherently inimical to the public interest, likely to transgress statutory authority, and hostile to public accountability. (One can pose these pragmatic political questions without prejudice to the larger moral questions which unilateral expansionism also raises.)

Histories of the CIA usually trace its covert operations back to the Special Operations of its World War II predecessor agency, the Office of Strategic Services (OSS). But the continuity glosses over an elemental difference. OSS Special Operations were designed to challenge the legal and political authority of our wartime enemies, chiefly Germany and Japan. Covert operations, more often than not, make a similar challenge; but as often as not they challenge authorities with which we are at peace, and indeed have recurringly challenged even our own government and laws.

From their inception to the present, many CIA operations have been covert, not just to deceive foreign populations, but at least partly because they were *designed* to violate U.S. statutes and Congressional will. A relevant example is the so-called "Defection Program" authorized in 1947 (by National Security Council Intelligence Directive 4, a document still withheld in full). Despite explicit Congressional prohibitions, this program was designed to bring Nazi agents, some of them wanted war criminals, to this country, to develop the covert operations capability of the United States.

Some of these agents helped supply the cadres and trainers for the nascent U.S. Special Forces or Green Berets, some of whose veterans help supply the training and operational backbone of today's contra army in Central America.[39] Others allegedly were among the Central Europeans who helped train the Cubans at the Bay of Pigs; their veterans' organization, Brigade 2506, is now a principal recruiting ground for contra supporters.

According to a U.S. special warfare veteran, William Corson, some of these ex-Nazis became pilots in the 1950-52 supply operation of Civil Air

Transport (later Air America) to opium-growing Chinese Nationalist (Kuomintang, or KMT) guerrilla forces in Thailand and Burma. Corson notes that those knowledgeable about an in-house murder and resulting "Thailand flap" have theorized "that the trafficking in drugs in Southeast Asia was used as a self-financing device to pay for services and persons whose hire would not have been approved by Washington (or condoned if discovered)."[40]

Another book, Alfred McCoy's *The Politics of Heroin in Southeast Asia*, documents that the KMT forces were accompanied by white advisers, and that they were supported with arms and equipment by an American company, Sea Supply, Inc.[41] In a sense, the Miami-based drug trafficking of the contras today can be traced back to this Miami-based corporation. As we shall see, its organizer, Paul L. E. Helliwell, had been a member of an OSS team in Kunming, Yunnan, that paid for its intelligence operations with opium.[42] Later Helliwell and three other members of this OSS team— Howard Hunt, Lou Conein, and Mitch WerBell—would work with drug-dealing Cuban veterans of the Bay of Pigs invasion. WerBell in turn would work closely with General John Singlaub, the leading "private" backer of the contras today.[43]

Two senior CIA officials, one of them Colonel Richard G. Stilwell, left the CIA after the "Thailand flap" of 1952. In 1959 U.S. intelligence officers would tell President Eisenhower that the Chinese Nationalist forces in Burma had caused "nothing but difficulty."[44]

The scandals arising from this drug traffic and murder caused the KMT supply operation to be officially "terminated" in 1952, with lasting consequences for the CIA. One was that the offending subordinate group, the Office of Policy Co-ordination (OPC), was merged into the Agency. This meant that the OPC "cowboys" who had relished their unsupervised use of former Nazis and drug traffickers were now theoretically subordinated to the somewhat more bureaucratic line of command in the CIA's Office of Special Operations (OSO). This was an unstable mix at the time, and it has been so ever since.

Thomas Powers has contrasted the free-wheeling, improvisatorial, "sometimes harebrained" style of the OPC "cowboys" with the professionalism of the OSO, who "not only distrusted the tradecraft of the OPC people, but on occasion went so far as to wonder just who they were working for, anyway."[45] That tension would last through three decades of CIA operations to the scandals of Contragate.

A second consequence with equal bearing on Contragate was that the severance of links to the Burma drug traffic was only cosmetic. As recorded elsewhere, the planes of Civil Air Transport, which had supplied the KMT troops in Burma, accepted a U.S. government contract to fly them out of Burma in 1954. But in fact it only removed those troops who were ready for retirement. Fresh KMT troops were flown in and Civil Air Transport continued to supply them.[46]

With Civil Air Transport in the 1950s, as with Southern Air Transport three decades later, the distinction between official and private had become blurred enough to permit the continuation of an operation that had been officially prohibited. What had up to now been an American operation became a KMT-Taiwanese one. However, since Civil Air Transport had a Taiwanese KMT corporate entity as well as an American CIA one, the planes, bases, and nature of the arms flow remained the same.[47]

The planes were now being sponsored by a new group, the Asian People's Anti-Communist League (APACL), which had been set up by the governments of Taiwan and South Korea. APACL, later the World Anti-Communist League (WACL), was set up with the assistance (as we shall see) of members of the CIA "secret team" in 1954, the year the United States "officially" wound up its Burma air supply operation. This support of APACL for the Burma air supply operation became clear in 1961, when Fang Chih, a KMT and APACL official, admitted responsibility, on behalf of the Free China Relief Agency, for an unlisted plane that had just been shot down over Thailand by the Burmese Air Force.[48] The Free China Relief Agency turned out to be a member agency of APACL, sharing offices with it at the same Taipei address. (Organized groups of ex-Nazi collaborators from Eastern Europe, later beneficiaries of the NSC-CIA Defection Program, have also been principal organizers of APACL/WACL from its outset.[49])

Despite the "private" Taiwan cover in the years 1954-61, sophisticated U.S. equipment continued to be shipped via mainland American air force bases to the KMT opium growers, until these were driven from Burma into Laos in 1961 and the CIA again took over.[50] In other words, the Civil Air Transport/Air America Burma drug supply operation never really closed down. On the contrary, it became a major factor in the 1961 reopening of the CIA's secret war in Laos, which continued, using local traffickers, Green Berets, and the renamed Air America, for the next fourteen years.[51]

That "secret" Laotian war of 1961-75, like the KMT Burma operation, involved air flights in and out of regions where the chief cash crop was opium. The CIA's prime Laotian protege, Phoumi Nosavan, who "had controlled the [drug] traffic for years," and his subordinate Ouane Rattikone, solved their fiscal crisis by having the U.S.-supported

Laotian government "become directly involved in the import and export of Burmese opium. This decision ultimately led to the growth of northwest Laos as one of the largest heroin-producing centers in the world."[52]

Despite official prohibitions, there is no doubt that, as a CIA investigation conceded, Air America planes flew opium out of isolated opium-growing areas, especially those held by Meo tribesmen in northeastern Laos, where land access was controlled by the enemy.[53] Top intelligence and military officials of both our Laotian and Vietnamese allies were involved in this traffic, which led among other things to the seizure in 1971 of sixty kilos of Laotian heroin (worth $13.5 million) from the suitcase of the chief Laotian delegate to the World Anti-Communist League.[54]

As we have seen, the CIA secret war in Laos and Vietnam was crucial in generating today's "secret team" behind the covert Iran-contra supply operation. It was in that Laotian war that the key players got to know each other: John Singlaub (now Chairman of WACL), Richard Secord, Theodore Shackley, Shackley's CIA assistant Tom Clines, and Felix Rodriguez (the anti-Castro veteran in charge of the contra air supply operation in El Salvador).

But in that same Laotian war the Contragate "secret team" of today was subordinated to the reconstituted ex-OPC "secret team" of the Burma KMT drug operation. In 1965 Richard Stilwell, released from the CIA after the "Thailand flap," returned to Thailand as U.S. military commander to oversee the secret war in Laos. Under Reagan, Stilwell returned from retirement to the Pentagon, to promote the Reagan build-up of special warfare forces (see Chapter IX).[55] William DePuy, Stilwell's deputy in 1952, also returned to Indochina under Stilwell in 1964, as the chief of the Vietnam SOG before Singlaub.[56] Stilwell's OPC deputy and successor, Desmond FitzGerald, perhaps the archetypal CIA "cowboy," had risen in the CIA to be Shackley's superior in the 1963 anti-Castro plots. FitzGerald's promotion in 1965 to be in charge of CIA operations was promptly followed by Shackley's transfer to Laos.[57]

Underlying the continuity between the Burma, Laos, and contra operations is the importance to all three of the drug traffic. As John Ranelagh has written of the KMT Burma army, it "never fought; it rapidly became a drug-producing operation instead."[58] Though the fighting in Laos was real enough, the question has frequently been raised whether America's "secret team" was helping to maintain a drug operation in support of their anti-communist war, or helping to maintain a war in support of a drug operation. Similar questions have been raised about some of the contra leadership and their U.S. supporters (at least in Costa Rica): is their primary motive to fight or to engage in the drug traffic (see Chapter VI).[59] In Miami the FBI has allegedly received an eyewitness report of cocaine being loaded on Southern Air Transport planes in Barranquilla, Colombia, at a time when the contra-supporting Southern Air Transport planes were in the Barranquilla area, as confirmed by flight records found in the downed Hasenfus plane.[60] (The airline has denied any involvement with drugs.)

A leading institution in this historic continuity has been the drug-linked WACL, which between 1984 and 1986 was the principal publicly identified source of funding for the contras. Since 1984, General Singlaub, as WACL World Chairman, has, in his own words, "quite frankly used the WACL organization...to meet with some people who are capable of contributing" to the contra cause.[61] Singlaub identified his three principal WACL sources as Latin America, Taiwan, and South Korea—the three areas where WACL members and their allies, as recently as the 1970s, have been recurringly linked to the narcotics traffic.[62]

There have been recurring rumors that profits from this same drug traffic have gone to finance an illicit lobby influencing and corrupting the American government. It is known that KMT officials in the U.S. narrowly escaped conviction on narcotics smuggling charges in the 1950s; and it has been alleged that the narcotics traffic was at this time "an important factor in the activities and permutations of the [KMT Taiwan] China Lobby."[63] This is of current concern because of the continuity between the bribery and other illegal activities of the China Lobby of the 1950s, the pro-Somoza and anti-Castro lobbies of the 1960s, the Chilean, Koreagate and Moonie lobbies of the 1970s, and the contra lobby today.[64]

Whether or not the American Mafia continues to play its historic role in the import of drugs from Latin America, one must be concerned by the possibility their ongoing contacts with that part of the CIA-"private" shadow network which is now supplying the contras.[65] Probably nothing ever did the CIA more harm than the decade of rumors, later proven correct, that it had collaborated with the Mafia to assassinate Fidel Castro. As Miami Station Chief from 1962 to 1965, Theodore Shackley did not inaugurate these contacts with Mafia figure John Rosselli, but he apparently helped maintain them in 1962, at a time when another CIA figure prepared an internal memorandum, "which falsely stated that the operation involving Rosselli was then being terminated," according to a Senate report.[66] According to that report, the Miami station chief (ie. Shackley) personally helped load a U-Haul truck with explosives, detonators, rifles, handguns, radios, and boat radar for Rosselli, to whom the keys of the truck were given.[67]

In a recent civil suit filed by attorney Dan Sheehan for the Washington-based Christic Institute, a non-profit religious legal foundation, it is alleged that Shackley's Mafia contacts did not end when Shackley moved in 1965 from Miami to Laos. It is a matter of record that in the same year a Miami syndicate representative, John Pullman, paid an extended visit to Hong Kong, and that Santo Trafficante, another figure in the CIA-Rosselli assassination plots, met with prominent Corsican gangsters in Saigon in 1968.[68]

The Christic suit charges that Shackley facilitated arrangements to sell opium from the Laotian guerrillas to Santo Trafficante, and that "in return, Shackley's organization received a fixed percentage of the income."[69]

It also alleges that arms from Shackley and Secord reached the contras via the firm of a Cuban called Rafael "Chi Chi" Quintero, once named by the *New York Times* as a business associate of Shackley and Clines.[70] *Business Week* has just identified Quintero as "a Cuban-American who played a key role in the Bay of Pigs invasion and in subsequent efforts to assassinate Fidel Castro."[71] And the *Wall Street Journal* has identified Quintero as involved, along with Clines, in the controversial NSC contra supply operation.[72]

If so, then two of the CIA's most notorious scandals, the post-war opium connection and the 1960s assassination connection, would appear to be origins of the supposedly "private" Contragate connection today.

The CIA's "Off-Loaded" Operations: The Nugan Hand Bank

Throughout the history of the CIA, exposures of scandals, such as supply operations to opium-growing guerrillas in Southeast Asia, have been followed by the resignation or forced departure of key officials. It has not always been clear, however, that by terminating the employment of the official the CIA intended to end its relationship to the operation. On the contrary, the CIA may merely have "off-loaded" the operation, in effect giving it a deeper cover by giving it a more private appearance (and, more important, a non-Congressional financial base).

We have seen how in 1954, when the CIA and its proprietary airline CAT Inc. terminated their support for the controversial Burma-KMT drug supply operation, the planes continued to fly for APACL (later WACL) and CAT Inc.'s Taiwan affiliate, CATCL. This privatization of controversial operations was carried out on a much larger scale in the period 1971-73, when the CIA was coming under increasing public and Congressional scrutiny for its alleged involvement in the Southeast Asian drug traffic.

In these years the CIA severed its formal connections with one of former Miami Station Chief Ted Shackley's Cuban exile groups (Operation 40) whose drug-running operations had become known to the Justice Department.[73] It also ostensibly "sold" its proprietary airlines Air America (formerly CAT Inc.) and Southern Air Transport, after Air America had been publicly identified as to some degree implicated in the narcotics traffic of Southeast Asia.

Just how much was changed by this legal off-loading is very much open to question. In 1985-86 two Cubans from Operation 40 (Felix Rodriguez and Luis Posada) were found to be overseeing supply operations for the contras, using planes flown by former Air America personnel and operated by Southern Air Transport.

The press subsequently learned that Southern Air Transport's Chairman and sole stockholder was James Bastian, who before the CIA divestment had been a vice-president of Pacific Corp., the CIA's parent holding company for Air America, and also Southern Air Transport's in-house attorney.

Between 1970 and 1973 a number of covert operators and subordinate personnel resigned or were dismissed from the Agency. But for one of the most notorious, Ed Wilson, departure from the CIA made little difference. When he was a career contract officer for the CIA, Wilson's job was to set up and run proprietary firms, sometimes profit-making, for his case officer, Thomas Clines. He continued to set up intelligence proprietaries and to deal with Clines after 1971, when he moved from the CIA to a deeper cover in a parallel and more secret intelligence network, Task Force 157, under the U.S. Navy. After 1976, when he was no longer a U.S. employee, his companies received no more government assistance, but his contacts with Clines and Clines' superior Ted Shackley continued.[74] He now went into business with another ex-CIA employee, Frank Terpil, who was apparently dismissed outright from the CIA in 1972.

Later Ed Wilson and Frank Terpil were both arrested for illegal smuggling of arms and explosives. Press exposure of the interrelated Wilson and Terpil scandals revealed that after their departures from the CIA the two men's "private" companies (some apparently authorized by Task Force 157 and some apparently not) continued to do business with both U.S. and foreign intelligence.[75]

Some of these companies and their personnel are close to the center of today's Contragate scandal. A Wilson-Terpil company at the heart of Wilson's illegal dealings with Libya was Inter-Technology, set up in the office of a Terpil sales company called Intercontinental Technology, which was doing business with Iran. Intercontinental's parent, Stanford Technology was run by an Iranian-American, Albert Hakim, who was later involved in both the Irangate arms deals and the contra supply operation.[76]

The Cuban exile assassin called Rafael "Chi Chi" Quintero was associated with Rodriguez and Posada both in Operation 40 and at the Ilopango contra supply base.[77] His former CIA case officer (and Wilson's), Tom Clines, who served under Shackley in both Miami and Laos, has also been linked to Colonel Oliver North's covert NSC operations.[78] Both Quintero and Clines were also associated in API, another company set up with assistance from Ed Wilson, as were Ted Shackley and yet another Operation 40 veteran, Ricardo Chavez.[79]

An affidavit filed by Dan Sheehan in the above mentioned lawsuit brought by the non-profit Christic Institute charges that Wilson and all of these associates (except Chavez, who is not mentioned) were allied in a "secret team" to continue covert operations which were being dropped by the CIA, and to finance these operations by their access to the Laotian and Caribbean drug traffic. It charges in particular that this long-established drug connection underlies the use of the Ilopango air base in an alleged contra arms-for-drugs operation, which is currently being investigated by the Miami FBI.

The affidavit charges that drug profits during the Laotian secret air war were deposited in a secret Ted Shackley bank account at the Nugan Hand Bank in Australia. Shackley denies the existence of any such arrangement or account. On the other hand, though they are not mentioned in the affidavit, facts published four years ago by Professor James A. Nathan in the Carnegie Endowment's prestigious magazine *Foreign Policy* corroborate what his Australian sources called Shackley's "long, close relationship with the Nugan Hand bank."[80] According to Professor Nathan,

> The bank's founders, along with Nugan and Hand, were four officials of Air America, a CIA property.... The director of [Nugan Hand's] Chiang Mai office [in Thailand] claimed on Australian television that he handled $2.6 million in less than six months. The money was garnered from the drugs transiting the area. The bank, he put it starkly, was a 'laundry' for Meo tribesmen and other poppy growers. The Bangkok office was run by the former CIA chief of station in Bangkok...records

from the Bangkok office were full of descriptions of troop deployments and arms sales in the region. Investigators found it hard to believe Nugan Hand was just a bank and not an abettor of U.S. intelligence.[81]

The article revealed that the bank's branch managers included U.S. Air Force General LeRoy Manor (who later collaborated with Secord and North on covert U.S. efforts to liberate the U.S. hostages in Iran), and Patry Loomis, a CIA employee who worked in Vietnam under Shackley and then helped Ed Wilson recruit a team of Green Berets to train Libyans. Ed Wilson himself was a close associate of the Nugan Hand Saudi representative, Bernie Houghton (through whom Wilson allegedly supplied 3000 weapons and 10 million rounds of ammunition to the CIA-backed rebels in Angola).[82]

The extraordinary Nugan Hand story, little known in the United States, was front-page news in Australia six years ago. It was there alleged that the Nugan Hand milieu may have played a role in the 1975 downfall of the left-leaning Gough Whitlam Labor Government, at a time when Shackley was still chief of the East Asia Division of the CIA.

Australian sources have given an even more sinister account than Professor Nathan of the extraordinary operations of Nugan Hand Bank, suggesting that the bank financed major drug deals in addition to laundering their profits. According to an Australian Royal Commission, Nugan Hand was the chief funding source for a series of major narcotics transactions which first brought heroin from the Golden Triangle to Australia in the early 1970s, at a time when the Nixon White House was giving a high priority to stopping the narcotics flow from the same sources to the United States.[83]

These stories are so well known in Australia that in March 1982 the CIA issued a rare public denial (for Australian eyes only): "The CIA has not engaged in operations against the Australian government, has no ties with Nugan Hand and does not involve itself in drug trafficking."[84] Technically, the CIA statement may be correct. In the relevant period 1973-75 Wilson was no longer working for the CIA, but (like Houghton) for the more shadowy parallel U.S. military intelligence network, Task Force 157. A company set up by Ed Wilson (who visited Australia in 1976 while still in Task Force 157) was alleged to have helped create the scandal that toppled Whitlam.[85]

If Wilson and Houghton (while still in Task Force 157) used the Nugan Hand bank to channel unauthorized support to CIA-backed rebels in Angola (in the face of Congressional opposition), then the off-loaded intelligence assets of the drug-linked Nugan Hand bank in the mid-1970s may well have been a close precedent for the drug-linked aid to the contras today.

The same "secret team" seems to have been involved in both operations. According to an informant quoted in an Australian government report on drug trafficking, when the Nugan Bank was being hurriedly closed in 1980, Tom Clines and Rafael Quintero called at the Geneva office of Nugan Hand; and, upon confirming that Houghton had left his travel case there, proceeded to remove a document from it. Clines reportedly said, "We've got to keep Dick's name out of this," meaning by "Dick" Richard Secord, the Iran-Contragate figure.[86]

In the same year, 1980, the new President of Nugan Hand, a Miami banker by the name of Donald Beazley, ceded control of a recently acquired British firm, London Capital Securities, to Ricardo Chavez, quite possibly, according to the same report, acting for Thomas Clines.[87]

The "secret team" may have been "off-loaded," but it would appear to have lost little of its cohesiveness and influence. In the early 1970s it would appear to have served the U.S. intelligence establishment, even after formal severance from the CIA. The available evidence suggests that it may be playing the same role today.

The "Secret Team" and the Wilson EATSCO Scandal

Back in 1980, of course, Shackley and Clines were still heros of that CIA minority of psy-war "cowboys" (mostly veterans, many of them fired by Jimmy Carter's CIA Director Stansfield Turner) who wished to see the agency return to the business of covert and proxy warfare. Many CIA veterans like Singlaub and his longtime OSS-CIA ally Ray Cline were actively supporting the Reagan-Bush ticket; and at least one senior CIA officer (Security Chief Robert Gambino) resigned from the CIA to join the Bush and Reagan campaigns (under Cline's son-in-law, Stefan Halper). The fact that under Carter the clandestine service had been reduced by 820 positions had produced, among men well trained in political warfare, a concerted will for revenge. Cline was a leader among those ex-CIA people who "now looked on with worry and concern."[88]

What personally concerned Shackley and Clines was the punitive drive which Carter's CIA Chief, Admiral Stansfield Turner, had mounted against the clandestine services, and especially those officials who had been involved in two interlocking scandals: the case of Michael Townley, the assassin of the Chilean Minister Orlando Letelier, and that of Edwin P.

Wilson, the renegade ex-CIA agent turned arms dealer and assassination specialist for Libya. Cline's friend and associate, Michael Ledeen, published an article in March 1980 (at the beginning of the Carter-Reagan campaign) "savaging Admiral Stansfield Turner for forcing Ted Shackley [Edwin Wilson's most senior CIA contact, by now a veteran of the anti-Allende operation] out of the agency."[89]

The election of Reagan meant a reprieve for the clandestine services. Michael Ledeen, in his new capacity as the Reagan State Department's expert on terrorism, was now in a position to help close off the investigation of those still in government who had been involved with Edwin Wilson, perhaps the world's most notorious ex-CIA terrorist.[90]

Shackley's "private" involvement in CIA covert operations appears to have been used by Ledeen to contain the expanding Justice Department investigation into the illegal activities of the ex-CIA terrorist and arms dealer Ed Wilson. Government auditors had learned that one of Wilson's companies (EATSCO), which had been set up to gain shipping contracts on U.S. arms sales to Egypt, "had fraudulently billed the Pentagon for some $8 million, in addition to the big profits it was already making."[91] Larry Barcella, the federal prosecutor on the case, had broadened the EATSCO investigation to include two CIA clandestine service veterans driven out by Turner, Tom Clines and Theodore Shackley, and two high-level men still in the Pentagon, General Richard Secord and Erich von Marbod. Witnesses told Barcella that the four men and Wilson each had a twenty percent share in the company, whose seed money had been supplied by Wilson. Allegedly, Clines and Shackley joined EATSCO after leaving the CIA; Secord and von Marbod, who generated the contracts, were hidden partners.[92]

These men were of course much bigger fish than Wilson. Shackley had been tapped to become CIA Director if Gerald Ford had been re-elected President; and he told Barcella that, except for the investigation, he could have been either the CIA Director or Deputy Director under Reagan.[93]

When auditors discovered the EATSCO fraud, von Marbod abruptly resigned, and General Secord, "the only one still in government service, was removed from his key position in the sale of arms to the Middle East, pending a polygraph." At this point Ledeen asked Barcella to lay off Shackley and von Marbod, saying that the "billing abuses...might have gone for a covert operation." Secord was reinstated by former CIA Deputy Director Carlucci, by then the number two man in the Defense Department. Then Barcella was taken off the EATSCO investigation, which ended with Clines (the only defendant) paying by plea bargain a $10,000 fine on behalf of his company.[94]

By this point in Barcella's investigation, Secord and von Marbod had alledgedly contributed to a covert operation paid for by padded arms sales contracts. This was the controversial sale of AWACS radar airplanes to Saudi Arabia—another deal where funds were siphoned off. According to intelligence sources, millions from this initial $3.5 billion contract have gone to arm the contras.[95]

Lt. Colonel Oliver North, "the administration's point man on the AWACS sale," later acted as the White House's chief liaison with the contras—working with Singlaub and Secord. (Although Secord officially retired in 1983, at the end of the Wilson *affaire*, he was later a member of the Pentagon's Special Operations Policy Advisory Group.) Both Singlaub and Secord have worked to supply the contras with modern counter-insurgency STOL (short-takeoff-and-landing) aircraft; and perhaps as many as four STOL planes have actually been delivered, via one of Secord's companies, to the contras in Honduras.[96]

Ledeen suggested to Barcella that the falsified billings might have been a cover for a covert operation. But that hypothesis can also be turned around. A covert operation, such as the contras, can become a justification for putting back into business a clandestine service that has been all but banished from government because of past excesses. That of course has happened. Because of the contras, the CIA airlines are flying again, the "swift boats" are being launched from their mother ships, and operations are once again being co-ordinated out of a possibly illegal CIA operations station in Miami. This is an almost certain formula for the involvement of CIA personnel in the drug traffic—perhaps the chief reason why Shackley's covert operations in Miami were closed down.

But a covert operation can also become a "CIA defense"—a cover for fraudulent profits from arms sales, and even for their diversion into illegal campaign contributions. Moreover, as we have seen from our historical review, it can easily become a cover for new illegal activities, particularly in that historical corollary to clandestine operations, the narcotics traffic.

The Cuban S-Force and Narcotics

So far we have studied the role played in the Iran-Contra arms scandal by a "secret team" or "shadow network," composed of Americans like Generals John Singlaub and Richard Secord, whose friendship during the

CIA covert war in Laos facilitated their collaboration in the "private" contra supply effort.

But for years the American "secret team" has been allied with a more autonomous, close-knit band of Cuban exiles, whose work for their American handlers has included assassination efforts, major terrorist operations, and the famous Watergate burglaries under President Nixon. Some members were arrested in 1970 in the Justice Department's Operation Eagle, which was announced as the largest federal narcotics enforcement operation ever up to that time.

The recent suit brought by the Christic Institute alleges that members of this Cuban "secret team," in conjunction with its U.S. intelligence allies, have also looked to the narcotics traffic to pay for its so-called "contra" operations. According to an affidavit filed by the Christic General Counsel, Daniel Sheehan, the profit from a drug-smuggling network organized by contra supporters who were Bay of Pigs veterans "was being used to help finance the purchase of military equipment, ammunition and explosives needed by the Contras to wage their private war against the Sandinista government."[97]

The political goal of this Cuban "secret team," and of at least some of its American handlers, has always been the overthrow of Fidel Castro. This political agenda has given them priorities different from those of any American president, Democrat or Republican, who has wanted to explore any degree of detente with the Soviet Union. This explains why so many in the Cuban team have turned for support to other right-wing governments like Argentina and Chile, whose own international intelligence operations have been financed by the same narcotics traffic.[98]

Today the two most prominent members of this second team are the Cubans in charge of loading the ill-fated Hasenfus supply plane at the Ilopango air base in El Salvador: Felix Rodriguez (alias "Max Gomez") and Luis Posada (alias "Ramon Medina"). But they are working in the contra supply operation with other ex-CIA Cubans, who have been recruited through Brigade 2506, the Bay of Pigs veterans association. Its president, Juan Perez Franco, who in 1985 made Brigade support for the contras official, is the same president who a decade earlier brought the Brigade to publicly support acts of terrorism.

One year later, in June 1976, Posada and Perez Franco, along with the Brigade's new president, Roberto Carballo, and its military chief, Armando Lopez Estrada, attended the small ten-man founding meeting of CORU, a 1976 Cuban terrorist alliance supported by the fascist governments of Chile and Argentina.[99] The *Wall Street Journal* reports Armando Lopez Estrada as saying that "on the instructions of a U.S. official in Costa Rica," he recruited Bay of Pigs veterans to advise the contras on the Costa Rican southern front.[100]

In retrospect, it is obvious that some if not most of CORU's terrorist operations were financed from the drug traffic. CORU interlocked with, and was funded by, the Miami-based World Finance Corporation (WFC), set up in 1971 by a Brigade 2506 veteran, Guillermo Hernandez Cartaya. The House Select Committee on Narcotics Abuse and Control later agreed with a local assistant U.S. attorney that WFC's activities included "political corruption, gunrunning, as well as narcotics trafficking on an international level."[101]

For example, Duney Perez Alamo, a WFC employee and former CIA agent, was also an admitted CORU member. His friend Gaspar Jimenez was arrested in 1976 for a CORU attempt at kidnap and murder in Merida, Mexico. According to the Miami Organized Crime Bureau, "Hernandez Cartaya financed and planned the Mexican action, with help from Perez Alamo." In March 1977 Jimenez escaped from a Mexican prison, apparently with the aid of $50,000 supplied by WFC.

According to Penny Lernoux,

> One of those who aided in the escape was Nestor 'Tony' Izquierdo, a Cuban exile formerly associated with the Defense Intelligence Agency. He was arrested while attempting to reenter the United States from Mexico, but was released on low bail when a retired Navy commander who had once worked with the DIA vouched for his 'good character.'...Government files further showed that Izquierdo's bond and legal fees were paid by WFC.[102]

The WFC had good relations with both the Washington establishment and, reportedly, the Mafia. One of its six founding stockholders and directors was Washington attorney Walter Sterling Surrey, a veteran of OSS. One of his WFC associates was, according to the Drug Enforcement Administration (DEA), an alleged narcotics wholesaler and member of the Trafficante Mafia family.[103] In 1981, after WFC had collapsed, Hernandez Cartaya was convicted and sentenced to five years for income tax evasion. His successor as "godfather" of the Miami narcotics traffic was another Bay of Pigs veteran, Jose Medardo Alvero Cruz.[104]

Like Rodriguez and Posada, Perez Alamo and Izquierdo were not average members of Brigade 2506; they were members of a much smaller elite of specialists trained in sabotage and other black arts. At least three members of this inner elite, which we shall call the S-Force, also were in touch with the renegade ex-CIA agent Ed Wilson.[105]

This S-Force had its origins in the eighty-man force of sabotage teams given special training in Panama and Florida for infiltration into Cuba at the time of the Bay of Pigs. According to Warren Hinckle and William Turner, many of these Cubans had been recruited from the ranks of the International Anti-Communist Brigade (IACB), a rag-tag private army funded chiefly by the dispossessed Havana casino owners with Mafia connections, and recruited and trained by the future Watergate burglar Frank Sturgis.[106] These origins may explain why so many of the S-Force members ended up taking over the narcotics traffic that had been associated with the Havana casinos, before the Cuban revolution eliminated such goings on.

Members of this smaller S-Force have been used for illegal purposes from at least 1971, when Howard Hunt attended the Brigade's tenth anniversary meeting to recruit some of the future Watergate burglars for the Nixon White House "plumbers" or "counter-intelligence" break-in teams.[107]

Hunt, seeking break-in specialists, went to the elite counter-intelligence operation of the CIA's station in Miami. Most of these 150 or so men were Bay of Pigs veterans who had subsequently been picked for further army training at Fort Jackson, and some, like Rodriguez and Posada, for officer training at Fort Benning. Some of this elite force were then recruited to work for the CIA. This counter-intelligence operation, identified in the *New York Times* as "Operation 40," finally had to be closed down in the early 1970s, after one of its planes crashed in Southern California with several kilos of cocaine and heroin aboard.[108]

Both Rodriguez and Posada, like their close friend the Watergate burglar Eugenio Martinez, have been identified as members of Operation 40.[109] The Fort Jackson trainees had their own, more restricted veteran's organization, the "Ex-Combatientes de Fort Jackson." Among those who took part in Hunt's first Watergate break-in, and were never arrested, were Angel Ferrer, the president of the Ex-Combatientes, and Felipe de Diego, identified in Watergate testimony as a member of Operation 40.[110]

Eugenio Martinez, a close personal friend of both Felix Rodriguez and Luis Posada, was an active member of Operation 40 on the CIA payroll when he was arrested, along with his American handlers Howard Hunt and James McCord, for the Watergate break-in of June 17, 1972. In 1981 Martinez was pardoned by newly elected President Ronald Reagan, a little noticed event that may have heralded the cementing of the Reagan-Contragate alliance.

Martinez, Rodriguez, and Posada were all members of an even more elite group within the Ex-Combatientes de Fort Jackson and Operation 40. They had been part of the much smaller S-Force of about 80 men trained for sabotage and other special operations, including assassinations in connection with the 1961 invasion. Although all three have been loosely called "Bay of Pigs veterans," in fact none of them went ashore there. Rodriguez and Posada had been infiltrated covertly into Cuba two months earlier. Martinez, a boat skipper, had taken Rodriguez in.[111]

It is this special advance sabotage force, or "S-force," that has had the most intimate and conspiratorial relationship with the American shadow network behind Contragate. "Sabotage" is perhaps a euphemism for the range of tasks this "S-Force" (as opposed to the larger "Ex-Combatientes de Fort Jackson," and still larger Brigade 2506) was trained for.

The most important of those tasks was the assassination of Fidel Castro. Business Week has identified Rafael "Chi Chi" Quintero, a member of the contra supply team at Ilopango and earlier one of the most important S-Force infiltrators, as a man "who played a key role in the Bay of Pigs invasion and in subsequent efforts to assassinate Fidel Castro."[112]

Quintero was later hired (along with Ricardo Chavez, another S-force veteran) for a business venture set up by his former CIA case officer Tom Clines; this venture also involved Theodore Shackley, Clines' former boss as head of the CIA Miami station.[113]

Richard Nixon learned to his regret the dangers of hiring Cubans with a different political agenda in order to bypass both the CIA and Congress. One can speculate that Ronald Reagan may be about to learn the same lesson.

The Contragate Cubans: A Trojan Horse?

Like Richard Nixon a decade earlier, Ronald Reagan, in order to bypass Congressional scrutiny in training and supplying the contras, turned to the right-wing ex-CIA Cuban Bay of Pigs veterans of Brigade 2506. The two Presidents' actions were similar but not identical; by the mid-1970s many Brigade 2506 members had turned against the United States government, and forged new alliances with foreign powers and groups that were overtly anti-Semitic and fascist.

This split became obvious in 1974, under Presidents Nixon and Ford, when Secretary of State Kissinger was reported to be preparing for normalization of relations with Cuba. (In March 1976 Posada's ally Orlando Bosch, who would soon become the ideological leader of CORU, was briefly jailed in Costa Rica during Kissinger's visit. Miami police had "picked up word that Bosch was planning the bombing assassination of...Kissinger. The apparent motive was Kissinger's earlier overtures to improve relations with Cuba."[114])

Many Brigade members responded to Kissinger's plans for detente with violence in Miami and overtures to fascists and neofascists in both Europe and Latin America. The most prominent of Brigade 2506's new alliances was with Chilean dictator Augusto Pinochet; at its April 1975 anniversary conference, it gave him its first Freedom Award. Speakers at the meeting denounced the United States for betraying their cause, and even threatened to storm the Kennedy Library in Boston if their flag there were not returned.[115]

Soon afterwards, for the first time in its history, Brigade 2506 began publicly taking credit for terrorist attacks against Cuba. In April 1976 Brigade President Juan Perez Franco was quoted as endorsing an attack on a Cuban fishing vessel in which a seaman was killed.[116]

In June 1976 former Brigade 2506 President Roberto Carballo joined leaders of three other avowedly terrorist organizations—the neofascist CNM of Felipe Rivero Diaz, the FNLC of Frank Castro, Alpha 66, and the Accion Cubana of Orlando Bosch—in creating a new terrorist alliance called CORU, the Congress of United Revolutionary Organizations. The purpose of CORU was to build political support for overthrowing Castro by performing hit jobs with and for right-wing governments, especially that of Pinochet in Chile and Somoza in Nicaragua.

That CORU alliance, uniting mainstream ex-CIA Cubans with mavericks accustomed to survive from the drug traffic, was a historic step towards the contra alliance with drug-trafficking Cuban exiles today. One sign of this continuity is the presence at Ilopango of Luis Posada, who attended CORU's founding meeting. That meeting was organized principally by FNLC chief Frank Castro, who has been named in connection with alleged arms-for-drug deals through Ilopango in support of the contras.[117]

CORU was also actively supported by Alpha 66, the Cuban exile participants in the World Anti-Communist League. Alpha 66 was particularly close to WACL's Guatemalan contingent the MLN, headed by their ally Mario Sandoval Alarcon (later an initial backer of the contras). In July 1976 Alpha 66 also expressed its ideological debt to the Mexican WACL leader Jorge Prieto Laurens, a member of a secret neofascist society, the Tecos, who had circulated at the Roman Catholic Vatican Council II a document denouncing "Jewish imperialism...the worst imperialism the world has ever seen."[118]

In September 1976, after publishing CORU "war communiques" promising that civilian airliners would soon be attacked, Brigade 2506's allegiance to CORU was publicly confirmed at a Brigade conference in September 1976, at which the keynote speaker was the Nicaraguan dictator Anastasio Somoza.[119] To make it even more plain that the Brigade and CORU had broken with the constraints of U.S. foreign policy, CORU delegates attended an October 1976 meeting in Rome to charter a new Fascist International, together with representatives of groups responsible for a spate of bombings and bank robberies in Europe.[120] Some of these same European neo-fascists began attending the Latin American meetings of WACL, where they were introduced by representatives of Chile and Argentina.

More importantly, CORU Cubans and European neofascists put together a series of joint terrorist actions and conspiracies designed to undermine U.S. foreign policy. In January 1977, for example, at a time when the United States was supporting Spain's first democratic election after the death of Franco, a CORU Cuban (Julio Carlos Perez) was arrested with an Argentinian and Mariano Sanchez Covisa, the leader of the Spanish "Guerrillas of Christ the King," for one of a number of gratuitous murders, part of a "strategy of tension" to prevent the elections from being held.[121]

Behind this "strategy of tension" was the so-called Aginter-Press, a group of former French intelligence officers, once banished to Portugal for their plots to overthrow French President Charles de Gaulle. One of them, Yves Guerin-Serac, was at the center of a plot to restore dictatorship to Portugal, where after the death of the dictator Salazar, official U.S. policy, as enforced by Ambassador Frank Carlucci, was again to support democratic elections.

Also prominent in this coup attempt were the same Spaniard, Mariano Sanchez Covisa, and "approximately 100 'anti-Castro' Cubans."[122] Just where these Cubans came from is not entirely clear. But in 1975 support for the coup came from a Fort Jackson sabotage-trained ex-CIA Cuban and top level drug trafficker, Alberto Sicilia Falcon.[123] At the same time the Brigade 2506 office in Miami became a recruiting ground for Cuban exiles willing to fight for the UNITA forces of Jonas Savimbi in the former Portuguese colony of Angola.[124] Inasmuch as these Cubans are not known to have arrived in Angola, and the ELP army was originally recruited for a coup in Angola, they may simply have become part of the CORU-Aginter-GCR alliance for a coup in Portugal.

For the next five years, Cuban exiles and other members of the Fascist International would meet at the annual meetings of CAL, the Latin American chapter of the World Anti-Communist League (WACL). Blas Pinar, the brains behind the 1977 murders in Spain for which Carlos Perez was arrested, attended the 1979 CAL Congress, as did the wanted Italian terrorist Elio Massagrande, whose bank deposit box was supposed to have contained the treasury for this conspiracy.[125]

WACL at this time was supported by four governments (Taiwan and South Korea, the founders, joined by Saudi Arabia and the Philippines) of which at least three were actively opposed to detente. As the United States moved toward coexistence in the 1970s, WACL moved in the opposite direction, toward a more open embrace of Nazi ideology and former war criminals. At least three WACL European Chapters (the German, the Austrian, and the Dutch) were taken over by former Nazi SS officers who had fought against America in World War II. In this same period some WACL members proclaimed themselves (in the words of the Norwegian chapter) united for freedom "from both World Communism and the international financial-imperialism."

It might seem surprising that this narco-fascist conspiracy, uniting the CORU-Brigade 2506 terrorist alliance, the WACL neofascists, and various European terrorists, should have been so swiftly and eagerly embraced by the incoming Reagan administration. But as we shall see in the next chapter, the shadow network had been busy for some years preparing for just this alliance.

IV.
The Growth of Reagan's Contra Commitment

Introduction: Private and Official Decision-Making

By any accounting, Washington's decision to create and support the contras was a consensual one, reached in the heart of the Reagan administration's professional bureaucratic apparatus. The relative weight of outside "shadow networks" and inside bureaucrats in generating the *formal* contra commitment is neatly summarized in an excellent book by Christopher Dickey, *With the Contras*:

> Before any hard and fast decisions on the Secret War were taken, several CIA 'old-timers,' released from service during the cutbacks of the 1970s, were in contact with anti-Sandinista forces, acting as private citizens to reassure them that once Reagan was elected, their lot would improve...But while some of these men eventually served as contract agents in the Secret War, their importance in creating it is, I believe, overstated. The paramilitary operation against Nicaragua *ultimately* was not just an out-of-control creation of conspiratorial ex-spies and right-wing ideologues but a conscious decision by senior administration officials who consider themselves pragmatic policymakers.[1]

Like other authors, Dickey locates this conscious decision making in the Senior Interagency Group on Central America set up under National Security Council guidelines and precedents, and initially responsible to

51

CIA Director William Casey and Robert McFarlane (then Secretary of State Haig's counselor).[2] Two names from this initial "Core Group" set up in 1981 would figure in the later Contragate story: Nestor Sanchez, a New Mexico-born CIA veteran of the Guatemalan "death squad" operations in 1967-68, (later representing the Pentagon), and Colonel Oliver North from the NSC staff.

Dickey's account, however, stresses the discontinuity between the "pragmatic" bureaucratic consensus of 1981, and the consensus of a year earlier under Jimmy Carter, when the message to Central American governments was not counter-revolution so much as "reform":

> Despite years of experience and seniority in the foreign service, most of the veterans associated with the Carter policy [in Central America] were fired, forced out or moved to obscure and distant posts. Carter's last assistant secretary was sacked. His principal deputy for Central America was transferred to Katmandu...[The men] brought in to replace them were, as one put it, 'action-oriented.'[3]

Clearly, then, the change in policy was not bureaucratic so much as political. The 1981 purge of those State Department hands who allegedly "lost Nicaragua," like the 1953 purge of those who allegedly "lost China," was undertaken to fulfill a campaign pledge, made in response to allegedly massive and illicit campaign contributions from the interested region. Those who acted to generate the change in policy were not just the self-important CIA "old-timers" to whom Dickey refers. The agents included these men's "anti-Sandinista" allies—most notably the deposed dictator Anastasio Somoza of Nicaragua, and after Somoza's murder in 1980, the Guatemalan death squad impresario, Mario Sandoval Alarcon.

In the late 1970s, as indicated in the last chapter, three of the foreign forces who would eventually back the contras (the governments of Taiwan and Argentina, and right-wing forces in Guatemala), had taken an important step to ensure themselves a voice in Washington for a new U.S. foreign policy in Latin America to replace President Carter's. All three moved to hire as their Washington lobbyist Michael Deaver, the man then managing the campaign of future presidential candidate Ronald Reagan.

After this, Deaver's Guatemalan clients, following visits from Reagan campaign representatives such as Richard Allen, Roger Fontaine and John Singlaub (the CIA "old-timer" and future WACL Chairman), began to raise funds for the Reagan campaign. On a BBC broadcast, these funds were estimated by former Guatemalan Vice-President Villagran Kramer as amounting to perhaps ten million dollars.[4]

Reagan, Deaver's Amigos, and the Death Squads

The group that Deaver represented in Guatemala, the Amigos del País (Friends of the Country), is not known to have included Mario Sandoval Alarcon personally. But ten to fifteen of its members were accused by former Guatemalan Vice-President Villagran Kramer on the BBC of being "directly linked with organized terror."[5] One such person, not named by Villagran, was the Texas lawyer John Trotter, the owner of the Coca-Cola bottling plant in Guatemala City. Coca-Cola agreed in 1980 to terminate Trotter's franchise, after the *Atlantic Monthly* reported that several workers and trade union leaders trying to organize his plant had been murdered by death squads.[6]

One year earlier, in 1979, Trotter had traveled to Washington as part of a five-man public relations mission from the Amigos. At least two members of that mission, Roberto Alejos Arzu and Manuel F. Ayau, are known to have met Ronald Reagan. (Reagan later described Ayau as "one of the few people...who understands what is going on down there."[7])

Roberto Alejos Arzu, the head of Deaver's Amigos and the principal organizer of Guatemala's "Reagan for President" bandwagon, was an old CIA contact; in 1960 his plantation had been used to train Cuban exiles for the Bay of Pigs invasion. Before the 1980 election Alejos complained that "most of the elements in the State Department are probably pro-Communist...Either Mr. Carter is a totally incapable president or he is definitely a pro-communist element."[8] (In 1954, Alejos' friend Sandoval had been one of the CIA's leading political proteges in its overthrow of Guatemala's President Arbenz.)

When asked by the BBC how ten million dollars from Guatemala could have reached the Reagan campaign, Villagran named no names: "The only way that I can feel it would get there would be that some North American residing in Guatemala, living in Guatemala, would more or less be requesting money over there or accepting contributions and then transmitting them to his Republican Party as contributions of his own."[9]

Trotter was the only U.S. businessman in Guatemala whom Alan Nairn could find in the list of Reagan donors disclosed to the Federal Election Commission. Others, who said specifically that they had contributed, were not so listed. Nairn heard from one businessman who had been solicited that "explicit instructions were given repeatedly: 'Do not give to Mr. Reagan's campaign directly.' Monies were instead to be directed to an undisclosed committee in California."[10]

Trotter admitted in 1980 that he was actively fundraising in this period in Guatemala. The money he spoke of, half a million dollars, was however not directly for the Reagan campaign, but for a documentary film in support of Reagan's Latin American policies, being made by one of the groups supporting Reagan, the American Security Council (ASC). The film argued that the survival of the United States depended on defeat of the Sandinistas in Nicaragua: "Tomorrow: Honduras...Venezuela, the Dominican Republic, Mexico...the United States."[11]

Deaver's Amigos and Trotter were in extended contact with the ASC over this project. In December 1979, and again in 1980, the ASC sent retired Army General John Singlaub to meet Guatemalan President Lucas Garcia and other officials.[12] According to one of Singlaub's 1979 contacts, the clear message was that "Mr. Reagan recognizes that a good deal of dirty work has to be done."[13] On his return to the United States, according to Pearce, Singlaub called for "sympathetic understanding of the death squads."[14] In 1980 Singlaub returned to Guatemala with another apologist for death squads, General Gordon Sumner of the Council for Inter-American Security. Again the message to Lucas was that "help was on the way in the form of Ronald Reagan."[15]

Jenny Pearce has noted that Singlaub's first ASC visit to Guatemalan President Lucas took place shortly after Lucas's meeting with Guatemalan businessmen, where he is "alleged to have raised half a million dollars in contributions to the [Reagan] campaign."[16] Since the 1984 Congressional cutoff of aid to the contras, Singlaub, as world chairman of the World Anti-Communist League, has been the most visible source of private support to the contras. He did this in liaison with both William Casey of the CIA and Col. Oliver North of the National Security Council staff.[17]

But Singlaub's contacts with the World Anti-Communist League go back at least to 1980, when he was also purporting to speak abroad in the name of Reagan. Did the help from Reagan which Singlaub promised Guatemalans in 1980, like the "verbal agreements" which Sandoval referred to at Reagan's Inaugural, involve commitments even then from Reagan to that fledgling WACL project, the contras?

Mike Deaver should be asked that question, since in 1980 he was a registered foreign lobbyist for three of the contras most important WACL backers: Guatemala, Taiwan, and Argentina.

Deaver, Taiwan, and WACL

Through his CIA contacts, Sandoval had also become the leader of the Guatemala chapter of the World Anti-Communist League. This chapter, partly organized by Howard Hunt, was a lasting spinoff of the 1954 CIA operation. WACL as a world organization however was principally the creation of two Asian governments which owed their survival to their well-organized lobbies in Washington. These two governments are Taiwan, which was represented in 1980 by Deaver; and South Korea, which is represented by Deaver today.

Through his long-time participation in WACL meetings, Sandoval has developed close relations with WACL's Taiwan organizers. It was largely through WACL that Taiwan picked up the task of training Central American police forces in "political warfare" (i.e. counter-terror), about the time that similar U.S. training programs were terminated by Congress in 1974. Today the Taiwanese embassy in Guatemala is second in size only to the American; and through Guatemala (and Sandoval) Taiwan has extended its influence to other Central American police forces. Deaver's double duty as a registered Taiwan agent and Reagan campaign organizer in 1980 helped generate one of the major controversies of that campaign. To understand it, one must go back to the origins of Deaver's public relations firm, Deaver and Hannaford, which he organized in 1974. Until that year both Deaver and Peter Hannaford had worked for Reagan in the California Governor's Office. In 1974, as Reagan retired to private life, the new firm undertook to book Reagan's public appearances, research and sell his radio program, and ghost-write his syndicated column. All this was arranged with an eye to Reagan's presidential aspirations, which Deaver and Hannaford helped organize from the outset.[18]

Nothing about this arrangement was especially remarkable until 1977, when Deaver and Hannaford registered with the Justice Department as foreign agents receiving $5000 a month from the government of Taiwan. This sum was not particularly large, and notably less than the $11,000 a month which the firm would receive in 1980 from Guatemala's Amigos. The fact remains that funds from three closely allied WACL countries, Guatemala, Taiwan, and Argentina, helped pay for the Deaver and Hannaford offices, which became Reagan's initial campaign headquarters in Beverly Hills and his Washington office.[19]

Questions of conflicting interest were raised when a Reagan column, said to have been written by Hannaford, argued that normalized relations with the People's Republic of China "could prove disastrous, not only for

Taiwan, but for the United States itself."[20] When Carter, undaunted, established full relations in late 1978, Reagan became one of the loudest critics of this action. In 1980 Reagan stumped the country with the catchphrase, "No more Taiwans, no more Vietnams, no more betrayals."

As Reagan's California team was melded into a national one, by the infusion of old Nixon supporters like William Casey and Richard Allen, Reagan's position on Taiwan appeared to soften. It was Allen's task at the Republican national convention to assure reporters that Reagan did not intend to "turn the clock back."[21]

However the more balanced position which Allen projected, and which the Eastern establishment press was eager to hear, was misleading. In May 1980 in Cleveland, almost three months after Casey had become Reagan's campaign chairman, Reagan said in reply to a question that "One of the things I look forward to most if I am successful in this re-election is to re-establish official relations between the United States Government and Taiwan." Although Reagan did not spell this out, such a step would have involved a repudiation of Carter's 1978 agreement which recognized that "Taiwan is part of China."[22]

Though the national press generally ignored Reagan's Taiwan position in May, they could not when on August 16 he repeated his pledge to establish "an official governmental relationship" with Taiwan. The occasion could not have been calculated to receive better press attention: Reagan's remarks were made as he was bidding *bon voyage* to his running mate George Bush, as he left on an image-building mission to Peking. As *Time* observed disapprovingly, Reagan's remarks "managed to infuriate Peking," and "create the impression of a rift between Reagan and Bush." When an embarrassed Bush tried to assure Peking officials that Reagan was not talking of relations "in a diplomatic sense," Reagan (in *Time*'s words) "undercut" Bush by telling a reporter he still stood by his Taiwan statement. In the end Reagan grudgingly backed off ("I misstated"), while an embarrassed Casey tried to dismiss the whole episode as "semantic mishmash."[23]

Reflecting the concern of the Eastern Republican establishment, *Time* analysed the problem as one of divisions between Reagan's "uncoordinated" staff. It claimed that the top echelon of California insiders (among whom it specifically named Deaver) was "insensitive," with "little Washington or national campaign experience. The outsiders—like Campaign Director Casey...—do have that valuable experience but exercise less influence over the candidate."

On the crunch level of foreign policy decision-making, the lack of coordination appears to have been primarily between Richard Allen, who carried the title of Foreign Policy Advisor, and Deaver. There was some irony in this, since Deaver and Hannaford were busy projecting images of Reagan and themselves as pragmatists, while Allen had once been under CIA surveillance for his links to Taiwan's Vietnam allies, and had subsequently been relegated by Nixon to a minor role.[24] On the issue of Taiwan, however, Deaver and Hannaford were the ideologues, and Allen relatively a pragmatist.

Though he had originated with the ideological right, by 1981 Allen had acquired far more experience as a registered foreign agent than Deaver and Hannaford; and underlying Reagan's Taiwan flap was the further irony that the great American patriot's foreign policy formulation was at this stage almost exclusively in the hands of registered foreign lobbyists.[25] But Allen had more varied and mainstream clients to worry about than Deaver—notably Japan, which had every interest in preventing Carter's China policy from being derailed. Twice Reagan's California team would use the pretext of Allen's Japan business profits to drop him—once five days before the election, and again permanently a year later. Little noticed at the time was the fact that the key architect in the plans for Allen's permanent removal was Deaver.[26]

The Restoration of Arms Sales to WACL Countries

Deaver's double duty as Taiwan agent and deputy campaign director was reported in the U.S. press, while his lobbying for Guatemalan businessmen has been noticed by radical Latin America watchers. No one has ever noted that through the 1980 campaign Deaver and Hannaford had one other international account: the military dictatorship of Argentina, by far the most notorious of Latin America's death squad regimes.

Argentina

Argentina's image problem in America was even more acute than Guatemala's. How to put a constructive face on the disappearance and presumed murder of between 6000 and 15,000 persons? The response of Deaver and Hannaford was to bring to the United States as apologist the junta's leading civilian, Economy Minister Martinez de Hoz, and allow him to address the United States through Reagan's radio broadcasts. Here is a sample of their description of what they called "one of the most remarkable economic recoveries in modern history."

Today, Argentina is at peace, the terrorist threat nearly eliminated. Though Martinez de Hoz, in his U.S. talks, concentrates on economics, he does not shy from discussing human rights. He points out that in the process of bringing stability to a terrorized nation of 25 million, a small number were caught in the cross-fire, among them a few innocents...If you ask the average Argentine-in-the-street what he thinks about the state of his country's economy, chances are you'll find him pleased, not seething, about the way things are going.[27]

Distasteful as this Deaver-Hannaford apologetics for murder may seem today, the real issue goes far beyond rhetoric. Though Deaver and Hannaford's three international clients—Guatemala, Taiwan, and Argentina—all badly wanted a better image in America, what they wanted even more urgently were American armaments. Under Carter arms sales and deliveries to Taiwan had been scaled back for diplomatic reasons, and cut off to Guatemala and Argentina because of human rights violations.

When Reagan became President, all three of Deaver's international clients, despite considerable opposition within the Administration, began to receive arms. This under-reported fact goes against the public image of Deaver as an open-minded pragmatist, marginal to the foreign policy disputes of the first Reagan administration, so that his pre-1981 lobbying activities had little bearing on foreign policy. The details suggest a different story.

Argentina could hardly have had a worse press in the United States then when Reagan took office. The revelations of Adolfo Perez Esquivel and of Jacobo Timmerman had been for some time front page news. This did not deter the new Administration from asking Congress to lift the embargo on arms sales to Argentina on March 19, 1981, less than two months after coming to office. General Roberto Viola, one of the junta members responsible for the death squads, was welcomed to Washington in the spring of 1981. Today he is serving a 17-year sentence for his role in the "dirty war."

Though the American public did not know it, the arrangements for U.S. aid to Argentina included a *quid pro quo*: Argentina would expand its support and training for the Contras, as there was as yet no authorization for the United States to do so directly. "Thus aid and training were provided to the Contras through the Argentinian defense forces in exchange for other forms of aid from the U.S. to Argentina."[28] Congressional investigators should determine whether the contemporary arms deals with Deaver's other clients, Guatemala and Taiwan, did not contain similar kickbacks for their contra proteges.

But aid for the contras was only one part of a covert Reagan grand design for Central America in which Argentina would play the active role. This involved, among other things,

> ...the training of more than 200 Guatemalan officers in 'interrogation techniques' (torture) and repressive methods...participation in the training at U.S. military bases of officers and elite troops of the Salvadorean army...training and combat leadership for incursions by Somocista bands based in Honduras...logistic and economic support for the...plot to overthrow the Sandinista regime...the despatch of at least fifty more officers to Honduras as para-military troops to intervene in counter-revolutionary activities throughout the region, particularly against Nicaragua ...the supply of arms and ammunition to the Guatemalan regime...direct participation in torture sessions in Guatemala, and—together with Israeli officers—the creation of an 'intelligence center' in that country.[29]

Argentina eventually became one of the two principal reasons why Reagan's first Secretary of State, Alexander Haig, resigned on June 25, 1982. (The other area of disagreement was over Israel's invasion of Lebanon.) Haig later charged that his official policy of siding with Britain against Argentina (supported by Reagan, whose closest personal ally abroad was Margaret Thatcher) had been seriously undercut, not just by Ambassador Jeane Kirkpatrick, but by someone above her in the White House.

> There were contacts made with Argentinian officials by the White House which were neither discussed with me nor cleared with me and which had the practical effect of confusing the issue...This helped confirm that the outcome [the Falkland Islands war] would be inevitable.[30]

William Clark, Reagan's official national security adviser, purported to refute this charge by saying that all of *his* contacts with foreign officials had been cleared with Haig. However it was Deaver, not Clark, whom Haig suspected of offsetting his tilt against Argentina. "At an NSC session...Haig had observed Kirkpatrick passing Deaver a note. Concluding that Kirkpatrick was using Deaver to prime Reagan...Haig told Clark that a 'conspiracy' was afoot to outflank him."[31] Haig's paranoia may have been justified. Soon Deaver (allied with Clark, whom Deaver had selected as Allen's replacement) was to play a principal role in dropping Haig, as he had earlier in dropping Allen.[32]

What reason could anyone in the White House have for putting U.S. relations with Argentina ahead of relations with the United Kingdom? It is hard to think of any reason more urgent than that of agreement for covert Argentinian support of the contras, "which was broken by U.S. support for Britain in the 1982 Falklands War."[33] Although some Argentine advisers remained in Honduras, the pull-out of the Argentine government produced a temporary setback in contra operations, followed in December 1982 by a major shake-up in the contras' nominal political leadership.[34]

Guatemala

Restoring arms deliveries to Guatemala proved a little more difficult than to Argentina. "The election of Reagan coincided with the bloodiest outbreak of Guatemalan death squad actions in history. Almost five hundred deaths a month, almost all attributed to the right, were being reported by the American Embassy, but even that figure was considered low by most other monitoring groups. Piles of mutilated bodies were being discovered every morning throughout the country."[35] President Lucas Garcia, alleged to have personally raised half a million dollars from Deaver's Guatemala businessmen for the Reagan campaign, was said in February 1981 by the *New York Times* (citing Amnesty International) to be directly supervising the security agency in charge of the death squads.[36]

The May 4 hearing of the Senate Foreign Relations Committee, in which the administration announced that it was disposed to give aid to Guatemala, followed two days of hard-hitting stories in the press about that country's increasing violence, including the murders of 76 leaders of the moderate Christian Democratic Party. When Congress balked at certifying that Guatemala was not violating human rights, the administration acted unilaterally, by simply taking the items Guatemala wanted off the restricted list.[37]

Taiwan

On the issue of restoring arms sales to Argentina and Guatemala there was no dissent within the Reagan administration, all of whom were eager to repudiate Carter's human rights policies as quickly as possible. The arguments against arms sales to Taiwan, however, were geopolitical as well as ideological. The more seriously one chose to believe in a Soviet threat, the more important it seemed not to threaten the growing strategic relationship between Washington and Peking.

Reagan was confronted with this geopolitical consensus as soon as he took office. After a year of fumbling, Haig (State), Weinberger (Defense) and Casey (CIA) united on a recommendation to Reagan: Taiwan should not receive the new weapons it was asking for. In August 1982 the State Department, after another visit to Peking by George Bush, announced a joint communique with China, in which the United States undertook to "reduce gradually its [weapons] sales [to Taiwan]...leading over a period of time to a final resolution."[38]

This result appeared to experts to represent a victory of "Geopolitics over Ideology."[39] But while the communique called for a reduction, arms sales to Taiwan in fact increased, to new levels of $530 million in 1983, and $1,085 million in 1984. Each new arms sales announcement was greeted with loud protests from Peking, and with increasing rumors and reports of Sino-Soviet rapprochement.[40] Once again, we now know that on the issue of Taiwan arms sales Haig at the State Department was being over-ruled by the Reagan White House staff.[41]

Deaver, WACL, and the Contras

The lobbying for increased U.S. arms sales came of course from at home as well as from abroad; and primarily from the American Security Council, the chief real-life incarnation of that military-industrial complex which President Eisenhower warned the country about a quarter of a century ago. Two prominent backers of the ASC (oilmen A.C. Rubel and Henry Salvatori) were also part of the trio of Los Angeles millionaires who had launched Reagan into politics after the Goldwater debacle of 1964.[42]

The third, Holmes Tuttle, lent his weight to the small meeting of May 1974 in Reagan's home where the decision was made for Reagan to begin his drive for the presidency. Four of Reagan's top aides attended that meeting: Meese, Nofziger, Deaver, and Hannaford. The Deaver and Hannaford agency was launched in 1974 as part of that presidential strategy.

The international clients taken on by Deaver and Hannaford— Taiwan, Guatemala, and Argentina—were longtime causes of the ASC as well.[43] More importantly, the ASC helped out Taiwan's foreign policy creation, the World Anti-Communist League, by setting up an American affiliate for it, the American Council for World Freedom (ACWF). The young executive secretary of the ACWF, Lee Edwards, was by 1980 the registered lobbyist for WACL's Taiwan chapter, and also of Argentina. Edwards also wrote a Reagan biography.

In 1976 Edwards' ACWF pulled out of WACL, on the grounds that it was becoming racist. The new U.S. WACL chapter, the Council on American Affairs (CAA), was however also headed by an ASC man: Roger Pearson of ASC's editorial board. By 1980, WACL had been largely taken over by former Nazis, SS men, Nazi collaborators, and outspoken anti-Semites. Most embarrassing, from the point of view of a "law and order" candidate like Reagan, was the presence at WACL conferences of wanted right-wing terrorist murderers, and, perhaps worse, bank-robbers.[44]

The Reagan team, both before and after the 1980 election, appears to have adopted a two-fold approach to the problem of right-wing WACL terrorism. On the one hand they fostered a careful program to improve WACL's image, badly tarnished after British and American WACL members had protested WACL's penetration by anti-Semites. On the other, they moved through Deaver's clients in Guatemala to make selected terrorists the lynchpins of the Reagan administration's policies in Central America.

Two men appear to have been central in this double policy: General John Singlaub, who after Reagan's election became WACL's new world chairman, and Mario Sandoval Alarcon, the Guatemalan godfather and WACL leader who got to dance at Reagan's inaugural ball. The public relations work for both men, at least prior to the election, was in the hands of Mike Deaver.

Singlaub was a long-time veteran of CIA and DOD "unconventional warfare" operations, which he once explained as including "terrorism, subversion and guerrilla warfare...sabotage...support to resistance groups ...black and gray psychological operations."[45] Singlaub was little-known until 1978, when he was transferred from his Army Command in South Korea for publicly denouncing Carter's announced plans to withdraw U.S. troops from that area. A spirited defense of Singlaub and his position was promptly prepared for one of Reagan's 1978 broadcasts by Deaver and Hannaford.[46]

Little noticed at the time was the fact that ten days before his retirement, in May 1978, Singlaub attended a meeting of right-wingers who "didn't think the country was being run properly and were interested in doing something about it." The meeting was hosted by Mitch WerBell, a conspiratorial colleague of Singlaub from their OSS days together at Kunming in China.[47] As we have seen, Singlaub then began a series of co-ordinated visits to Central America, with Generals Graham and Sumner, laying the basis for Reagan's current support of the contras in Nicaragua. Singlaub's visits focused on Guatemala, where in 1982 WerBell would support a coup attempt by the National Liberation Movement (MLN) of Mario Sandoval Alarcon and Lionel Sisniega Otero.[48]

Singlaub's link-up with Sumner in 1980 was particularly significant to the Guatemalans, since for a year Sumner had been one of the most prominent contra contacts in Washington who was "looking for some way to help Nicaraguans who wanted to fight" the Sandinistas.[49] After the election that most prominent supporter would become Singlaub himself, by a series of events which seem to have been pre-arranged.

The most important event was the creation of a new United States chapter of WACL, to replace one which had been taken over by crackpots and racists. Singlaub did this on November 22, 1981, four days after a secret approval by Reagan of a CIA plan to begin direct assistance to the contras.[50]

The weeks after Reagan's election had seen a number of rapid developments. Some of Sandoval's contra group, headed by Colonel Enrique Bermudez who had been Sumner's contact, departed for training in Argentina. (This was training in terrorism; and one of the trainers is now wanted for his leadership of a cell attempting, by bombings and kidnappings, to destabilize the new Argentine civilian government.[51]) The Salvadorean death squad leader, Major Roberto d'Aubuisson, entered the United States illegally (the Carter administration refused to issue him a visa), and had conferences "with members of the Reagan transition team and with members of the staff of...Senator Jesse Helms."[52]

Meanwhile Singlaub flew to Australia to address WACL's Asian contingent, the Asian People's Anti-Communist League (APACL). He correctly predicted that there would be closer relations between the U.S. and WACL countries, and hinted that he himself would be helpful even though he would not be a member of the new administration.[53] This public healing of the rift between WACL and the United States had begun the previous July in Geneva, when the nominal head of WACL's U.S. chapter (a white racist who had once urged his state of Mississippi to secede from the Union) was upstaged by the presence at the WACL Conference of Singlaub's close friend Ray Cline. Cline was another strong Reagan supporter and a foreign policy adviser; he flew to Taiwan after the election to convey the message that "the new Reagan Administration will enhance U.S. relations with Taipei without damaging ties with Peiping [sic]."[54]

Singlaub, WACL, and LaRouche

In the light of WACL's subsequent importance to the Reagan policy of supporting the contras, it is significant that the approaches of Cline and Singlaub to WACL began before the 1980 election. Singlaub and Cline were the logical team to consolidate the Reagan-WACL alliance, since their acquaintance with WACL's members and drug-financed intrigues went back to the 1950s, if not earlier. Singlaub had first met Cline, along with four future backers of CIA-Cuban operations (Howard Hunt, Paul Helliwell, Lucien Conein and Mitch WerBell) in a small OSS mission at Kunming in China, at the very center of the World War II KMT drug traffic. According to the *Wall Street Journal*, OSS payments at this base were frequently made with five-pound shipments of opium.[55] The sixth and most mysterious of these men, Mitch WerBell, would himself be indicted on drug smuggling charges in 1976, two years before he began an extended and little-noticed relationship with John Singlaub and Lyndon LaRouche.

The other five men from the OSS Kunming mission went on into the CIA, and in the 1950s served in or supported CIA covert operations in Asia. Helliwell, from his law office in Miami, organized the arms supply to General Li Mi's drug-growing KMT troops in Burma, as he would later organize support for the CIA's Cuban sabotage teams in Miami (see Chapter III).[56] Lucien Conein went on to be the CIA's liaison with the Corsican gangsters of Saigon; and, according to Alfred McCoy, "did not pass on" to Washington the information he learned about the large shipments of drugs these Corsicans were making to Europe, while they gave the 1965 Saigon government "a fixed percentage of the profits."[57] Howard Hunt was in 1954 assigned to a black propaganda psychological warfare operation based in Tokyo.[58]

More directly impinging on what became WACL were the activities of Cline as CIA station chief in Taiwan (1958-62), and Singlaub as deputy CIA station chief in South Korea (ca. 1950-52). Cline is said to have helped Taiwan found its Political Warfare Cadres Academy at Peitou, which has through its training program developed a conspiratorial Latin American fraternity of thousands of military and security officers, including Roberto d'Aubuisson. In this way the Kuomintang created in Latin America "carbon copies of what they had created in Taiwan: a politicized military whose first loyalty was to the party, then to the military, and finally to the nation."[59]

All of this was in fulfilment of recommendations drafted in 1959 by General Richard Stilwell for a special Presidential Committee under

General William Draper reporting to President Eisenhower: that the U.S. help develop "higher level military schools" with political-economic curricula in the Third World, to encourage local armies to become "internal motors" for "socio-political transformation."[60]

Former U.S. intelligence officers have also suggested that the funding of APACL, and of the initial preparatory meetings in 1958 for WACL, came from U.S. Embassy Counterpart funds in Taiwan to which Cline had access.[61] As CIA deputy chief in South Korea during the Korean War, Singlaub is also said to have had a hand in developing what eventually became the Korean Central Intelligence Agency, the other chief partner in setting up APACL.[62]

In 1954, when APACL was founded in Taiwan, its first Latin American affiliate was founded in Mexico City by Howard Hunt. Hunt did so in his capacity as political and propaganda chief of the CIA operation in Guatemala; but his creation (the Interamerican Council for the Defense of the Continent, or CIADC) would survive to be involved in other CIA-backed coups as well, notably the Brazil coup in 1964.[63] The CIADC soon became a vehicle for the international plotting of two of Hunt's young Guatemalan proteges: Lionel Sisniega Otero, who in 1954 was employed on clandestine radio operations by Hunt's assistant David Phillips, and Sisniega's mentor, the future "Godfather," Mario Sandoval Alarcon.[64]

By accident or by design, the simultaneous creation of APACL and CIADC in 1954 also had the effect of creating a conspiratorial China Lobby for Taiwan overseas, at precisely the time that the activities of the old conspiratorial China Lobby in Washington were being exposed and neutralized. When the first provisional steering committee for a combined WACL was announced from Mexico City in 1958, its General Secretary was veteran China Lobbyist Marvin Liebman, who earlier had organized Washington's "Committee of One Million" in support of Taiwan. Lee Edwards, Liebman's successor at the Committee of One Million, organized the first U.S. Chapter of WACL, with officers from the leadership of the American Security Council.[65]

From the China Lobby bribes of the early 1950s to the contra raids of the 1980s, there have been continuing reports linking Taiwan's and WACL's activities to profits from the international narcotics traffic (see Chapter III). The situation was aggravated by the evolution of the 1950s China Lobby into the 1960s Cuban exile-Somoza Lobby, particularly when ex-CIA CORU Cubans like Orlando Bosch, dropped from the CIA for their terrorist and/or drug trafficking activities, were simply picked up by Somoza.

It made sense that Somoza, when his long-time backers were abandoning him in 1979, should have tried to hire Shackley's associate Tom Clines to work for him, along with Bosch. Shackley and Clines, by coincidence or not, personified the CIA-mafia connection that successive CIA Directors found impossible to eliminate. When Richard Helms closed down anti-Castro operations in Miami, dispersed its U.S. and Cuban personnel, and sent Shackley and Clines to manage the covert war in Laos, the two men were moving from a local drug-linked operation to a more distant one. Significantly, the Florida mob went with them. Two years after they were transferred to Laos in July 1966, Santos Trafficante, a key figure in the CIA-mafia assassination plots against Castro, was seen contacting local gangsters in Hong Kong and Saigon.[66]

But the Shackley-Clines links to Latin America increased as their former agents were dispersed there. One of these men was John Martino, an old mafia casino associate of Santos Trafficante in Havana. In 1970, posing as a mafia representative, John Martino became a business associate of President Arana, and the CIA control for Mario Sandoval Alarcon—two of the Guatemalans who attended Reagan's 1981 inaugural ball.[67]

We see then that the Reagan-WACL alliance was forged by two men, Ray Cline and John Singlaub, whose connections to WACL's Asian patrons went back three decades or more. One's first assumption is that, as loyal Americans, they would be more likely to approach WACL on behalf of Reagan than the other way round. Singlaub, in particular, has a reputation of being a "straight arrow," a "boy scout," for whom subversive intrigue would be anathema.

There are nonetheless disturbing indications that Singlaub, at least, may have been working for a hidden agenda that went far beyond naive loyalty to a Republican presidential candidate. It is hard to explain his dealings in the same period 1978-82 with his former Kunming OSS colleague Mitch WerBell, and more importantly with WerBell's employer since 1977, Lyndon LaRouche. About his political activities with the LaRouche movement Singlaub has at the very least been less than candid. What makes this disturbing is that the LaRouche movement was then suspected of looking for a dissident general to lead a military coup.[68]

We have already seen that in May 1978, ten days before his retirement, Singlaub attended a meeting of right-wingers who "didn't think the country was being run properly and were interested in doing something about it." The meeting was hosted by Mitch WerBell, who in 1982 would travel to Central America in support of an attempted Guatemalan coup on behalf of WACL leaders Mario Sandoval Alarcon and Lionel Sisniega Otero.[69] WerBell's career of covert activities in the Caribbean also involved work for Cuban dictator Batista in 1959, Dominican Republic dictator Imbert in 1965, and a coup operation (said by Hinckle and Turner to have had possible Mafia backing) against Haitian dictator Duvalier in 1966.[70] WerBell, when Singlaub visited him in 1978, had recently evaded separate indictments for arms smuggling and for narcotics trafficking.[71] WerBell was also in touch with "Secret Team" members such as Ted Shackley and Richard Secord, and allegedly was paid once through the drug-linked Nugan Hand Bank (see Chapter III) when he conducted "operations for U.S. intelligence."[72] More importantly he was also in touch with Cuban Bay of Pigs veterans suspected of involvement in the CORU assassination of Orlando Letelier.[73]

WerBell, when Singlaub visited him in 1978, was employed as the "personal security adviser" to Lyndon H. LaRouche, then the leader of the so-called National Caucus of Labor Committees (NCLC), a group which previously had posed as left-wing but in fact harassed anti-nuclear and other left-wing demonstrations with the help of the right-wing domestic intelligence group known since 1979 as Western Goals (backed primarily by WACL donor and Texan millionaire Nelson Bunker Hunt). Singlaub and another leader of his U.S. WACL chapter (Anthony Kubek) joined the advisory board of Western Goals.[74] Though Singlaub left Western Goals in 1984, the organization is controlled today by Carl Spitz Channell, who in 1986 met with Oliver North "five or ten times" about his TV advertising campaigns against political candidates opposed to contra aid.[75]

In 1979 General Singlaub conceded to the *New York Times* that he had met with two of LaRouche's party officials at the home of WerBell, but claimed that he had

> ...since rejected the organization. "It was so clear to me after the first three or four contacts that they wanted something from me," the general said. "They hounded me for months, they flooded me with documents, they showed up at places where I spoke."
>
> "I think they're a bunch of kooks of the worst form, General Singlaub went on. "I've been telling WerBell that if they're not Marxists in disguise, they're the worst group of anti-Semitic Jews [sic!] I've encountered. I'm really worried about these guys; they seem to get some people."
>
> The general was asked if any mention was made in his talks of the possibility of a military coup in the United States—an idea that has recently received currency in the party as a way to put Mr. LaRouche in power. "Well, it didn't come up in that form, but it was suggested that the military ought to in some way lead

the country out of its problems," General Singlaub replied. "I guess I stepped on them pretty hard on that, and it never came up again. It was one of the first things that made me realize they're a bunch of kooks."[76]

Singlaub's worries about a LaRouchean military solution to America's problems, although expressed so strongly in this interview, do not appear to have been very profound or long-lived. According to Scott and Jon Lee Anderson, in 1982 Singlaub returned to WerBell's counterterrorist training camp in Powder Springs, Georgia, to lecture WerBell's trainees. Many of these were security forces for the organization of Lyndon LaRouche, then the anti-Semitic leader of the so-called U.S. Labor Party, whose security director was WerBell.[77]

The Strategy of Tension: CAL, P-2, Drugs, and the Mafia

Reports linking WACL to drugs became particularly flagrant in the period 1976-80, as the rift between WACL and Carter's CIA widened, and as a new Argentine-dominated affiliate of WACL in Latin America (the Confederacion Anticomunista Latina, or CAL) plotted to extirpate radical Roman Catholic priests and prelates fostering liberation theology.

A high-point or low-point of the CAL plotting was reached in 1980, when Argentine officers, bankrolled by the lords of Bolivia's cocaine traffic, installed the Bolivian drug dictatorship of Luis Garcia Meza. Two of the Argentine officers involved turned out to be wanted Italian terrorists, Stefano delle Chiaie and Pierluigi Pagliai; together with the veteran Nazi fugitive and drug trafficker Klaus Barbie, the neo-fascists seized the radio station as a signal to launch the coup.[78]

Barbie and delle Chiaie were both deeply involved in the CAL project to identify and exterminate leftists and radical priests. Through this project delle Chiaie had advised d'Aubuisson by 1979; and at the September 1980 meeting of CAL in Argentina, delle Chiaie and d'Aubuisson met and arranged for weapons and money to be sent to d'Aubuisson in El Salvador.[79]

That 1980 CAL Conference was presided over by Argentine General Suarez Mason, today a fugitive wanted on charges arising from the Argentine junta's death squads. In attendance were Bolivia's dictator, Garcia Meza, wanted by U.S. drug authorities for his involvement in cocaine trafficking, and Argentine President Videla, today serving a life sentence for his policies of mass murder and torture. A featured speaker at the conference was Mario Sandoval Alarcon, who had brought his protege d'Aubuisson and arranged for him to be put in touch with delle Chiaie.

What was being brokered at the September 1980 CAL Conference was nothing less than an "Argentine solution" of death squad dictatorships from Buenos Aires to Guatemala City. The inspiration and direction of this scheme was however not just Argentine, but truly international, involving the Italo-Argentine secret Masonic Lodge P-2 (of which General Suarez Mason was a member), and possibly through them the financial manipulations by insiders of the Milan Banco Ambrosiano and Vatican Bank.[80]

P-2 has come under considerable scrutiny in Italy, where it began, because of its on-going involvement in intelligence-tolerated coup attempts, bank manipulations, and terrorist bombings. All of this has contributed to a right-wing "strategy of tension," a tactic of developing a popular case for right-wing order, by fomenting violence and disruption, and blaming this when possible on the left. Stefano delle Chiaie was perhaps the master activist for P-2's strategy of tension, assisted by a group of French intelligence veterans working out of Portugal as the so-called press agency Aginter-Presse.[81] The Aginter group had their own connections to WACL in Latin America before delle Chiaie did, especially to the Mexican chapter (the so-called "Tecos") and to Sandoval's WACL chapter in Guatemala.[82]

According to the Italian Parliamentary Report on P-2:

> P-2 contributed to the strategy of tension, that was pursued by right-wing extremist groups in Italy during those years when the purpose was to destabilize Italian politics, creating a situation that such groups might be able to exploit in their own interest to bring about an authoritarian solution to Italy's problems.[83]

Delle Chiaie was a principal organizer for three of the most famous of these incidents, the 1969 bomb in the crowded Piazza Fontana of Milan (16 deaths, 90 injuries), the 1970 coup attempt of Prince Valerio Borghese (a CIA client since 1945), and the Bologna station bombing of August 2, 1980 (85 deaths, 200 injuries). In December 1985 magistrates in Bologna issued 16 arrest warrants, including at least three to P-2 members, accusing members of the Italian intelligence service SISMI of first planning and then covering up the Bologna bombing.[84] One of these 16 was P-2's leader Licio Gelli, who had spent most of the post-war years in Argentina.

A small group of anarchists, penetrated by delle Chiaie's man Mario Merlino, were blamed at first for the Piazza Fontana bombing, even though Sismi knew within six days that delle Chiaie was responsible, and Merlino had planted the bomb.[85]

After 1974, when the right-wing "strategists of tension" lost critical support with the ending of the Greek, Portuguese, and Spanish dictatorships, they appear to have looked increasingly for new friendly governments in Latin America. Delle Chiaie began to work for Chile's service DINA in 1975, the first contacts having been made through Aginter by Michael Townley, who would later murder Letelier with the help of CORU Cubans for DINA.[86] (Delle Chiaie is said to have come from South America to Miami in 1982, with a Turkish leader of the fascist Grey Wolves who was a friend of the Pope's assassin Mehmet Agca.[87])

The P-2's support for Latin American terror seems to have been in part a matter of internal Roman Catholic politics: an attempt by one faction to use right-wing death squads to eliminate the Church's liberation theologians and moderate Christian Democrats. Both the contras and Mario Sandoval Alarcon were part of the anti-liberationist campaign: the contra radio maintained a steady propaganda campaign against the Maryknoll Sisters in Nicaragua; Lau of the contras murdered Archbishop Romero of El Salvador; and Lau's patron Sandoval, at the 11th WACL Conference in 1978, denounced the "intense Marxist penetration...acting within the highest echelons of the Catholic hierarchy."[88] During the two years after the CAL adopted the Banzer Plan in 1978, "at least twenty-eight bishops, priests, and lay persons were killed in Latin America; most of their murders were attributed to government security forces or rightist death squads. That number multiplied after 1980 as civil war spread through Guatemala and El Salvador."[89] We have already seen how Reagan's termination of the Carter "human rights" policies was followed by the decimation of the Guatemalan Christian Democrats.

The CAL/P-2 connection was and remains a drug connection as well. The terrorist delle Chiaie has been accused of ties to some of the French Connection heroin merchants who had relocated to Italy; while CAL Chairman Suarez Mason, according to the Italian magazine *Panorama*, became "one of Latin America's chief drug traffickers."[90]

This Latin American WACL drug connection appears to have been originally put together by former Argentine Interior Minister Jose Lopez-Rega, a P-2 member and Gelli intimate who was responsible for restoring Peron to power in 1973 and arranging for European experts in "dirty war" tactics to launch death squad tactics against the terrorist left. Lopez-Rega was later said to have been directly involved with other P-2 members in the Argentine-Paraguayan cocaine traffic, and to have used French members of the Ricord drug network as terrorists for his underground AAA (Alianza Argentina Anticomunista).[91] Ex-CIA Cuban exile terrorists involved in the drug traffic also worked with the AAA, as well as for Somoza.[92]

Paraguayan Intelligence Chief Pastor Coronel, a CAL participant and death squad co-ordinator, was also a smuggling partner of the Corsican drug kingpin in Latin America, Auguste Ricord, whose network trafficked with the Gambino Mafia family in New York.[93] Michele Sindona, the author of the Ambrosiano-Vatican Bank connection to P-2, had his own connections to the Gambino family, which surfaced when in 1979 he used them to stage his own "abduction" to avoid a New York court appearance.[94] According to Penny Lernoux, "the P-2 crowd obtained money from the kidnappings of well-to-do businessmen in Europe and from the drug traffic in South America. Sindona's bank laundered money from the notorious [Italian] Mafia kidnappers of *Anonima Sequestri*, who worked with ... Ordine Nuovo."[95] Significantly, Mario Sandoval Alarcon has also been accused of resorting to the kidnapping of rich coffee-growers in Guatemala to get financing for his political faction.[96] Since the fall of the Argentine junta and Suarez Mason in 1982-83, the AAA, abetted by delle Chiaie, has also taken to bank robberies and kidnapping.

P-2, the Republicans, and Ledeen

But P-2 had equally strong links to both the CIA and the Republican Party. Under President Nixon, the CIA allocated $10 million for centrist and right-wing parties in the 1972 Italian elections. The U.S. Embassy in Rome was acutely divided over whether the money should go through Sindona, who appeared to have "a direct line to the [Nixon] White House," or Italian Intelligence Chief Vito Miceli, implicated in a 1970 CIA-financed coup attempt with delle Chiaie. Both Sindona and Miceli, as it happened, were part of the P-2 connection.[97]

Sindona's U.S. investments were partnered by the Continental Illinois bank headed by Nixon's first Treasury Secretary, David Kennedy, and his interests were represented by the law firm of Nixon and his Attorney General John Mitchell. "In Italy, Sindona orchestrated the efforts of the neo-Fascist deputy Luigi Turchi to garner support for Nixon's election campaign. Sindona even offered $1 million, on condition of anonymity, to CREEP treasurer Maurice Stans. The offer was refused."[98] Turchi's efforts were co-ordinated by Philip Guarino of the Republican National Committee, a P-2 associate later implicated in the plotting to help Sindona escape prosecution.[99]

We have seen how in 1980 Cline's associate, Michael Ledeen, published an article (at the beginning of the 1980 election campaign) "savaging Admiral Stansfield Turner for forcing Ted Shackley [one of Edwin P. Wilson's senior CIA contacts, a veteran of the anti-Allende operation] out of the agency."[100] A year later Michael Ledeen, in his new capacity as the Reagan State Department's expert on terrorism, was now in a position to help close off the investigation of those (specifically Shackley and von Marbod) who were being investigated along with Edwin Wilson, perhaps the world's most notorious ex-CIA terrorist.[101]

Ledeen's efforts in 1980 on behalf of Shackley were paralleled by a dirty tricks campaign on behalf of Reagan in alliance with P-2 members of the Italian intelligence service SISMI. The chief of these, Francesco Pazienza, was a financial consultant of Roberto Calvi at the Banco Ambrosiano. Pazienza was ultimately indicted in an Italian court (with Ledeen as an unindicted co-conspirator) for luring President Carter's brother Billy into a compromising relationship with Qaddafi during the 1980 presidential campaign. According to Edward Herman and Frank Brodhead, the prosecuting judge

> ...had evidence that "SISMI was the architect of the scandal over Billy Carter," and that the material in this case was gathered mostly by Pazienza and by his American friend Michael Ledeen...." Pazienza availed himself of SISMI both for the use of some secret agents and for the expenses of organizing the scandalous plan. It seems that the organizers got a huge payoff for 'Billygate.' Moreover, [SISMI chief] Santovito [a P-2 member] and Pazienza got great advantages in return from American officials."[102]

Ledeen published his Billygate stories in three pro-Israeli publications: the *New Republic* of Martin Peretz, and two journals controlled by Sir James Goldsmith, the chairman of the Banco Ambrosiano-linked oil company BRISA (see below), and later one of the multimillionaires consulted by Reagan in his Project Democracy.[103]

In 1980 Ledeen was also in high gear, allegedly again with assistance from Pazienza, as a propagandist for the notion of a terrorist threat requiring a beefed-up U.S. intelligence response. Given access in 1980 to a Czech defector from twelve years earlier (Jan Sejna), Ledeen elicited from him the information, which Sejna had never volunteered in his extensive CIA debriefing, that the Soviet Union maintained a network of terrorist training camps as part of its plan for global domination. According to Herman and Brodhead, Ledeen had Sejna reaffirm the contents of a purported document on Soviet sponsorship of terrorism which Sejna had willingly claimed to be authentic a decade earlier, and which was in fact a CIA forgery shown to Sejna for the purposes of testing his credibility.[104]

This document and corroboration then became central to the case built by Ledeen and his friend Claire Sterling to show that the KGB and Bulgarian drug traffickers had plotted to have the Turkish fascist Mehmet Agca kill the Pope.[105] This story was of course augmented by the "confession" of the assassin, whose testimony was later discounted as not credible. This confession now appears to have been generated by P-2 SISMI agents linked to Ledeen, among whom may or may not have been Pazienza.[106]

What inspired Michael Ledeen's zeal on behalf of Reagan and the shadow network? European journalists have suggested that an unspecified "huge payoff" to the SISMI P-2 organizers of Billygate was followed by a payment of at least $120,000 plus expenses from SISMI to Ledeen in 1980-81, after Ledeen "sold old U.S. intelligence reports to SISMI at stiff prices."[107] But there are indications that Ledeen had an affiliation, not just with SISMI, but (like his ally Pazienza) with P-2. There are unexplained stories that "Ledeen had links with Gelli...and that Ledeen, on behalf of the State Department, had tried to buy 480 P-2 files photocopied by the Uruguayan interior ministry" after a raid provoked by the P-2 scandal revealed by the investigation of Sindona.[108]

It is obviously a convenient arrangement when P-2 contributions and favors to a right-wing U.S. President can be followed by the release of $10 million in unvouchered CIA funds for political use by P-2. No doubt their knowledge of such arrangements must have fuelled the zeal of Carter and Turner to cut back on the CIA's clandestine services. Conversely, the CIA's cutback on clandestine operations and subventions spelled both political and financial disaster for parallel operations, such as Wilson's and Sindona's, which had fattened on CIA handouts. The end of U.S. intelligence subsidies to Wilson's company Consultants International is clearly responsible for Wilson's move into the illegal Libyan deals for which he was eventually jailed. The same drying up of the CIA cash flow to right-wing assets appears to have contributed to the failure of Calvi's Banco Ambrosiano; and of another intelligence-related bank whose operations interlocked heavily with Wilson's: the drug-linked Nugan Hand Bank of Australia.[109] Thus CIA reforms had the effect of building a powerful coalition of both Americans (ousted CIA clandestine operators, the Taiwan-Somoza lobby, the ASC) and foreigners (WACL, P-2), determined to restore the clandestine operations which had been cut back by four different directors of central intelligence (Helms, Schlesinger, Colby, and Turner).[110]

Whatever the details, it appears that the P-2 Republican connection remained as healthy in 1980 as it had been in 1972. Licio Gelli, the head of P-2, was invited by Republican bigwig Phil Guarino to Reagan's inaugural ball.[111]

P-2, the Calvi Scam, and Nicaragua

By 1980 the fate of Calvi's Banco Ambrosiano (and hence indirectly of P-2) depended largely on an anti-Communist turnaround in Central America. In 1977 Calvi had developed close relations with the increasingly isolated Nicaraguan dictator Anastasio Somoza, and opened a subsidiary (the Ambrosiano Group Banco Comercial) in Managua. Through another of his Ambrosiano-controlled companies, Central American Service, Calvi began prospecting for minerals and oil. As the Nicaraguan situation deteriorated in 1978-79, Calvi's Managua subsidiary received a steady flow of funds from Calvi's Bahamas subsidiary, which had come under the scrutiny of Italian government investigators.[112] By 1979,

> Calvi (probably with Gelli's intercession) was on good terms not only with the then dictator Anastasio Somoza, but also with the ever more menacing Sandinista opposition. To the end of his life [in 1982] he retained a Nicaraguan diplomatic passport, and in 1979 Calvi attempted to lobby the Rome government for an increase in coffee imports from Nicaragua...[O]f the foreign banks in Managua at the time of the left-wing takeover in...1979, Ambrosiano's subsidiary was the only one not to be nationalized by the new revolutionary regime.[113]

Calvi had obviously established a bridge to the Sandinista junta's bankers, Alfredo Cesar and Arturo Cruz, and their allies such as Alfonso Robelo. By 1982 both Cruz and Robelo were working with the contras.[114]

In every account of the P-2/Banco Ambrosiano billion-dollar scam, the role of Somoza's Nicaragua is prominent. According to one source, it was Gelli who "smoothed the way" for Calvi's use of Somoza's offer of bank secrecy, "after several million dollars had been dropped into the dictator's pocket."[115] In this period the Italian construction magnate Mario Genghini (whose name was also on Gelli's P2 lists) "was one of the biggest foreign investors in Nicaragua."[116] In 1978, to avoid an investigation by the Bank of Italy, Calvi "moved the axis of [his international] fraud to Nicaragua"; one year later, as Somoza's position worsened, the fraud was moved to Peru.[117]

In 1981 Bishop Paul Marcinkus of the Vatican Bank "held a number of secret meetings with the convicted Calvi, which resulted in the Vatican Bank officially admitting an increase in its outstanding debts of nearly $1 billion. This was the sum that was owed to the Calvi banks in Peru and Nicaragua as a result of their having loaned, on Calvi's instructions, hundreds of millions of dollars" to companies allegedly under Marcinkus's control.[118] Just one of these companies, Bellatrix, received $184 million for P-2's political purposes, which included Gelli's purchase of Exocet missiles for Argentina during the Falkland Islands War.[119]

P-2's political purposes also clearly involved the election of Ronald Reagan in 1980:

> On April 8, 1980, Gelli wrote from Italy to Phillip Guarino...
> "If you think it might be useful for something favorable to your presidential candidate to be published in Italy, send me some material and I'll get it published in one of the papers here."...The favorable comments about Ronald Reagan, carefully placed by Licio Gelli, duly appeared in Italy. In January 1981, Licio Gelli was an honored guest at the presidential inauguration. Guarino later ruefully observed, "He had a better seat than I did."[120]

In 1981, the period of its Argentine grand design for Central America, the Reagan administration appears in turn to have been exploiting P-2 pathways. One of its first envoys to Argentina and Guatemala for the grand design was General Vernon Walters, a major figure in the Brazilian military coup of 1964, and reportedly a prime architect in the blending of the various contra forces into a united FDN under Enrique Bermudez in 1981.[121] "In May 1981 General Vernon Walters...visited Guatemala as a 'goodwill ambassador' of the Reagan Administration. At the same time, though, he was representing BRISA [Basic Resources International SA], which was seeking permission to export more oil. The Guatemalan military granted the request."[122]

The fate of Calvi and his allies, by then ominous, was tied up with the fortunes of BRISA, whose chairman, as previously mentioned, was Sir James Goldsmith. In 1977 the Guatemalan government (with Mario Sandoval Alarcon as Vice-President) had awarded an oil concession to BRISA, one of whose board members was Calvi's representative Antonio Tonello. In March 1981, as the Italian investigation of Sindona led to Gelli's files and Calvi's name, the Calvi case was nearing its denouement. On May 20, 1981, exactly one week after Walters' visit to Guatemala for Reagan and BRISA, both Calvi and Tonello were arrested (and soon convicted).

The CAL-Reagan-Helms Triangle

In 1980 the incoming Reagan administration had links to the Latin American chapters of WACL, not just through P-2, but even more directly through Republican Senator Jesse Helms. Indeed Helms became a focal point for U.S. intelligence and Republican connections to CAL in Latin America, following a visit in 1975 to WACL headquarters in Taiwan. Helms also travelled to Argentina (via a WACL Conference in Rio) in April 1975; and at least two of his aides, Ramon Molina and Nat Hamrick, returned, along with Daniel Graham, in early 1976, shortly before the Argentine generals' coup of March 24. Helms, according to Ramon Molina, "actually encouraged the military to move in and depose President Peron."[123]

The president in question was not Juan Peron, who had died in June 1974, but his widow, Isabelita, who was deposed in March 1976. This event followed from the more significant ouster in July 1975 of her mentor Jose Lopez Rega, the original fascist architect of the P-2/Italian terrorist presence in Argentina. The Argentinian army was responsible for both ousters, each of which followed a visit by Helms or his aides.

The presence on the 1975 Helms delegation of two other associates (Victor Fediay and J. Evetts Haley), and the subsequent involvement of Daniel Graham, may help explain why the relatively inexperienced Senator from North Carolina (he had been elected in 1972) would involve himself in an Argentinian military takeover. In 1975 Fediay (a Russian emigre and prewar Polish fascist) and Haley (a Texas rancher) had just helped with Richard Allen to broker a request (which was eventually turned down) for U.S. backing behind a Eurofascist secessionist coup in the Azores (sponsored by the so-called Aginter-Presse intelligence service, with which delle Chiaie was affiliated).[124] One can imagine that the message to the Argentine military was similar: the U.S. could support a military take-over, perhaps even death squads and terrorists like delle Chiaie, but only if the Lopez Rega connection to the newly forming Fascist International in 1975 was eliminated.

This U.S.-Argentine connection in 1975-76 (Helms, Molina, Hamrick, Richard Stone, and Daniel Graham) would become the hard core Reagan-Sandoval-contra connection after 1980.[125] We have seen how Graham and Singlaub assured Guatemalans in 1979 that "Mr. Reagan recognizes that a good deal of dirty work needs to be done."[126]

It was Helms who (after his aide John Carbaugh met d'Aubuisson at the September 1980 CAL Conference) received Sandoval's protege d'Aubuisson on an illegal visit in December 1980.[127] (Since that time Carbaugh has worked closely with Mario Sandoval Alarcon's nephew, Carlos Midence Pivaral, to fashion a more marketable and "Republican" image for d'Aubuisson's new party, ARENA.[128]) Stone, a lobbyist for Guatemala in 1980, became Reagan's special ambassador to Central America.[129] In 1981-82, Hamrick, while on Helms' staff, would lobby, together with the head of the Costa Rica WACL chapter, for a friendly base for the contras in that country.[130]

But the most significant member of the Helms Argentine connection may have been Ramon Molina, a Cuban-American Bay of Pigs veteran who in 1976 was the apparent point of contact between his two employers, Nicaraguan dictator Somoza and Senator Helms.[131] In 1975-76 Molina appears to have been Somoza's connection to renegade ex-CIA Cubans, like Orlando Bosch, whose CORU assassination activities extended to Argentina by August 1976.[132] It would appear that, just as in the 1972 election Manuel Artime (another ex-CIA Cuban accused of drug trafficking) emerged as the connection between Nixon, Somoza, and the Watergate burglars, so in the 1980 election Ramon Molina emerged as the connection between Reagan and Somoza.[133]

The Helms camp has been very much of a right-wing embarrassment to the Reagan administration since it took office: in 1984 Helms put the life of Reagan's Ambassador to El Salvador at risk by leaking secret CIA data. In 1976 and in 1980, however, candidate Reagan was very much dependent on winning the support of Helms and his international WACL network. In 1976 the Reagan campaign appointed David Keene, an old Liebman sidekick and WACL participant, to be chief delegate hunter in the southern states. In 1980 a campaign aide, Belden Bell, travelled to Latin America and met both Deaver's Amigos and Ramon Molina.[134] What may have interested the Reagan campaign in Molina was his capacity as a representative of Somoza's personal fortune, in whose employ he used his CIA training as a strong-arm man and enforcer (he allegedly once broke the jaw of a South Carolina concrete businessman). Somoza, until his assassination in September 1980, was said to be funding terrorist activities through CAL as a way of building an international neofascist coalition for his return.[135]

Reagan, the Contras, and Narcotics

Such then was the state of WACL when Singlaub began his missionary activities to it on behalf of Reagan in 1979-80. It might be said in defense of their policies that WACL represented an old U.S. intelligence project out of control; and that Singlaub has worked to bring it back under control. Alternatively, the WACL collaboration might be seen as a kind of "constructive engagement" with neofascism, offering right-wing governments equipment and support services, in exchange for their renunciation of death squad politics that would never play well in Peoria.

It is clear that the Reagan administration has since backed away from many of its old CAL proteges, usually after revelations linking them to the drug traffic. It has relegated d'Aubuisson to the background, after a plane belonging to one of his financial supporters was detained in Texas with a cargo of $5.9 million in cash. It has helped extradite Pagliai (the younger of the two Italian terrorists) from Bolivia, after Pagliai was detected by the DEA at a high-level drug-traffic meeting in 1981.[136]

Eventually the Reagan administration helped ease both the Bolivian and the Argentine dictatorships out of power. After the failure in 1982 of a Guatemalan coup plot by Sandoval's associate Lionel Sisniega Otero (plotting with WerBell, the OSS colleague of Singlaub and Cline), the U.S. eventually accepted a civilian government headed by a Christian Democrat, of the party targeted by Sandoval and Sisniega for extermination.

In marked contrast, the Reagan commitment to the contras has been unswerving. Modifications to its policy have been limited to a search for better personnel, as Congressional opposition mounted to the contra record of raping peasants and torturing social workers to death. In September 1982 the CIA reorganized the contra directorate, and sent a new station chief to Honduras, with the task "of getting the Argentines out and getting the war back under control."[137] In late 1983 the CIA began its own covert operations against Nicaragua, cutting out the contras, and reorganizing their FDN directorate yet again.[138]

However the CIA, inevitably, was faced with a disposal problem. A handful of contra field officers were executed for various crimes, chiefly the murder of one of their peers. But the CIA was reluctant to send Argentine terrorists back to their home country at a time when the civilian government was barely establishing itself. Ricardo Lau, the murderer of Archbishop Romero, was detached from the contra hierarchy, but remained in Honduras to be the mastermind of the death squad operation of the CIA's and CAL's Honduran protege, General Gustavo Alvarez

Martinez.[139] Alvarez was the point-man for the CIA-contra presence in Honduras, and even the godfather to the adopted daughter of the new CIA chief. When he was ousted in 1984 the CIA changed its station chief yet again, and Lau reportedly left for another country.

These cosmetic changes of personnel do not appear to have reached to the level of eliminating the old CAL presence in the contras. Enrique Bermudez, the link between Sandoval's Guardia proteges and Washington, has remained through each successive FDN shake-up. As for the international drug traffickers, their interest in maintaining the contra status quo in Honduras was revealed when the FBI broke up a drug-financed plot in Miami to assassinate the elected Honduran president and restore Alvarez to power.[140]

Since December 1985 it has become clear that the CIA contra operation has become as intermingled with drug trafficking as the old CIA Cuban exile operations which had had to be closed down in Miami (see Chapter III). In December 1985,

> ...the Associated Press cited a CIA report alleging that a "top commander" of the Costa Rica-based guerrillas had "used cocaine profits to buy a $250,000 arms shipment and a helicopter."...Two Nicaraguan smugglers convicted in the largest cocaine seizure in West Coast history—430 pounds— admitted that they passed drug profits on to the contras...A leading Bay Area fund-raiser for the Honduras-based Nicaraguan Democratic Force, the largest contra group, was identified in 1984 by the Drug Enforcement Administration as "the apparent head of a criminal organization responsible for smuggling kilogram quantities of cocaine into the United States."[141]

The possibility that the contra operation serves as a cover for the Latin American drug connection does not seem to have occurred to the Reagan administration. On the contrary, its pressures to resume Congressional aid to the contras this year were not deterred by the revelation that the FBI was "examining assertions that cocaine was smuggled [into the United States] to help finance the rebels' war effort."[142] Since then former Ambassador Robert White has charged that the Administration has attempted to kill this FBI inquiry. The stage has been set for a potentially explosive Senate investigation.

Watergate, Contragate, and Foreign Campaign Contributions

Why would the Reagan administration, whose ideology is supposed to be one of patriotism mellowed by pragmatism, have such a huge investment in a cause that is so controversial here as well as in Latin America? The Reagan response is to point to the alleged human rights violations by their opponents, and to the Caribbean basin's proximity and strategic importance. But it has been said in response to both arguments that the contras, by their excesses and sheer incompetence, are weakening rather than strengthening support for the U.S. in the area.

A different question is whether the funds from Guatemala, P-2, Somoza, and other WACL sources, helped generate the private "verbal agreements" that Sandoval Alarcon referred to. The recycling of profits and AID funds from foreign countries back into American elections is perhaps one of the largest and least discussed scandals of the last three decades. WACL countries in particular, whose survival and affluence so often depend on U.S. support, have repeatedly been at the center of such rumors.

This would seem to be an appropriate topic for any Senate investigation into any illegal contra activities and cover-ups. But Congress in the past has proven most reluctant to pursue the question of illegal foreign funding in electoral campaigns. Renata Adler has described how the Congressional inquiry into Watergate faded at the point when traces were uncovered of large funds pumped into the Nixon campaign from the Far East.[143] Nor did Republicans pursue similar allegations that dogged the campaign of even that cleanest of candidates, Senator George McGovern. Silence on such matters serves the interests of both parties.

Some of the points made by Renata Adler, a member of the staff investigating Nixon for the House impeachment inquiry, bear closely on the Reagan-WACL connection. She referred to theories "that Nixon was driven from office by a conspiracy within government itself—more specifically, within the CIA." And she drew attention to the inability of the CIA "to give any satisfactory account" of its involvement in the Southeast Asian narcotics traffic (where its airline Air America collaborated with members of Taiwan's WACL Chapter in supplying the opium growers of the Golden Triangle).[144]

Adler did not refer specifically to the very efficient sabotaging of the Nixon White House by Howard Hunt, nor to the fact that Hunt's White House services went into their disastrous high gear after the June 1971 departure of Kissinger for Peking.[145] But she specifically named Anna Chan Chennault, perhaps Taiwan's top lobbyist in Washington, as someone who had raised campaign funds for Nixon from the Philippines, Hong Kong, Japan, and South Korea.[146] Citing evidence too complex to review here, she concluded that "the South Vietnamese administration, not wanting peace to be at hand just yet, used some of the enormous amounts of money we were pouring in there to bribe our Administration to stay in."[147]

The bribes were in the form of illicit foreign campaign contributions— possibly in 1968, and more clearly in 1972. Though she refers to him only as a Nixon "White House official," Adler refers to two distinct sub-plots where in each case a principal suspect was Richard Allen, the man who in 1980 became Reagan's principal foreign policy adviser.[148] In the 1968 case,

> Mrs. Chennault's activities had aroused the suspicions of the Washington intelligence community, and a plethora of agencies seemed to be watching her closely. According to published reports, the FBI tapped her telephone and put her under physical surveillance; the CIA tapped the phones at the South Vietnamese embassy and conducted a covert investigation of Richard Allen. Then, a few days before the election, the National Security Agency...intercepted a cable from the Vietnamese embassy to Saigon urging delay in South Vietnam's participation in the Paris peace talks until after the [U.S.] elections. Indeed, on November 1, her efforts seemed to have paid off when President Nguyen Van Thieu reneged on his promise to Lyndon Johnson...

and announced he would not take part in the exploratory Paris talks.[149]

There are enough similarities between Allen's career and Deaver's (both men having gone on from the post of White House official to become the registered foreign lobbyist of Asian countries) to suggest that Adler's hypothesis for the origins of Watergate (bribery by illicit foreign campaign contributions, and the potential for blackmail thus created) might help explain the workings of the Contragate mystery as well. In 1980 as in 1968 the WACL coalition apparently decided to conspire against an American Democratic incumbent, the main difference being that in 1980 the role both of illicit foreign funds and of American intelligence veterans appears to have been more overt.

Congress should certainly investigate this possibility. But there is also a chance of a searching and objective inquiry in the special prosecutor's examination of the affairs of Mike Deaver. Deaver is already under scrutiny for his lobbying activities in South Korea. Some of these involve the U.S.

Ambassador in Seoul, Richard Walker, a WACL participant since as far back as 1970.

Deaver's connections with South Korea go back at least to February 1981, when he "ushered President Chun Doo Hwan of South Korea into the Oval Office to meet Reagan."[150] Chun was in fact the first of the WACL dictators, shunned by Carter, to be received into the Oval Office. In a sense his visit, like Sandoval's, was a trial balloon for Reagan's new policy of tilting towards WACL and away from Carter's support of "human rights."[151]

Chun's visit to Reagan is said to have followed a period of intense involvement in Latin American WACL intrigue by CAUSA, the political arm of the South Korean Unification (Moonie) Church. (The links between Moon's church and the South Korean Central Intelligence Agency are so overt that a decade ago they provoked a U.S. Senate investigation.[152]) CAUSA officials are reported to have offered $4 million for the Garcia Meza Bolivian coup of July 17, 1980; and one of them is said to have had worked directly with Klaus Barbie in organizing the coup.[153] When Congress ordered a cutoff of military aid to the contras in 1984, CAUSA worked with Refugee Relief International, a creation of Singlaub and of WACL, to ferry non-military supplies to the same contra camps. An informed observer said that "the 'big three' countries that were expected to aid the contras [militarily] were Israel, South Korea, and Taiwan."[154] Robert Owen, said to have served with Singlaub as a cut-out contact between the National Security Council and the contras, is a former registered lobbyist for South Korea.[155]

It is unlikely that Deaver's lobbying activities were more than a small part of the apparatus securing the Reagan-WACL connection. The full story, if it could be told, would probably lead to grey intelligence-political alliances that were already in place when Deaver was a young boy. Undoubtedly Cline and Singlaub, not to mention Reagan himself, would know more about such matters.

Singlaub, at least, probably faces a Congressional investigation in the months ahead. But Contragate is not a narrowly bureaucratic or administrative scandal. Deaver's post-1984 lobbying activities have already suggested to federal investigators that he may have violated U.S. statutes. Thus he too can be made to talk about how these connections were forged. Under oath.

V.
Israel and the Contras

It is no accident that Israel, rather than, for example, South Korea, which has also sold its share of arms to Iran, was caught in the thick of things when the two-legged Irangate scheme was exposed in November 1986. For Israel was almost certainly the intellectual author of the plot to make Iran pay for the war against Nicaragua and Israel had already been selling arms to the contras, training them, and otherwise helping Reagan to circumvent Congressional restrictions on the contra program. To find the roots of this behavior we must return to Israel's earliest days.

Surrounded by Arab states whose hostility endured from the rout of their armies and uprooting of the Palestinian population as the Jewish state established itself, Israel has from its outset sought international contact beyond its confinement in the Eastern Mediterranean. Its Labor Zionist government propounded a doctrine calling for the establishment of good relations with the peripheral, non-Arab states of the region: Ethiopia, Turkey, and, of course Iran.

Looking farther afield, in the mid-1950s Prime Minister David Ben-Gurion attempted to involve Israel in what would later become the Nonaligned Movement, but was at the time a loose gathering of nations emerging from colonialism. Israel was barred from the now-historic 1955 meeting at Bandung, Indonesia, because it was seen as an outpost of European colonialism.

Israel next turned to Africa, where, after some vigorous behind the scenes wooing of Ghana's founding leader Kwame Nkrumah,[1] Israel's anticolonialist credentials (based on having fought the British when they ruled Palestine) were accepted.[2] As African nations were granted independence, Israel commenced a program of development assistance on the continent that was nothing short of spectacular, given Israel's size, its resources and its own recent establishment.

In Africa, and in part of Asia as well, Israeli technicians set up experimental farms, taught agricultural methods, established medical programs and "workers banks," helped develop infrastructure including roads, harbors and, for Ghana, a shipping line, and undertook youth training, labor union leadership training, and cooperative formation.[3] Israel also established courses for foreign students in many of these subjects so that by the end of 1970 15,000 foreign students had been to Israel to study.[4]

Development programs run by Israel were successful because the Israelis technicians came from a small country rather than recent colonial masters, and because the Israelis made it a practice to work alongside their students.

However there was also a less savory side to these programs. "For many years...the United States sent millions of dollars in covert aid to Israel for operations in Africa that included training several African intelligence services."[5] During the tenure of the Labor government (until 1977) European Social Democratic regimes also supported Israeli development activities.[6] Understandably, Israel ammassed an enormous intelligence capability in sub-Saharan Africa. The big powers often consulted or coordinated with Israeli operatives.[7] Military training and arms sales were also a part of Israel's outreach to Africa, along with its humanitarian gestures. As a result of all this, by 1968 32 African nations had established diplomatic relations with Israel.[8]

In the mid-1960s Israel expanded the programs which had been so successful in Africa (and in parts of Asia as well) to Latin America, a region which needed little courting as its already established governments had provided an important bloc of supporting UN votes in 1947 when that body was considering the partition of Palestine into Palestinian and Jewish states.[9]

After Israel's 1973 war the Organization of African Unity called for a diplomatic embargo of Israel, and all but three African governments—Malawi, Swaziland and Lesotho, all within the tight embrace of South Africa—either already had or shortly thereafter severed diplomatic relations. Israel was then left with little choice but to focus on the Asian nations with which it had relations and on Latin America.

Following the 1973 war, which in turn had followed the 1967 war during which Israel had occupied territory belonging to Jordan, Syria and Egypt, the perception of Israel as an underdog beset by rapacious neighbors was wearing out. In much of the world Israel was criticized for its occupation of Arab territory, its oppression of Palestinians in that territory, its intransigence in the face of all opportunities for peace, and, increasingly, its close links with South Africa.[10] Also around this time, Israel's focus was shifting from development to military power. By 1980 Israel would be railing at the "petro-power" of the Arab governments of the Gulf—which, it claimed had turned Africa against it, with promises of funding for major infrastructural projects—and selling $1 billion worth of arms to a curious assortment of customers, including some of its former African friends. While clinging to as much as it could of the old patina of the days when it was a "light unto the nations," Israel had redefined itself into an arms merchant.

The Dictates of Israel's Arms Industry

Well before there was a state, there was an arms industry, producing small arms which the Jewish settlers in Palestine used against the Arab inhabitants they found there.[11]

In the late 1930s and early 1940s arms acquisition by unconventional means, including smuggling war surplus from the U.S., became a preoccupation of Zionist leaders. After the United Nations approved the partition plan establishing a Jewish national homeland in Mandatory Palestine, great energy was expended securing weapons from a mostly-unwilling world for the fight that was expected, following the withdrawal of the British colonialists.[12]

The difficulty experienced in obtaining weaponry, when combined with the legacy of the recently abated Holocaust, seems to have produced a certain mindset in the leaders of the new state of Israel. To call it determined would be to understate it.

> The Holocuast reconfirms the perspective that there are those who seek the destruction of the Jews and that Jewish survival should not depend on the guarantees or efforts of others. Thus, Israel sees that it must rely on its own defense capability to ensure its survival and protect its people.[13]

Emblematic of this grim determination was the decision in 1952 to commit the fledgling nation to the expensive and politically risky development of nuclear weapons.[14]

A similarly far-reaching commitment to establish an arms industry was made in 1967, when France, at the time Israel's major source of weapons (and nuclear technology), cancelled contracts for major weapons systems. French President de Gaulle was angered by Israel's decision to go to war. Always resistant to political pressure, Israeli leaders determined to become self-sufficient in arms.[15]

The investment was a political one, without a thought to economies of scale[16]—which would have shown it to be foolish. Actually Israel had had the beginnings of a parastatal military industry from 1948, built up around the secret munitions workshops of the pre-state period.[17] In the late 1960s and through the 1970s new companies were founded and major weapons systems produced. Much of the technology for the weapons Israel manufactured came from abroad, first from France, then from the United States. Investment also was needed from abroad, most notably from U.S. firms establishing joint ventures or subsidiaries[18] and from the government of South Africa which agreed in 1976 to subsidize research and development on major Israeli weapons systems.[19]

Israel's army is ranked among the best in the world, and it is very large in proportion to the country's tiny population, but no major arms-producing state manufactures weapons solely for its own military. In order to lower the unit cost of weapons, they produce more than they need and try to export the difference. In Israel's case the problem was compounded because Israel's possible markets were severely limited. NATO countries for the most part produce for themselves and each other, and likewise for members of the Warsaw Pact. With some notable exceptions (Ethiopia, Indonesia, and recently the Peoples Republic of China) the socialist and Islamic countries shun Israel. Since the 1973 break, most African nations have also kept their contacts with Israel to a minimum. What remained were the ASEAN nations, the pro-Western Asian grouping, Latin America, and the pariah, or untouchable, nations such as South Africa, Taiwan, Chile, and Guatemala. Latin America, where many countries fall into none of these categories and most of the rest fall into the pariah category, became Israel's premier market, although recently Israel has picked up some sales in Europe.[20]

The typical Israeli customer, wrote one leading analyst of Israeli arms exports,

> ...is most likely to be a non-western country with a defense-conscious government, rightist in orientation, in which the military is either the actual or proximate locus of power. It is confronted by a security threat originating either domestically

or from a neighboring country.... [L]ike Israel, it, too, is isolated diplomatically and under international criticism, and therefore encounters problems in meeting military requirements from other sources of supply.[21]

Israel never managed to produce even half of its own military gear.[22] But it did become hooked on arms exports, which represented 31 percent of industrial exports in 1975,[23] and are now thought to comprise 30 to 40 percent of Israel's industrial output.[24]. Twenty percent of the industrial labor force works in arms production.[25] By aggressively marketing its products where it could, by 1980 Israel had managed to boost its exports to over the $1 billion mark.[26] With the possible exception of 1983,[27] they have remained at that level, and are now above $1.25 billion.[28] Moreover, since these numbers are estimates based on observations and accounts of transactions in the international media—the Israeli government releases no information on its arms sales—if anything, they are too low.

Yet these sales were never enough, especially after 1985, when Israel's defense budget began to suffer regular cuts and orders from the military dropped as part of an anti-inflationary program. The military industries were faced with the necessity of increasing exports to save jobs.[29]

The export statistics do not begin to describe the power wielded by the arms producers, much less the "pro-arms lobby," a wider group including top ranks of the Israeli military, directors of various industries, unions whose members depend on incoming weapons orders for their livelihood, and several Israeli leaders with close ties to arms industries including Shimon Peres, who as a protege of Ben-Gurion at the defense ministry, is credited with being the architect of Israel's arms producing sector, and Moshe Arens, a former president of Israeli Aircraft Industries.

Some critics even charge that the defense ministry, at the apex of the arms producing sector, has taken over Israeli foreign policy. That policy is directed, they say, for short term objectives which often foreclose the possibility of longer term diplomatic aims which might bring Israel out of its isolation. Under the sway of this system, Israel's overall "conduct of external affairs...tends to be unsystematic, with a strong emphasis upon short-term contingency planning and crisis management."[30] "Because of the feeling which has taken root that weapons must be sold at almost any price, countries described as 'dirty' are attracted to us as to a magnet," lamented the military columnist for Israel's leading daily. "The irony is that many of these countries are even ashamed to publicize the fact that they purchase weapons from Israel, as though we were lepers."[31]

Compounding this situation is the process by which sales are approved. It is conducted in secrecy by four men—the prime minister, the defense minister, the foreign minister, and the minister of trade and industry—who convene as the Ministerial Committee on Weapons Transfers.[32] As with Israel's part in Irangate, other cabinet ministers are kept in the dark and, similarly, the Knesset, Israel's parliament has neither the authority nor the will to veto arms sales.[33]

None of this has been without its effect on Israel's mainstay, the United States, which has played a crucial role in Israeli arms marketing in several respects. Much of what Israel has to sell contains U.S. technology and thus needs Washington's permission before it can be exported, or, as was the case with some of the sales to Iran, came to Israel through its U.S. military assistance grants. As the *Jerusalem Post* reported in March of 1985, its economy in serious enough trouble to warrant a supplementary U.S. aid package of $1.5 billion, Israel targeted the United States as an untapped market for its weapons exports.

An interesting intersection with the U.S., and one with much bearing on Israel's relationship with the contras, is the search for markets. Israel has asked the U.S. to set aside certain markets for exclusive Israeli exploitation.[34] It has requested help in marketing, and it has requested U.S. financing for its weapons sales to impoverished governments. It has also asked that recipients of U.S. military aid be allowed to purchase Israeli weapons, an unprecedented break with the traditional "buy American" practice, considered to be the underpinning of U.S. military assistance.[35]

None of these elements were operative when Israel first began marketing its military wares in Central America in 1973. Israel simply pushed into the market itself, introducing its new products at fairs and with a shipboard showroom. Aided by contacts developed during the previous decade when it had conducted technical assistance programs in the region, Israel sold its castoff French combat jet aircraft to El Salvador and in 1975 to Honduras—these were the region's first jet fighters and first supersonic jets, respectively, and the buyers had not yet made peace following a shooting war in 1969—and a variety of armored vehicles, patrol boats, counterinsurgency aircraft and small arms to these two nations and to Nicaragua and Guatemala.[36] Before very long, however, Israeli sales would increase and that increase would be thanks to events in the U.S., which created sales opportunities for Israel.

Opportunity in Central America

The same Carter human rights doctrine that brought campaign contributions from wealthy Guatemalans to Ronald Reagan brought orders to the Israeli arms industries. By 1978 Nicaragua, El Salvador and Guatemala were found guilty of human rights violations connected with insurgencies arising from longstanding social and political inequities. U.S. military aid was terminated and all three of these nations then turned to Israel to fill the gaps left by withdrawal of U.S. aid.

As part of this windfall Israel supplied the military regime of El Salvador with over 80% of its weaponry for the next several years, including napalm for use against the Salvadoran civilian population. Israeli advisers trained the Salvadorans in counterinsurgency and installed a computerized intelligence system able to track insurgents and, by monitoring utility usage, pinpoint safe houses.

It is almost certain that these advisers remained after 1981 when Washington made the cause of the Salvadoran landowning oligarchy its own and resumed military aid. The Israelis thus helped the U.S. exceed the congressional limitation of U.S. advisers in El Salvador at any one time. According to a member of El Salvador's short-lived First Junta (1979-80), Israeli advisers who came to train officers of ANSESAL, the Salvadoran secret police originally established by the CIA and closely linked to the infamous death squads, remained in El Salvador as late as 1983.[37]

Although increasing U.S. military assistance cut into the amount of business available to Israel, Israel continued its relationship with the Salvadoran military, most recently providing a sophisticated "pacification" plan which involves the forcible resettlement of civilians into communities under military control. Following the failure of confidently announced U.S. plans to "win the hearts and minds" of the long suffering Salvadoran populace, the Israeli program (funded by the World Bank, the U.S. and West Germany) is a *quid pro quo* for El Salvador's decision to move its embassy in Israel from Tel Aviv to Jerusalem.

If Salvadoran "model villages" follow the pattern of those Israel has helped establish in Guatemala, their "citizens" will soon be growing fancy vegetables for export in exchange for barely enough food for their families, turning a profit for their military "guardians." The agricultural operations under Israeli advisement are likely to order Israeli high tech farming equipment and Israelis have invested heavily in Guatemala's agricultural sector. Already some Salvadoran officers are trying to imitate Guatemala's involuntary "self defense" forces, an integral part of its "pacification" program.[38]

Since 1977 the Guatemalan military has relied heavily on Israel for each phase of its anti-insurgency campaign. Israeli advisers appeared on the scene when the military government was engaged in killing and dispossessing the largely Mayan highland communities in an effort to squash the

Indians' support for a revolutionary movement inspired by the incredible inequality of land ownership. Over the following eight years, Israeli weapons and advisers helped the Guatemalan military halt the growth of the insurgency—by a mass carnage of at least 10,000 which some observers have not hesitated to call genocide.

Israel, according to Benedicto Lucas Garcia, brother of head of state (1978-1982) Romeo Lucas Garcia, and former chief of staff of the Guatemalan Army, "did not provide us with large amounts, but it was the only [state] which provided us with military support so that we could deal with the guerrillas."[39] The arms might not have been numerous enough to please Lucas, but in 1983 a *Time* reporter marveled that "the Israelis have sold the government everything from anti-terrorism equipment to transport planes. Army outposts in the jungle have become near replicas of Israeli army field camps."[40]

Moreover, Israel also provided Guatemala with two computer centers, one of which, located in an annex to the Presidential Palace, was used to monitor dissidents and compile and disseminate death lists. Israel has also been instrumental in providing advice and direction for Guatemala's audacious program of long term social control: four "poles of development" with dozens of "model villages" in which are interned indigenous peasants driven off their land or captured by the army. Wrested from their corn-oriented culture and under direct military control, the peasants grow export crops. This social experiment—the Guatemalan officer who directs the program compared the model villages to Israeli kibbutzim—has enjoyed support from the U.S. religious right. South Africa is also known to be assisting with the "resettlement" program.

Nicaragua escaped the same fate, but not for want of Israel's attention. In the late 1970s, dictator Anastasio Somoza Debayle, last of a dynasty that had run Nicaragua as a family fiefdom since 1933, was faced by an insurrection of virtually the entire population, and in 1978, at the latter stages of events, the Carter Administration finally cut off U.S. assistance. Somoza was then faced with a fairly rigorous informal embargo; no country seemed willing to sell him weapons.

The Israelis were quick to take up the slack, and from September of that year until the following July when he was ousted, Israel sold Somoza 98 percent of the weapons he used against the Nicaraguan population.[41] Those included not only Uzi submachine guns and "thousands" of Israeli-made Galil assault rifles,[42] but large quantities of ammunition, surface-to-air missiles (the FSLN, the Sandinistas, had no air force)[43], nine combat-armed Cessna aircraft and two Sikorsky helicopters,[44] which Somoza's Guard used as platforms for machine gun strafing. Sometimes they rolled 500 pound bombs out the helicopter doors.[45]

With the tacit permission of the Carter Administration,[46] the Israelis continued to ship arms to Somoza until the end of June 1979. Three weeks before the dictator was forced to flee, Washington said "enough," and Israel recalled supplies (including two patrol boats) that were then on their way to Nicaragua.[47] From exile, Somoza fretted about the ship that was recalled to Israel: "Somewhere in Israel there is a large consignment of arms and ammunition which could have saved Nicaragua."[48] Someday, his men would reclaim that cargo, but killed in Paraguay in 1981, Somoza would not live to see that, nor would he see how hard Ronald Reagan would work to restore Nicaragua to his National Guard.

In response to criticism occasionally leveled at it in subsequent years, Israel has always insisted that it stood by Somoza because of a debt dating back to the 1930s. At that time, and again following World War II, Anastasio Somoza Garcia, the father of the toppled dictator, vouched for weapons purchased in Europe by the pre-state Zionist military forces, the Haganah. The Zionists who dealt with him paid Somoza extremely well at the time,[49] so it is somewhat ludicrous for the Israelis to argue that they were honor bound to help his son murder thousands of Nicaraguans decades later. However, they have gotten by with this line of defense, since no one with any leverage over Israel has challenged it, and the arms sales were very lucrative, probably amounting to $250 million.[50]

Israel, the White House Junta and the Contras

The lack of criticism from where it mattered—the U.S. Congress and influential liberal and progressive constituencies in the U.S.—to any of its arms dealings in Central America emboldened Israel to cooperate with the Reagan Administration in supporting the contras in the early days of the program. But there came a time, as early as the summer of 1983, when the administration wanted more from Israel than Israel was willing to risk. The tension that arose then persisted and almost certainly set the course for the scheme which would become known as Iran-Contra affair.

Whatever else the story demonstrates, it shows clearly that Israel might cooperate extensively with the administration or its covert agents in many parts of the world, but it is far from the supine proxy that such a role suggests. The dickering back and forth which went on over what Israel could do for the contras was never completely resolved: when the federal furniture is rearranged following the investigations of the affair, there will be even greater pressure on Israel to stand up in public with the contras. But much money and many weapons changed hands while the relationship grew up around that point of contention. The participants' divergent wishes about Israel's role with the contras resulted in the linking of two operations, which were eventually exposed as the Iran-Contra scandal.

"Strategic" Cooperation

Until the U.S.-approved Iran arms sales began, U.S.-Israeli collaboration in the war against Nicaragua appears to have been carried out in the framework of a series of agreements. Israel's Likud government, which took office in 1977, had always pursued concessions from the U.S. to help it develop and market weapons. Some elements of what Israel desired were incorporated in a Memorandum of Agreement signed by the two countries in March 1979. Four months after the Reagan Administration was sworn in, Secretary of State Alexander Haig signed a commitment extending the privileges of the 1979 pact.

On November 30, 1981 the administration signed a Memorandum of Understanding (MOU) on Strategic Cooperation with Israel. In addition to provisions aimed at boosting Israel's weapons industry, the MOU bound the two countries into a loose mutual defense pact (aimed, as quickly became *de rigeuer* in the Reagan years, at the USSR) and covered cooperation in Africa and very likely other areas of the developing world. Although this agreement was suspended almost immediately when Israel angered Washington with its surprise annexation of the Golan Heights, "its spirit and some of its initiatives continue under the 1979 MOA."[51] (Defense Minister Ariel Sharon said the suspension of the MOU did not hurt Israel as the U.S. would pay interest for the delay in its implementation.[52])

The cooperation was unspecified in the MOU, but an Israeli official said it was left to be evolved.[53] The Israelis wanted—and until David Kimche took his leave from the Foreign Ministry shortly before the Iran-contra scandal broke, continued to want—U.S. funding to entice African nations to reestablish diplomatic relations with them.[54] Defense Minister Ariel Sharon said that Washington had promised Israel money for its activities in Africa.[55] (Sharon arrived in Washington to sign the MOU for Israel immediately after having traveled through Africa. He urged the Reagan Administration to sell arms to South Africa so it too could help in the fight against communism.[56])

Israel was also eager for the formal pact because it believed that the connection would boost public perception of Israel as a "strategic asset" of the United States, rather than Washington's biggest foreign aid client— although the goal of the perception engineering was in part to obtain more U.S. aid.[57]

Judging from the way the Israelis would keep seeking it, Washington never put a great deal of money into Israel's Africa operations. And whatever spirit of the 1979 Memorandum survived Israel's 1982 invasion of Lebanon and, in the aftermath, Prime Minister Begin's arrogant rejection of the timid peace plan proffered by President Reagan, was quite withered.

Moreover, with the resignation of Secretary of State Haig and his replacement by George Shultz, a longtime employee of the giant Bechtel construction firm with close business ties to Arab governments, Israel and its U.S. backers expected relations to get worse. Instead, then Deputy Secretary of Defense Frank Carlucci—he has since been appointed national security adviser—persuaded Shultz to work with Robert C. Ames, the CIA senior officer for the Middle East. Moshe Arens, Israel's ambassador at the time and his aide Benjamin Netanyahu (since Israel's ambassador to the UN) made the reeducation of Shultz their personal project, building a personal relationship with the Secretary of State. The "real turning point" came at the end of 1982, when Shultz tried to block a $200 million addition to Israel's U.S. assistance, proposed by Congress at the behest of AIPAC (the American Israel Public Affairs Committee, Israel's registered lobby in the U.S.). He lost and acknowledged the lobby's power—and Israel has regarded him as a firm friend ever since.

That summer four Shultz assistants began to press the secretary to establish closer links with Israel. One of the four was Undersecretary of State Lawrence Eagleburger, who would later be assigned to act as U.S. liaison on bilateral covert activities. When the group had completed their position papers arguing for "strategic cooperation" with Israel, Shultz and Robert McFarlane, at the time national security adviser, went to see the President and sold him the new policy, over the opposition of CIA Director Casey and Secretary of Defense Weinberger. They argued that it would help contain Soviet expansion in the Middle East.

The political correspondent for Israel's military radio credited Robert McFarlane with the breakthrough. "It is stressed in Jerusalem that even before the massacre [the October bombing of marine headquarters] in Beirut, a tendency had emerged in Washington toward increasing cooperation with Israel in the wake of deliberations in the U.S. capital after Robert McFarlane became the new national security adviser."[58]

In late October 1983 President Reagan signed National Security Decision Directive 111, establishing strategic cooperation with Israel.[59] Israel's Prime Minister Yitzhak Shamir arrived in Washington the following month to discuss the pact—he described it as, in part, "a dialogue on coordinating activity in the third world"[60]—and it was formally signed the following March.[61]

Largely unknown in this country, in Israel the new pact was leaked before it was even signed, much less discussed, after a visit to Israel by Under Secretary of State Lawrence Eagleburger. The conservative Israeli paper *Ma'ariv*, said that early in November Eagleburger told Prime Minister Shamir that "the president would like to meet with a personality or personalities from the most senior echelons in Israel."

Ma'ariv pointed out that what the White House wanted was "substantive, and not just intended to shut Israel up and justify the AWACS deal with Saudi Arabia," and that it finally recognized Israel "as a real asset." The paper speculated that Eagleburger, Secretary of State Shultz, "and the members of the National Security Council advocating a pro-Israeli line are currently enjoying Reagan's support," over those aligned with Defense Secretary Weinberger.

Ma'ariv said that the Reagan Administration admitted that it had dealt harshly with Israel over Lebanon and, "during the invasion of Grenada, when the United States used all the explanations Israel used to explain its invasion of Lebanon within the framework of the Peace for Galilee Operation, which the United States did not find satisfactory."[62]

Shamir left Washington with promises of increased U.S. aid, short term economic credits, concessions on the sales of Israeli weapons systems to the U.S., and an administration commitment to a Free Trade Agreement.[63] Shortly thereafter, the Defense Department relented in an ongoing standoff and released technology packages for the Lavi aircraft Israel was developing.[64] To the media, Secretary of State Shultz acknowledged that there was "no *quid pro quo* in the new arrangement with Israel, that the United States received no major concessions in return."[65] Clearly the administration was propitiating Israel and there was only one conceivable reason it could have been doing so: it wanted Israeli help with the contras.

Well before the U.S. invasion of Grenada, and while the State Department was still fashioning its new pro-Israeli policy, a bilateral committee spearheaded by Robert McFarlane began what would become twice-yearly meetings. In 1982, as an aide to Secretary of State Alexander Haig, McFarlane had been sent to Israel to discuss Haig's vision of a conservative Middle East alliance. McFarlane's interlocutor had been David Kimche, director-general of the Israeli foreign ministry. When McFarlane moved over to the White House he established links between Kimche and senior State Department officials, launching what came to be known as the U.S.-Israel Political Military Committee. The committee 'which would meet every spring and fall (alternately in Washington and Jerusalem)' was set up "to look at the big picture," meaning everything but what is euphemistically known as the Middle East "peace process."[66] It would later be subsumed under the 1984 strategic agreement.

At the first meeting of the group, in June 1983, discussion was mainly on cooperation in the developing world, centered especially on Central

America—on "the intention of the U.S. Administration to get Israel to supply the armies of the pro-American regimes there," with funds "the U.S. cannot directly transfer to its allies in the region...paid to Israel directly from the United States."[67]

During the same time frame the White House was starting to appreciate Israel for what it could do to promote administration aims in Central America and Israel's willingness to "assist" the U.S., administration officials had said, helped to improve strained relations between the two countries.[68] An Israeli account said that such cooperation was the *only* "aspect of cooperation...to be energetically pursued during the last two years."[69]

Israel had allowed $21 million to be reprogrammed from its foreign assistance to El Salvador in 1981,[70] before Congress had had an opportunity to cave in to the new Reagan Administration's demands for major military aid for the Salvadoran regime. Israel already had the Guatemalan situation well in hand, and it had reinforced the words of UN Ambassador Jeane Kirkpatrick to debt-ridden Costa Rica: if you want aid you must create an army.[71] And it was involved in a low-key way with the contras.

Early Days with the Contras

There are several stories about how and when Israel began arming and training the contras. One of them is that the Israelis helped launch the contras soon after Somoza was overthrown in 1979.[72]

Some say that after the fall of Somoza, associates of Edwin Wilson and Thomas Clines transferred a "security assistance program" they had going with Somoza to the contras. [73] If another account is true, that this network "began funneling aid to Somoza via Israel and EATSCO," then possibly it is also true that Israel took part in the network's activities in Honduras on behalf of the remnants of Somoza's secret police, whom they were said to have "outfitted" between August 1979 and January 1981, when the Reagan Administration was sworn in.[74]

Most sources set the date Israel became involved a year or two later. According to one account, in early 1982 after contras holding U.S. weapons were shown on U.S. television (causing, at the time, embarrassment), some former Israeli intelligence officials approached the CIA, which was just getting back into gear after having been reduced during the 70s and was having trouble finding untracable weaponry with which to equip the contras, with an offer to supply such weapons. The high U.S. official who related this version said that Washington authorities had assumed that the offer had the backing, awareness or sponsorship of the Israeli government. It came during a period when Israel was rejecting requests through "normal diplomatic channels" for weapons and funds for the contras. The CIA, he said, turned the offer down.[75]

Another version has it that an arrangement was made with Israel in the early 1980s to supply the contras with East bloc equipment[76] under which Israel agreed to sell the CIA light arms and shoulder-fired missiles for both the contras and the Afghan rebels. "Then [w]hen the Israelis presented their bill for $50 million earlier this year, [1986] the CIA pleaded poverty, paying $30 million in arms, not cash."[77]

Former FDN Director Edgar Chamorro said that Israel was among the international supporters that the contra leaders spoke of in 1982 to promote themselves.[78]

In December 1982 the FDN leadership had met with then Defense Minister Ariel Sharon in Honduras. It is certain that an arrangement was made at that time to funnel Israeli-held East bloc arms to the contras through Honduras.[79] In addition, it is likely that Sharon, in cahoots with the head of Honduras' armed forces, Gustavo Alvarez Martinez, made Washington a strings-attached offer to take the contra program under his wing. Just as the aftermath of his invasion of Lebanon was turning nasty, Sharon had turned up unannounced in Honduras with the director of the Israeli defense ministry and David Marcus Katz, Israel's Mexico-based arms agent.[80]

It was soon determined that Sharon and Alvarez were trying to close a deal for Israel's Kfir C-2 jet fighter planes. Also on the table were smaller weapons systems and some of the weapons Israel had captured in Lebanon; these were being offered free, with the taker to pay the freight.[81]

As the Kfir contains a U.S.-made engine—otherwise it is made in Israel, based on the French Mirage—Israel needed U.S. permission to sell the aircraft to Honduras. Previously Washington had refused to sell Honduras (or Mexico, for that matter) the F-5 because it did not want to introduce a new level of sophistication in the region's aircraft. It was feared that if Honduras acquired such an advanced plane, Nicaragua would be forced to obtain the equivalent MIG from the East bloc, a move which the administration had made it clear would be regarded as a "provocation."[82]

Even though there could be no deal for the Kfir without the blessing of the U.S., Alvarez and Sharon agreed to the sale of 12 of the aircraft,[83] at a price of $100 million. Honduras had no money, so Sharon asked the Reagan Administration to finance the deal, after the manner that had been set forth in the MOU.[84]

The only thing that could possibly have tempted the Reagan White House into such a deal would have been a Sharon-Alvarez proposal to take over the contras, which were in the process of being abandoned by their Argentine trainers. Both were certainly motivated for the undertaking. Alvarez was an obsessive anti-communist and an advocate of the Argentine-style security state. Whether against Nicaragua or his domestic oponents, he advocated "preventive" war without frontiers.[85]

In analyzing Israel's involvement in the Iran-contra scandal, the senior political columnist of Israel's major daily *Ha'aretz* recalled Ariel Sharon's approach to foreign policy:

> The Iranian affair resulted from the belief that no action is too big for Israel as an international mini-superpower. Ariel Sharon, who once said that Israel is strong enough to reach the gates of Odessa, was the natural candidate even before the outbreak of the war in Lebanon, to approach the U.S. with the suggestion of intervention in the Iran-Iraq war. Within the framework of the strategic understanding with the U.S., he offered the U.S. Israel's services in a war torn Central America, notifying the Americans of our readiness to participate in blocking the Soviet threat wherever we possibly can.
>
> Even after Sharon, Israeli diplomacy lived quite comfortably with the notion that we can, and should, play some role in every possible world arena.[86]

Whether with reluctance or out of concerns about Sharon, who would shortly be forced to surrender the defense portfolio when Israel held him partly responsible for the massacres in the Sabra and Chatila refugee camps after the invasion of Lebanon, the Reagan Administration did not go for this deal. In 1986, with its contra war coming apart following the discovery of the "private" supply network, the Kfir deal would be revived and the administration would lean toward granting financing for the Israeli planes in hopes that they would be more acceptable to Congress than the F-5s the U.S. had wanted to sell Honduras.[87] But if anything, the Sharon-Alvarez episode awakened the administration's interest in working with Israel.

Israeli advisers, well distributed in Central America, were almost certainly working with the contras when Sharon made his bid. In early 1983, 50 Israeli specialists in guerrilla and psychological warfare were said to have gone to El Salvador and Honduras.[88] That summer intelligence sources said that Israel was providing "special" guerrilla training to the contras.[89]

The following year President Daniel Ortega told Balfour Brickner, rabbi of the Stephen Wise Free Synagogue in New York, that Israeli military advisers had been working with the contras in Honduras.[90]

Israeli advisers were well paid, probably by the CIA, making $6,500—$10,000 a month compared with the $5,000-$7,000 being paid to Argentine advisers.[91] and, although the Israeli government always claims that such trainers are mercenaries, running loose through the world (the Israeli army graduates many, many of them, skilled in suppressing the smallest manifestation of Palestinian nationalism) to make their fortunes, in fact they were almost certainly sent by the Israeli government.

An Israeli mercenary who had served in Central America said that Israelis were training *and supervising* the contras. He said they were recruited by "foreigners with excellent Israeli connections." Another Israeli mercenary said that the Defense Ministry was aware of the Israelis working with the contras and that they use IDF (Israeli Defense Forces) manuals and catalogs.[92]

A 1983 U.S. National Security Agency document revealed a request to Israel to arm the contras[93] and the first reports of Israeli weapons reaching the contras appeared.

The earliest report of Israeli weapons to the contras was of 500 AK rifles in July 1983.[94] These were delivered to the Costa Rica-based ARDE (Revolutionary Democratic Alliance).

In 1983 and early 1984 Israel devoted much of its attention to ARDE. This was undoubtedly part of an effort to preserve the "clean" image of ARDE's leader Eden Pastora. In what would ultimately be his undoing, the former "Commandante Zero" made his identification with social democracy and his participation in the anti-Somocist insurgency a point of pride. Pastora often swore that he never got money from the CIA, although in the early days of its war against Nicaragua the agency was supporting Pastora—quietly, in the hopes that he could gain a following in the Socialist International. According to one report, Pastora was a CIA informer during the years he was part of the Sandinista Directorate.[95]

Disturbingly, ARDE leaders made frequent reference to having received funds from Jews, or Jewish groups in the United States. It is still not known whether this was a euphemistic reference to Israel or whether one or more Jewish organizations in this country has been funding the contras.

In June 1983 ARDE leader Eden Pastora had been ready to fold, with only $3,000 left. In September ARDE boasted of "increased donations from individuals in Venezuela, Colombia, Mexico, Peru and some European countries, as well as "private American organizations and some

Jewish groups." Pastora was able to increase his guerrilla force from 300 to between 2,000 and 3,000 and was planning to arm an additional 2,000 to 3,000. He was also receiving weapons from Israel described as captured in Lebanon.[96]

Alfonso Robelo, at the time political leader of ARDE, said the mercenary grouping received "financial aid from German and Venezuelan citizens, Mexican organizations, U.S. Jewish organizations, as well as from Germans and Cubans in exile." He said he did not care where they got the funds they gave ARDE.[97] Another time Robelo reeled off a list of ARDE backers that included "the democrats of Venezuela and Mexico, the Nicaraguan exile community [colonias nicaraguenses] and the Jewish communities of the United States."[98] Yet another time Robelo said "we are receiving help from many democrats and private companies in France, Spain, Venezuela, Mexico, Colombia, and even Jews."[99]

In any event, it is known that Israel itself sent considerable quantities of arms, and advisers as well, to ARDE in Costa Rica. Referring to the armaments he had received, Pastora said "only the CIA or the Israelis could give us these."[100]

Another reason for the Israeli-ARDE connection was that the Israelis had been very active in Costa Rica since the accession of Luis Alberto Monge to the presidency. Monge had made good on a campaign pledge to move Costa Rica's embassy to Jerusalem, and Costa Rica, which had prided itself on having no army, was receiving Israeli weapons and training for its security police and two newly-created special tactical squads. Israelis also carried out various "intelligence activities" in Costa Rica.[101]

When the contras were just getting under way, Israel's ambassador in San Jose supplied them with passports and aliases so that they could travel through Central America.[102] Pastora told one reporter that the Israeli ambassador had tried to sell him weapons.[103] Israel's parastatal Tahal was working with U.S. AID to develop plans for a border barrier, comprising roads, electronic barriers, and an agribusiness/settlement scheme.[104] Ultimately a scaled-down version of the plan was begun.[105]

It later became known that Israeli arms also reached ARDE through Panama. In the autumn of 1985 Alvin Weeden, a Panamanian attorney and former secretary general of the Popular Action Party (PAPO) said that Gen. Manuel Antonio Noriega, commander-in-chief of the Panama Defense Forces, obtained the "materiel needed by the Southern Front to continue its struggle" from Israel. Noriega then distributed the supplies to ARDE, and, according to Weeden, in the process made himself some money.

Weeden said his information came from Dr. Hugo Spadafora. Spadafora, a Panamanian physician who had fought with other guerrilla movements, had been fighting with ARDE and had enlisted Weeden to represent him in declarations he planned to make about Noriega's malfeasance and links with narcotics traffickers. Spadafora was murdered soon after. Weeden says the physician had left ARDE because of Pastora's close connection with Noriega.[106]

In October 1983 FDN Director Edgar Chamorro said that the Honduran-based main mercenary force had received 2,000 AK-47s from Israel.[107]

Jack Terrell, now at the International Center for Development Policy, said he was in Honduras when an Israeli arms shipment arrived for the contras. Terrell said that in November 1984, when he asked FDN chief Adolfo Calero for Uzis and 9 mm ammunition for a commando raid on Managua, Calero told him "I'll get this as soon as I can. We're expecting two ships in from Israel in February. When they get in, you will get your stuff. Terrell said that the Uzis arrived and were given out to the contras.[108] (The choice of weapon might have been influenced by the fact that Nicaragua still uses some of the arms Somoza acquired from Israel.)

Terrell said the sales were made by Israeli arms dealers acting with "at least the tacit support" of Tel Aviv and that he learned in Honduras that the documents covering the shipment were signed by Honduran officials (who made 30 percent on the deal) and were then sold to the contras. Terrell also said that he learned in early 1985 that Calero's brother Mario Calero had been to Israel to buy 10,000 AK-47s, said to have been captured in Lebanon.[109]

Later, especially after ARDE collapsed following the CIA's decision to eliminate Pastora, Israel's main action would shift to the contras in Honduras. But as far as the administration was concerned, Israel never did quite enough.

Israel Disappoints the Reagan Administration

During the summer of 1983 the Reagan Administration had tested Israel's willingness to participate in its plans for Central America and discovered that Israel was not ready to go the distance. There had followed a demonstration of both picque and pressure from the White House. At that time the administration would have wanted help with supplying the contras in the field and training them. The Argentine officers who had at first performed those tasks had been withdrawn, following the administration's backing of Great Britain in the Malvinas-Falklands War. The administration would also have wanted Israel's open political support of its contra policy, which was becoming controversial and unpopular.

When Israel was not forthcoming, "senior Reagan Administration officials" let it be known through "a foreign source" that Israel was sending some of the arms captured in Lebanon to Honduras "for eventual use by the contras." The circuitous sources even listed the arms: artillery pieces, mortar rounds, mines, hand grenades and ammunition. The administration told the *New York Times* that Honduras would pass most of the arms Israel supplied on to the contras.

The same sources explained that the arms shipments were indicative of an "enlarged" Israeli role in Central America"—more like a surrogate for the U.S. and less like the independent supplier of arms Israel had been in the past. It was revealed that the administration had encouraged Israel to increase its presence in the region "as a way of supplementing American military aid to friendly governments and supporting insurgent operations against the Nicaraguan Government."

U.S. officials themselves confirmed the report, and said the Administration, braced for a congressional refusal to provide funds for the contras, was looking for "new lines of support to Nicaraguan rebels."

Israel's response at the time was clear. An Israeli diplomat denied that Israeli activities were related to U.S. policies and said that there had been no change "in Israel's role as an arms supplier." Israel would make arms sales and provide trainers, but it would not take the heat for the politically unviable program.

Spurious Charges of Anti-Semitism

The administration coupled its 1983 public "appeal" to Israel with what it perceived to be a special reason for Jews to support the president's contra program: Sandinista "anti-Semitism." As one in a series of efforts the Administration was making to promote its policy of backing the contras to special interest groups, the White House Office of Public Policy arranged a briefing for Jewish groups. During the Jewish briefing Isaac Stavisky and Abraham Gorn were introduced as Nicaraguan Jews who had fled their country, the victims of "anti-Semitic persecution" by the government. At the briefing the President accused Nicaragua of anti-Semitism, and Rabbi Morton Rosenthal, the director of the Anti-Defamation League's Latin America division told reporters that Stavisky and Gorn—"Nicaraguan Jews" the Rabbi generalized—had been driven out by the Sandinistas, who had expropriated their property and seized the synagogue in Managua.[110]

There would be other similar pitches from the president, mostly focused on Nicaragua's links with the PLO, Libya and Iran. At the July 20 briefing and for many months afterwards the White House gave out a document entitled "The PLO in Central America" under the masthead of *White House Digest* seeking to show by means of crudely drawn cartoons the connections between the PLO and various "terrorist" organizations around the world. The FSLN [Sandinista National Liberation Front] was of course included, but so were defunct groups such as the U.S. Black Panther Party, and so were organizations that had long since become electoral formations in their respective countries. The document, said to be warmed-over Israeli propaganda, was identical to one given out by JINSA [The Jewish Institute for National Security Affairs].[111] These pitches reflected the administration's fevered thinking that, given Israel's popularity in the Congress and the strength of Israel's Jewish supporters in the U.S., "American cooperation with Israel can, during any U.S. military activities in the Caribbean, make the difference between success and failure in the House of Representatives."[112]

None of the other ploys used to appeal to Jews, however, caused nearly as much consternation as the charges of anti-Semitism. These drew attention when Rabbid Rosenthal put out a bulletin charging that the Nicaraguan government had forced the entire Jewish community into exile and confiscated Jewish property, including the synagogue in Managua, converting it to a children's club. Rosenthal initially said that the Nicaraguan Jews "blame their plight on the relationship of the Sandinistas and the Palestine Liberation Organization."[113] But attention rapidly narrowed to the charges of Sandinista anti-Semitism.

In fact, however, the charges had been discounted even before they were publicized at the White House. Four days before the debut there of Stavisky and Gorn the U.S. embassy in Managua sent a cable to Washington. The ambassador wrote:

> ...the evidence fails to demonstrate that the Sandinistas have followed a policy of anti-Semitism... Although most members of Nicaragua's tiny Jewish community have left the country and some have had their properties confiscated, there is no direct correlation between their Jewish religion and the treatment they received.[114]

Literally dozens of subsequent investigations further discredited Rosenthal's charges. Sergio Nudelstejer, who heads the American Jewish Committee's Mexico office said that the Jews left Nicaragua because of "factors other than anti-Semitism, including their belonging to the propertied classes." A press release issued by the World Jewish Congress said Panama City Rabbi Heszel Klepfisc had been to Nicaragua in September 1983 and found that there was an "anti-Israel" tendency, but no anti-Semitism.[115] New Jewish Agenda, the Council on Hemispheric Affairs, and other organizations sent teams to Nicaragua and concurred with Klepfisc's determination.

Rabbi Rosenthal and his White House backers were not deterred. Relatives of the "exiled" Jews reappeared in 1985 as part of a campaign launched to lobby for $14 million in contra aid. Billed as "conservative Nicaraguan Jews" Elena Gorn and Sarita and Oscar Kellerman joined contra leaders in a national campaign "to convince American Jews that the Sandinista government is anti-Semitic and anti-Israel." The campaign specifically targeted Jewish members of Congress and members of Congress with large Jewish constituencies who had opposed contra aid. The three exiles joined contra leaders for Washington press conferences and then met individually with members of congress, at synagogues and with "conservative" groups. They called fresh attention to the old charges of Nicaraguan anti-Semitism.[116]

During the 1986 campaign for contra aid Rosenthal reissued his "White Paper" on Nicaraguan "anti-Semitism" and distributed it to every member of Congress.[117]

Only later would it be known that the whole campaign was cooked up by the CIA. Edgar Chamorro, a former FDN official who is now a critic of the contras, told of a spring 1983 meeting with three CIA officers in Coral Gables, Florida during which the idea was hatched to "target" American Jews "by making the case that the Sandinistas were anti-Semitic."

They knew that the two men they planned to invite to speak at the White House had been persecuted for their collaboration with Somoza, but Chamorro said the CIA operatives thought it would be "valuable" propaganda.

Chamorro said, "They said that the media was controlled by Jews, and if we could show that Jews were being persecuted, it would help a lot."

Chamorro said that Israel was not directly targeted in this campaign, but that "the White House event coincided" with the administration's leaked reports of a greater Israeli role.[118]

Rabbi Rosenthal, whose special task this cause became, simply kept reiterating his accusations.[119] In a further irony, a real Nicaraguan anti-Semite was discovered. It was Bishop Miguel Obando y Bravo, who shamelessly worked with the U.S. government to create strife in Nicaraguan church and society. During an October 1984 sermon he preached in

Managua, Obando y Bravo repeated the "Jews-killed-Jesus" calumny. When questioned by Rabbi Ronald B. Sobel, chair of the ADL Intergroup Relations Committee, Obando did not respond to Sobel's letter. [120]

The Kimche-Eagleburger Committee

In November 1983, following Prime Minister Shamir's visit to the White House, Undersecretary of State for Political Affairs Lawrence Eagleburger and Foreign Ministry Director-General David Kimche were appointed to be coordinators of strategic cooperation outside the Middle East.[121]

The administration had suffered a setback in October when the Congress slapped controls on CIA funding for the contras. After the Boland Amendment a series of administration meetings was held in December 1983 and January 1984. President Reagan put his weight behind CIA director Casey's proposal to find another means of supporting the contras,[122] redoubling administration interest in sending Israel against Nicaragua. Israel was at the bottom of its worst economic crisis ever, making it, presumably, more susceptible to the administration's entreaties.[123] The administration kept talking to Israel.[124]

1984: Crucial Aid and an Impasse

In the spring of 1984 Israeli support for the contras "became crucial to the war's continuation." Robert R. Simmons, who in 1984 was staff director of the Senate Intelligence Committee said that the Iran-contra affair would not "be fully understood until the events of 1984 are fully looked at."[125] The last covert money was spent on March 8, 1984.[126]

Prime Minister Shamir told Seymour Reich, president of B'nai B'rith International, that the Reagan administration had approached Israel "several times" about supplying aid to the contras.[127]

A former U.S. official "who routinely reviewed intelligence reports" said that the Reagan administration made "at least two attempts in 1984 to use Israel to circumvent a Congressional ban on military aid to the contras."[128] That former U.S. official or another one said that the Israelis had refused to supply "bridging financing," weapons and training and then later refused a request to launder and pass along U.S. funds to the contras.[129]

As the administration pressured Israel to help it get around congressional restrictions on arming the contras, Israel begged the U.S. to keep its involvement secret out of fear of Congressional anger.[130] It was a sign of the administration's desperation in April 1984 that after its "quiet diplomacy" had failed to produce the desired results and with Congress dead set against funding the contras in the wake of reports that the CIA had mined Nicaragua's major harbors and David Kimche due in Washington for the April 1984 meeting of the political-military committee, the administration pulled out all the stops.

In Israel, news leaked that at this third meeting of the political-military committee Kimche would be discussing setting up a special fund to finance Israeli assistance in Central America and Africa—"to improve Israel's position in Africa."[131]

An Israeli paper reported from Washington that the U.S. had proposed making Israel a conduit for U.S. aid to anti-Communist forces in Central America and that the U.S. would establish a fund "independent of the government budget to finance projects suggested by Israeli experts."[132]

Kimche would be pressing for U.S. Agency for International Development (AID) contracts to undertake agricultural and technical assistance programs in Africa, said the *Jerusalem Post*. In exchange, it was expected that the administration would push for "a higher Israeli political profile in support of U.S. policy in Central America," which was currently under fire in Congress.

This high profile would consist not only of increased Israeli aid to the contras: "The administration would like to see Israel encourage its own supporters in the Congress, the Jewish community and elsewhere to become more assertive in backing the "contras."[133]

In Israel diplomatic sources acknowledged that discussions in Washington would be about the setting up of a special fund which would cover programs in Central America and Africa—"this is nothing new," these sources said—but they would not say if the fund would cover military aid.[134]

The State Department said the U.S. had "no intention of providing funds to third countries for the purpose of supporting covert activities in Central America."[135] However, requests were coming at Israel from a number of directions in a seemingly orchestrated manner.

"CIA Director William J. Casey is considering the possibility of asking another country, such as Saudi Arabia, to send money to the Contras until the funding problem is solved, according to one well-placed source, but no decisions have been made," reported the *Washington Post*.[136] The CIA later admitted having "unofficially" asked Israel and Saudi Arabia to support its covert operations against Nicaragua and its sources explained that the satellite information Israel had been getting from CIA

Director Casey was "so valuable" that the Israelis might have been expected to be eager to please the CIA by helping out with the contras.[137]

A contra chorus line went into action. The FDN announced that because Congress had not authorized the $21 million asked by the administration for continuation of the contra program it would ask Israel for aid. An unnamed FDN official said the organization's leaders were to meet that day with U.S. intelligence officials "to discuss their options for finding new funds." FDN chief Adolfo Calero said, "We have looked for private money, but there isn't enough. We need a government. We think the Israelis would be the best, because they have the technical experience."

Another contra official offered the view that Israel might be willing to assist the contras "as a favor to the Reagan administration," and out of consideration for the $2.6 billion in aid it received from the U.S. that year.[138]

Simultaneously ARDE leader Eden Pastora deplored the condition of anonymity under which non-U.S. aid was given to ARDE. He said "I continue to complain about these people who call themselves democrats and who are ashamed of supporting us.... In this way we lose political support."[139]

Bosco Matamoros, Washington representative of the FDN, also called on Israel to aid the contras. He said the interests of Israel and the contras "overlap" because the PLO was aiding Nicaragua. He also noted the "anti-Semitism" of the Nicaraguan government and the flight of Jews from Nicaragua.

Matamoros said that after PLO Chairman Yaser Arafat visited Managua in 1982, Nicaragua became closer to Libya. He also warned that there was an "increase in anti-Semitism and anti-Israeli feeling in other countries in Central America, where rebels are being helped by the Sandinistas and the PLO."

While neither confirming or denying whether the contras were getting arms, advice, or training from Israel, Matamoros said he was speaking "only of policy, not of military matters, so as not to embarrass Israel or the FDN." He added that his mother was Jewish—her name was Salomon—and that he hoped to visit Israel soon.[140]

Once before when an aid cutoff had been threatened, the contras had spoken of using Israel as a substitute. In June 1983, when asked about reports that the U.S. would not continue providing aid to the contras, Marco Zeledon, one of the directors of the FDN, said "If this should be the case Israel would be a good candidate."[141]

In one of the more curious, heavy-handed episodes of the whole affair, Fred Francis, Pentagon reporter for NBC News, reported from Honduras at the site of a contra air drop operation. Francis said NBC had "learned" that Israel, "at Washington's urging, has armed a quarter of the rebel army." Live on camera (but not loquacious) Enrique Bermudez, FDN commandante, told Francis, "We received some weapons from the, the, that Israeli government took from PLO in Lebanon."

The gist of the report, a voiceover on footage made during a trip "into Nicaragua" on a C-47, is that Washington keeps the contras on a tight reign and won't let them win. Soon they might be abandoned altogether, and, concluded Francis, "forced to turn again to Israel and others to save themselves from becoming refugees of a war lost in a divided Washington."[142]

Israel attempted to fend off some of the attention without attracting more. "Israeli observers" interpreted the statement of Enrique Bermudez that the FDN is receiving weapons from Israel "as an American tactic to link Israel with Reagan Administration policies" in order to prevail over congressional resistance to its funding proposals. The CIA "keeps a tight reign" on the contras, it continued, and Bermudez would never have spoken "without CIA approval or encouragement."[143]

Israeli Embassy spokesman Victor Harel said he knew nothing of the contra request and said "We are not involved in any activity to overthrow any government in this part of the world, even if it is a very unfriendly government."[144] But Israel "was so worried that increased Israeli aid to the contras might create bad publicity and difficulties in Congress" that Col. Aviem Sella—at the time studying in New York and running spy Jonathan Jay Pollard—was asked to find out what Israelis working with the contras were doing.[145]

Washington was rife with "speculation that the Reagan Administration, seeking to get around Congress' cutoff of covert-action funding for the contras, wants Israel or some other third country to take over financing and direction of the guerrilla campaign"[146] and there was a report that "some Administration officials in recent weeks have talked privately about the possibility of persuading friendly governments, such as Israel to help." A State Department official said that "hawks" thought that Israel ought to help out because "it shares our concerns about the Soviets."[147]

The political—military committee meeting was held on April 26. Both sides insisted that no agreement had been reached on funding Israeli aid programs and that the U.S. had not asked Israel to become involved in the contra program.[148] However, National Public Radio said that the idea of "joint U.S.-Israeli foreign aid was discussed," and noted speculation about a new fund that the U.S. would create "ostensibly for non-military aid projects which reportedly would allow the U.S. to funnel extra money for covert aid which could then be channeled by Israel when needed."

In an apparent effort to dampen the speculation, Kimche had a breakfast meeting with reporters after his meeting with State Department officials, and he emphatically denied any Israeli contacts with or arms sales to the contras. He said Israeli policy is to only sell arms to "constitutionally organized countries and not to unofficial organizations." He said that Israel might have been mentioned in conjunction with Soviet-made arms supplied to the contras, but any such aid was "without our consent and without our knowledge." He noted that stories of Israeli arms going to the contras might have come from the contras "in the hopes that members of Congress sympathetic to Israel would then look more favorably on U.S. covert activity."[149]

Kimche "acknowledged that the talks had included discussion of how Israel might increase its technical assistance programs in Third World areas, including Central America." He said the aid would be limited to "peaceful projects." However, he reiterated, "I haven't come to arrange how Israel is going to take over the contras."[150]

He said that Israel had decided "some time ago" against supporting the contras for two reasons: Prime Minister Shamir didn't want to have a debate on Central America during the Israeli election campaign then getting under way; Israel did not want to alienate Congress, upon which it depends for its aid.[151]

Apprently Kimche had come to Washington at least part way inclined to go along with the administration's desires. There was at least some Israeli sentiment in favor of an open role with the contras for Israel. UN Ambassador Benjamin Netanyahu had tried several times to get Israel to supply aid to the contras. Netanyahu's efforts began when he was an attache at the Israeli Embassy.[152] Then the Israeli Embassy warned Kimche's ministry "that the growing controversy over the administration's policy in Central America could damage Israel's standing with Congress."[153]

It is unlikely that Kimche's committee assignment was his only Washington contact. When Yitzhak Shamir moved from the foreign ministry to the premier's office in 1983 after the sudden resignation of Menachem Begin, he appointed no one to succeed him, leaving Kimche to function as *de facto* foreign minister.[154] The April meeting in Washington would be the last with Lawrence Eagleburger as a counterpart. Kimche's new interlocutor would be Richard Armacost.[155] During his April visit Kimche was also set to meet with members of the NSC.[156] It is possible that the committee continued to meet, but it is also worth wondering whether the actual functions of the committee were transferred to the little White House junta led by NSC staffer Oliver North. In addition to his meeting with Eagleburger (and the assistant secretaries for Africa and the Middle East, who also took part in that session) Kimche met with Langhorne Motley, who was then assistant secretary of state of Inter-American affairs.[157] That post was later assumed by Elliot Abrams, a friend of Oliver North, who once said that the Nicaraguan government was anti-Semitic because it recognized the PLO,[158] and served on the task force assigned to promote the war against Nicaragua.[159]

In autumn 1984 Kimche met with another White House body, the President's Task Force on International Private Enterprise. Headed by Reagan insider Dwayne Andreas, the task force was staffed by former U.S. AID employees who worked out of an office in suburban Virginia. Its ostensible purpose was to increase the participation of the private sector in foreign aid, which the Reagan philosophy has consistently approached as an unexploited profit-making opportunity for U.S. business interests (thus the constant equation of starvation in Africa with the quasi-social control of agriculture and marketing in many parts of the continent). It also had the appearance, and probably the capacity as well, of serving as a front for unmonitored distribution of funds for activities abroad.[160] Israel was the only foreign government included in the planning process.[161] David Kimche was "the only non-American to appear before the committee."[162]

Nonetheless, whatever else Kimche had negotiated,[163] from the standpoint of the contra backers, the stumbling block remained as it had been the previous year: Israel feared running afoul of Congress.

However, Israel was apparently willing to assist in a joint attack on Nicaragua. A former diplomat said, "They are willing to go in with us in the open, but to get the onus for assisting the contras while the U.S. is standing aside and keeping their hands clean? No."[164] The following year the White House would make crude efforts to change this political reality. For the moment though, it showed its exasperation. U.S. officials said there was no foreign aid money for the Israeli aid projects.[165] The administration bought several aircraft from Brazil, Israel's rival in the arms trade, purportedly for use by the Honduran military.[166]

Apparently congressional Democrats did not feel alienated when Israel increased its covert aid to the contras. They simply professed not to know anything about it.[167] Meanwhile, it soon became obvious that Israel had agreed to step up the tempo of the covert assistance it provided to the contras.

Several contra leaders said that they had made arrangements to get Israeli assistance. Government sources said "Israel provided some type of well-concealed financial assistance to U.S.-backed guerrillas called contras," worth several million dollars. It "appeared" to be going to the contras through a South American intermediary. They said that Washington might be reimbursing Israel through its U.S. military or economic assistance.[168]

"Knowledgeable sources inside and outside the U.S. government who asked not to be identified said they believed that Israel would help U.S. allies in Central America if Congress reduced its military assistance to those nations," said a report at the end of May. These sources said that "administration and State Department officials are delighted by Israel's role in arming Central America"—although they doubted that Israel and other third countries could replace the $177.4 million that the U.S. spent on the region 1983. Several international arms traders said that indirect reimbursement of Israel by the United States would not be difficult.[169]

Between March and September 1984, $15 million came to the contras, by one estimate—an average of $2.5 million a month. FDN leaders, "government officials" and "White House sources" said that the source of the funds were big U.S. corporations and the governments of Israel, Guatemala, Venezuela, Taiwan, Honduras, El Salvador and Argentina. Israel's share of that total was estimated at just under $5 million.[170] That sum was further broken down into contributions of "Soviet- and Chinese-made weapons believed captured in Lebanon" and cash payments "that help contras meet their $800,000 monthly payroll."[171]

The Israeli Embassy again denied that Israel was providing funds to the contras. Victor Harel, press counsellor said, "We deny it completely. Israel is not providing any aid to the Nicaraguan rebels, in any form." Harel said Kimche's denials of the previous April "remain operative today" and reiterated that Israel "can't prevent" arms it has sold to other countries in the region from reaching the contras.[172] But it looked as though an arrangement had been made that was fairly acceptable to both sides.

An Evolving Modus Operandi

In early 1985 both Reagan Administration officials and members of Congress said that Israel had again stepped up aid to the contras, but denied that U.S. foreign aid was funneled through Tel Aviv, El Salvador or Honduras.[173] The denial came as the Reagan Administration began signaling its desire to find a legal way to send aid through third countries. In March 1985 it said it was considering asking "friendly" Asian countries to support the contras. Taiwan and Thailand were mentioned[174] and it was never made clear whether U.S. aid or the friendly countries' own resources would be used. An administration official said both U.S. aid recipients and non-recipients were under consideration.

Ominously, an administration official said "Right now there is a proscription from any third country providing assistance. Well, might the Congress not wish to reconsider that?"[175]

After a few such feelers on this score produced negative reactions from Congress, the pronouncements ceased. The White House announced that it had "rejected a series of proposals for indirect financing of the Nicaraguan rebels."[176] But the conniving continued.

In July 1985 the Reagan Administration not only got $27 million "non-lethal" aid out of Congress for the contras, it also figured out a way to "legalize" shaking down U.S. aid recipients for contributions to the mercenaries. (Incidental but not unrelated to this process, the $12.6 billion foreign aid bill containing contra aid—the first foreign aid bill since 1981 to stand on its own rather than skulk in a continuing resolution—won the votes of a number of liberals because it also contained $4.6 billion in U.S. aid for Israel. Rep. Howard Berman (D-CA) called it "critical assistance."[177] The House leadership either did not try to separate the contra aid from the aid to Israel or was unable to do so.[178])

The president signed the foreign aid bill containing the $27 million on August 8.[179] Before he signed it, however, while the bill was in a House-Senate conference the White House ordered surgery on one of its amendments. Named for Senator Claiborne Pell (D-RI), the offending language forbid the Reagan Administration from making a formal or informal arrangement with U.S. aid recipients to aid the contras. Unless the Pell Amendment was removed, it was threatened that the president would veto the entire bill. The State Department explained that the amendment might prevent the president from soliciting "nonlethal" aid from Israel, Taiwan, South Korea, and other such allies, some of which had already spoken to the White House about donations.

In a highly unusual move, Sen. Pell, Foreign Relations Chairman Richard Lugar (R-IN) and White House and congressional staff sat down together and rewrote the amendment. The new language read:

> ...the U.S. shall not enter into any arrangement conditioning expressly or impliedly the provision of assistance under this act...upon provision of assistance by a recipient to persons or groups engaging in an insurgency...against the government of Nicaragua.

Both houses of Congress passed this language before they adjourned for the summer.[180] Henceforth the administration was allowed to put the arm on aid clients—just not to the point of threatening to cut off their aid!

The following week it became evident that the heat was off Israel, as contra boss Adolfo Calero catalogued contributions for reporters: "A lot of people help on weapons. Gen. Singlaub, some Germans, some French. The people who help us are not government people, but governments can give leaves of absence or it can be a retired person. We have no Israeli dealings. They have not given or sold us anything."[181] Earlier that year a reporter for National Public Radio had seen Israeli-made artillery pieces at the FDN's main camp in southern Honduras.[182]

Although information is now coming to light about arms shipments made by the Secord-Hakim-North junta through Portugal and France, there have been very few reports of weapons coming from Europeans for the contras. As to financial contributions that might have been used to purchase weapons, Edgar Chamorro insists that the occasional reports of such money from Europe are a "smokescreen." "Money only goes through Europe to be laundered," he says.[183]

In 1986, in a scenario at least as ironic as the forcing of Iran to finance the war against Nicaragua, Richard Secord shook down the government of Saudi Arabia for funds for the contras. The Saudis gave in after being reminded that the administration had stuck its neck out and "defied the powerful pro-Israeli lobby" to get the AWACs sale through Congress. Secord himself had lobbied for the sale. Secord then used the Saudi money "to acquire Soviet-made weapons from Egypt, from Israeli-held stocks captured in Lebanon, and from international arms dealers."[184]

During the years Congress limited funding for the contras, CIA Director Casey and UN Ambassador Vernon Walters traveled to a number of U.S. clients and urged contributions. Both Israel and Egypt donated money in response to these pleas "when reminded of the substantial U.S. aid they receive."[185]

It was not all giving though. While some of the money that Israel volunteered is said to have been passed through Oliver North,[186] it is more than likely that the money Israel gave was immediately recycled in Israel for weapons, a pattern that was to be repeated when the siphoning off of the Iran profits commenced. (The same pattern which ensures that much of U.S. foreign aid is spent on U.S. weapons or civilian imports.) Former contra leader Edgar Chamorro has pointed out that arms dealers do not seek out the contras, nor do the mercenaries often make purchases on the open market. He explained that "a very few people, close to the White House, tell the FDN how to get weapons...Calero is told by the people in charge where to go to buy weapons. They even make the connections."[187]

Genesis of the Idea

When Canadian investors came asking for their money and the plot started to unravel, hints in intelligence cricles that money from the Iran operation was going to the contras jelled into hard fact. While the facts were not quite so hard regarding who had initiated this angle of the operation, the preponderance of the evidence laid the intellectual authorship (and at least some of its execution) at Israel's door. Israel would have every reason to put two and two together: generating funds from Iran would be an obvious way to get the administration, with its constant pleas to do more for the contras, off its back. That aspect of the operation was begun in January 1986, the same month when the President had signed the finding legitimizing the arms sales to Iran.[188]

David Kimche, who had been Israel's main contra contact with the U.S. as well as the point man in the early part of the Iran scheme, was the logical villain in the piece. Robert McFarlane had great admiration for Kimche's intellect: "He gave McFarlane much of what passed for an intellectual construct," a State Department official said, adding, "of course it helped that McFarlane thought the Israelis knew everything."[189] When he made his confession, Oliver North told Attorney Gen. Meese that the idea had originated with Kimche.[190] Kimche vehemently denied suggesting shunting the funds, calling North an unmitigated liar.[191]

The Senate Intelligence Committee's report seized upon the exchanges on the subject which North reported he had had with Amiram Nir, Prime Minister Peres' "terrorism" adviser. Various sets of notes taken by Justice Department personnel during Meese's November 23 questioning of North quote North as saying that Nir suggested using the arms sales profits for the contras, that the two discussed the contras, that North "also recalled turning down other Nir suggestions that U.S. funds to Israel or Israeli's [sic] own funds could be used to support the Nicaraguan resistance."

More tellingly, the report continued, "Other notes of that interview reflect only that Nir told North in January that the Israelis would take funds from a residual account and transfer them to a Nicaraguan account."[192] That suggests that the scam had already been decided upon— probably by North's and Nir's superiors, which would be a far more egregious challenge to Congressional sensibilities. Obviously, it was much less threatening to construe this vital element in the affair as the concoction of renegade aides rather than a deliberate high level piece of collusion between the Israeli government and the White House—a conspiracy in which Israel left an adoring Congress out in the cold. Perhaps with this in mind the report totally ignored North's earlier statements about Kimche. It mentioned several other possible sources of the idea of diverting the funds—Albert Hakim, Manucher Ghorbanifar—without weighing or analyzing the discrepancies presented by the varying attributions. It also failed to take into account the relative bargaining positions of Israel and the U.S., with Israel repeatedly urging a reluctant White House to continue with the arms sales to Iran.

The normally cautious *Times* of London said that "the Senate Intelligence Committee had been given secret evidence strongly suggesting that the plan to divert money from the Iran arms operation to the Nicaraguan Contras was first put forward by Mr. Shimon Peres, then the Israeli Prime Minister."

According to the *Times* Amiram Nir had simply conveyed the suggestion to Oliver North and Vice Admiral John Poindexter, the President's national security adviser, during a January meeting.[193]

It was also reported that Adnan Khashoggi suggested the idea to Gen. Secord, who passed it on to North.[194]

Whichever Israeli official or agent conceived the idea of overcharging the Iranians to generate cash for the contras, it was a somewhat risky gambit for Israel. There was always the (very slight) chance that Congress might be really angry and cut back on Israel's aid.[195] In view of that risk, even though it had every appearance of being a concession to the administration in exchange for its participation and legitimization of the arms sales to Iran, it is no surprise that Israel would insist on making itself some money selling arms to the contras. A recycling of cash for arms would have been the least Israel would have demanded from the NSC junta for the risks to which it was putting its congressional image.

Miami-based contra leaders suggested that was the reason FDN leader Calero insisted that he had never received any of the money the Israelis funneled through Switzerland. "I imagine that the money was handed directly over to the arms suppliers and the arms were sent to us," said one. "These things are all handled by the U.S. and Israel," he added, claiming to be unaware of the exact logistics of the transfers.[196]

Massive Israeli Arms Shipments

After the administration doctored the Pell Amendment it was reported that the contras had received "substantial new arms shipments."[197] There was another surge in the spring of 1986, when proceeds from the Iranian arms sales began to reach the contras in the form of weapons. An arms expert estimated that the Israelis had sent the contras "thousands" of AK-47s. Seventy AK-47s and 100,000 rounds of AK-47 ammunition were among other items on the plane shot down by Nicaragua on October 5, 1986.[198]

During the 1985-86 period Israel sent at least 6 shiploads of East bloc assault rifles, grenade launchers and ammunition to Honduras for the contras.[199] Some of the 400 tons of weapons shipped by Southern Air Transport to Ilopango Air Base in El Salvador came from Israel, via Portugal.[200] One shipment, a "significant quantity" of East bloc arms (interestingly, the only Israeli arms shipment to the contras to be mentioned in the Senate Intelligence Committee's report) was offered by Israeli Defense Minister Yitzhak Rabin on September 12, 1986. They were to be picked up during the following week and taken on a foreign-flag vessel to Central America. Admiral Poindexter had corresponded with Oliver North about the Israeli shipment and wrote North a note characterizing the deal as a "private deal between Dick [Secord] and Rabin that we bless," and telling North to "go ahead and make it happen."

An Israeli source confirmed that the shipload of weapons had indeed been on the way to Central America. He said that it had been recalled after the scandal broke.[201]

In a briefing he prepared for President Reagan in advance of a scheduled September 15 meeting with Prime Minister Shimon Peres, Poindexter advised Reagan to thank Peres for the shipment "because the Israelis held considerable stores of bloc ordnance compatible with arms used by the [contras]."[202] Such shipments might have been a regular feature of the "strategic" relationship between the U.S. and Israel, or that blessed deal might have been a unique occasion. Many, if not most of the Israeli shipments went through private Israeli dealers, who exist for just such business.

"Private" Dealers

Ya'acov Nimrodi, who figured prominently in the arms-to-Iran dealings, also handled "shipments" of arms for the contras, which were paid for with several million dollars, given by the Israeli government to the contras at the request of CIA Director Casey.[203] A former employee of Nimrodi's International Desalination Equipment Co. said the sales were made through a U.S. company owned by Nimrodi and the dealer had done the deal as a "favor" to the contras, taking only a "small fee" for himself.[204]

Pesakh Ben Or, a big Israeli arms dealer based in Guatemala and Miami, owns Eagle Israeli Armaments and Desert Eagle. In late 1984 (at the earliest) Ben Or gave the Israeli defense ministry sale documents bearing the signature Col. Julio Perez, chief of logistics in the Honduran

Army's Ordnance Corps. In a telephone conversation Col. Perez confirmed the documents and verified his signature.[205]

In all, Ben Or is known to have sold three shipments to the contras through the Honduran military. The consignments included such items as RPG-7 grenade launchers, which the Honduran army does not even use! The contras do use them.[206]

As likely as not, the SA-7 surface-to-air missiles which the contras use to try to bring down Nicaraguan helicopters, came from Israel. The contras bought the missiles "by the dozens" starting in mid-1985.[207]

Opinions vary as to whether Ben Or or Sherwood, a U.S.-based company widely understood to be an Israeli operation,[208] was the source. A report in *Defense and Foreign Affairs* "suggests that Ben Or may have supplied the Soviet SAM-7 missiles."[209]

Moreover, Ben Or's operation and Sherwood are connected by a tangle of other Israeli arms dealers. At the time it was selling arms to the contras, Sherwood employed Pinhas Dagan and Amos Gil'ad, an Israeli transport officer, in senior positions.[210] Michael Kokin, president of Sherwood, confirmed that Pinhas Dagan and Amos Gil'ad were once Sherwood employees.[211]

Gil'ad was an acquaintance of Gerard Latchinian, arrested by the FBI in an assassination plot against Honduran President Roberto Suazo Cordoba. Gil'ad introduced Latchinian to Pesakh Ben-Or.[212]

Latchinian, whose role in the assassination plot was to obtain the necessary weapons, had at one time employed Emil Sa'ada[213] who was identified by Honduran military sources as one of two former Israeli military men who had "helped arrange" arms shipments to the contras in deals dating back to 1984.

The other Israeli was Yehuda Leitner, who said he worked for Sa'ada in Honduras. Sa'ada runs a melon growing operation called Acensa and also a business called Shemesh Agrotech. Leitner was also employed by ISDS, a "security expertise" exporter in Israel which confirmed his employment.

Both Sa'ada and Leitner denied having sold arms and charged they were being scapegoated in the shuffle resulting from the Iran-contra scandal and from rivalry among regional arms deals, "including Marcus Katz."[214]

David Marcus Katz "helped broker [a] deal with the contras in 1985," according to an associate of his interviewed by the *Miami Herald*.[215] And to bring the connection around full circle, Pesakh Ben Or began his career as chauffer to Katz.[216]

The Israelis vehemently denied *any* arms shipments to the contras, or any contact with them at all—though they were just a shade less vehement when it came to "private deals" put together by their middlemen. (These they said they couldn't control, a contention which most Israeli arms dealers hotly challenge.[217]) A congressional investigator said the Israelis use the middleman technique so that they can maintain "plausible deniability" of their operations.[218] Privately, senior Israeli officials conceded that David Marcus Katz and Pesakh Ben Or "appear to have acted in semiofficial capacities in previous arms dealings."[219]

Israel or its associated arms dealers might also have participated in the diversion of U.S. arms to the contras. A former U.S. Army combat pilot and supply officer now working as an arms expert for a conservative Washington think tank said that he had quizzed "Americans who had visited rebel training and supply camps in Honduras, and their conclusion was that the U.S. Defense Department was the ultimate source, through theft, cut-out deals with Israel and other governments, of most of the rebel arms." The arms expert said that major items such as batteries and aircraft parts had been accounted as discarded scrap and "had actually been diverted in good working order to the rebels."

Former CIA senior arms analyst David MacMichael said that there had been a great deal of stolen ordnance and much that was reported used in training at an Alabama base could have gone to the contras.[220]

Direct Contact with the Contras

Although kept carefully under wraps, there was also direct contact between Israel and the mercenaries. "It is extremely rare for us to go to Israel," said a contra leader. "We do not have a formal relationship with the Israelis. We work with them quietly, usually outside Israel. There is no need for us to go directly to Israel." Referring to Israel's wish to deny any links to the contras, one of the leaders commented, "you wouldn't believe how hard it is to ship arms from Israel to Honduras."[221] Contra leaders said that they normally obtained arms from Israel through the Israeli embassy in Guatemala.

Yet in addition to the visit by Mario Calero, at least one other contra went to Israel seeking arms. Julio Montealegre, a Miami-based, high ranking aide of Adolfo Calero, spent two weeks in Israel in late January and early February 1986[222]—just as the first of the arms shipments authorized by the Presidential finding would have gone to Iran and some of the profits from those sales diverted to Israel to purchase arms for the contras.[223]

According to contra sources, Montealegre went "to talk to some people."[224] Bosco Matamoros, the FDN's UNO Washington spokesman, said the reports of a visit were "speculation," but two contra leaders in Miami said he was indeed in Israel in late January and early February 1986.

"He was gone about 15 days," said one leader. "He did not say why he was going there."[225]

There was speculation that he was seeking the last cargo of arms which Somoza bought from Israel. The arms were paid for, but never delivered.[226] In a bit of a reverse from the line taken by their U.S. publicists that the contras are not Somoza's direct descendants, the contras were claiming what they considered to be their inheritance: "We have been trying to get those arms for a long time," said one of the contra leaders.[227]

The Israelis and the contras also seemed to be making direct contact on other levels. Soon after the second shoe of the scandal dropped, Adolfo Calero told the New York correspondent for IDF Radio that "one time I met with Gen. Simhoni, but not in relation to anything that is going on now. I heard that he might be of service to us once he retired."[228] Gen. Uri Simhoni was until last summer the Israeli military attache in Washington. He was apparently also an intimate of the fevered inner circle that ran operations out of the White House. During the November 1985 interception of the aircraft carrying the Achille Lauro hijackers, Simhoni was in the White House situation room.[229]

Another Israeli spoke anonymously on the state-run television: "I conducted negotiations with the contras. They need light weapons, ammunition.... They want advisers from Israel." He said there were more Israelis working with the contras, and that relations between the two groups were "outstanding," so sympathetic that, in his words, "you feel after a day like you've known them for years."[230]

Some of those instructors, said a report right after the New Year, were training the contras at U.S. Army bases in Honduras. The report said that the Israelis were paid by the Honduran government, but that Israeli military sources said the payment might be from "American sources or intelligence groups."[231]

The Jewish Campaign

Clearly subordinate to the murder and mayhem perpetrated on Nicaragua by the contras was the administration's attempt to rearrange the Jewish body politic, to effect a 180 degree shift in its attitude toward the contras. In 1986, after Israel presumably relieved itself of some of the heat by funneling profits from the Iran arms sales to the contras, President Reagan's attention was directed to Israel's support system in the U.S. The first and obvious aim of this exercise was to enlist Jewish support for funding for the contras. Another was to soften up public opinion to a possible future overt Israeli role in the contra program.

Those Jews who supported the contra program hooked onto the administration's campaign with alacrity. It has been the hope of several right wing Jewish groups to force a shift to the right among Jewish organizations. They argue that, as they have become more affluent, Jews have continued to vote as liberals—against their own interests, these rightists argue. Underlying that line of argument is the hope (which was shared by Israel's Likud government and to a lesser degree by some Labor leaders) that U.S. Jews will ally themselves with the pro-arms, militarist right, likely to support military spending on Israel.

It was also hoped that Jews would align themselves with the religious right, in reaction to the mainline churches' insistence on an evenhanded approach to the Middle East. This was of course what was behind the appalling friendship between Menachem Begin and Jerry Falwell and the much more sinister fawning of Pat Robertson on the Israeli intelligence services. These religious figures made a great deal of money taking superstitious Biblebelters to Israel, after convincing them that the already embattled state would be the scene of the last battle of Armageddon as the televangelists read it literally from the Bible.

All this left the majority of Jewish voters cold. Jewish males were the only white ethnic group which voted against President Reagan in 1984. But in the Washington world of perceptions a few photo-opportunities and the cunning press release can sometimes overwhelm the most compelling reality.

On March 5, 1986 Reagan entertained leaders of major Jewish organizations to lobby for his contra aid bill. He assured them that "I would not consider any measure, including arms sales to moderate Arab nations, if I thought it might endanger the security of Israel." Then he told them "there's a vote coming up in Congress of utmost importance, and I have to tell you, I need your understanding and support." The vote was for $100 million in lethal aid for the Nicaraguan contras. In his pitch Reagan underscored Nicaragua's connections with the PLO, Iran and Libya.

"If the Sandinistas are allowed to consolidate their hold on Nicaragua," he told his guests, "we'll have a permanent staging ground for terrorism. A home away from home for Qadhafi, Arafat and the Ayatollah, just three hours by air from the U.S. border."[232] (This was typical Reagan rhetoric of that period; on March 6 the president had made his famous statement that members of Congress must choose between supporting his administration or supporting communism.[233]) He also told the Jewish leaders that Jews should support contra aid because U.S. credibility with allies in Latin America and with Israel was at stake.

Also lobbying for the $100 million contra aid bill, Vice President Bush told an Agudath Israel (religious and conservative) leadership gathering that the Nicaraguan government had used "Nazi-like tactics" against the Nicaraguan Jewish community. Bush also spoke about Nicaraguan connections with the PLO.[234]

During the White House meeting the chairman of the Conference of Presidents of Major Jewish Organizations (MAJO), Kenneth Bialkin, endorsed the Reagan policy, but he stressed that he could not endorse it on behalf of the entire Jewish community which the conference purports to represent.[235] It did not occur to Bialkin, whose organizational base, the Anti-Defamation League supposedly exposes and protests prejudice against Jews, that the President's cynical pandering might be anti-Semitic.[236]

In the *Congressional Record* of March 19 Rep. Vin Weber (R-MN) inserted a letter signed by prominent Jews such as Max Fisher and Jack Stein (former head of MAJO) stressing the connections between the PLO and Nicaragua and saying that Libya had given Nicaragua $400 million over 4 years and trained its political police. The same day Robert Mrazek (D-NY) inserted an American Jewish Congress resolution opposing contra aid.[237]

In the March 20th vote on contra aid, 21 of the 30 Jewish members of the House voted no. The administration continued with its pressure on Jews, even entertaining Wall Street crook Ivan Boesky (in his hey day a heavy contributor to Jewish causes) along with ultraright Jewish Senator Chic Hecht (R-NE).[238] An early May news release by Sen. Rudy Boschwitz (R-MN) reiterated the fraudulent ADL anti-Semitism charge. To counter the impression that all Jews supported the contras, the Union of American Hebrew Congregations sent a letter refuting the anti-Semitism charges to all members of Congress saying that the 1.3 million Jews represented by the organization oppose military aid to the contras.[239]

During the 1986 battle over contra aid, Israeli diplomats also "discreetly encouraged American Jewish bodies" to lobby Congress in favor of the $100 million the President was asking for the contras.[240]

About this time—a month after Foreign Minister Shamir had been in Honduras and said nice things about the Contadora process[241]—there began to come from Israel very hostile statements about Nicaragua. Shamir said that, in exchange for its assistance to the Nicaraguan government, the PLO had set up a base in Nicaragua.

He told a group of high school students that terror was "an international monster spread over continents" and that Libya and Nicaragua were aiding it. He "congratulated the United States on its antiterror war in South America, saying that Israel favors cooperation for the suppression of terror."[242]

After the Iran-contra scandal broke, the Israelis shifted their approach and began to claim that they had made diplomatic overtures to Nicaragua, but that Nicaragua had rebuffed every attempt.[243]

Where Did the Money Go?

Three months after it was divulged that funds were being shunted from the Iran operation to the mercenary war in Central America there was still no accurate estimate of how much money was actually involved. The first figure mentioned, $10 million to $30 million was drawn from the air by Attorney General Meese, interpolated from a statement made by Oliver North.[244]

An "Undated Memorandum" discovered in Oliver North's office mentioned $12 million from an arms sale to Iran that would be used to purchase supplies for the contras. When questioned, North said he had obtained the figure from the Israelis, who would disburse the funds.[245] After a White House briefing Rep. Jim Wright (D-TX) was able to provide a breakdown of one transaction: Iran had paid the Israelis $19 million. $3 million of that had gone back to the Pentagon, $4 million went to arms brokers and $12 million went to the Swiss accounts for the contras.[246] Other sums were bandied about: $30 million to $50 million in accounts earmarked for both the contras and the Afghan guerrillas;[247] "the bulk" of $15 million from a May arms shipment that Ghorbanifar had told arms dealers Khashoggi and Furmark was "earmarked for Central America."[248]

When considered in tandem with the question of who, among the many that have been mentioned, moved the money from Iran to its final destination and who took a piece of it along the way, it can only be surmised that the network through which it was funneled was intentionally tangled—or that there were several networks shuffling a great deal more money than has yet been reckoned.

Some of the money went to the Israeli government, which, according to Oliver North, established the prices that Iran would have to pay.[249] One source, a private individual in the Middle East whose name was said to be "familiar from recent reports on this matter," said that $10 million was placed in Swiss bank accounts by Lt. Col. Oliver North and Amiram Nir and then transferred to the Israeli government by Nir for purchase of East bloc arms for the contras. According to this version, the $10 million from Brunei was used to cover money given to the Israelis.[250]

Exactly who did the banking in Switzerland (and in other offshore locations) is also not totally clear. Attorney General Meese's original announcement said that it was "representatives of Israel."[251]

Albert Hakim's lawyer (who also represented Oliver North) told Assistant Attorney Gen. Charles Cooper that the money from the February shipment of TOW missiles and another shipment in May went "through Israelis into Hakim's financial network." Hakim distributed the money to other accounts.[252]

Oliver North said that after meeting with Amiram Nir in January 1986 he "contacted Adolfo Calero and as a result of that contact three accounts were opened in Switzerland." North said he gave the numbers of the accounts to "the Israelis," who arranged for the deposits and that the money was deposited, and the contras were appreciative.[253] Calero has denied having received any money at all and the Israelis insisted it was the CIA which opened the Swiss bank account in which profits from the Iran arms sales were deposited. They said Iranian "counterparts" got the money from Iran and made the deposits.[254]

The Senate Intelligence Committee report says that a Credit Suisse account was used by North, Hakim and Richard Secord for Iran arms sales proceeds. It also notes that it had obtained information (of "unknown reliability") about profits being deposited in Credit Fiduciere Services, the Secord/Shackley/Clines Swiss bank, and then funneled to CFS' subsidiary in the Cayman Islands.[255]

On November 26 the *Los Angeles Times* reported that it had learned a week earlier from an Israeli businessman that Adnan Khashoggi had arranged for the Iranians to put money into a Swiss account run by Ya'acov Nimrodi. A senior Israeli official said that Israeli middlemen "meddled" with a Swiss bank account and that their meddling might be connected with the disappearance of millions of dollars from the account.[256] The missing money might be the money sought by Canadian associates of Roy Furmark. When CIA Director Casey asked Oliver North about the whereabouts of Furmark's friends' money, North said either the Israelis or the Iranians had it.[257]

Another Israeli report spoke of two other bank accounts—one for logistical expenses, to which the Israelis had access. That account also noted that before January 1986 Israelis had had access to an account in which Iran deposited money.[258]

On December 16 the *Washington Times* reported that, in addition to Adnan Khashoggi, "Swiss bankers identified other 'intermediaries' as Israeli arms merchants who used the names Arnon Milchen, Shlomo Cohen, Marcus Kritz and Al Schwimmer."[259]

Kritz is very likely the Mexico-based Israeli arms dealer David Marcus Katz. Al Schwimmer, one of the major Israeli dealers, was involved in the initial phase of the joint U.S.-Israeli arms sales to Iran.

Arnon Milchan is an arms dealer and movie producer who has been involved in Israeli arms sales to South Africa. He has admitted laundering some of the more than $100 million spent by the South Africans during the 1970s in an attempt to improve the white government's image abroad. (This scandal later became known as Muldergate.) More recently Milchan purchased in the U.S. on behalf of the Israeli government 810 electronic switches known as krytrons, which can be used to detonate nuclear weapons explosions. Israel and South Africa collaborate on an advanced nuclear weapons program.[260] Shlomo Cohen is the name of the Israeli ambassador to Honduras.

As to what portion of the Iran profits actually went to the contras, in cash or in kind, North said that Amiram Nir decided on that. Confirmation of North's statement is contained in one of Prime Minister Peres' denials: after Meese's shocking announcement on November 25 1986 Peres telephoned him and said that Israel had only told the Iranians where to put the money, and how much to put in each account![261]

If there is any question that Israeli arms merchants or government entities were on the receiving end of at least some of the money, it ought to be dispelled by the information North provided to the Attorney General: that when a price was set (presumably not by Israelis) for an October 1986 shipment of 500 TOWs and no money for the contras was included because $100 million approved by Congress the previous summer had become available, Nir was upset.[262] Also in October, as the operation unraveled, a CIA memorandum to Director Casey and his lieutenant Robert Gates spoke of the risk that Ghorbanifar might disclose to the press an account charging that the U.S. government had failed to keep several promises to him and that both the U.S. and Israeli governments had acquired substantial profit from the Iran arms transactions, some of which was redistributed to "other projects of the U.S. and Israel."

The memo also alluded to "indications of funds needed for some unknown purpose by an Israeli official."[263]

The Attractions of Obscurity

Over the many hearings, investigations, and other dissections of the Iran-contra affair, Israel's purposes are likely to remain obscure to the public. Israeli citizens, be they officials, arms dealers, or civilian witnesses are not bound by U.S. law to testify or cooperate in investigations. Israel has already made it clear that it will shield its citizens who were involved in the affair behind its national sovereignty and will only cooperate to the extent necessary to placate public opinion.

And that, given the well-oiled media machinery of Israeli loyalists in the U.S., is a very limited proposition. As was seen during the invasion of Lebanon, when the cameras focus in too close a vast cry will go up, charging media imbalance and probably also anti-Semitism.

The Congress, which had many opportunities to examine Israel's activities in Central America and to discourage them, understands the problems attached to those activities all too well but members of Congress would be the first to admit (if only they dared) that they are powerless to restrain Israel. Organizations dedicated to reversing the post war trends in U.S. foreign policy are also unlikely to depart from their ingrained tendency to avoid confrontation with Israel.

Israel's immunity to U.S. law and the silence it has created around itself by years of methodical intimidation will protect it through the bloodletting ahead. These built-in attractions are also likely to make Israel the vehicle of choice for the next tragic and avoidable essay in covert foreign policy.

VI.
Contragate:
The Disposal Problem

Lessons of the Bay of Pigs

The long-simmering, brutal war for Nicaragua may take years to conclude. But it's not too soon to begin considering the consequences of probable defeat for the administration's proxy war against the Managua regime.

The $100 million in U.S. aid now flowing to the contras is a mere down payment for violence yet to come. Yet no one supposes it will purchase a contra victory. On the contrary, short of a U.S. invasion to decide the outcome, the money and supplies will only delay and embitter the collapse of the CIA's contra-waged counterrevolution.

Ironically, U.S. policy will make Washington's allies, the contras, bleed as much as its enemies. Used as instruments of geopolitical policy, most of the contras will likely be abandoned and forgotten once the president's attention moves on to other regions.

The syndrome is well known to students of other CIA-sponsored paramilitary campaigns, including the Kurdish revolt against Iraq and the resistance of the Hmong tribesmen in Laos to Pathet Lao and North Vietnamese troops. In both cases, withdrawal of U.S. support ensured defeat for U.S.-allied guerrilla armies.

But the most notorious abandonment occurred during the 1961 Bay of Pigs invasion by CIA-trained Cubans against the Castro regime. The failure of the Cuban people to rise in revolt led to the ignominious defeat of the landing.

"We didn't call the Cubans of Brigade 2506 [the invasion army] that in 1961, but they were our contras," observes David Atlee Phillips, former chief of Latin American and Caribbean operations for the CIA.

The Bay of Pigs fiasco seared the CIA officers who planned that disastrous landing. "It is my worst memory of abandoning an ally, but it isn't the only one," Phillips recalls. "In my 25 years with the CIA, I was aware of too many instances in which allies and agents were left stranded after a successful operation or dumped after a failed one.... Our covert-action operations are too often tactical missions, short-term ventures for short-term ends. We ask people to take risks for us without fully comprehending the logistical—and moral—commitments we have made to them."[1]

But there is another troubling aspect to such covert commitments. Allen Dulles, CIA director at the time of the Bay of Pigs invasion, called it the "disposal problem"[2]: What do you do with an army of trained, armed, indoctrinated and fiercely committed warriors once you no longer need them? How do you contain or safely vent their anger, resentment and energy?

These possibilities will soon apply no less to the contras of Nicaragua than they did to the contras of Cuba. Even Pentagon leaders with responsibility for Central America have been heard to wonder, "How are we ever going to cut this thing off?"[3] The lessons of Cuba are thus vitally relevant to policy choices today.

President Kennedy faced a disposal problem as soon as he took office and inherited the Eisenhower administration's plan for an invasion of Cuba by CIA-trained exiles. Dulles warned him of the difficulty and embarrassment of calling off a plan so far advanced. Kennedy felt he had little choice. "If we have to get rid of these men," he rationalized just before authorizing the invasion, "it is much better to dump them in Cuba than in the United States, especially if that is where they want to go."[4]

But the plans failed and the "disposal problem" only worsened after Castro defeated the invaders and humiliated their sponsor. More bitter than ever, and fanatically committed to Castro's downfall, the exiles became a galloping horse that threatened to master its rider.

"You train them and put them in business," veteran CIA office Ray Cline noted, "it's not that easy to turn them off."[5] Or, as one militant Cuban who landed at the Bay of Pigs later put it, "Everyone thought they could wash their hands of it. But when the day came to wash their hands, they could find neither soap nor water, and their hands stayed covered in mud."[6]

Kennedy subsequently hit on a two-track approach to disposal: He cracked down on exile raiders operating against Cuba from U.S. soil while encouraging them to find offshore bases with CIA support. So long as their attacks could be directed away from U.S. targets and citizens, the CIA would continue to supply weapons, speed boats and even planes for use from Nicaraguan and Costa Rican staging areas.[7]

But the strategy became a political issue of national significance after some anti-Castro guerrillas vowed resistance to Washington and some politicians—notably Richard Nixon—denounced Kennedy's efforts to "quarantine" the exiles. In New Orleans, Carlos Bringuier of the Revolutionary Student Directorate (DRE) pledged that his group "would continue efforts to liberate Cuba despite action by the United States to stop raids originating from U.S. soil."[8] Eventually the FBI, CIA and at least two committees of Congress would take seriously the possibility that right-wing extremist exiles may have taken revenge by assassinating Kennedy.

Kennedy's successors had no greater success in "disposing" of the violent and poorly adjusted minority of exiles for whom guerrilla war had become a way of life. "The problem was never worked out to everyone's satisfaction because it was so difficult," explains Phillips. "Some people entered American society with no trouble. But some who were revolutionaries were inclined to become terrorists. Terrorism among Cuban exiles became a real problem."[9] Indeed, exile bombings and assassinations wracked this nation from Miami to New York since the early 1960s.

Some exiles, moreover, put their clandestine training to use in the lucrative field of drug smuggling. By the early 1970s, law enforcement officials estimated that no fewer than 8 percent of the Bay of Pigs army had been arrested or convicted of drug crimes.[10] Many terrorists, in turn, financed their underground operations by importing marijuana, cocaine or heroin.

Still other exiles became professional guerrillas, signing up for CIA missions in the Congo, Bolivia, Vietnam or Central America; joining the intelligence agencies of other Latin nations like Venezuela or Costa Rica; or taking on domestic missions like the Watergate burglary of June 1972, led by former Bay of Pigs political officer E. Howard Hunt.

Drugs, terrorism, political destabilization: The American people and, indeed, people throughout the world, have paid a heavy price for the U.S. government's unleashing a war it could not contain. The contra war is far from concluded, but already it shows all the signs of producing a monster that will attack its creator.

The Terrorist Blowback

Mention "terror" and the average American thinks of fanatical Iranian mullahs or Palestinian hijackers—but the greatest terrorist threat to the United States in recent times has originated not overseas, but much closer to home, with Cuban exile extremists bent on avenging the loss of their homeland.

Their bombings and assassinations, on U.S. soil and around the Caribbean, reached a crescendo in the mid-1970s, and have tapered off since only gradually. But the Cuban exile terrorists may someday be succeeded by an equally militant group of Nicaraguan exile terrorists, if the contras are similarly sent into battle and then hung out to dry.

Orlando Bosch, a longtime leader in the anti-Castro movement, epitomizes the exile terrorist frustrated by the loss of official support. In an orgy of violence in 1968, his group blew up a Japanese freighter in Tampa, damaged a British vessel off Key West and bombed eight diplomatic or tourist offices in New York and Los Angeles to punish nations doing business with Cuba. Bosch was finally arrested while firing a bazooka against a Polish freighter in Miami Harbor.

Sprung from jail four years later with help from powerful Florida politicians,[11] Bosch went abroad to carry on his crusade. "His main goal," according to one reporter who interviewed him in jail, "was to forge alliances with friendly governments in [Somoza's] Nicaragua, the Dominican Republic, Costa Rica and Venezuela—all countries with powerful Cuban exile communities." He bombed embassies in Caracas and Buenos Aires and arranged the murder of two Cuban diplomats in Argentina. On instructions from the Chilean military junta, he went to Costa Rica to assassinate a prominent Chilean leftist and—as an added bonus—plotted to kill Henry Kissinger who was due to arrive at the same time. In 1976, he played a prominent role in a meeting of 20 exile terrorist leaders who gathered in the Dominican Republic to form an umbrella organization for their desperate acts: Coordination of United Revolutionary Organizations (CORU).[12] At least four other exiles from that elite terrorist fraternity later turned up in Central America as military backers of the contras.[13]

Offered up to the United States as a parole violator by both Venezuela and Costa Rica, Bosch had nothing to worry about. The Justice Department didn't want him back.[14] Washington had solved its "disposal problem" by sending him abroad to attack pro-Cuban targets.

Bosch was only one of many exiles who turned CIA training in demolition, assassination and irregular warfare into tools of a lifelong trade.

For years these exile terrorists, the flotsam and jetsam of the failed covert war against Castro, sponsored by benefactors at the highest levels of government, got the upper hand of law enforcement agencies.

"I realize that part of what is happening in Miami today has sprung out of the Central American era," reflected Bay of Pigs leader Manuel Artime in 1977. "You must understand it was with an enormous patriotic sense these men went into training and it is bad to kick them out to the street. Because out of frustration and misguided patriotism come some senseless acts, like terrorism."[15]

Artime himself was hardly the innocent social observer. Responsible for a lethal commando raid against an innocent Spanish freighter in 1964, Artime later used his influence to free Bosch from a Costa Rican jail.[16]

Nor was Artime's sponsor, the CIA, any more innocent. It built the very infrastructure of terror. Michael Townley, who hired Cuban exiles to assassinate former Chilean ambassador Orlando Letelier in Washington, D.C. in 1976, said, "The one thing I found out in Miami...[was that] due to all the stuff that they had obtained from the CIA...you could buy plastic explosives on any street just like you'd buy candy—weapons, explosives, detonators, anything that you wanted—and it was exceedingly cheap."[17]

Today a similar infrastructure of terror supports the Nicaraguan contras in the CIA-backed struggle against the Sandinistas. The violence it feeds has already spilled over to neighboring countries in Central America. And it may be only a matter of time before the terrorist methods it encourages also turn against the United States—an example of what intelligence professionals term "blowback."

Like the Bay of Pigs Cubans who apparently got their deadly training in Guatemalan camps from East European SS veterans recruited by the CIA,[18] many contras in turn have learned their trade from veteran Cuban exile terrorists.

Those former Cubans gravitated to the contra cause from the start for ideological reasons. For those emigres, indeed, Central America became a prime "disposal" ground in the Reagan years just as it had been under Kennedy. Felipe Vidal, a Cuban-American active in Costa Rica on behalf of the contras, explained:

> During the 1970s the form of [our] struggle was terrorism against Castro in Mexico, France, Barbados and the United States. President Carter created this wave of Cuban [exile] terrorism because he began to negotiate with Castro. Once Reagan got into power, there was no need for these organizations because the government's policy coincided with the Cuban community's. In 1982, when Reagan came to Miami, he

told us he was willing to support Cuban revolutionaries outside the U.S., just as long as nothing went on inside the U.S. So that's why we're here.[19]

Central America was not the only theater of Cuban exile-contra collaboration. Some of the earliest pro-Somocista contra contingents got their training in the backwaters of Florida, under the benign eye of Washington. The former director of Orlando Bosch's New York terrorist operations set up a training camp in 1981 to "share intelligence and coordinate maneuvers" with ex-Nicaraguan National Guardsmen and ruthless military representatives of Guatemala and Chile.[20]

But the real work went on in obscure facilities in Honduras and Guatemala, where feared Argentine counterguerrilla specialists, fresh from an extermination campaign that took the lives of at least 9000 civilians in their own dirty war, came to teach the contras (and local death squads) what they knew of killing. The Argentinians included Army intelligence specialists and paramilitary thugs who had carried out the bloody work back home. Their method of urban counterinsurgency was simple but effective: kidnap suspects, question them under torture, kill and then repeat. They called it the "cleaning operation."[21]

Such techniques were appreciated by one Salvadoran rightist who told an American reporter, "The Argentines were a great help to the death squads (in Guatemala). Before, they used to kill right away. The Argentines taught them to wait until after the interrogation."[22]

The head of the CIA-financed Argentine training mission in Honduras in 1981 was Col. Osvaldo Ribeiro, an urban warfare expert nicknamed Little Bullet. Based more on his own experience than the objective situation facing the contras, Ribeiro and his colleagues counseled a campaign of urban terrorism, not rural guerrilla war. The Argentines had no scruples about killing prisoners, which became a regular contra practice.[23] They had willing students: Many of the contra commanders were themselves graduates of Argentine military academies.[24]

Joining the Argentine trainers were at least two notorious Cuban CIA veterans. One of these was Felix Rodriguez, who helped blow up a Spanish freighter in 1964 under Manuel Artime's direction, interrogated Che Guevara just before his murder in 1967, and advised on counterinsurgency tactics in Vietnam. After his 1981 stint with the Argentines in Honduras, Rodriguez moved on to El Salvador where he handled contra supply shipments at Ilopango air force base.[25]

(One of his cohorts in that later contra supply operation was a fellow CIA special warfare expert, Luis Posada, who joined Orlando Bosch in a series of attacks on Cuban sugar mills and fishing boats in the 1960s. In

1971, Posada allegedly took part in a CIA-sponsored plot to murder Castro in Chile.[26] As a top officer in Venezuelan intelligence, where he worked with several other Cuban exiles still reporting to the CIA, Posada arranged protection for Bosch while the latter engaged in political bombings and murders throughout Latin America. The two met again during the June 1976 terrorist summit in the Dominican Republic to form CORU. After CORU took credit for the October 1976 bombing of a Cubana Airlines jet, which killed all 73 passengers aboard, Venezuelan authorities arrested Posada and Bosch for plotting the deed. In Posada's papers were found a map of Washington, D.C. with the work route of former Chilean ambassador Orlando Letelier, murdered in September 1976 by Cuban exiles working for the Chilean secret police, DINA.[27])

Yet another Cuban on hand to serve the Argentinians in 1981, according to CIA-trained saboteur and contra supplier Rafael Quintero, was Dionisio Suarez. Suarez attended the CORU meeting in the Dominican Republic with Posada and was later indicted as a conspirator in the 1976 Letelier assassination.[28] He apparently joined the nascent contra movement in Guatemala on a Costa Rican passport.[29] Before then, but after jumping bail on the Letelier case, Suarez reportedly "set off a bomb aboard a TWA airliner, firebombed the Soviet UN mission, and informants said he was in Union City the day before the Cuban diplomat was gunned down in New York."[30] Suarez apparently belonged to a CIA unit that trained Nicaraguan exiles in sabotage and demolitions.[31]

Argentine methods, responsible back home for the "disappearance" of thousands of civilians under the military dictatorship, quickly took root with the contras. A 1982 Defense Intelligence Agency report noted that one typical contra operation included "the assassination of minor government officials and a Cuban adviser."[32] The CIA officer in charge of the covert war, Duane "Dewey" Clarridge, admitted in 1984 that the contras were routinely murdering "civilians and Sandinista officials in the provinces, as well as heads of cooperatives, nurses, doctors and judges." Clarridge said "there were no rules, no restrictions and no restraints at all on what the contras did inside Nicaragua."

Still he justified the killings: "After all, this is war—a paramilitary operation."[33]

Indeed, a CIA-prepared briefing manual instructed the Nicaraguan rebels on the "Selective Use of Violence for Propagandistic Effects." Employing the standard euphemism for assassination, it advised readers "to neutralize carefully selected and planned targets such as [judges], police and State Security officials, CDS chiefs, etc."[34]

Apparently the contras took that advice. "Frankly, I admit we have killed people in cold blood when we have found them guilty of crimes," said Edgar Chamorro, a director of the Nicaraguan Democratic Front, in 1984. "We do believe in the assassination of tyrants. Some of the Sandinistas are tyrants in the small villages."[35] Later, when Chamorro had left the contra movement in disgust, he described the process in more detail:

> FDN units would arrive at an undefended village, assemble all the residents in the town square and then proceed to kill—in full view of the others—all persons suspected of working for the Nicaraguan government or the [Sandinistas], including police, local militia members, party members, health workers, teachers, and farmers from government-sponsored cooperatives."[36]

Today the policy of terror seems as firmly implanted as ever. Reporters have documented the contras' strategy of targeting rural clinics, schools and agricultural cooperatives in order to undermine the Sandinistas' hold on the countryside.[37] The human rights organization Americas Watch reported in 1987 that the contras "still engage in selective but systematic killing of persons they perceive as representing the government, in indiscriminate attacks against civilians...and in outrages against the personal dignity of prisoners. The contras also engage in widespread kidnapping of civilians, apparently for purposes of recruitment as well as intimidation; a significant number of the kidnap victims are children."[38] Independent study missions to Nicaragua and the admissions of a former top security officer to the contras have confirmed these findings.[39]

No less troubling, the practice of terror against Nicaragua is leaving a bloody stain throughout the region. Nicaraguan exiles, like the Cubans before them, have become freelance killers in the service of shadowy death squads established and coordinated by CIA-trained Central American security forces.

A former top Salvadoran intelligence official charged in 1985 that the contras' intelligence chief Ricardo Lau—a former torturer and hatchet man for Nicaraguan dictator Anastasio Somoza—had been paid $120,000 to arrange the assassination of El Salvador's Archbishop Oscar Romero in 1980. The killing was apparently carried out by two former Nicaraguan National Guardsmen along with two Salvadoran soldiers. The former intelligence chief also accused Lau of having "played a key role in training the death squads" blamed for upward of 50,000 deaths in El Salvador, from his base in Guatemala.[40] Reportedly helping Lau in that latter task were Argentine torture experts and several Cuban-Americans working for the CIA and military.[41]

Lau bore further responsibility for political killings in Honduras, a country with no tradition of such brutality. With his help, Argentine advisers and anti-Sandinista contras joined CIA-advised Honduran security forces to systematically eliminate suspected Honduran leftists between 1981 and 1984, according to U.S. and Honduran officials. These death squad victims totalled more than 200 during that period. Locals began talking of the "Argentine method" as a new import. CIA officials "looked the other way" when people disappeared, according to one American official there. The violence tapered off only after the ouster of the CIA-backed, Argentine-trained and notoriously corrupt Honduran military commander, General Gustavo Alvarez Martinez.[42]

Even so, the terrorist violence continues there, if more sporadically. The Honduran army major who first exposed the existence of these death squads was found, torture-murdered and largely decomposed, near the Nicaraguan border in September 1985.[43] A year earlier he had publicly charged the CIA with establishing a secret Honduran military intelligence unit responsible for political killings and he had accused the anti-Sandinista FDN with doing much of the dirty work.[44] Police later charged three contras with his savage murder.[45]

In Guatemala, such violence had long been institutionalized by security forces organized by the CIA, trained by Argentine and Chilean torture specialists and supported by Israeli computer and weapons experts.[46] From his sanctuary in Guatemala, the Somocista torturer Lau was by late 1980 directing the "September 15 Legion," a group of former Nicaraguan National Guard officers financed by the Argentines and one of Somoza's cousins, in the "bloody underworld of politics and crime" controlled by Guatemalan veterans of the 1954 CIA coup. "There were robberies and kidnappings, threats and extortions," reports Christopher Dickey. "There were murders. Market vendors at the bus terminal in Guatemala City's fourth zone were prey to the operations described as 'recuperating funds'.... And other actions were more political. There were jobs for the Guatemalan police and for certain Salvadoran exiles." And joining them all were members of the Argentine military formerly detailed to Somoza's Nicaragua.[47]

By no means were all the contras so friendly toward the fascist element in Latin politics. But with the Argentinians in control of the purse-strings (as proxies, by the summer of 1981, for the CIA), the more democratic opponents of the Sandinistas carried little weight. Even honest conservatives could not call the shots. In late 1981, six major contra officers in the September 15 Legion rebelled against their leaders, demanding the ouster of Lau and his allegedly corrupt boss Col. Enrique Bermudez on grounds of "misuse of funds," "negligence of duty," "lying," and "lack of patriotic spirit." But the Argentine bosses prevailed. Bermudez and Lau purged their enemies.[48]

Nicaraguan exiles and their fellow Latins have no monopoly on anti-communist terror in the region. According to at least two direct partici-pants, a group of American mercenaries and a White House representative met in Miami in January 1985 to discuss plans to assassinate the U.S. ambassador to Costa Rica, Lewis Tambs. According to one of the mercenaries in on the planning, the same team had planted the bomb in May 1984 that aimed to kill Eden Pastora, the dissident contra leader who had fallen from favor with the CIA. Now they talked of bombing the U.S. embassy in San Jose and making it look like a Sandinista job. As an added bonus, a cocaine drug lord would pay for the operation in revenge for Tambs' prior anti-drug crusade while ambassador to Colombia. The defection and arrest of several of the participants ultimately nixed the plot.[49]

And so the circle begins to close back on the United States. A much-feared Cuban-American terrorist, Frank Castro, once declared, "I believe that the United States has betrayed freedom fighters around the world. They trained us to fight, brainwashed us how to fight and now they put Cuban exiles in jail for what they had been taught to do in the early years."[50]

Ten years from now, will embittered Nicaraguan exiles be making the same pronouncements in Miami, New York or San Francisco? Will the United States once again inherit the terrorism it sponsors abroad?

An Army of Smugglers

The First Lady tells kids tempted by drugs to "just say no." But her advice goes unheeded by some of the CIA's closest allies.

America's drug problem today is arguably, in large measure, an outgrowth of the "secret war" against Fidel Castro begun under Presidents Eisenhower and Kennedy. And America's drug problem of tomorrow may similarly grow out of the Reagan administration's "secret war" against the Sandinistas.

The connection isn't fanciful. Over the years, federal and local law enforcement officials have found CIA-trained Cuban exiles at the center of some of this nation's biggest drug rings. They had the clandestine skills, the Latin connections, the political protection and the requisite lack of scruples to become champion traffickers.

"A great many of the drug smugglers in Miami today are Bay of Pigs veterans," notes one Florida drug prosecutor who requested anonymity. "That's why they're so tough. They are intelligence trained. That's why we're having such a tough time."[51]

In 1974, a joint federal-state drug task force reached the same conclusion while investigating meetings between exiles and mobsters in Las Vegas. The Cubans were all Bay of Pigs veterans and criminal associates of Santo Trafficante, Jr., the Florida mob boss recruited by the CIA in 1961 to murder Castro.

"The CIA not only taught these individuals how to use weapons but made them experts in smuggling men and material from place to place under Castro's nose," the task force report observed. "This training seems to be applied here."[52]

In 1970, strike forces in 10 cities around the country rolled up one of the biggest hard-drug networks of all time, said to control 30 percent of all heroin sales and up to 80 percent of all cocaine in the United States.[53]

One of the ringleaders was a Cuban exile veteran of Operation 40, a secret CIA counterintelligence and assassination program set up at the time of the Bay of Pigs invasion.[54] This 150-man operation was quietly disbanded in the late 1960s after one of its planes crashed in California with several kilos of heroin and cocaine aboard.[55]

Among the reported employees of this Cuban drug kingpin were two exile brothers, Ignacio and Guillermo Novo, who won a certain notoriety by firing a bazooka against the United Nations building in 1964. Guillermo was later convicted of being an accessory to the 1976 murder of former Chilean ambassador Orlando Letelier in Washington, D.C. (a decision overturned on appeal).[56]

Those brothers, who reportedly financed their organization from drug sales, were represented at the infamous summit conference of exile groups in June 1976 at a site in the Dominican Republic. In attendence, as we have seen, were such alleged terrorists as Orlando Bosch and Luis Posada, both arrested later in Venezuela for planning the bombing of a Cubana Airlines jet.

Another exile representative at that terrorist convention was Frank Castro, a Bay of Pigs veteran and head of the Cuban National Liberation Front. Castro, who received special guerrilla training at Fort Jackson, has been linked by investigators on the staff of Sen. John Kerry, D-Mass., to the contra cause.[57]

Castro was a key operative in the smuggling organization of a fellow Bay of Pigs veteran who imported no less than one-and-a-half million pounds of marijuana before his arrest in 1981. Also implicated was an exile whose steamship company served the CIA in its abortive 1961 invasion of Cuba.[58]

Last but not least, Frank Castro was a close friend and parachute-training partner of Rolando Otero, one of Miami's most notorious bombers. Before his capture, Otero took out an FBI office, two post office buildings, a Social Security office, a bank and an airport locker. In 1983 he was convicted of a giant marijuana conspiracy.[59]

The list could continue *ad infinitum.*

These men were not born drug criminals. They became smugglers for several reasons: to finance the anti-Castro struggle, to punish the host country that let them down, to apply the only skills they knew and to re-experience the thrill of clandestine operations.

Precisely the same motives may someday spur another CIA-created and CIA-trained group of exiles, the Nicaraguan contras, into replacing the Cubans as America's premier drug smugglers.

The process has already started. In late 1984, two reporters for the Associated Press wrote that "Nicaraguan rebels operating in northern Costa Rica have engaged in cocaine trafficking in part to help finance their war against Nicaragua's government, according to U.S. investigators and American volunteers who work with the rebels."

The smuggling was reported to involve "individuals from the largest of the U.S.-backed counterrevolutionary, or contra, groups, the Nicaraguan Democratic Force (FDN) and Revolutionary Democratic Alliance (ARDE), as well as a splinter group known as M3."

Their sources confirmed that "two Cuban-Americans used armed rebel troops to guard cocaine at clandestine airfields in northern Costa Rica. They identified the Cuban-Americans as members of the 2506 Brigade, the anti-Castro group that participated in the 1961 Bay of Pigs attack on Cuba."[60]

After numerous denials, the Reagan administration finally admitted that one contra group—formerly but no longer supported by CIA funds—helped a Colombian trafficker move drugs to the United States in return for money and materiel.[61] Adolfo Chamorro, one of the leaders of this group (ARDE), was arrested in April 1986 by Costa Rican authorities in the company of two Cuban exiles and held on suspicion of drug trafficking.[62]

The administration's reticence on this subject owes less to ignorance than political interest. Thus one convicted smuggler, a former crop-dusting pilot from Arkansas, claims to have flown 1500 kilograms of cocaine from the farm of a CIA operative in Costa Rica to the United States. "It was guns down, cocaine back," he said. The two-way traffic was conducted "with the full knowledge and cooperation of the DEA and the CIA," he claimed.

His partner, convicted smuggler and speed-boat champion Jorge Morales, confirmed, "The CIA was very, very aware of it."[63]

Whatever the extent of official administration complicity, anecdotal evidence abounds of broader contra involvement with drugs. Two smugglers convicted in the 1983 "frogman" case—which netted federal agents 430 pounds of cocaine off a Colombian freighter in San Francisco harbor—admitted their connection to the anti-Sandinista cause. One of them, a former member of Somoza's air force, testified that the proceeds of his deals "belonged to...the contra revolution." The other said he deposited hundreds of thousands of dollars from cocaine profits in the coffers of two Costa Rica-based contra groups and helped arrange arms shipments for Fernando Chamorro, a "hard-drinking, hell-raising" leader of a small contra group in Honduras.[64]

A Nicaraguan exile now living in Costa Rica, Norwin Meneses-Canterero, has been named by a DEA report as "the apparent head of a criminal organization responsible for smuggling kilogram quantities of cocaine to the United States." He himself admits trafficking in cocaine "for about six months" in 1982; the DEA first suspected him of criminal drug activities back in 1976, when his brother was chief of the Managua police. Meneses, according to former contra members, "helped finance at least four contra functions" in the United States "and sent a truck and video equipment to FDN members in Honduras." He was also reported to have visited the FDN's military commander, Enrique Bermudez, in Honduras in 1983.[65]

At a 1986 drug trial in Costa Rica, according to CBS Evening News, "the government presented wire-tapped phone conversations between Horacio Pereira, charged with drug dealing, and contra leader Huachan Gonsalez. In the conversations the men discuss large amounts of cocaine they were sending to the United States. The wire-tapped phone calls show the drug dealers have ties to the highest level of contra leadership in Costa Rica."[66] Pereira supplied the the frogman case defendants with cocaine and was an associate of Meneses.[67]

In May 1986, Costa Rican agents arrested a Cuban exile carrying 204 kilos of cocaine at a small air landing strip. A Costa Rican arrested later in the same case denied knowledge of any drugs but said he had been asked by the Cuban to help smuggle arms for the contras.[68]

One former FDN guerrilla, who left the FDN in 1982 out of disgust over the "corruption" in its higher ranks, charged that "Troilo Sanchez, brother of Aristides Sanchez who is a member of the FDN directorate, was caught in Costa Rica with pillows full of cocaine." Troilo, who allegedly sold 200 pounds of cocaine for $6.1 million, is also the brother-in-law of contra political leader Adolfo Calero.[69]

Summing up a group of similar tales, CBS correspondent Jane Wallace reported in 1986: "According to many in the private aid network some of the same secret routes used to bring weapons to the contras carry cocaine back to the United States. Contra suppliers taking advantage of their covert connections to run cocaine (sic)."[70]

One beneficiary of these air operations was said to be Jorge Ochoa, co-leader of Colombia's giant drug cartel. A contra-Ochoa connection seems more than plausible. One prominent Nicaraguan rebel, M3 leader Sebastian Gonzalez Mendiola, was charged by Costa Rican authorities in November 1984 with drug trafficking. He subsequently told U.S. authorities that the Colombian cocaine cartel was paying his group $50,000 to help move a 100 kilogram cocaine shipment.[71]

One of the contras' Miami-based weapons smugglers supplied an assassination weapon to a group of Colombian hit men who murdered the U.S. government's chief witness against Ochoa, Barry Seal.[72] Seal, indicted in 1972 for a heroin-for-guns deal with anti-Castro exiles in Mexico,[73] began smuggling marijuana and cocaine on a regular basis in 1977. In that capacity Seal became well acquainted with the cocaine-wholesaling Ochoa family. Turned as an informant by the Miami DEA, Seal helped federal drug agents indict the major heads of the Colombian drug cartel: Jorge Ochoa, Pablo Escobar and Carlos Lehder.[74] In the same period, Seal was said to have become "a key asset in an elaborate logistics network of 'private' suppliers, fund-raisers, transporters and advisers recruited by the White House to circumvent congressional restrictions on U.S. aid to the contras."[75] One of the planes he had flown on drug runs as a DEA informant was later shot down over Nicaragua while on its way to a supply drop for the contras.[76]

Ochoa's partner Pablo Escobar also has direct ties to the contra cause. According to a Miami-based Cuban exile involved in arms smuggling to the Nicaraguan rebels, Escobar offered to finance a plot by U.S. mercenaries and other contra backers to assassinate the U.S. ambassador to Costa Rica, Lewis Tambs. The bombing would serve to discredit the Sandinistas. And, of most interest to Escobar, it would eliminate the man who had previously led Washington's anti-drug crusade in Colombia as ambassador to Bogota.[77]

The same Cuban informant said "It is common knowledge here in Miami that this whole contra operation in Costa Rica was paid for with cocaine. Everyone involved knows it. I actually saw the cocaine and the weapons together under one roof, weapons that I helped ship to Costa Rica."[78]

One result of the U.S. covert war against Nicaragua will thus surely be to make nonsense of the anti-drug push so lavishly funded by Congress. Washington has given less scrupulous elements of the contras all the training, support, connections and motive to graduate into the top ranks of the international drug underworld. They are well on their way to climbing the ladder.

A Region Under Fire

The fragile democracies—and dictatorships—of Central America and the Caribbean have never been the same since the CIA dumped in their midst a small army of well-trained, well-financed and well-armed Cuban exile guerrillas after 1961.

The failed Bay of Pigs invasion let loose upon the region a force of zealots without a home to call their own. Their subsequent coup attempts, bombings, invasion plots and assassination conspiracies have perilously destabilized an already unstable region.

With the formation of another, even larger guerrilla army—the Nicaraguan contras—the Reagan administration may be setting the stage for another round of regional political turmoil far more harmful to U.S. interests than anything the Sandinistas could do in Nicaragua.

Costa Rica

Few nations ever suffered the indirect brunt of U.S.-sponsored "covert" wars against leftist targets in this hemisphere more than Costa Rica, Central America's showcase democracy.

By late 1963, Costa Rica was host to two CIA-sponsored anti-Castro training camps. From there (and similar camps in Nicaragua) exile commandos under the direction of future Somoza business partner Manuel Artime infiltrated Cuba for hit-and-run sabotage missions. In May 1964 a team attacked a Cuban sugar mill, destroying 70,000 bags of sugar. Four months later another fired on a Spanish freighter off the coast of Cuba, killing the captain and two crew members.[79]

But Costa Rica was sadly mistaken if it hoped to buy immunity from rightist subversion.

In 1965 its security forces shut down the camps, ostensibly after discovering a smuggling operation in their midst. Actually, the exiles had been plotting with Nicaraguan dictator Anastasio Somoza, Dominican Republic military officers and local right-wing extremists to assassinate Costa Rican government leaders and install a right-wing dictatorship.

According to a contemporary news account,

> The Cubans involved apparently believe a rightist government would be more willing to back military attacks on Cuba. Members of the neo-Nazi group are understood to have been given military training in the Cuban camp. With arms provided by the Cubans, the reports say, this group had planned to assassinate President Francisco Orlich; Jose Figueres, former president and one of the original leaders of the Latin America democratic left; and Daniel Oduber, former foreign minister and front-runner in the presidential election scheduled for next February.[80]

The right-wing Free Costa Rica Movement (MCRL), founded in 1961 with U.S. support to mobilize the nation against Castro, was almost certainly implicated in that plot.[81] It was also accused of plotting the assassination of President Jose Figueres in 1970 and a coup in 1971, with help from a Guatemalan death squad leader, following a series of political openings by the elected government to the Soviet Union.[82] MCRL may again have been implicated in a coup attempt in 1974, with support from Cuban exiles and the Chilean secret police, this time after the foreign minister made overtures to Cuba.[83]

Today the Free Costa Rica Movement reportedly still maintains close relations with Guatemalan death squads and a Miami-based Cuban exile organization, Alpha 66. Always prepared for future emergencies, its 1000-member paramilitary branch trains with Israeli Galil rifles, mortars and even anti-aircraft weapons, some of which were reportedly bought from a CIA-linked American rancher in northern Costa Rica.[84] The MCRL has led the call for the creation of U.S.-trained counterinsurgency forces, in a country whose constitution bars the formation of a standing army.[85]

Today the MCRL plays an important support role in the U.S.-sponsored contra war. One of its leaders, Bernal Urbina Pinto, a protege of the late Spanish dictator Francisco Franco, helps direct the Latin branch of the World Anti-Communist League, which has supplied arms and money to the contras. In 1981 he reportedly "met with Argentine military agents and exiled Nicaraguan National Guardsmen to plot the overthrow of the Sandinista regime."[86] Two representatives of the MCRL also conferred with an Argentine intelligence office that year to discuss means of pressuring the Costa Rican government to support contra operations; at the same time "there was talk with assistants to the Costa Rican foreign minister of setting up an incident in which the Sandinistas would appear to have made attacks inside Costa Rican territory," possibly including the assassination of dissident contra leader Eden Pastora, a thorn in the side of the Somocistas.[87] In recent years, MCRL followers have disrupted the Legislative Assembly, mounted a riot outside Nicaragua's embassy (killing two civil guardsmen), and attacked the Central America Peace March.[88]

Ironically, given this history of MCRL-sponsored violence, one of the movement's founders, the American-educated Benjamin Piza Carranza, ran the Ministry of Security from September 1984 until the late spring of 1986. A strong contra sympathizer, he reportedly owed his job to U.S. pressure.[89] He did little to curb what one of his predecessors in that post charged was a disturbing shift toward the "extreme right" and to "anticommunist hysteria" fed by groups like the MCRL.[90] For example, his security forces did nothing to prevent the MCRL's attack on the Nicaraguan embassy in June 1985, despite having advance warning.[91]

Even apart from the Free Costa Rica Movement, the contra rebellion has profoundly polarized the nation and introduced violence and militarism into its politics.

In December 1980, for example, a detachment from the September 15 Legion, the Somocista core of the fledgling contra movement, was sent by a group of Argentine advisers to knock over a left-wing radio station broadcasting revolutionary propaganda. The military junta under President Roberto Viola in Buenos Aires wanted it silenced in order to quiet the voice of exiled members of the Argentinian Montonero guerrilla movement. The Legion's first major military operation failed, however, as Costa Rican police picked up the unsuccessful saboteurs.[92]

That wasn't the end of the story, however. The MCRL stepped up its campaign to discredit the radio station and succeeded in having its license canceled.[93] Ten months after the attack, five commandos from a splinter group of the September 15 Legion hijacked 20 passengers and three crew members aboard a plane from Costa Rica's national airline. The terrorists threatened to kill the entire lot if Costa Rica did not free the jailed Legion members. Costa Rica met the demand, releasing the prisoners to El Salvador. The five hijackers and six free prisoners were detained by authorities in San Salvador—only to become the targets of rescue by a right-wing Salvadoran terrorist squad that attempted to take Salvadoran citizens hostage.[94] Later the same contra group bombed a Nicaraguan 727 jet in Mexico City and a Honduran plane in Managua.[95]

The presence of as many as 8,000 armed contras and free-floating Nicaraguan exiles in northern Costa Rica made life tense and often dangerous for local citizens. Costa Ricans complained of armed bands robbing cattle, kidnapping families, intimidating local news broadcasters, trafficking in drugs and arms and pillaging small rural communities.[96] Border provocations by contra forces have, on occasion, brought Costa Rica close to war with Nicaragua.[97] With only a token security force at its disposal, the central government could not easily call the shots.

Nor, under the conservative, anti-Sandinista administration of President Luis Alberto Monge[98] and Security Minister Piza, did the government always want to restrain the contras or preserve the country's neutrality. According to U.S. mercenaries jailed in Costa Rica, the Civil Guard during Monge's administration regularly supplied logistical information, vehicles and sanctuary to contras on the southern front.[99]

The U.S.-supported contra struggle hastened Costa Rica's slide toward a partisan, militarized state by raising a host of new security problems that only Washington (and Israel) could help solve. In response to the drug epidemic brought by the contras and their air strips, for example, the United States conducted an "anti-drug" helicopter operation in the country in the spring of 1984 and proposed establishing a police training school under the auspices of the Drug Enforcement Administration, which took over foreign police training from the CIA in the mid-1970s.[100] In 1986, the U.S. Southern Command in Panama laid plans with Costa Rica to help establish two naval facilities, ostensibly to control drug traffickers.[101]

On the military front, the pressures of war pushed Costa Rica steadily into Washington's arms. In 1982, following contra-provoked tensions between Nicaragua and Costa Rica, the once-pacifist nation set up a "Special Intervention Unit" for counterterrorist and security functions, with U.S., Israeli and West German assistance.[102] In 1984, after a cabinet shakeup triggered by MCRL agitation, the new security minister, Benjamin Piza, arranged training of Civil Guard units in Honduras and Panama under U.S. auspices. The course work included anti-guerrilla operations, explosives, nocturnal navigation, and aerial mechanics. The next year, without first obtaining approval from the Legislative Assembly, Monge and Piza also invited into the country a contingent of U.S. Special Forces to shape four Civil Guard companies into a special reaction battalion against the Sandinistas.[103] The two leaders upgraded the right-wing, civilian paramilitary Organization for National Emergencies into an official rural police reserve force under the president and security minister.[104] And Piza was reported to have helped the CIA-backed FDN contras set up a southern base in Costa Rica to challenge Eden Pastora's out-of-favor ARDE group.[105]

Senior statesman Jose "Pepe" Figueres, who had three times served as Costa Rica's president, decried such moves as "the beginning of militarism in our country."[106] But they paid off in terms of U.S. aid, which climbed from zero in 1980 to $18.35 million in 1984-85.[107]

Under President Oscar Arias, elected in February 1986, Costa Rica has taken some steps to reassert its neutrality despite heavy economic pressure from Washington.[108] Arias, who has nothing but criticism for the Sandinistas, nonetheless blames the contras for frightening away domestic capital, foreign investment and tourism. His government closed an air strip in the north used as a base for guerrilla operations and drug trafficking, shut down contra medical clinics, barred their military leaders from entering the country and beefed up border security to prevent the establishment of guerrilla camps.[109]

And in late 1986 Arias expelled a prominent veteran of countless CIA-sponsored anti-Castro attacks, Armando Lopez Estrada. In 1976, Lopez Estrada helped found that decade's most notorious Cuban terrorist organization, CORU, along with several fellow exiles who would later become prominent in the anti-Sandinista struggle.[110] Now he had been caught with two grenades strapped to the underside of his car. "The U.S. government sent me to Costa Rica to do intelligence work," he explained, "and serve as liaison to...the Nicaraguan contras with the purpose of providing them with advisors and military equipment."[111]

El Salvador

At the opposite political extreme from Costa Rica lies El Salvador, a country torn by war and burdened by a series of oligarchies and dictatorships throughout most of its history. But much like Costa Rica, it has suffered painfully from the intervention of Cuban and Nicaraguan exiles primed for war by the CIA.

Anti-Castro groups in Miami, for example, trained Salvadoran death squad killers in return for financing from wealthy Salvadoran exiles in the United States.[112] And the demands of the CIA-sponsored contra war have undermined the civilian leadership in El Salvador by bolstering the autonomous status of Air Force commander Gen. Juan Rafael Bustillo.[113] Out of his airbase Ilopango, the Cuban CIA veteran Felix Rodriguez helped coordinate the contra supply operation. Bustillo, a favorite of the CIA and known as "the great untouchable strong man of the death squads,"[114] was able to force the ouster of the government's defense minister in the spring of 1983. "The air force is very jealous of its independence," admitted the armed forces spokesman.[115]

Guatemala

The target of a successful CIA coup in 1954, Guatemala was the host to Cuban exile guerrilla bases throughout much of the 1960s. As in Costa Rica, some exiles even rose to high positions in government. The country naturally became a home to Cuban plotters throughout the region.

In 1973, certain exiles reportedly conspired to use Guatemala as a launching pad for a "triple coup"—not against Cuba but against three wayward neighbors in Central America: Costa Rica, Honduras and Panama.[116]

But also like Costa Rica, Guatemala enjoyed no immunity from right-wing Cuban exile plotters despite its hospitality. In 1978, the interior minister charged that Guatemala's fascist National Liberation Movement (MLN) was conspiring with anti-Castro Cubans and mercenaries from the military dictatorships of Argentina and Chile to seize power.[117] The MLN took credit for the March 1982 coup that (with Israeli assistance) unexpectedly brought to power General Jose Efrain Rios Montt. It has been held responsible for several coup attempts since then led by the MLN's number two man, Lionel Sisniega Otero.[118]

Sisniega once proudly called the MLN "the party of organized violence."[119] In 1960 the party founded Guatemala's notorious death squad Mano Blanco (White Hand), which butchered thousands of moderate-to-leftist students, union leaders and politicians.[120] In its embrace of violence, the MLN has even kidnapped wealthy businessmen to raise money for election campaigns.[121] The MLN has also been responsible for subversive acts throughout Central America. It provided support and sanctuary for Salvadoran and Nicaraguan death squads,[122] and financing for the Free Costa Rica Movement in its 1971 coup plot.[123]

The party's leader, Mario Sandoval Alarcon, is a veteran of the 1954 CIA coup. An admirer of Spain's Falange movement and Chile's neofascist Patria y Libertad, Sandoval once boasted, "I am a fascist."[124] Like his close Costa Rican collaborator Urbina Pinto, Sandoval is active in the pro-contra World Anti-Communist League headed by retired U.S. general and ex-CIA officer John Singlaub. A guest at Ronald Reagan's 1981 inaugural ceremony, Sandoval facilitated and inspired the terrorist and death squad collaboration between Nicaraguan contras and CIA-funded Argentine advisers in Guatemala that same year. He provided the land on which the first group of Somocista exiles trained with the Argentines before moving to Honduras.[125] And his party is now training hundreds of Guatemalans to assist the contras in overthrowing the Sandinistas.[126]

Argentina

Though far from the scene, Argentina itself has suffered the consequences of its involvement in the contra war. Thus one contra trainer, a former security and intelligence agent under the Argentine military junta, was later implicated as the head of a right-wing terrorist cell bent on destabilizing the country's revived democracy. Police raids in Buenos Aires in mid-1985 turned up caches of arms, sophisticated electronic equipment and uniforms. Authorities linked the rightists to arsenal robberies, kidnappings, extortion and several bombings. And several had ties to a mid-1970s death squad, the Argentine Anti-Communist Alliance, that carried out murders with the help of Cuban exiles and other foreign nationals.[127] One of those Cubans was Luis Posada, who later joined the contra supply network.[128]

But neither Costa Rica, Guatemala, El Salvador nor Argentina faces anything like the "disposal problem" that will confront Honduras when the Nicaraguan contras are turned loose as were the Cubans two decades ago.

Honduras

Once home to as many as 20,000 anti-Sandinista guerrillas, Honduras has an army of only 17,500 men.[129] It can hardly tell the contras to behave or go away. Its top military officers now fear the country will face "Lebanonization" if the contras fail to win back their homeland and instead make Honduras a permanent base for guerrilla warfare and terrorism.[130]

Honduran president Jose Azcona walks a fine line between the contras, Washington and his own U.S.-supplied military. "He is in a delicate position," said Ramon Zuniga, a professor at the University of Honduras. "He has so little real power that he must try not to antagonize any part of the armed forces."[131]

Although Azcona has complained to the Organization of American States that the contras' presence on Honduran soil "causes constant friction," he supports Washington's aid to them. His logic is revealing: He says he wants to keep the rebels from "becoming an uncontrollable group" of bandits within his country if they lose U.S. backing.[132]

But they have already become bandits. Some contras have been implicated in death-squad murders of local Honduran leftists.[133] Recent bombings of the Honduran Human Rights Commission and of the car of a prominent radio news director appear to be linked to the contras and their radicalization of the country's security forces.[134]

Other Nicaraguan rebels have been linked to bribery and corruption in the armed forces. In one particularly notorious incident in August 1986, the heads of the Honduran Public Security Force and of military intelligence arranged a raid on the residence of an opposition deputy, apparently to muscle in on the enormous profits he and a rival group of army officers made selling supplies to the contras.[135]

Economic disruption brought by the contras has soured the lives of thousands of Honduran citizens. The Nicaraguan rebels have taken over 20 villages and made another 30 uninhabitable near the southern border.[136] Coffee growers in the area have been ruined; in the first half of 1986 alone they lost $2 million owing to cross border battles between the contras and Sandinista forces. "The government should expel all foreign troops and affirm Honduran sovereignty over its own territory," declared Wilfredo Castellanos, vice president of the Association of Coffee Producers. "The crisis will worsen soon if this does not happen because of the new (U.S.) aid program."[137]

Echoing his sentiments, the president of the Honduran congress declared in October 1986 that "the anti-Sandinista rebels will have to leave Honduras. We want Honduras to be free from such irregular armed groups and to have a climate of peace and tranquility."[138] The same month, a conservative deputy introduced legislation calling for the contras' ouster from Honduras. "They point their rifles at Nicaragua now but one day they may have to aim them at us just to survive," he warned.[139] Foreign Minister Roberto Suazo Tome raised the specter of "internal conflict" if the United States withdrew its support of the contras. "How are we going to feed them?" he asked. "How are we going to disarm them?"[140] President Azcona himself declared in no uncertain terms, "The government of Honduras wants the contras fighting in Nicaragua, not in Honduras."[141]

Costa Rica, El Salvador, Guatemala and Honduras are all relatively weak nations. But not even the mighty United States can expect immunity from the "blowback" of its contra war, any more than it could during and after its prior war against Castro.

We have seen how CIA-sponsored Cuban exile extremists left their legacy of drug trafficking, bombings and assassinations in this country and fed the anticommunist hysteria of the time that sanctioned extraordinary violations of democratic principles by agencies of the U.S. government, ranging from terrorism abroad to domestic spying at home.

It was almost predictable that Richard Nixon, who planned the Bay of Pigs invasion in the Eisenhower White House, would later turn to former Bay of Pigs CIA officer Howard Hunt and his still-loyal band of Cuban exiles to engage in political burglaries, "dirty tricks" and even one assassination plot before Watergate blew up in their faces.[142]

The contra struggle will almost certainly leave a similar legacy of crime and political disorders if the United States refuses to heed the lessons of recent history. In the name of anti-communism, Washington has again set up a powerful movement it cannot entirely control. The contras, like the Cubans, will not be "disposed" of quietly; they will return to haunt us for years to come.

VII.
Arms for Iran:
History of a Policy Disaster

The controversy over the 1985-86 arms-for-hostages deals with the Khomeini regime has rocked the Reagan administration like no other foreign policy debacle. Yet the roots of the policy were firmly implanted back in the Nixon-Kissinger era; only the implementation bears the unique stamp of the Reagan contracting-out strategy.

U.S. policy toward Iran since 1972 has varied remarkably little, even through a revolutionary change of regimes. Indeed, at least as far back as 1954, when the State Department organized the Iranian Consortium of U.S. and British oil companies in the aftermath of a CIA-sponsored coup that brought the Shah to power, Washington has recognized the enormous value of Iran's oil reserves and strategic position vis-à-vis the oil-rich Gulf states and the Soviet Union.[1]

President Nixon and his national security adviser Henry Kissinger shaped U.S. policy toward Iran according to their realization that the Vietnam War had sapped America's resources to the point where the unilateral exercise of U.S. power was no longer a viable option. Following the terms of the "Nixon Doctrine" enunciated in June 1969, the United States would henceforth rely on regional gendarmes to keep order, discourage insurgencies and neutralize Soviet gains. Unlike earlier attempts at regional alliances like CENTO, this new form of power sharing would rely on individual pro-American nations to carry out Washington's aims.[2]

Kissinger remarked in his memoirs that he envisioned for Iran the role of filling "the vacuum left by the British withdrawal" from the Middle East and South Asia, a region "now menaced by Soviet intrusion and radical momentum." Iran's subcontractor role, moreover, "was achievable without any American resources, since the Shah was willing to pay for the equipment out of his oil revenues."[3] Undersecretary of State Joseph Sisco publicly spelled out Washington's conception of the Shah's role: "Iran, by virtue of its population, its economic and military strength, and its geographic position along the northern shore of the Persian Gulf, is destined to play a major role in providing for stability in the Gulf and the continued flow of oil to consumer countries."[4] Kissinger himself spoke of ensuring a favorable security climate in the Persian Gulf by "thickening the web of interdependence" between Iran and the United States.[5]

In late May 1972, during a visit to Tehran after their historic summit in Moscow, President Nixon and Kissinger made the Shah an offer too good to refuse: unlimited access to America's non-nuclear arsenal, along with support in quelling the Kurdish revolt.[6] The Shah in turn graciously agreed to guarantee the flow of oil and to act as the West's "protector" in the Gulf area.[7] So eager was the White House to close the deal that it ignored the Pentagon's warning that sales of sophisticated U.S. arms would be "counter-productive" to the security of both the Persian Gulf and the United States.[8]

This bargain had dramatic consequences, far beyond even Iran and the United States. In late 1973, as the Organization of Petroleum Exporting Countries was putting the squeeze on the Western consumer countries, the Shah himself led the militants in favor of what would soon become a four-fold price increase that would shock the world economy. Saudi Arabia made urgent appeals to Washington, offering to unload its huge reserves and beat the price down if the administration would rein in the Shah and so minimize the political risk for the Saudi royal family. Their appeals fell on deaf ears. Instead, the State Department resisted efforts by the major oil companies to break OPEC through joint negotiations.[9]

Finally the Saudis could not help but conclude where the administration's real interests lay. Their oil minister, Sheik Ahmed Zaki Yamani, observed cynically in a secret cable to Washington, "There are those amongst us who think that the U.S. administration does not really object to an increase in oil prices. There are even those who think that you encourage it for obvious political reasons and that any official position taken to the contrary is merely to cover up that fact."[10] Yamani complained to the U.S. ambassador in his country, James Akins, that Secretary of State Kissinger "is speaking lower oil prices but in secret doing everything possible to jack them up." Akins himself confirmed the minister's impression in a memorandum for his secret files, revealed years later.[11]

Jerome Levinson, chief counsel to the Senate Subcommittee on Multinational Corporations, concluded similarly after a study of the relevant documents that "The commitment to Iran is the fundamental commitment to which all else is subordinated."[12]

In effect, Kissinger supported the oil price hike at the expense of world consumers as a clever means of financing the Shah's weapons purchases and boosting Iran as a regional power. Although American commuters and other energy users would suffer, Kissinger no doubt reasoned, the vital American defense sector would be saved from the pain of inevitable Vietnam War spending cutbacks. Moreover, the Shah had agreed to recycle much of his oil wealth back through U.S. banks into long-term U.S. government securities, as part of an agreement with the Treasury Department to disguise the volume of his investments.[13] While the U.S. economy would be hit by the price hikes, our competitors in Europe and Japan would suffer much greater setbacks. To Kissinger and the constituencies he served the bargain looked good.

Indeed, so long as the Shah stayed on the throne, the deal served one definition of the U.S. national interest. The Shah was a team player. At Washington's behest, he sent arms to Somalia and helped crush an insurgency in Oman.[14] Kissinger notes that Iran was "the sole American ally adjoining the Soviet Union which did not permit the overflight of Soviet transport planes into the Middle East." The Shah, true to his word, did not join the oil embargo in 1973-4, continued to sell oil to Israel and South Africa, and supported Sadat's peace quest.[15] He flew squadrons of F-5s to Saigon in 1973 to tilt the military balance in Gen. Thieu's favor. He agreed to consider providing arms to Chad on behalf of the CIA. He provided a base for U.S. listening posts that gathered intelligence on the USSR and Afghanistan—and Saudi Arabia. And he was a key partner in the so-called Safari Club, an informal, anti-Soviet alliance of Middle East and African nations that included Saudi Arabia, Morocco, Egypt, Ivory Coast and Senegal.[16]

In the equally short term, the bargain also brought windfalls to certain private interests. A number of Eastern banks began specializing in the profitable recycling of petrodollars; chief among these, at least as far as Iranian oil funds were concerned, was Chase Manhattan Bank. Its chairman, David Rockefeller, was a longtime friend of the Shah, an alleged recipient of huge payments from the National Iranian Oil Company, and longtime mentor to Henry Kissinger, who would become chairman of Chase's international advisory committee.[17]

Chase had taken a leading position in the Iran market by the 1960s, bolstered by Rockefeller's personal relations with the Shah. In 1972 it opened a merchant bank in London in 1972 in order to capture the business of extending oil-financed Eurodollar loans to Iran. By the next summer, the bank had a major taste of success: a $250 million syndicated loan to Tehran, the largest ever arranged to that time.[18] And in 1974 Chase created an important new joint venture in Tehran, the Iran-Chase International Bank.[19]

The potential profits to Chase skyrocketed after Kissinger's decision not to contest the Shah's inflationary price strategy. Iran's oil revenues skyrocketed from about $6 billion in 1973 to more than $20 billion in 1974.[20] By 1975, Chase was handling $2 billion a year in Iranian transactions.[21]

But above all these oil revenues vastly enriched U.S. defense manufacturers.[22] The Shah's hunger for weapons was nearly insatiable. In line with Kissinger's goal of making Iran a pillar of regional security, the Shah announced plans to develop one of the "most advanced armed forces" in the world, sufficient to defend the Indian Ocean as well as the Persian Gulf.[23] In 1974, the Shah spent fully 14 percent of his country's gross national product on American arms.[24] In 1977, his purchases amounted to $4.2 billion, making Iran the largest foreign buyer of U.S. arms.[25] In the decade as a whole, the Shah bought more than $17 billion worth of U.S. military equipment.[26]

Defense engineering firms and weapons manufacturers threatened by the phasing out of the Vietnam War found an immense new market that promised to serve them in the process of realizing the geo-political ambitions of Kissinger and the Shah.[27] Some companies, employing Vietnam veterans with special skills, literally organized whole units of the Iranian military and sold them the relevant equipment.[28]

One of the more ambitious contractors was the politically powerful Brown & Root construction company, which built many of the biggest military bases in Vietnam. It took the lead position on an $8 billion project to build a vast new port at Chah Bahar—without competitive bid. The Shah's aim was to make the port a staging area for projecting naval power into the Indian Ocean (with a fleet to be built by Litton Industries); the U.S. Navy saw the opportunity to base a carrier task force for the same purpose and gain its first serious presence in that region. Brown & Root stood to make a fortune. And some Iranians made out handsomely from the deal, too. According to Barry Rubin, an historian of U.S. relations with Iran, "Top Iranian officers, including the navy commander and the admiral charged with negotiations for the massive Chah Bahar harbor-drydock complex, were jailed for embezzling millions of dollars."[29]

So much money poured through the pipeline that the arms sales process spun out of control. Technically unsophisticated soldiers could barely operate, much less maintain, the state-of-the-art aerospace equipment coming their way. Iran's ports couldn't even unload the materiel fast enough to keep from choking. Still the Shah ordered more, impressed by write-ups of new weapons in arms trade journals and reports from trusted informants. Company representatives rushed to feed his fancy.

Pentagon consultants and military assistance specialists viewed the U.S. military mission in Iran as a center of commercial intrigue—in the words of one, "captured by the aerospace industry." In the most notorious case, the CIA and Rockwell International pushed on Iran a gigantic electronic spying and communication system called IBEX. Described by one trade journal as "the most ambitious intelligence program in the entire Middle East," IBEX was derided by a Pentagon reviewer as a "straight electronics boondoggle." Even Richard Helms, the former CIA director-turned-ambassador to Tehran, castigated it privately.[30]

The IBEX project smelled for reasons beyond its doubtful contribution to Iran's defensive needs. Rockwell paid huge bribes to Iran's air force commander (and the Shah's brother-in-law), Gen. Mohammed Khatemi, to win approval for the $500 million project.[31] Other military contractors, including Bell Helicopter, Northrop and Grumman, hired agents who bribed Iranian officials with handsome commissions, often amounting to millions of dollars.[32]

The practice was condoned by some U.S. officials as a means of keeping the Iranian military dependent on the American presence.[33] Jonathan Kwitny writes,

> The curious thing about these particular commissions is that the sales were made through the U.S. government, which bought the planes from Northrop and Grumman, and sold them to the government of Iran. Why were the commissions paid?... All these companies rely for their business on huge contracts with the U.S. Defense Department. So it would obviously be easy for the government to arrange to have corporate payments overseas underwritten by American taxpayers. Domestic contracts that were otherwise legitimate could simply be padded to contain the payoff money.[34]

But not everyone approved of these methods. Ambassador Helms told a representative of Defense Secretary James Schlesinger that he had "never seen...so many people out of control" in the Pentagon. The Shah himself complained that "the chicanery of Pentagon officials and their military and civilian representatives" was "intolerable."[35]

A few far-sighted analysts in Washington warned that the Shah's insatiable appetite for weapons, combined with the Iranian public's growing disgust over the ostentatious wealth, corruption and secret police brutality that came in tandem with the arms trade, could together spark a revolt against the Shah and his American backers.[36]

In 1975, Defense Secretary Schlesinger, a persistent critic of the dizzy pace of arms sales to Tehran, drafted for President Ford a memo questioning whether "our policy of supporting an apparently open-ended Iranian military buildup will continue to serve our long-term interests." Kissinger blocked the memo and two months later Schlesinger was gone from his post.[37]

A staff report issued by the Senate Foreign Relations Committee in 1976 complained that Nixon's *carte blanche* policy toward the Shah had "created a bonanza for U.S. weapons manufacturers, the procurement branches of the three U.S. services and the Defense Security Assistance Agency." If there "were to be a change in government," the study warned, the small army of Americans in Iran could become "hostages" of radical elements. But the report offered no clear way out of the hole Washington had dug itself into: "The United States cannot abandon, substantially diminish, or even redirect its arms programs without precipitating a major crisis in U.S.-Iranian relations."[38] And no one could afford to ignore the warning of Deputy Secretary of Defense William Clements, that any curb on the export of arms would "decrease the potential contribution of sales...to strengthening both free world security and the U.S. balance-of-payments position."[39]

A State Department economist suggested in 1977 that by devoting a quarter of all public funds to the military, the Shah would "have insufficient resources to head off mounting political dissatisfaction, including discontent among those groups that have traditionally been the bedrock of support for the monarchy." Certain CIA analysts pointed out that the Shah's military was simply too backward and poorly trained to absorb the tidal wave of sophisticated armaments coming their way. Their superiors did not listen; such predictions did not fit with prevailing American policy.[40] As late as August 1978 an official CIA estimate concluded that "Iran is not in a revolutionary or even a 'prerevolutionary' situation."[41]

Ignorance alone does not explain the intelligence community's failure to alert decision makers to the coming upheaval. The CIA's own operational arm was so deeply implicated in arms-for-oil deals with Iran that the agency could not objectively assess their impact. The CIA not only financed local sales offices of U.S. defense contractors in order to gain intelligence, it undertook at the direction of the National Security Council "to select certain contractors who had a high expertise in certain areas and help them sell high-dollar projects surreptitiously" in order to recapture some of the $20 billion-a-year the United States was spending on Middle Eastern oil.[42]

Thus the military binge continued unabated, led by a 201-strong U.S. Military Assistance Advisory Group, the largest in the world by 1975.[43] To Tehran came thousands of uniformed and civilian Americans who daily reminded the Iranian people of U.S. complicity in the Shah's policies. As of December 31, 1977, there were 7,674 Americans in Iran working on military contracts.[44] Some of these individuals were former Pentagon officers who now represented military contractors hoping to sell their wares in Iran.[45]

The Iran Team

Among the Americans were several especially important figures who would reappear in connection with the controversial contra supply and Iran arms deals of the Reagan years. Admiral Thomas Moorer, three months after stepping down as the controversial head of the Joint Chiefs of Staff under President Nixon, visited Iran in December 1974 as a representative of Stanwick International, which had a contract to manage repairs for Iran's navy.[46] Moorer's real interest was in advancing the Chah Bahar port project. "So great was his zeal for this extension of American naval power," write Ledeen and Lewis, "that Moorer far exceeded his authority and had to be restrained by Secretary of Defense James Schlesinger."[47] Today Moorer sits on the board of directors of the American Security Council, a right-wing group associated with Singlaub that pushes a militant Central America policy.

While still heading the JCS, Moorer oversaw a shadowy naval intelligence operation called Task Force 157, which specialized in using private corporate fronts to gather information on Soviet naval activities.[48] One of its agents, the notorious Ed Wilson, appeared in Iran in 1974, claiming to work for Moorer—and SAVAK, the savage Iranian secret police.[49]

Iranian officials certainly could see Wilson had high-level connections. Wilson had already been introduced in 1971 by Thomas Clines, his former CIA case officer, to Colonel Richard Secord in Washington; by 1975 they were all together again in Tehran, where Secord headed the Air Force Military Advisory Group, which in effect represented the U.S. arms merchants before the Shah.[50] According to his Pentagon biography, Secord "acted as chief adviser to the commander in chief of the Iranian air force and managed all U.S. Air Force programs to Iran as well as some Army and Navy security assistance programs."[51] That job would have given Secord a direct role (with the CIA) in the shady sale of IBEX and possibly (with Moorer) an interest in the U.S. Navy's plans for the Chah Bahar facility.

Later, Wilson would claim to have joined his former CIA control officers Ted Shackley and Tom Clines in a fraudulent Egyptian arms transport venture, EATSCO. Secord was also named in connection with the firm; he denied having a business relationship with it but ultimately left the Pentagon as a result of an official investigation of his ties to Wilson.

A fifth alleged associate of EATSCO, Erich von Marbod, had worked closely with Secord to arrange covert financing for CIA-directed Thai guerrillas fighting in Laos in the early 1970s.[52] After that war ended, he led a Pentagon mission to Tehran beginning in September 1975 to evaluate and bring order into the chaotic U.S. arms sales program.[53] He worked with Clines during that assignment in Iran.[54] Von Marbod proved almost as controversial as the practices he was sent to clean up; the Shah reportedly considered him an undesirable agent of Northrop, E-Systems and Teledyne and asked that he be fired.[55] After leaving Iran to head the Defense Security Assistance Agency, Von Marbod championed the Carter administration's controversial proposal to sell Iran 8 Airborne Warning and Control System (AWACS) planes, a system blasted by the General Accounting Office as too advanced for Iran's needs and overpriced. The GAO suggested darkly that Carter's rationale for the deal was so thin that "there may be other undisclosed reasons underlying the proposed sale."[56]

Members of this close-knit crowd, which came together first in Vietnam and then in Tehran, would later become the key to the covert policy scandals of the Reagan administration in Central America and Iran. Of these individuals, Secord and Clines were directly involved with contra support activities and the Reagan arms-for-hostages deal.

Shackley, too, played a role in later events. He held discussions with a key Iranian arms broker in late 1984 that paved the way for later arms-for-hostage trades with Tehran.[57] From 1980 to 1983 he consulted for a shadowy firm—Stanford Technology Corp. which had picked up several electronics intelligence contracts in Iran, including one for SAVAK, the Shah's secret police.[58] The firm was, fittingly, also the home of another key player in the Reagan-era Iran story: the Iranian-born Albert Hakim.

Hakim, Stanford Technology Corp.'s founder, fit right in with this tight-knit group of Tehran-based Americans. He was introduced to Secord in Iran by Ed Wilson, who did business with Libya out of Hakim's office in Switzerland.[59] (Wilson allegedly tried to arrange a lucrative Egyptian electronics contract for Hakim through Ted Shackley in 1976.[60]) In Iran, Hakim made a handsome living selling military equipment from such firms as Olin Corp., Hewlett-Packard and his own Stanford Technology Corp. Hakim's STC had a $5.5 million contract to supply the notorious, CIA-promoted IBEX project, which Secord oversaw.[61]

Secord reportedly helped Hakim win another, $7.5 million contract with Iran's air force for a sophisticated telephone monitoring system to allow the Shah to keep track of his top commanders' communications.[62] The Shah's secret police, SAVAK, operated the equipment.[63]

Hakim's business methods were as controversial as his products: He arranged the latter communications deal through the air force commander, Gen. Mohammed Khatemi, who Hakim bribed on at least one other deal and who also received hefty payoffs for approving the IBEX contract.[64] Hakim was also paying off top Iranian air force officials to win military contracts for Olin Corp. In a 1983 lawsuit, Hakim described the "total financial network" he established in Iran to funnel kickbacks to officials in return for contracts.[65] "We have more class than using the word 'payoff,' " he testified.[66]

Hakim's bribes were in line with the CIA's strategy of boosting U.S. military sales and political influence by gaining corrupt leverage over foreign military commanders; Hakim in turn furnished the CIA with valuable intelligence.[67] Years later he would work with Secord and several CIA officials in laundering money through Swiss banks for U.S. arms deals with Iran and the contras.[68]

This group's privileged position at the vortex of the U.S.-Iran arms connection under the Shah, like the policy that made their mission possible, did not last long. The combination of blatant corruption, grotesque waste of scarce development funds on arms and ubiquitous presence of U.S. advisers helped spark a national revolt against the Shah's misrule.[69] With his downfall, so went the strategy of employing Iran as America's surrogate in South Asia and the Indian Ocean. Only a few months into the Khomeini era, Iran's deputy prime minister—a man later linked to the Reagan arms-for-hostages negotiations—would announce the cancellation of $9 billion in arms contracts with the United States signed under the Shah.[70]

Contributing to the bitter divide between Washington and the new, post-revolutionary Iran, ironically, was the agitation of Henry Kissinger and his mentor David Rockefeller. Both felt genuine loyalty to the Shah;

both had an interest, moreover, in preventing the Khomeini regime from withdrawing the deposits of the National Iranian Oil Company from Chase. With the help of former Chase chairman and ARAMCO attorney John J. McCloy, the three mounted a vigorous lobbying campaign within the Carter administration to admit the exiled Shah into the United States for medical care—despite explicit State Department warnings that such a move could trigger an embassy takeover and hostage crisis.[71] Kissinger's pleas carried particular weight; his position could help make or break the SALT II treaty in the Senate.[72]

In the end, incorrect or purposely falsified reports of the Shah's medical condition and of Mexico's willingness to readmit the Shah after treatment—and possibly threats by the Shah communicated through Rockefeller to cash in billions of dollars worth of U.S. government securities—convinced President Carter to admit the exiled ruler to the United States. The consequences proved disastrous for all but the Chase Manhattan Bank.[73]

The Reagan Years

Iranian policy has proved no less a disaster now for Ronald Reagan, who played Carter's difficulties into an election victory in 1980. Reagan's troubles stemmed not only from his willingness to bargain for the hostages, but also from his commitment to the same geopolitical assumptions that underlay U.S. policy toward Iran in the post-World War II era.

Again, those assumptions boiled down to oil and anti-communism. As Reagan himself explained the thinking behind his policy,

> Iran encompasses some of the most critical geography in the world. It lies between the Soviet Union and access to the warm waters of the Indian Ocean. Geography explains why the Soviet Union has sent an army into Afghanistan to dominate that country and, if they could, Iran and Pakistan. Iran's geography gives it a critical position from which adversaries could interfere with oil flows from the Arab states that border the Persian Gulf. Apart from that geography, Iran's oil deposits are important to the long-term health of the world economy."[74]

The administration's search for "moderates" in the radical Khomeini regime was more accurately an effort to cultivate anti-Soviet mullahs against a wing favoring an equidistant policy between the superpowers, represented by leftist Iranian President Ali Khamenei. If Khomenei were edged out by the more anti-Soviet Rafsanjani, the White House apparently believed, an Iran strengthened by U.S. arms and higher oil prices could better resist Soviet influence and serve U.S. aims in Afghanistan.[75]

Although the arms side of this policy sparked an explosive controversy that still rages, the Reagan administration's oil diplomacy was perhaps no less scandalous. By helping Iran raise oil prices and replenish its depleted treasury, this policy permitted Iran to procure vast new stocks of arms on the world market—regardless of Washington's own sales policies—at the direct expense of the American consuming public.

In preliminary discussions with U.S. representatives of the National Security Council, the Iranians stressed their interest in achieving higher oil prices and in acquiring the "defensive" arms needed to protect their oil installations, particularly the facility at Kharg Island, from Iraqi air attack. Low prices and disrupted production facilities cut Iranian oil revenues from $16 billion to only $6 billion in 1986.[76]

The White House went along with these requests, just as it had satisfied the Shah's oil-for-arms demands. The Hawk surface-to-air missiles and Phoenix air-to-air missiles that Iran acquired have dramatically limited Iraq's control of the air and thus safeguarded Iran's oil installations. And on the oil price front, before the talks became a world scandal, U.S. and Iranian negotiators were actually drafting a "protocol" that would have ended the formal state of hostility between the two countries and thrown Washington's support behind a world price of $18 per barrel.[77]

The shift in oil policy was signalled by Vice President George Bush's visit in the spring of 1986 to the Gulf States. He asked his Saudi hosts to "stabilize" world oil prices "as part of our national security interest."[78] At the time, Bush appeared only to be catering to his Texas financial constituency (oil producers and bankers dependent on their revenue); now it appears he was also supporting Iran's high-price policy against Saudi Arabia's more moderate position. Indeed, in a report to the Khomeini regime, an Iranian arms agent cited Bush's repeated calls for higher oil prices as evidence of Washington's good faith in the arms-for-hostages negotiations.[79] Riyadh had been keeping production rates up, among other reasons, to punish radical states and quota-busters like Iran and Libya, and to discourage the long-term conversion of energy consumption away from oil to renewable resources. Bush, to the Saudis' surprise, undercut that strategy as part of the administration's covert pro-Iran tilt.

From Bush, Saudi Arabia got the message to get on board with the winning team or face an implacably hostile Iran in the future.[80] In October 1986, Saudi Arabia's King Fahd received Iran's petroleum minister, Gholam Reza Aghazadeh; in the aftermath, Fahd agreed to seek an $18 per-barrel price for OPEC oil and ousted his own oil minister, Sheik Ahmed Zaki Yamani, whose full production policy had been viewed by Iran as the near equivalent of a declaration of war. Saudi Arabia has reportedly even refined oil for fuel-short Iran. Fahd decided to cement this economic alliance after he learned of Washington's own overtures to Tehran and saw Iraq's poor showing on the battlefield. As Iran's petroleum minister put it, "The Saudis had no choice."[81]

American foreign policy functions most smoothly when strategic considerations mesh with domestic interest groups. The high-price oil policy was no exception. Though it flatly contradicted the Reagan administration's professed faith in the free market, it neatly served the interests of the Republican Party's most generous campaign supporters. Thus Bush's former national campaign finance chairman and colleague in the oil business, independent Houston producer Robert Mosbacher Sr., told the *New York Times* of his conviction that higher oil prices were essential to the well-being of the domestic oil industry. He added that "some of the people close to the President" had probably told Reagan of the national security implications "if the price of oil stays too low."[82] (Mosbacher is also a director of the Georgetown Center for Strategic and International Studies, the employer of Michael Ledeen, the NSC's "consultant" on the Iran deal.)

Not surprisingly, U.S. oil industry executives are reported to be "smarting from the loss of two men they considered friends at the White House—former National Security Adviser Robert McFarlane, a key player in the arms deal, and his successor, Vice Adm. John M. Poindexter... Industry sources said McFarlane and Poindexter understood better than most in the administration the connection between a strong domestic oil industry and national security."[83]

Playing the Anti-Soviet Card

The first success of U.S. policy in post-Shah Iran occured not in 1985 but 1982-83, when the CIA helped pass along to Khomeini details on Tudeh party activities and KGB penetration of the Tehran regime, based on the revelations of a KGB major who defected to the British earlier that year. Armed with the information, Khomeini's forces banned Tudeh, arrested or killed as many as 4,000 leaders and supporters, and expelled at least 18 resident KGB agents.[84] As David Newsom, former U.S. undersecretary of state, remarked with satisfaction, "The leftists there seem to be getting their heads cut off."[85]

The CIA may have helped trigger that bloodbath, but the mullahs had earlier left no doubt of their attitude toward the Soviet Union. Even before the purge of the Tudeh party, Tehran had renounced the 1921 Treaty of Friendship (which gave the Soviets legal cause for military intervention), cancelled construction of a natural gas pipeline to the Soviet Union, and condemned the Soviet invasion of Afghanistan—all this despite receiving arms from Soviet client states with Moscow's approval.[86]

The massacre of the Tudeh party ended any real prospect of a pro-Soviet coup. Even so, the specter of Soviet intelligence inroads in Iran continued to haunt administration officials primed to think in simplistic terms of cold war rivalries. Ignorant of the depth of Iranian hostility toward the atheistic superpower to the north, and possibly misled by Israeli-inspired intelligence reports, the White House misread the intentions of Iranian leaders whose pragmatism extended as much to Moscow as to Washington. Tehran was not about to fall into the Soviet orbit, but it was adept at playing off all powers for maximum advantage.

By the spring of 1985, hundreds of Soviet technicians were reported to have dispersed throughout Iran, helping that country build and operate power stations, gas fields and other large engineering projects.[87] Rafsanjani, the "moderate" speaker of the Iranian parliament, announced that June that "We intend to increase and expand our relations with the Soviet Union."[88]

That apparent expansion of Soviet influence had been cemented by arms, Washington might well have noted. On April 1, 1985, Iran's assistant deputy foreign minister told the *Financial Times* that Iran was "hoping for some indication from Moscow that it is prepared to scale down its level of military supplies to Iraq in return for better relations with Tehran." He also indicated that "while Iran appreciates that it could not expect the Soviet Union to supply tanks or aircraft directly, there are, of course, many other routes through which such weaponry could be delivered. Syria and Libya, both of which are substantial purchasers of Soviet arms, would be seen in Tehran as possible conduits."[89]

Two months later, Iran negotiated a deal with Libya to obtain Soviet-made Scud missiles. The Soviets stepped up arms deliveries to Iran via Czechoslovakia (chemical weapons equipment, light arms) and Poland (antiaircraft guns, rocket-propelled grenades, parts for armored equipment).[90] Since then, nearly half of all Iranian arms spending has gone to Soviet-bloc purchases.[91]

On May 17, the head of the CIA's National Intelligence Council, Graham Fuller, produced a report on Soviet gains in Iran, warning that the

United States might be left out in the cold in case of a Khomeini government collapse. Press leaks at the time reported U.S. intelligence estimates that the Soviet Union had 600 agents in Iran "poised to direct Iranian communists in a post-Khomeini power struggle."[92] Fuller, along with several NSC officials, advocated overtures to Iran based on this bleak analysis.[93] These assessments may have been erroneous; they may even have been disinformation produced by the Israelis or by certain CIA and NSC officials to steer the White House in a predetermined direction.[94] What matters here is that the administration acted in part on the basis of these warnings.

White House overtures to Iran did not stop the ayatollahs from exploiting the Soviets' own interest in achieving a rapprochement with the Islamic regime in Tehran. In August 1986, Iran agreed to resume natural gas deliveries to the Soviet Union for the first time since 1979. One month later, the Iranian-Soviet Chamber of Commerce held its first meeting in Tehran to announce plans to increase bilateral trade to $1 billion.[95] In December, Iran and the Soviet Union signed a protocol to expand cooperation in commerce, banking, construction, transportation, fisheries and technology.[96] In seeking commercial contacts to the north, the Khomeini regime was simply returning to a policy long followed by the Shah himself.

But the Reagan arms policy appears to have achieved at least one of its aims: relations between Iran and the Soviet Union soured for a time in the wake of revelations that at least some of those arms were transshipped to the anti-Soviet Afghan guerrillas across Iran's border.[97] The government newspaper *Izvestia* accused Tehran of cooperating "with the forces of imperialism in carrying out an undeclared war against the Democratic Republic of Afghanistan." It charged further that Iranian air and land forces had "carried out more than 60 acts of aggression" on Afghan territory in 1986.[98]

The October Surprise: An Hypothesis

Although details are still lacking, the country now knows that the Reagan administration counted on a handful of highly trusted individuals within the NSC and private sector to implement this covert strategy of enticing Iran back into the U.S. orbit. Given the common background of several of these men, the disturbing possibility arises that the Reagan camp used them even before the November 1980 election as "moles" within the Carter camp to keep tabs on that administration's own Iran-hostage strategy and election chances.

The discovery that the Reagan campaign had acquired copies of the briefing books used by Carter to prepare for the 1980 presidential debate sparked a brief scandal in 1983 known as "Debategate." Subsequent investigations by a congressional committee proved that the Reagan forces had infiltrated their rival's camp with one or more spies. By most accounts, this project was led by Reagan's campaign chairman, the intelligence veteran William Casey.[99] Indeed, Casey boasted in the summer of 1980 of running an "intelligence operation" against the Democrats.[100]

The penetration of Carter's government and campaign went far beyond a few "bent" campaign workers.[101] And its objective, far more than the debate briefing books, was inside news of secret Carter initiatives to salvage the hostages held in Iran. Much as Richard Nixon and Anna Chennault maneuvered to sabotage the 1968 Paris peace talks by establishing a pipeline to South Vietnam's president,[102] some of Reagan's top strategists may have hoped to make use of advance knowledge of Carter's plans to upset an untimely rescue of the embassy captives.

Time magazine reported in 1983 that,

> Casey did indeed set up a political intelligence-gathering apparatus for the Reagan campaign. But it was not simply a casual use of retired military officers asked to stay alert for any U.S. aircraft moves[103] that might signal the Reagan camp that Carter was about to gain the freedom of the U.S. embassy hostages in Iran—the 'October surprise' that Reagan's political aides feared. Instead, cooperative former agents of both the FBI and CIA were used to gather political information from their colleagues still active in the two agencies.[104]

Washington reporter Elizabeth Drew suggests the stop-Carter movement was staffed by intelligence veterans outraged by the massive cutbacks ordered by CIA director Stansfield Turner (among whom Ted Shackley and Tom Clines were premier figures) and by "retired military officers and other strong supporters of the military" who were angered by "what they considered Carter's 'weakening' of America's defenses."[105]

Evidence abounds of the existence of a classic intelligence operation against Carter, focused on the "October surprise." In August 1980, Jack Anderson ran an explosive series of columns alleging that Carter had chosen a "tentative invasion date" in mid-October for a punitive assault on

Iran. Anderson claimed he had been supplied documents by someone working with the National Security Council. (Some source had also been supplying Reagan foreign policy adviser Richard Allen with staff reports going to National Security Adviser Zbigniew Brzezinski.) Anderson's mystery informant claimed that Carter had ordered the invasion "to save himself from almost certain defeat in November." Carter's people claimed the report was false. According to Carter press secretary Jody Powell, "If someone on the NSC staff confirmed the authenticity of these documents, much less described the President's motives for the non-existent orders, he was lying."[106]

In September 1980, someone delivered to the *Washington Post* a document purporting to be a CIA estimate warning that 60 percent of the hostage rescue team would be killed or wounded. The implication was that Carter had played callously with human lives in April to advance his political interests. The document has been called a forgery; however it cited the correct secret code-name for the mission.

Hearst reporter John Wallach, known for his outstanding sources in the intelligence community, informed the Reagan campaign's senior foreign policy adviser, Richard Allen, in October 1980 that a hostages-for-spare parts exchange might take place "at any moment, as a bolt out of the blue." The same day, a Chicago television station made national headlines with "news" that such negotiations—remarkably reminiscent of those the Reagan camp later attempted—were nearing completion. A congressional investigating committee later learned that the source was "a highly placed member of the U.S. intelligence community" who hoped that "publicizing the secret hostage negotiations would have delayed a pre-election release of U.S. hostages in Iran, to the benefit of the Reagan-Bush campaign."[107]

The same month, conservative columnists Evans and Novak claimed that Carter adviser Lloyd Cutler had been to Geneva to arrange a deal to bring out the hostages before the election in return "for military equipment vital to the Iranian war effort." The column included authentic-sounding details about weapons being transferred from Philadelphia Navy Yard warehouses for shipment to Iran.[108]

Worst of all, however, may have been a pre-hostage rescue mission leak—in the guise of an imaginative exercise—by veteran intelligence agent Miles Copeland. Writing in the *Washington Star* on April 20, 1980, just before the actual mission took place, Copeland outlined his scenario for rescuing the embassy captives. Its remarkable faithfulness to the real operation suggests that Copeland had tapped the "old boy" network to blow the mission's cover.[109]

The overwhelming evidence of a Reagan penetration of the NSC and top military and intelligence circles prompts inevitable speculation about the identity of the moles. No evidence yet exists to implicate any of the following individuals in campaign dirty tricks. But all have in common two suggestive characteristics: a key role in the Carter Iran operation or NSC, followed by an especially trusted and political role in the Reagan presidency:

* Donald Gregg—A veteran CIA officer, Gregg was detailed to the national security council as CIA liaison in 1979. When Reagan took office as president, Gregg became George Bush's top national security aide—a political assignment. In that position, he worked closely with Oliver North and the Shackley-Clines protege Felix Rodriguez on the Central American operations.[110]

* Albert Hakim—This shady military sales agent, taken under the wing of Gen. Secord in the late 1970s, had a "sensitive intelligence" role in the 1980 hostage rescue and helped procure jeeps, vans and other vehicles for the desert operation. In particular he seems to have worked for the CIA near the Turkish border, just where Oliver North was operating in the same period. Hakim shed no tears over Carter's downfall following the mission's failure; on the contrary "he couldn't have been happier when the Carter Administration ended," one of his former consultants said.[111] In 1985-1986, on North's behalf, Hakim established the network of financial and corporate conduits used to launder Iran arms money and supply the contras in the face of congressional opposition.

*Robert McFarlane—A Marine lieutenant colonel, McFarlane was an assistant to Sen. John Tower of Texas on the Armed Services committee in the Carter years. He reportedly came to the attention of the Reagan camp by authoring a report blasting Carter for the hostage rescue mission.[112] More remarkably, he approached Reagan campaign adviser Richard Allen with a plan, and an Iranian exile to help implement it, for the Reagan camp itself to free the embassy hostages before the November election.[113]

* Oliver North—As Marine Corps major, North led a secret detachment to eastern Turkey to assist the 1980 Iran hostage rescue mission, then worked with Secord on a second rescue plan. The next year he joined Reagan's National Security Council where he organized and carried out covert operations.[114]

* H. Ross Perot—This remarkable entrepreneur, who employed several former Green Berets to spring two former employees from an Iranian jail, was brought onto Brzezinski's "Military Committee" of advisers on the rescue effort.[115] In early 1982, President Reagan appointed Perot to the President's Foreign Intelligence Advisory Board, where he met NSC covert operator Oliver North. North tapped Perot in two failed ransom attempts for Brig. Gen. James Dozier, kidnapped in 1981 by the Red Brigades, and William Buckley, the CIA station chief in Lebanon, taken hostage in 1984.[116]

* Richard Secord—Gen. Secord helped organize the botched April 1980 hostage rescue and was deputy to the head of a planning group for another rescue attempt in 1980 that never got off the ground. In the Reagan years, North and McFarlane would tap him as a key intermediary both in the contra supply operation and the Iran negotiations.[117] Working closely with him on those ventures in 1986 were at least three other key officers involved in the first Iran hostage mission: Robert Dutton, Richard Gadd, and John Cupp.[118]

* Larry Stearns—Col. Stearns was director of special operations at the Joint Chiefs of Staff in 1980, one of the key offices where the Iran hostage rescue mission was planned.[119] In the Reagan years, after retiring, he worked with the contra supply network.[120]

VIII.
Irangate:
The Israel Connection

The conduct of foreign policy through covert channels presents certain obvious pitfalls, above all the danger of exposure and subsequent political backlash from the public and unconsulted members of Congress and the executive branch. But another, less appreciated risk is of manipulation by the individuals and governments to whom covert policy implementation is contracted out.

As the Tower Commission noted, "Private or foreign sources may have different policy interests or personal motives and may exploit their association with a U.S. government effort. Such involvement gives private and foreign sources potentially powerful leverage in the form of demands for return favors or even blackmail."[1]

Such manipulation can occur by rogue agents within the operation itself. Thus renegade CIA agent Ed Wilson made millions of dollars selling his terrorist know-how to Khadafy and other buyers under cover of the aura of intelligence connections surrounding his own career and that of his many friends. Investigators looking at his activities could never be sure whether they had stumbled across a "sanctioned" operation or a purely criminal one.

Such manipulation can also take place at the hands of foreign governments. In the case of Iran, the evidence suggests that certain Israeli officials and businessmen took advantage of trusting and ambitious members of the Reagan NSC to advance their own interests at the expense of the administration.[2] Contrary to Washington's express wishes, Israeli leaders covertly supplied Tehran with arms and vital spare parts in order to punish the Arab regime of Saddam Hussein in Iraq; then they convinced the White House to endorse that very same violation of official U.S. policy. Playing off Washington's faith in Israeli intelligence, and using American and Iranian intermediaries who served their interests, Israeli officials effectively choreographed the entire affair.

The official story from Israel is quite different, of course. Leaders there have insisted they merely tried to do a good deed at Washington's behest. "From the very beginning of this operation we have acted on behalf of the United States," one senior Israeli official claimed. "Everything we did, including shipping arms to Iran, we did with the explicit approval of Washington. We offered them our good offices and assets, and they used them."[3] Or as Prime Minister Yitzhak Shamir sweepingly declares, "Everything attributed to Israel has no basis in reality."[4]

But unofficial Israelis question this pat story. Yo'el Marcus, writing in *Ha'aretz*, was biting in his dismissal of the innocent claims of his own government officials:

> The contention that our involvement is only recent, at the request of the United States, is very dubious. For about 7 years now bits of information have been published in the world press which prove that Israel and/or Israelis are involved in assistance to Khomeini's Iran. It began before the Lebanese war, continued during it, and is still going on. There is even room to fear that Israel is the moving force behind the whole idea of assistance to Iran. Evidence of this lies in the fact that as early as July 1980 the Jewish lobby was actively trying to convince the administration that the shipment of military spare parts and equipment to Iran would help in getting the hostages (members of the U.S. Embassy in Tehran) released!... It is exactly the same thesis, only now with different hostages."[5]

Even Israeli insiders, speaking not for attribution, contradict the denials of the top leaders, Shimon Peres and Yitzhak Shamir. One "knowledgeable Israeli source" who spoke to the *New York Times* "said the idea for the parts shipments to Iran was initially broached with the United States by Israel, which had been covertly supplying Iran since the fall of Shah Mohammed Riza Pahlevi in 1979. 'We had the contacts and we approached the Americans. We said: Look, we have these contacts, why don't you take advantage of them?'"[6]

And as the top Israeli intermediary on the Iran arms deals himself admitted, "We activated the channel; we gave a front to the operation, provided a physical base, provided aircraft."[7]

The Israeli Interest in Iran

To appreciate the accuracy and implications of these unofficial versions, one must recall the extent of Israel's involvement in Iran during the entire period of Khomeini's rule.

Israeli interests in non-Arab Iran became prominent as early as the 1950s, when Mossad, Israel's foreign intelligence agency, cooperated with the CIA in establishing the Shah's secret police, SAVAK. A 1979 CIA report on Mossad notes that:

> The main purpose of the Israeli relationship with Iran was the development of a pro-Israel and anti-Arab policy on the part of Iranian officials. Mossad has engaged in joint operations with SAVAK over the years since the late 1950s. Mossad aided SAVAK activities and supported the Kurds in Iraq. The Israelis also regularly transmitted to the Iranians intelligence reports on Egypt's activities in the Arab countries, trends and developments in Iraq, and Communist activities affecting Iran."[8]

Cooperation between Israel and Iran touched many fields, including oil, trade, air transport, and various forms of technical assistance. But their most important mutual interest was in the military sphere.

Like the United States, Israel cemented its relationship with Iran by the exchange of arms for oil, which both sides kept alive through the worst of the OPEC oil embargo. The Iranian arms market was worth at least $500 million a year to Israel.[9] The Shah bought everything from Gabriel anti-ship missiles to advanced communications equipment.[10] In 1977, Israel arranged a $1 billion arms-for-oil deal around Operation Flower, a joint Israeli-Iranian project to build a nuclear-capable surface-to-surface missile.[11] And like their American counterparts, certain Israelis also seem to have been part of the corrupt nexus through which top Iranian political and military leaders were enriched through arms sale commissions.[12] "When the Israelis decide to change their policy," one top State Department official told a reporter in the mid-1970s, "the first place the Israeli jet touches down is Tehran. Moshe Dayan is in and out of there quite frequently."[13]

No Israeli representative in Iran during the Shah's reign was more significant or influential than Ya'acov Nimrodi, Israel's military attache. He reportedly helped organize and encourage the rebellion of Kurdish tribesmen against Iraq, the Shah's main political and military rival in the region.[14] As the chief government agent for Israel's burgeoning arms industry, known as an all-purpose "fixer," Nimrodi was intimate with the Shah and his generals. "I was in partnership with the Shah," he told friends.[15] (Among other coups, Nimrodi sold the Iranian army on the Uzi submachine gun.[16]) And as the Mossad agent who could properly boast of having "built" SAVAK into an efficient if brutal intelligence service, he was no less intimate with the keepers of the Shah's secrets.[17] With the arrival of the Khomeini regime, Nimrodi kept open his lines of communication as a private arms dealer who would become central to the Reagan arms-for-hostage talks.

Though Israel, along with the United States, suffered a grievous loss with the fall of the Shah, its leaders concluded that lasting geo-political interests would eventually triumph over religious ideology and produce an accommodation between Tel Aviv and Tehran. The onset of the Iran-Iraq war in 1980 gave Israeli leaders a special incentive to keep their door open to the Islamic rulers in Iran: the two non-Arab countries now shared a common Arab enemy. As Israeli Defense Minister Ariel Sharon told the *Washington Post* in May 1982, justifying Israeli arms sales to Tehran, "Iraq is Israel's enemy and we hope that diplomatic relations between us and Iran will be renewed as in the past." Four months later he told a Paris press conference, "Israel has a vital interest in the continuing of the war in the Persian Gulf, and in Iran's victory." Such views were not Sharon's alone; Prime Ministers Itzhak Shamir (Likud) and Shimon Peres (Labor) shared them too.[18]

To this day, prominent Israelis still argue that strategic calculus unashamedly. Retired Gen. Aharon Yariv, former head of military intelligence, told a conference at Tel Aviv University in late 1986 that "it would be good if the Iran-Iraq war ended in a tie, but it would be even better if it continued." Otherwise, Iraq might open an "eastern front" against Israel.[19] The carnage of human life didn't figure in the equation at all. Uri Lubrani, Israel's chief representative in Iran under the Shah and Nimrodi's superior in Mossad, recently justified continued arms sales because "Khomeinism will disappear and Israel and the United States will again have influence in Iran."[20]

One other consideration, rarely articulated, also swayed successive Israeli leaders: money. According to Gary Sick, an expert on Iran who served on the NSC under Presidents Ford, Carter and Reagan, "Israel acknowledged that arms sales were good business. One out of 10 Israeli workers is employed in arms-related production; military items constitute more than a quarter of Israel's industrial exports."[21] The distinguished Israeli defense correspondent Ze'ev Schiff states that Israel's pro-Iran policy has been "guided by a ravenous hunger for profit rather than by strategic considerations..."[22]

This hunger was all the more acute in view of severe unemployment that hit the Israeli arms industry in 1979 after the Iran market shriveled. Nimrodi, the Mossad-agent-turned-arms-dealer, recalled that when he reported to the Israeli government on the millions of dollars to be had from arms sales to Khomeini's Iran, "people's eyes lit up here. They have been laying people off in the defense industry, and this meant jobs."[23]

The Arms Channel Opens

Israel lost no time supplying the new Khomeini regime with small quantities of arms, even after the seizure of the U.S. embassy. The first sales included spare parts for U.S.-made F-4 Phantom jets;[24] a later deal in October 1980 included parts for U.S.-made tanks. Israel informed Washington, only "after the fact, when they were far down the line and right into the middle of the thing," according to a former State Department official. To Begin's *ex post facto* request for approval, "the answer was instant, unequivocal and negative," writes Gary Sick, the Iran expert on Carter's NSC.[25]

The White House was in fact aghast to find that its embargo had been flatly violated. "We learned much to our dismay," Brzezinski noted later, "that the Israelis had been secretly supplying American spare parts to the Iranians without much concern for the negative impact this was having on our leverage with the Iranians on the hostage issue." Secretary of State Edmund Muskie demanded that Israel cease its shipments; Prime Minister Begin promised to comply. In fact, however, the supply line stayed open without Washington's approval, carrying tank parts and ammunition.[26]

Why didn't the administration crack down? One reason is simply that no president since Eisenhower has ever really punished Israel for acting against U.S. interests. Prime Minister Begin bombed the Iraqi nuclear reactor, invaded Lebanon, annexed the Golan heights and speeded up the settlement of the occupied West Bank much to the Reagan administration's embarrassment, but considerations of military strategy and Israel's political clout in Congress always gave the client state the upper hand.

Moreover, the administration could rarely prove what it suspected. Israel did its best to disguise these shipments by using layers of foreign brokers to cloak their source. Notes *Ha'aretz* correspondent Yo'av Karny, "The cloak of secrecy that surrounds Israeli arms exports is so tight that one can compare it to the technique for smuggling hard drugs."[27] When caught in the act, Israeli officials maintained they were simply selling domestic arms, not embargoed U.S. weapons. "Whenever we would get word of shipments," one American official explained, "the State Department would raise the issue with Israel, and we would get the standard lecture and promises that there were no U.S. weapons involved."[28]

That standard lecture was clearly false, though Washington may have lacked usable evidence to prove it. U.S.-made weapons were very much for sale. On 24 July 1981, Israeli arms dealer Ya'acov Nimrodi—later to play a vital role in the arms-for-hostages negotiations—apparently signed a deal with Iran's Ministry of National Defense to sell $135,842,000 worth of arms, including Lance missiles, Copperhead shells and Hawk missiles.[29] A sale of such magnitude must have had Israeli government acquiescence.[30] Nimrodi's close personal friend Ariel Sharon, a wartime comrade from the 1948 struggle,[31] likely kept tabs on, if he did not direct, the private dealer's sales with Iran.

Sometime the same year, David Kimche, director general of Israel's foreign ministry, apparently approached Secretary of State Alexander Haig and his counselor Robert McFarlane to discuss proposed Israeli shipments of $10 million to $15 million in spare parts to "moderates" in Iran. Kimche may have been referring to a contract to supply 360 tons of tank spares and ammunition—worth about $28 million, twice his estimate—to Iran by air via Cyprus.[32] But Haig denies that he ever approved any such shipments, a claim strengthened by the admission of Israeli officials that they went ahead based only on Haig's alleged failure to disapprove.[33] In any case, the shipments in question paled beside what Nimrodi was then arranging.

In November 1981, Israeli Defense Minister Sharon visited Washington, shopping for approval of similar arms sales. His U.S. counterpart, Caspar Weinberger, flatly turned him down. Sharon then went to Haig, hoping for acquiescence from the State Department. Again, McFarlane handled many of the discussions with Sharon and Kimche; this time Haig unequivocally opposed any violation of the embargo.[34]

In numerous discussions with Israeli officials thereafter, administration decision makers flatly refused requests for permits to ship U.S. arms to Iran, and strenuously discouraged Israel from sending its own weapons to the radical Khomeini regime.[35] Undersecretary of State Lawrence Eagleburger at one point summoned the Israeli ambassador to protest his country's continued sales—only to be assured that they had been stopped.[36] And officials who ran Operation Staunch, the project to block Iran's access to the world arms market, were never discouraged from extending their efforts to Israeli-linked deals.[37]

Yet as in 1979-80, Israel pursued its policy anyway, in flat violation of its arms reexport agreements with the Pentagon.[38] In a May 1982 interview with the *Washington Post*, Sharon claimed that Israeli shipments had been cleared "with our American colleagues" months earlier and that details of all the shipments were supplied to the administration. Later that year, Israel's ambassador Moshe Arens declared that Israel's arms sales were cleared at "almost the highest levels" in Washington, "inconsequential" in size, and designed to undermine the Khomeini regime.[39] Both times the State Department flatly contradicted the Israelis' claims.[40] At least Sharon and Arens were more credible than Foreign Minister Shimon Peres, who declared after the Irangate scandal broke in 1986 that "Israel's policy is not to sell arms to Iran."[41]

All the standard propaganda themes and practices were in place. Israel would continue seeking approval for arms sales on the basis of their potential political leverage, but would ship arms willy-nilly while falsely claiming Washington's sanction.

And those shipments would continue to be enormous in size, estimated by experts at the Jaffee Institute for Strategic Studies in Tel Aviv at $500 million in value from 1980-83. Other arms market experts have put the total value at more than $500 million a year, including aircraft parts, artillery and ammunition.[42]

Anecdotes abound in the world press relating to Israeli sales to Iran:

* In March 1982, the *New York Times* cited documents indicating that Israel had supplied half or more of all arms reaching Tehran in the previous 18 months, amounting to at least $100 million in sales.[43]

* Foreign intelligence sources told *Aerospace Daily* in August 1982 that Israel's support was "crucial" to keeping Iran's air force flying against Iraq.[44]

* An alleged former CIA agent reportedly visited Israel in 1982, met with the chief of staff of the Israeli Defense Forces and head of military intelligence, and "struck a deal with them involving the transfer of weapons and equipment, captured by Israel during the Lebanon war, to Iran."[45]

* Israeli sources told *Newsweek* that "they sold the Iranians much of the light weaponry and ammunition that the Israeli

army had captured during its invasion of Lebanon; subsequently, they sold overhauled jet engines, spare parts for American-made M-48 tanks, ammunition and other hardware—$100 million worth in 1983 alone."[46]

* *Newsweek* also reported that after an Iranian defector landed his F-4 Phantom jet in Saudi Arabia in 1984, intelligence experts determined that many of its parts had originally been sold to Israel, and had then been reexported to Tehran in violation of U.S. law.[47]

* In 1984 and early 1985, a single one of Israel's many European brokers, based in Sweden, reportedly shipped hundreds of tons of TNT and other explosives to Iran, often by way of Argentina, worth 500 million kroner.[48]

* The Milan weekly *Panorama* reported that Israel had sold the Khomeini regime 45,000 Uzi submachine guns, antitank missile launchers, missiles, howitzers and aircraft replacement parts. "A large part of the booty from the PLO during the 1982 Lebanon campaign wound up in Tehran," the magazine claimed.[49]

* Manila newspapers have reported since the Irangate scandal broke that former armed forces chief of staff Gen. Fabian Ver, a crony of Ferdinand Marcos, supplied phony end user certificates to allow Israeli intermediaries to divert U.S. arms to Iran in 1984.[50]

Washington Enters the Picture

Israel finally succeeded in penetrating Washington's defenses at a time of crisis for the administration. An Iranian-backed terrorist group seized the CIA's Beirut station chief, William Buckley in March 1984. Buckley's encyclopedic knowledge of terrorism, and familiarity with every CIA agent in Lebanon, made him a priceless catch, particularly since the destruction of the CIA station in the Beirut embassy bombing had left the United States with few eyes and ears in the region. "I thought it was vital to get him out," Casey declared. Yet the CIA's Herculean efforts to rescue him failed at every turn.[51] Desperate for help, the Reagan administration turned to the Israelis in early 1985.[52]

The nature of the approach almost guaranteed the outcome. The key emissary—and a pivotal figure in the entire Iran story—was Michael Ledeen, an NSC consultant with a passion for cloak and dagger.[53] Ledeen had extremely close ties with Israel. His wife Barbara is an assistant in the Pentagon office of Stephen Bryen, who was investigated by the FBI in the late 1970s after an eyewitness alleged that he passed secrets to Israel. In 1981 Ledeen was a founder of the Jewish Institute for National Security Affairs, a Washington group that lobbies for Israeli defense interests. His co-founders included Bryen and Richard Perle, another Pentagon official associated with the Israeli arms industry.[54] And only a few weeks after its 1982 invasion of Lebanon, the Israeli armed forces invited him to tour the conquered territory.[55]

Ledeen planted the notion of exploring an opening to Iran with National Security Adviser McFarlane by claiming, supposedly on the basis of discussions with a European intelligence official in April 1985, that the timing was favorable.[56] Then at his own initiative, but with McFarlane's approval, Ledeen visited Israel in early May 1985 to pursue the idea unofficially. There he met with government officials to discuss means of contacting Iran's "moderates." "He was involved in the creation of the idea that we have to have some kind of relations with the Iranians," said his wife Barbara.[57]

Ledeen says he asked Israeli Prime Minister Shimon Peres what could be done to further the cause of better U.S.-Iranian relations.[58] Peres did not turn for answers to his intelligence professionals, as he would were his aim merely to exchange information. Instead he convened a tight-knit group of arms dealers including his longtime confidant Al Schwimmer, the American-born founder of Israel Aircraft Industries.[59]

Schwimmer, according to some Israeli news accounts, came up with the arms-for-Buckley formula. He also brought in his lifelong friend and partner in the arms business, Ya'acov Nimrodi.[60] Nimrodi, the Mossad agent and former Israeli military attache, had acted as a sales agent for Schwimmer in the Shah's Iran. As we have seen, evidence suggests that Nimrodi was also involved in shipping arms to Khomeini's Iran.

Fellow career Mossad officer David Kimche, then director-general of the Foreign Ministry, came on board to steer the negotiations. Ledeen's chief contact in Israel, Kimche proved to be an ardent advocate of reopening relations with Iran's "moderate" elements. In fact, Kimche appears to have been one of the architects of Israel's arms sales to Iran ever since 1980.[61]

Leading these Israelis was Shlomo Gazit, former director of military intelligence and president of Ben Gurion University.[62]

Peres also knew and trusted a fifth, non-Israeli, member of the team: Adnan Khashoggi, a wealthy Saudi arms broker and business partner of Nimrodi who frequently acted as an intermediary between moderate Arab governments and Israeli officials. Khashoggi would finance some of the U.S. arms deals with Iran.

According to the Tower Commission, this group supplied the "catalyst" for the entire Iran catastrophe by "proferring a channel for the United States in establishing contacts with Iran."[63] That channel was Manucher Ghorbanifar, a former SAVAK commander and Iranian arms dealer living in exile.[64] Khashoggi had apparently known him for years.[65] To this group he promised the necessary contacts with "moderates" in Iran—and Buckley's release—in exchange for arms.[66] In particular, he claimed to have access to Iranian Prime Minister Mir Hussein Musavi and Khomeini's heir apparent, the Ayatollah Hussein Ali Montazeri.[67] With Ghorbanifar, however, the truth was always hard to determine. He was branded dangerously unreliable by the CIA as early as 1980, repeatedly demonstrated himself a liar and finally flunked several CIA lie detector tests hands down.[68] Ghorbanifar was even said to have tried to trade intelligence for protection of several drug-trafficking associates.[69]

Yet the truth about Ghorbanifar is much more sinister than that he failed some lie detector tests and struck nearly everyone who dealt with him—except Ledeen and the Israelis—as a "fabricator and wheeler-dealer who has undertaken activities prejudicial to U.S. interests."[70] Far more telling is the published report that Ghorbanifar "had worked for Israeli intelligence before the fall of the Shah."[71] Until 1979 he was a partner in Starline International, a shipping firm run largely by Israelis that moved Iranian oil to Israel.[72] By 1986, if not long before, Ghorbanifar was directly on Israel's payroll.[73] CIA Director William Casey judged him unstable but noted that he "he appears to respond generally to...direction" from a top Israeli official involved in the Iran arms negotiations.[74] Ghorbanifar is said to have been the source of the fanciful story about a Libyan assassination team dispatched to murder President Reagan in 1981. According to the *Washington Post*, "the CIA believed he was tied to both the Iranian and Israeli intelligence services, and that he had made up the hit-squad story in order to cause problems for one of Israel's enemies."[75]

Probably unbeknownst to McFarlane and other American officials, Ghorbanifar and the others assembled by Peres had already met in late 1984—if not earlier—to discuss ways of reordering U.S.-Iran relations. Far from simply responding to American queries, Kimche, Nimrodi, Schwimmer and Ghorbanifar had been making plans months before the White House asked for Israel's help in contacting Tehran.[76] Nimrodi himself admits his government's chief interest in these early talks was in reaping profits and jobs from arms sales to Iran.[77] Ledeen was simply the most suitable intermediary in the summer of 1985 for influencing Washington to that end.

The Ledeen contact in mid-1985 may not have been this group's first effort to lobby the United States for arms-for-hostages deals through Ghorbanifar. In November 1984, when the Israeli group had formed, its Iranian front-man made contact with the former high-ranking CIA officer Ted Shackley in West Germany. Ghorbanifar claimed an unselfish interest in bringing Iran back to the Western fold. "He feared that Iran would become a Soviet satellite within the near term—three to five years," Shackley reported back to the administration. "He rhetorically asked what can we do, for despite our ability to work with the 'moderates' in Iran, we can't get a meaningful dialogue with Washington. Ghorbanifar suggested ransoming the hostages for cash as a first step."[78]

Ghorbanifar's approach to Shackley may have been more calculated than the latter has let on. Shackley had worked as a consultant to Stanford Technology, run by Ghorbanifar's fellow Iranian and one-time partner in arms deals, Albert Hakim.[79] Hakim, as we shall see, succeeded by 1986 in occupying center stage in the financial end of the U.S.-Iranian transactions.

In May 1985, Shackley revived the Ghorbanifar gambit—with historic consequences—at a meeting with his friend Michael Ledeen to discuss the hostage situation. According to Shackley, Ledeen said members of the U.S. government wanted to know in that connection whether the Ghorbanifar channel were "still open."[80]

These reports, taken together, suggest the possibility that the entire Irangate affair was stage-managed by Israeli agents from the beginning. Certainly they put a whole new light on Kimche's crucial assurances to National Security Adviser McFarlane that Ghorbanifar was trustworthy and reliable.[81] They explain the pains taken by the Israelis to exclude the CIA—Ghorbanifar's nemesis—from any knowledge of the arms deals. Above all, they add special resonance to the Tower Commission's finding that "it was Israel that pressed Mr. Ghorbanifar on the United States. U.S. officials accepted Israeli assurances that they had had for some time an extensive dialogue that involved high-level Iranians, as well as their assurances of Mr. Ghorbanifar's *bona fides*. Thereafter, at critical points in the initiative, when doubts were expressed by critical U.S. participants, an Israeli emissary would arrive with encouragement, often a specific proposal, and pressure to stay with the Ghorbanifar channel."[82]

Some Israeli accounts shift the responsibility by suggesting that the Saudi participant in the 1985-86 deals, Khashoggi, was the "key figure" in putting the whole deal together.[83] Such an emphasis points the finger directly or by implication at the Saudi royal family with some of whose members Khashoggi once enjoyed good relations.[84] Some accounts, for example, have Khashoggi introducing Nimrodi to Ghorbanifar and thus setting the whole chain of events in motion. Such a role makes little sense, since Nimrodi knew the former SAVAK agent from the days of the Shah.[85] As the Mossad agent who as much as anyone built SAVAK, Nimrodi would have enjoyed close relations with Ghorbanifar, whether or not the latter worked directly with Israeli intelligence. And both men reportedly knew Maj. Gen. Secord during his service in Iran in the mid-1970s.[86]

Moreover, Khashoggi was more likely an agent of the Israelis than of the Saudi regime, with which his relations were often "severely strained."[87] He introduced Israeli officials, including Sharon, to Sudanese president Nimeiri in the early 1980s, paving the way for the airlift of Falasha Jews from Ethiopia.[88] His London-based lawyer was involved with several Israelis in some gigantic arms deals with Iran, said to have the approval of Prime Minister Shimon Peres.[89] He arranged the sale of Egyptian arms to Israel for resale to South Africa.[90] He greeted Peres at the Regency Hotel in New York on his first visit to the United States as prime minister.[91] He was a business partner of Nimrodi and is reportedly a "close friend" of the Mossad veteran David Kimche.[92] Khashoggi was hardly able to manipulate the Israelis; he was simply their agent.

As the Tower Commission noted in its report, this group of Israeli insiders and Israeli agents was seeking "U.S. approval of, or at least acquiescence in" its own program of arms sales to Iran. But there was another consideration, a corollary to Israel's perceived strategic interest in helping Iraq's enemy: "In addition, elements in Israel undoubtedly wanted the United States involved for its own sake so as to distance the United States from the Arab world and ultimately to establish Israel as the only real strategic partner of the United States in the region."[93]

Ledeen returned to Washington as a *de facto* emissary representing this group's aims. In particular he advanced and supported the Israelis' proposal to use Ghorbanifar as an intermediary. But Ghorbanifar demanded 500 TOW anti-tank missiles as a sign of good faith. Israel would not ship them without U.S. approval.[94] Thus began the critical period of policy making at the NSC. Ledeen, backed by McFarlane and North who both respected Israeli opinion to the point of admiration,[95] vigorously promoted the Ghorbanifar plan "inside and outside the government."[96]

McFarlane should have recognized Ledeen's account as skewed to Israel's self-interests. An April 1985 National Intelligence Estimate "indicated that Israel had its own reasons to promote the sale of arms to Iran and described those interests that diverged from U.S. policy," according to a draft report of the Senate Select Committee on Intelligence report on the

Iran affair. "The NIE also described the informal relationship that the Israeli Government maintains with Israeli arms dealers, facilitating their activities even when the Government of Israel officially supported the U.S.-led embargo of weapons for Iran." McFarlane did not see that analysis, however.[97] McFarlane testified that "if he had known that the Israelis had previously shipped arms to Iran it would have made him less responsive to later Israeli proposals to resume shipments."[98]

When George Shultz learned of Ledeen's back-channel mission, the secretary of state gave McFarlane a lesson. Complaining that State should have been consulted, Shultz warned that Israel's agenda "is not the same as ours," that depending on Israeli intelligence assessments "could seriously skew our own perception and analysis of the Iranian scene" and that the Israeli-brokered initiative "contains the seeds of...serious error unless straightened out quickly." McFarlane promised to "turn it off entirely."[99]

The June 14, 1985 hijacking of a TWA jet to Beirut immediately turned it back on again. McFarlane once again raised the possibility of opening lines of communication to Tehran with Israel's help.[100]

McFarlane may well have been influenced by a draft National Security Decision Directive submitted to him only three days before the hijacking by two of his most pro-Israeli aides, Donald Fortier, the NSC's executive secretary and Howard Teicher, the council's Israeli-educated Middle East expert.[101] In May they had closely directed preparations of a National Intelligence Estimate on Iran warning of a pro-Soviet takeover in the chaos that would follow Khomeini's death unless the West could "blunt Soviet influence" by filling "a military gap for Iran." The best strategy, this NIE concluded, was to encourage friendly states [read Israel] to sell arms to Iran to keep the country out of Moscow's corner.[102] Now in their June 11 draft directive, Fortier and Teicher cited the very intelligence estimate they had shaped as reason to "encourage Western allies and friends to help Iran meet its import requirements...including provision of selected military equipment..." Fortier wrote McFarlane on the side, "the Israeli option is the one we have to pursue, even though we may have to pay a certain price for the help."[103]

CIA Director Casey "strongly endorsed" the thrust of the draft directive, but its argument failed to impress Defense Secretary Weinberger. "This is almost too absurd for comment," he scribbled. "It is based on the assumption that there is about to be a major change in Iran and that we can deal with that rationally. It's like inviting Khadafy over for a cozy lunch."[104] Secretary of State Shultz similarly complained that the proposed directive "is contrary to our interest in containing Khomeinism and in ending the excesses of this regime."[105] Yet the proposal to unleash Israel was about to receive a new round of support.

Three weeks after the hijacking, David Kimche, one of Ledeen's main contacts and director general of Israel's foreign ministry, flew to Washington to make the same case as Fortier and Teicher.[106] Kimche argued it would be "criminal" not to take advantage of the new Iranian contact Israel had made.[107] Ghorbanifar had warned the Israelis that Iran would "become a second Lebanon, in larger and more dangerous dimensions" or else "part of communist Russia" if moderate mullahs were not strengthened against the radicals.[108] From that assumption, Kimche argued that the hostages could only be freed, and Iranian moderates cultivated, with generous shipments of weapons.[109] Such arms would supply the Iranians with "evidence of American good faith," he maintained.[110]

Reinforcing Kimche's message was the visit to McFarlane by Prime Minister Peres' personal adviser and emissary, Al Schwimmer, on July 13, the day of President Reagan's cancer operation. The American-born arms dealer claimed that Ghorbanifar had made contact with a pro-Western faction in Iran and could both free the hostages and open a political dialogue if only Israel were granted permission to ship U.S. made TOW missiles to Iran.[111]

A few days later, McFarlane took up with the convalescing Reagan the general proposition of using an Israeli contact to establish a channel to Iranian policy makers. What happened next is particularly in dispute. The national security adviser may or may not have mentioned arms and Reagan may or may not have authorized an approach to Israel's contact Ghorbanifar. The recovering president may not have been fully attentive, but he was receptive at least to exploring a political opening with Iran.[112]

Meantime, the Israelis were taking no chances. In early July, Kimche arranged for Ledeen to meet with Al Schwimmer, the confidant of Israeli Prime Minister Peres, in Washington. The Israeli arms dealer spoke glowingly of Ghorbanifar and encouraged Ledeen to meet the Iranian as soon as possible. Leeden got McFarlane's approval to meet Ghorbanifar while taking a "vacation" in Israel later that month.[113]

Their meeting in late July was top-heavy with arms dealers: Schwimmer, Nimrodi and Ghorbanifar attended along with Kimche. Leeden came away impressed by Ghorbanifar's "great quantity" of information on politics in Tehran and with his tantalizing promise that arms sales might induce Iran to release William Buckley and stop sponsoring further terrorism. Ledeen chose to discount the CIA's apparently well-founded suspicions about the Iranian's credibility.[114] Indeed, Ledeen has since called

Ghorbanifar "one of the most honest, educated, honorable men I have ever known."[115]

In case the administration did not get the hint, Kimche returned to Washington at the beginning of August and reiterated to McFarlane what Ledeen had already reported: Iran could produce the hostages only in return for TOW anti-tank missiles and other U.S. arms.[116].

On August 6, McFarlane made his case to Reagan, Bush, Shultz, Weinberger, CIA Director Casey and White House Chief of Staff Don Regan. Once again stories differ as to the outcome. The secretaries of state and defense, at least, opposed any arms sales. But McFarlane testified (contrary to Regan) that he carried the day and won the President's approval for an initial Israeli shipment of TOWs. Reagan did not issue an official "finding" to lend legal authority to the new policy.[117]

Then, claiming to speak for the president, McFarlane told Kimche that the administration would "condone" an Israeli shipment of arms to Iran and would replace the TOW missiles.[118] The national security adviser put Ledeen in charge of handling arrangements with Kimche to receive the hostages.[119] The first two arms shipments, financed by Khashoggi, were delivered in Iran on August 19 and September 14. On that latter date, his Lebanese abductors released the Rev. Benjamin Weir.[120] Another shipment of HAWK anti-aircraft missiles followed in November, brokered by retired Maj. Gen. Richard Secord with help from the CIA.[121]

With those first shipments, the process of hooking Washington was underway. Israel's hope must have been to keep the White House from disrupting the much larger Israel-Iran arms traffic that flourished while the administration agonized over the fate of U.S. hostages. Certain law enforcement agencies, on the other hand, could not so easily be constrained without endangering the White House's secret. Operation Staunch remained in effect—to the dismay of certain smugglers linked to the Israeli government.[122]

Key Israeli officials thus had every incentive to maintain their leverage in Washington and suppress White House doubts as long as possible. Those doubts were growing fast. By December 1985, National Security Adviser McFarlane had become disenchanted with the one-sided negotiations and the obvious failure of Ghorbanifar's contacts in Tehran to achieve the hostages' release. McFarlane obtained presidential approval on December 7 to stop further arms shipments; the next day, he flew to London to call off the Israeli and Iranian middlemen. Ledeen, too, was told his services were no longer needed. Kimche argued in vain that the Iranian connection was still viable and promising; in particular he defended the credibility of Ghorbanifar, who struck McFarlane as a "man of no integrity."[123]

McFarlane resigned from office as of December 11; the opportunity was thus ripe for an end run around his parting policy shift. All through December, North, Ledeen, Ghorbanifar, Richard Secord (North's private agent) and an Israeli representative of Peres, Amiram Nir, continued to meet.[124] On a private trip to Europe, the NSC "consultant" met Ghorbanifar again, then returned to brief CIA officials, including Casey, on the Iranian's immense potential value. More important, Ledeen arranged for Ghorbanifar to visit Washington and charm top administration officials in person. Ledeen told government associates that Ghorbanifar was a "wonderful man...almost too good to be true." Although the arms dealer flunked every significant question asked him on a CIA lie detector test, Oliver North decided to keep him on.[125] Just why North and Casey continued to use Ghorbanifar remains something of a mystery.[126] One reason may be that the Iranian claimed, and North believed, that the Khomeini regime would order the hostages killed if Washington jettisoned Ghorbanifar and called off the arms deals. North also believed he could control Ghorbanifar adequately through Secord.[127]

Israel's pressure on Washington to resume its arms-for-hostages policy intensified. On January 2, 1986, according to the Tower Report, "just when the initiative seemed to be dying," Prime Minister Peres sent his special terrorism adviser, Amiram Nir, to Washington with "news" that logistical problems had been cleared up and the Iranian "moderates" were willing to bargain again in good faith. Nir asked the administration to reconsider its termination of arms dealings with Iran.[128] As bait, he suggested that Israel might release some Shia prisoners held in southern Lebanon—along with 3000 TOW missiles—to expedite the release of American hostages.[129] Shultz remained suspicious that Israel simply wanted to "get itself into a position where its arms sales to Iran could not be criticized by us" or cut off by Operation Staunch, the official embargo effort against Tehran. But President Reagan, desperate to get the hostages back, was persuaded to give the Israel channel another chance.[130]

A memorandum for the president, prepared by Oliver North and delivered in summary by National Security Adviser John Poindexter on January 17, supplies powerful evidence of Israel's crucial role in initiating the resumption of U.S. arms sales to Iran in 1986:

> Prime Minister Peres of Israel secretly dispatched his special advisor on terrorism with instructions to propose a plan by which Israel, with limited assistance from the US, can create conditions to help bring about a more moderate government in Iran...

> The Israeli plan is premised on the assumption that moderate elements in Iran can come to power if these factions demonstrate their credibility in defending Iran against Iraq and in deterring Soviet intervention. To achieve the strategic goal of a more moderate Iranian government, the Israelis are prepared to unilaterally commence selling military material to Western-oriented Iranian factions. It is their belief that by so doing they can achieve heretofore unobtainable penetration of the Iranian governing hierarchy. The Israelis are convinced that the Iranians are so desperate for military material, expertise and intelligence that the provision of these resources will result in favorable long-term changes in personnel and attitudes within the Iranian government. Further, once the exchange relationship has commenced, a dependency would be established on those who are providing the requisite resources, thus allowing the provider(s) to coercively influence near-term events.

North saved the strongest enticement for last. "They also point out," he noted, "...this approach through the government of Iran may well be our only way to achieve the release of the American hostages held in Beirut." Indeed, the whole deal ultimately rested on their fate. "If all of the hostages are not released after the first shipment of 1,000 weapons," North stated, "further transfers would cease."[131]

As evidence cited earlier proves, Peres's offer to "commence" arms sales was disingenous in the extreme. Such sales had never stopped. And his proposal to "penetrate" and control the Iranian government with them was no less misleading in view of the failure of past sales to change Tehran's behavior.

According to North's memo, the Israelis asked only for "an assurance that they will be allowed to purchase U.S. replenishments for the stocks that they sell to Iran." Such an arrangement, the NSC official noted, would violate U.S. laws; but the "objectives of the Israeli plan could be met" legally if the CIA, acting under a presidential order, "purchased arms from the Department of Defense under the Economy Act and then transferred them directly to Iran after receiving appropriate payment from Iran."

Although Weinberger and Shultz still firmly opposed further sales, Nir won over CIA director Casey, Attorney General Edwin Meese and National Security Adviser Poindexter. Together they convinced Reagan on the 17th to authorize—without notification of Congress—a renewed round of arms shipments for the purpose of moderating Iran's government and "furthering the release of the American hostages held in Beirut..."[132] But now, for the first time, Washington would supply arms directly to

Tehran: Israel would merely "make the necessary arrangements" for the deal.[133]

It was an extraordinary decision, even if the finding merely sanctioned an ongoing policy. For in writing, it put the President on record as violating his own arms embargo, bargaining with terrorists over hostages and potentially tilting the military scales in favor of America's sworn enemy, Iran. Thus began "Operation Recovery."

Thereafter, various Americans, chiefly from the CIA and North's own private network, took the lead in making the arrangements and bargaining with Tehran. But—contrary to accounts that minimize Israel's role in the latter stages of the affair—Nir worked closely with Khashoggi to line up bridge financing for the deals.[134] Nir further sat in on meetings the Americans had with Ghorbanifar and went—disguised as an American—to meetings with Iranian government representatives in Tehran. Prime Minister Peres personally appealed to the White House to include Nir in the delegation to Tehran, where he could keep tabs on the developing arms trade and report back to Israel.[135]

North claims further that it was Nir who first broached the scheme of financing the contras with profits from the sale of arms to Iran in the decisive month of January 1986—a strategy seconded by Ghorbanifar, the expatriate Iranian arms dealer supported financially by Israel.[136] Further investigation may determine the truth of North's allegation, but the record is clear that Israel had already grossly overcharged Iran for the August/September 1985 arms shipments and thus established a precedent for generating profits that could be used for other ends.[137] North may have believed that since the money came from Iran, not the United States or Israel, it could be diverted without actually breaking the law.[138]

Investigators believe some of these proceeds went to Swiss bank accounts controlled by North's private agents, Albert Hakim and Richard Secord. To fellow NSC officials, North described Hakim variously as vice president of a European company set up to "handle aid to resistance movements" and as the man who "runs the European operation for our Nicaraguan resistance support activity."[139] According to his lawyer, Hakim arranged for the Iranians to purchase TOW missiles in February 1986 in exchange for a contribution to the contras, and "the money from that sale was routed through Israelis into Hakim's financial network."[140] Hakim was not a disinterested observer in this affair. He appears to have had a personal financial stake in arms deals with Khomeini's Iran.[141] One top CIA operations officer worried that Hakim was involved in arms transactions of his own "that might or might not be legal" and that might conflict with White House plans.[142] But no less important to understanding his role may be the fact that he was reportedly an Iranian Jew with "strong Israeli military-type ties."[143]

Outside Central America, some of the Iran money may also have been diverted to purchase anti-aircraft missiles from Israel for the Afghan rebels.[144] The same bank account may have also financed military shipments from China. That materiel reportedly went both to Afghanistan and, via the Portuguese territory of Macao, to the former Portuguese colony of Angola to help the UNITA guerrilla movement.[145] A growing body of evidence suggests that the administration's private contractors circumvented the Clark Amendment barring aid to UNITA in the same way that they bypassed the Boland Amendment regarding the contras.[146]

Still other profits went to Israel's foreign intelligence agency, Mossad, "for its undercover operations in Europe and the Middle East," according to Jack Anderson. "Casey went along with the secret diversion of money to Mossad," Anderson learned, "because in the past Mossad has undertaken delicate intelligence jobs for the CIA on request."[147] Israeli press accounts indirectly support this story.[148]

Last but not least, Ghorbanifar reportedly saw to it that several million dollars ended up in the coffers of top Iranian government officials and in the hands of financiers of the very group that kidnapped the Americans in Beirut.[149]

Any time the administration began to have second thoughts about this dangerous policy, Israeli officials were there to steer the White House back on track. In February 1986, for example, Prime Minister Peres wrote President Reagan, urging him "not to give up" and to "be patient that the policy would bear fruit."[150] George Shultz later complained that "every time he was told the deal was dead, some Israeli would come over and stir the flames."[151]

The White House, in any case, was hooked. As Casey and others pointed out, there was no turning back: Cancelling the talks could make the situation "turn ugly" either at the expense of the hostages or the administration, which was now hostage itself to potential leakers like Ghorbanifar or Khashoggi.[152]

Thus were the ransom negotiations kept alive and intensified until one faction in Iran (around Montazeri) leaked details of the deals to a Beirut newspaper,[153] followed by Attorney General Ed Meese's revelation in late November 1986 of the illegal siphoning of money from Swiss accounts maintained for the Iran arms deals to pay for contra supplies.

Israeli pressure and manipulation, it must be stressed, could never have succeeded without the administration's consent, and would never have worked without a predisposition in the White House for resorting to back-channel policies contrary to declared policy.

In retrospect, however, the Reagan administration was particularly vulnerable to Israeli offers of "assistance" because the CIA had developed no assets of any value inside Iran. "We had nothing going in Iran," one official said.[154] "We really had no alternative" to depending on Israel, McFarlane explained in a similar vein. With the fall of the Shah, he noted, the CIA suffered "an enormous loss of the means of collection in Iran that still gives us an imperfect picture of what is going on in Iran."[155]

Thus when the Israelis came up with Ghorbanifar as their window on Iran's "moderates," NSC staffers with little knowledge of the Middle East and limitless faith in Israeli intelligence prowess took the bait. Not only did Israel win Washington's sanction for arms shipments, it advanced the goal of strengthening Iran against its supposed long-term enemy, Iraq.

But the administration was vulnerable above all because it chose to undertake so much of its foreign policy in secret, without the benefit of public debate and at the mercy of more experienced covert operators. The relatively unsophisticated staffers on the NSC were no match for professional Israeli Mossad agents like Kimche and Nimrodi, or the champions of Israel's cause within the administration, like Fortier, Teicher, and Casey. Consumed by the operational details of their clandestine deals, they never stopped to assess the enormous risks either of exposure or of tilting the balance of the war in Iran's favor. In the case of Iran, at least, the administration effectively subcontracted not only policy implementation but policy formulation—and paid the price.

IX.
Secret Wars and
Special Operations

As Congress explores reforms to prevent further breakdowns of law and accountability at the top levels of government, legislators should not ignore one of their own obscure but vital contributions to the recent scandals. Even as Congress has demanded a more open foreign policy, it has promoted a significant expansion of special operations and unconventional warfare capabilities—necessary components of U.S. military forces, but ones that may conceal a perilous capability for unaccountable action by presidents, their advisers or rogue agents.

The realm of military special operations lies beyond the day-to-day reach of the intelligence committees, and often beyond even the knowledge of all but a handful of officials in the executive branch. The hallmark of most special operations units—stealth and deception—keeps the American public in the dark no less than the enemy. In the wrong hands, their activities can no less easily be kept secret from Congress as well.

And just as the special operations fraternity provided the training ground for most of the undercover specialists who are today notorious for their role in the illicit Iran and contra networks—including Oliver North and Richard Secord—so it will constitute the recruiting pool for similar abuses in the future.

Special operations units, broadly defined, include the Green Berets, Army Rangers, Navy SEALs, Air Force Special Operations Wing, the Delta Force antiterrorist commandos and related signal, civil affairs and psychological warfare units. Depending on the unit in question, their specialized skills and training include "underwater demolition, sabotage, foreign weapons expertise, wilderness survival, parachuting, scuba, hand-to-hand combat, sniper, pathfinder, camouflage, escape and evasion, aerial resupply and extraction, intelligence gathering, interrogation and psychological operations."[1]

Such forces took their model from the irregular warfare units of the Office of Strategic Services (OSS), the World War II-era predecessor to the CIA. In the postwar years, their first mission was to support America's earliest "contras": East European emigres, some of them veterans of Nazi military formations, who hoped to roll back Soviet control of their homelands.[2] They first saw major action during the Vietnam War, working closely with the CIA on clandestine raids and guerrilla warfare throughout Indochina. Since the 1960s they have spearheaded U.S. training and counterinsurgency efforts in Latin America, ranging from the capture of Che Guevara in Bolivia in 1967 to recent support for government troops in Honduras, Costa Rica and El Salvador.[3]

In the last few years they have served in the 1980 Iran hostage rescue mission, the Grenada invasion and even the Los Angeles summer Olympics.[4] Special Forces training teams undertook missions in 35 countries in the Reagan administration's first term.[5] The Army Special Operations Command is currently training forces for five separate regions: the Pacific, North Africa, Persian Gulf, Germany and Latin America.[6]

Special Operations: A Growth Field

In the last few years, the special operations sector of the U.S. military has grown at a rate unprecedented in peacetime to meet such diverse "low intensity" challenges as classic counterinsurgency, anti-terrorist missions and support of anti-communist insurgencies that meet the tests of the "Reagan Doctrine."[7]

In the first five years of the Reagan administration, special operations forces (SOF) grew in manpower by 50 percent, with a goal of doubling to more than 20,000 by the end of the decade.[8] Budgets directed to unconventional warfare have sextupled during the Reagan presidency.[9] The Pentagon's five-year plan from fiscal 1988-1992 calls for spending $10.4 billion on special operations.

Since 1982, several bureaucratic changes have given SOF heightened stature within the military to match their increased resources. The Army put all its special operations units under one command at Fort Bragg in 1982; the Air Force followed suit in 1983. In early 1984 the Joint Chiefs of Staff created the Joint Special Operations Agency to advise them on command and control of the SOF in all the services. And each of the unified theater commands set up Special Operations Commands to guide their SOF capabilities.[10] Today such units actually have representation at the level of the National Security Council.

The theory and practice of special operations enjoy a powerful constituency within the Pentagon, especially on the civilian side. These boosters cite the terrorist threat as one rationale for augmenting such forces. But today, as in President Kennedy's era, special operations units above all offer the illusory promise of allowing the United States to intervene successfully in the Third World "without U.S. involvement in large-scale armed conflict and with minimal cost in lives and resources," according to the U.S. Army.[11]

President Kennedy's explanation of their mission in 1961 could have come from President Reagan's mouth two decades later:

> It is clearer than ever that we face a relentless struggle in every corner of the globe that goes far beyond the clash of armies, or even nuclear armaments. The armies are there. But they serve primarily as the shield behind which subversion, infiltration and a host of other tactics steadily advance, picking off vulnerable areas one by one in situations that do not permit our own armed intervention...We dare not fail to see the insidious nature of this new and deeper struggle. We dare not fail to grasp the new concepts, the new tools, the new sense of urgency we will need to combat it—whether in Cuba or south Vietnam.[12]

In 1982, Defense Secretary Weinberger justified the current buildup of special operations forces as essential "to project United States power where the use of conventional forces would be premature, inappropriate or infeasible." The sort of "low-level conflict" most suited to special operations forces, he maintained, "will pose the threat we are most likely to encounter throughout the end of this century."[13] Deputy Assistant Secretary of Defense Noel Koch told Congress in 1984 that "Special Operations Forces...provide us a precisely tailored capability" for resisting "insurgency and international terrorism in every region of the Third World." And according to Undersecretary of Defense Fred Ikle, these forces will give the United States the ability to match the Soviets in "all means—terrorist, covert, arms shipments, what have you—to topple governments or support governments..."[14]

The Risks of Intervention

In fact, as military officers have been the first to stress, the use of such forces entails great risks of unintended escalation and overcommitment. Lt. Gen. John Chain, then Air Force deputy chief of staff for operations, warned in 1984 that relying on the Special Forces is "like carrying a loaded gun," tempting but dangerous to use before the nation is committed to war.[15] Policy makers attracted by the low visibility and supposed effectiveness of special operations forces may be disposed to deploy them without adequate political support at home. Dispatched as a limited beachhead of American troops in "low intensity conflicts," they may require conventional support when the going gets tough. Above all, they may entangle the country in the far-reaching consequences of their covert missions, without Congress even being notified under the War Powers Act.[16]

Thus in Indochina, special operations forces made up the low-visibility spearhead of the Kennedy administration's first, and ultimately disastrous, commitment of forces. On May 11, 1961, a National Security Action Memorandum directed the military to "expand present operations" of one special unit "in guerrilla areas of South Vietnam under joint MAAG [Military Assistance Advisory Group]-CIA sponsorship and direction" and in Laos to "infiltrate teams" trained by the CIA and Special Forces to attack Vietcong lines of communication "under light civilian cover." Assisting in those operations were Navy SEAL frogmen and a CIA proprietary airline (VIAT) using pilots from Taiwan who could "provide plausible denial that the Vietnamese or U.S. governments were involved in operations over North Vietnam."[17] These special units reported directly to the CIA or Defense Intelligence Agency, bypassing normal military channels.[18]

By 1963, an average of four Vietnamese teams trained by the Special Forces were entering North Vietnam each month to conduct "harassment and psychological operations."[19] Before year's end these infiltration missions, considered essentially futile by the CIA, were transferred to military control "as part of a worldwide replacement of CIA leadership of clandestine paramilitary operations." Specifically, the operations were run by the Special Operations Group (operating undercover as the "Study and Observation Group"), which reported in practice not to local military commanders, but directly to the Special Assistant for Counterinsurgency and Special Activities in the Joint Chiefs of Staff, a post established after the Bay of Pigs invasion.[20]

A relative handful of military covert operators had a disproportionate effect on the war's political development. SOG's clandestine raids on North Vietnam in 1964 triggered the infamous reprisal attack on U.S. naval vessels in the Gulf of Tonkin, the single greatest watershed in the early history of that war's escalation. Later, U.S. special forces, possibly without Washington's full knowledge and apparently against strenuous opposition from the State Department, helped destabilize the neutral regime of Cambodia's Prince Sihanouk, contributing to the escalation of war into his country and the ultimate collapse of that society into barbarism.[21] Finally, special military units attached to the CIA helped carry out the notorious Phoenix program, which arranged the murder of tens of thousands of civilians suspected of sympathy with the Vietcong. Revelations several years later of the staggering abuses involved ultimately helped swing American public opinion further against the war.[22]

Where Abuses Flourish

William Jackson, an aide to Sen. Alan Cranston, D-Calif., argues that the real purpose of special operations forces is "to fight undeclared war, that is, a war kept secret from the American press. They specialize in the 'gray zone' between military and intelligence operations. Thus, the armed forces of the United States are engaged in covert military operations designed to circumvent the law and avoid congressional oversight."[23]

The clandestine nature of special forces encourages the same sort of abuses that have characterized the CIA, with one major difference: what goes on in the shadowy recesses of the military is much less well studied or understood. The intelligence oversight committees acknowledge having little expertise in this realm.[24] As Senator Patrick Leahy, vice chairman of the Senate Select Committee on Intelligence, has noted, "the new reliance on covert paramilitary action as a normal instrument of foreign policy—even as a substitute for foreign policy—has strained the current oversight process to the breaking point."[25]

Congress can only guess at what really goes on. In 1983, for example, an obscure embezzlement trial of a former two-star Air Force general revealed the existence of a secret Swiss bank account used to finance CIA and military special operations[26] and "bribes to foreign officials." What's more, the account was managed not only by the military but also by the chairman of the board of Lockheed Aircraft—an invitation to abuses and conflicts of interest that can only be imagined.[27] Many other defense contractors keep such Swiss accounts, according to retired Air Force intelligence chief, Maj. Gen. George Keegan. In effect, the military has taken over—or at least complemented—the CIA's longstanding practice of supervising the laundering of overseas corporate political payoffs.[28]

This financial scandal, like others that have plagued military special operations,[29] grew out of what one military judge called the "extraordinary means" used to "circumvent accountability for money." Army special operations units laundered their funds and made purchases on the commercial market through front companies to avoid leaving any trace of their finances or activites.[30] Such practices appear to be a legacy of the Vietnam era, when the CIA bequeathed to military Special Forces their lucrative if unorthodox funding and support system.[31]

But "extraordinary means" have also been used to circumvent accountability for policy no less than for money.

In 1985, after revelation of yet another financial fraud, the Army disbanded a supersecret group of at least 250 officers called Intelligence Support Activity (ISA). Created in 1981 in the aftermath of the failed Iran hostage rescue operation, and owing its existence to lobbying by CIA-and-special-operations veteran Richard Stilwell,[32] ISA conducted classified missions in Nicaragua, El Salvador, parts of Africa and Southeast Asia. ISA backed the contras, supported the freelance efforts of Special Forces veteran James "Bo" Gritz[33] to find remaining U.S. POWs in Laos, and played a role in the rescue of Army Brig. Gen. James Dozier, kidnapped by the Red Brigades in Italy.[34] ISA reportedly carried out covert activities for more than a year without proper presidential authorization, congressional oversight or initially even knowledge of the CIA director. ISA also supplemented its $10 million budget from Special Operations Division funds and with equipment from the Drug Enforcement Administration. The Army admitted that ISA "had been watched insufficiently closely."[35]

Frauds and embezzlement are the least of the problems posed by special operations missons. Sen. James Sasser, D-Tenn., warns of "a real danger that these Special Forces could be used by CIA programs and thus skirt congressional review." His worry is more than theoretical. The two sectors in fact routinely swap personnel.[36] Undersecretary of Defense Fred Ikle boasts accurately that "there has been very good cooperation since the start" between the CIA and military special operations forces.[37] "We gave the Agency pretty much anything they wanted," said one aide to the former CIA officer, Nestor Sanchez, who was until 1987 the top Pentagon officer for Latin America. "There is a terrible gray area about what to do in semi-declared wars. It helps to have the (Pentagon) and CIA working together in this situation."[38] As military units have become adept at setting up private front companies, purchasing civilian planes for cover and bugging foreign trading companies, the line dividing them from the CIA has all but vanished.[39]

The failure of Congress to understand the intimate links between Pentagon and CIA covert operations has seriously limited its review of presidential policies. The Church Committee's investigation of the CIA's complicity in the overthrow of Chilean President Salvador Allende, for example, neglected to examine the role of military intelligence and Navy SEAL teams in the 1973 coup.[40] (Much like the later Iran and contra plots, the Nixon administration's military coup plans were never discussed at full NSC meetings and were known only to a tiny circle of White House and CIA officials.)[41]

Congress was similarly ignorant of the true scope of military cooperation with the CIA in mounting a bloodbath against tens of thousands of Guatemalan civilians during the 1960s. U.S. counter-insurgency experts established within the Guatemalan military the ruthless 1st Special Forces Company, modeled on the Green Berets, and the Special Air Squadron, modeled on the U.S. Air Force 1st Air Commando Squadron (with which Richard Secord served in the 1960s). The Air Force-funded RAND corporation attributed the success of such forces to "the psychological impact of terror tactics," ranging from death-squad killings to indiscriminate napalming of villages. Contrary to congressional authorization and official Pentagon policy, U.S. Special Forces personnel and pilots almost certainly took part directly in these extermination campaigns. Nestor Sanchez was a CIA veteran of this bloody era.[42] The horrifying reports of abuses finally moved Congress in 1977 to cut off all aid and most training to the Guatemalan military. But in 1982 a reporter discovered that at least one Special Forces adviser was still in the country, teaching skills ranging from demolition to ambush techniques.[43]

A more contemporary example of CIA-military "cooperation" was the Pentagon's provision of physical facilities in Honduras to the CIA to evade congressional funding restrictions on the intelligence agency.[44] Through "Project Elephant Herd" in 1983, the Defense Department also supplied $12 million in military supplies, including 3 rocket-equipped planes, to the CIA at no cost for use by the contras.[45]

More infamous yet was the CIA's translation of a 1968 Green Beret lesson plan—advocating selective assassination as an effective tactic of special operations—to instruct the Nicaraguan contras in "Psychological Operations in Guerrilla Warfare."[46]

News of special forces activity inside Nicaragua itself—where members of a secret Army helicopter unit have reportedly flown in support of the contras[47]—further brings home the pertinance of Sasser's warning and highlights the dangers of escalation, without congressional authorization, inherent in the Reagan doctrine's support of anti-communist insurgencies through covert military channels.

The Special Operations Samurai

The perils inherent in such secret operations can only multiply as the covert infrastructure within the military expands. And those perils will persist even if Congress finally reins in the special operations forces. The legacy of past operations will haunt the United States, and the world, for a long time to come. Thus veterans of special operations in the Vietnam era today form a freelance pool of agents trained in the ways of money laundering, logistics, safehouses and dummy front companies. Under the right guidance, they have the knowledge and contacts to run a private foreign policy even against prevailing public policy.

That capability was demonstrated in microcosm by the rogue CIA and naval intelligence veteran Ed Wilson, himself a protege of the special operations afficionado Thomas Clines, who supervised Wilson's activities for the CIA from Cuba to Laos.[48] In the late 1970s, Wilson began turning his clandestine skills to a highly profitable end: supplying Gadhafy's Libya with advanced explosives, timing devices and military training.

To the latter end, Wilson recruited more than a hundred ex-Green Beret sabotage, explosives and unconventional warfare experts.[49] He hired them for legitimate work, then shipped them off for the illicit training program. His chief recruiter was a former Green Beret who fought in Laos under Ted Shackley before joining the CIA; this veteran in turn plugged into the network of highly trained special operations experts through an active-duty Special Forces master sergeant who had participated in many CIA-directed military actions in Latin America and Southeast Asia.[50]

Among their recruits was the chief parachute drop instructor at the Fort Bragg Special Warfare School; a top helicopter pilot for Air America, the CIA proprietary that flew supply missions in Laos and North Vietnam; and two employees of the top secret Naval Weapons Center in China Lake, California who had developed weapons for the CIA and Pentagon for special warfare in Vietnam.

To help Gadhafy launch an attack in Chad, Wilson enlisted an elite Special Forces veteran to plan the invasion in conjunction with several French mercenaries, former members of the extremist Secret Army

Organization (OAS) that attempted to assassinate French President Charles de Gaulle in the early 1960s. And Wilson hired yet another Green Beret vet, whose five tours of duty in Indochina had taken him on missions deep into Laos, as an enforcer to murder his own and Gadhafy's enemies. (Previously Wilson had made a $30,000 down payment to Rafael Quintero, a former CIA contract agent and alleged Castro assassination plotter, for one "hit" that never came off.[51]) For such services Libya paid Wilson $1.2 million a year.[52]

Even as Wilson was breaking U.S. laws in the most sordid fashion, the Pentagon was giving him official cover indirectly through its own clandestine programs. Thus the head of the Defense Security Assistance Agency, Erich von Marbod, allegedly gave retired CIA officer and Wilson business associate Thomas Clines a contract in 1978 to gather information on Soviet weapons sold to Libya. Clines in turn hired as his agent Wilson's chief aide in Libya, Douglas Schlachter.[53] Thus Wilson could more believably claim—as he often has—that his terrorist supply contract in Libya was really a sanctioned covert operation.[54]

Other employers of special operations veterans have made similar claims. Recruited to "sell their skills to unfriendly governments and repressive regimes" with claims of CIA sponsorship, "former Green Berets, accustomed to handling sensitive and often unconventional covert tasks for the CIA while on active duty, assumed that the jobs had been approved by the Government," according to the *New York Times*. Their freelance work has encompassed such locales as Egypt, Zaire, Honduras, Mexico and Argentina. Chilean government agents recruited several ex-Green Berets in 1981 to conduct training exercises in Chile and counter-terrorist operations in El Salvador, purportedly on behalf of the U.S. government (see chapter VI). Several Special Forces and Navy SEAL veterans worked for Nicaraguan Gen. Anastasio Somoza on sabotage and assassination missions.[55] And a Marine Corps intelligence officer who trained with the Delta Force and served as an instructor for a the Navy SEAL team became the security chief for contra political boss Adolfo Calero.[56]

The Iran-Contra Group

Nowhere is the capability of these retired practitioners of covert warfare for subverting an open foreign policy more graphically demonstrated than in the current Iran and contra scandals. Nearly every field operator named in either case had long experience in past unconventional battle-fields, above all in the gray zone between CIA military special operations forces.

Several of these individuals had been set up in business after military retirement with Pentagon contracts that "offloaded" sensitive SOF logistics missions onto their private companies. These firms, in turn, provided the essential infrastructure for "contracting out" foreign policy from the National Security Council.[57]

The administration's access to these clandestine specialists provided the key to subverting the will of Congress and the American people. The private network of loyal covert operators, tapped by NSC officials in the name of patriotism or anticommunism, lay far outside the normal bounds of congressional oversight.

* On the CIA end, Theodore Shackley and Thomas Clines, who ran sabotage operations against Cuba from the huge Miami CIA station in the early 1960s and then graduated to command the covert paramilitary war in Laos later in the decade,[58] were both reportedly involved in the Iran affair. Clines further arranged arms shipments for the contras.[59]

* Working with Shackley and Clines on anti-Castro infiltration and sabotage raids in the early 1960s were such Cuban CIA agents as Felix Rodriguez, Rafael Quintero and Luis Posada. Rodriguez worked with U.S. Army Ranger units to track down Che Guevara in 1967, then served as a special airmobile counterinsurgency expert in Vietnam with Shackley (and George Bush aide Donald Gregg) before turning up in El Salvador as a leader of the undercover contra supply operation. Quintero and Posada joined him there—Quintero after working for CIA agent-turned-terrorist Ed Wilson, Posada after escaping from a Venezuelan prison following his imprisonment for blowing up a Cuban passenger airline.

* One of this CIA group's closest associates—and the single most important nongovernmental organizer of the secret NSC operations in Central American and Iran—was retired Gen. Richard Secord. Assigned to a special Florida-based air wing in 1961, where he may well have supported CIA operations against Cuba, he was first sent to Vietnam as a special warfare expert in 1962. In 1966-68 he was attached to the Shackley-Clines CIA station in Laos, where he directed and flew secret supply missions for their covert war. He was detailed once again to the CIA secret war in Laos in 1973. In 1980, he helped plan two hostage rescue missions in Iran.[60] He is said to have participated in overseeing the Army's shadowy Intelligence Support Activity. Secord reportedly took advantage of another secret Army unit's Swiss bank account, which remained active after the unit's

disbandment, to aid the contras in 1985.[61] Until 1985, Secord served as a member of the Pentagon's Special Operations Policy Advisory Group.[62]

* The highly effective front man for the White House aid effort in Central America was retired Gen. John Singlaub. Singlaub was the covert warrior *par excellence.* An OSS veteran and then CIA officer responsible for China and Korea, Singlaub later directed the CIA-linked Special Operations Group infiltrations of North Vietnam, Laos and Cambodia during the Vietnam War—provocative raids conducted with no consultation of Congress.

* His Vietnam-era colleague, then-Air Force Major Harry Aderholt, oversaw special air operations for the CIA in Laos and was Richard Secord's deputy there. Today head of the Air Commandos Association and unconventional warfare editor of *Soldier of Fortune,* he is active with Singlaub in private Central America aid missions.[63] With Singlaub and CIA/military unconventional warfare veteran Edward Lansdale, Aderholt was tapped by Fred Ikle in the Pentagon in May 1984 to advise the military on counterinsurgency tactics in Central America.[64]

* Army Special Forces Master Sergeant John Cupp, a veteran of the elite counterterrorist Delta Force team, retired in December 1985 from the Low Intensity Conflict branch of the Pentagon's Joint Special Operations Agency. He subsequently recruited at least three other Delta Force veterans to help direct contra operations against Nicaragua.[65]

* Edwin Dearborn, a former CIA pilot in Laos, Cambodia, Vietnam and the Congo, is now an aide to Singlaub and helping to advise and train the fledgling contra air force, commanded by Col. Juan Gomez, a former pilot in Somoza's National Guard.[66]

* Col. Robert Dutton oversaw airlift and special operations in the Air Force's Office of Special Plans, which carried out jobs for the CIA. Upon retiring in April 1986, he went to work for Secord at Stanford Technology. Under that cover, he reportedly helped the contras obtain supplies and arranged at least one arms delivery to Iran in October 1986.[67]

* Richard Gadd, a former Air Force lieutenant colonel who served under Dutton at the Air Force Office of Special Plans, later became the liaison between Joint Special Operations Center at Fort Bragg and Joint Special Operations Agency, created to unify Green Berets, Air Force commandos and Navy SEAL units. After retiring in 1982, Gadd set up several private firms to which the Pentagon contracted out sensitive missions for the Delta Force and similar units. One such firm, Airmach, handled secret arms deliveries to the Nicaraguan contras. His American National Management Corp., run with Secord, reportedly included among its clients Southern Air Transport and Stanford Technology, the two firms

most prominently linked to the Iran and contra scandals. One ANMC document boasted, "Special procedures and system methodology have been developed for discreet and expedited services which transcend military disciplines."[68] Gadd reportedly arranged with Clines for arms shipments from Portugal to the contras.[69]

* Richard Meadows was a member of Singlaub's "Studies and Observation Group," which mounted numerous secret missions in Laos and North Vietnam. In 1970 he helped plan the failed Son Tay POW camp raid. After retiring in 1977, he became a civilian adviser to the Army's Delta Force anti-terror team and then a key participant in the 1980 Iran hostage rescue mission. After working briefly for H. Ross Perot, the Dallas billionaire who bankrolled Oliver North's hostage ransom schemes, Meadows moved on to work in Central America, possibly for the contras.[70]

* Andy Messing, a reserve major with Army Special Forces, worked with the NSC's Oliver North to get help from the military in airlifting supplies to the contras. With Aderholt's Air Commandos Association, he has arranged the delivery of medical supplies from World Medical Relief to Guatemala's rural counterinsurgency program.[71]

* H. Ross Perot, the Dallas billionaire owner of Electronic Data Systems, supplied private funds to help the NSC's Oliver North ransom American hostages held in Lebanon, above all the former CIA station chief William Buckley. Although not himself a special operations veteran, he bankrolled Arthur Simons, a former Special Forces colonel and veteran of White Star missions in Laos and the Son Tay POW camp raid,[72] in the successful 1979 rescue of two EDS employees in Iran. Perot then advised President Carter's national security adviser, Zbigniew Brzezinski, on the 1980 embassy rescue mission. And he played a role, with the Army's shadowy ISA, in supporting both "Bo" Gritz's POW searches in Laos and the rescue of Gen. James Dozier, kidnapped by the Red Brigades in Italy.[73]

* Larry Stearns, now a retired Army colonel, directed special operations at the Joint Chiefs of Staff from 1980-82 before reportedly going to work in a private capacity with Richard Gadd's contra supply operation.[74]

* Other, lower-ranking special forces veterans have joined private mercenary fronts like Civilian Military Assistance for action in El Salvador and Nicaragua. Two Americans shot down over Nicaragua in a CIA-supplied helicopter in 1984 were members of the 20th Special Forces Group, attached to the Alabama National Guard.[75] And many of the contra supply pilots, including William Cooper and Eugene Hasenfus, were veterans of Air America and similar CIA air operations that supported Special Forces operations in Laos.

The Controllers

Given the overwhelming representation of special operations veterans in the undercover implementation of White House policies in Iran and Central America, it should come as no surprise that all the key administration overseers of special operations forces played at least some role in those affairs as well. Their involvement, barely publicized or investigated, deserves greater scrutiny.

Until the spring of 1986, the head of the Special Planning Directorate, with policy responsibility for all special operations, was Noel Koch, deputy assistant secretary of defense for international security affairs. Senator William Cohen, R-ME, praised him as "instrumental in revitalizing special operations" and as "the champion of special operations on policy matters."[76] He supervised many of Gen. Secord's activities in the Pentagon before the latter "retired." Koch battled the traditional services to beef up the special units; his foes in turn planted rumors that Koch had suspect loyalties to Israel.[77] According to testimony before Congress, Koch attended a February 1986 meeting with Oliver North, Secord, and two CIA officials to help arrange the Iran arms deals.[78]

Koch's boss, Richard Armitage, also oversees special operations, but may lose some of that responsibility in a recent Pentagon reorganization. A former aide to Erich Von Marbod in Vietnam, he has been accused in the Christic Institute's lawsuit of involvement in the 1970s-era drug trade associated with CIA covert operations in Southeast Asia.[79] Along with Koch, Armitage oversaw Michael Ledeen's consulting for the Pentagon on terrorism. In 1986 Defense Secretary Weinberger assigned him to help manage the secret delivery of U.S. arms to Iran.[80]

Armitage in turn reports to Undersecretary of Defense Fred Ikle, a staunch advocate of special operations capabilities. Ikle sits on the interdepartmental "208 Committee" that plans covert operations, and heads a Pentagon "special coordination staff" that supplies weapons and transportation for CIA operations. He has advocated a particularly militant line against the Sandinistas.[81] Some Senate conservatives believe Ikle fired a former aide to prevent the Iran arms deal from leaking to Congress.[82]

Ikle's main adviser on Central America until January 1987 was Nestor Sanchez. Sanchez took as tough a line as Ikle from his post as assistant secretary of defense for inter-American affairs. A veteran CIA officer with immense experience in the Western Hemisphere, Sanchez worked closely with Gen. Secord, Koch and others on secret military operations to aid the contra effort.[83] He helped place Felix Rodriguez in El Salvador to direct the contra supply effort and approved a "private" shipment of East bloc arms to Central America in 1986.[84] He reportedly left the administration under a cloud, owing to his involvement with the contras.[85]

Finally, Oliver North, the NSC officer who ran amok carrying out covert administration policies, reportedly met Singlaub and Secord as a young Marine officer in Vietnam assigned to counterinsurgency missions. He claims to have been "in the Special Operations Force, team commander" and to have undertaken "classified missions" in Laos.[86] Years later, put in charge of counterterrorist and other special operations at the NSC, North called upon this highly experienced group of clandestine operators for top secret missions of his own, knowing they had the contacts, skills and deniability needed to pull off projects that would otherwise have leaked within days.[87]

The Responsibility of Congress

Such individuals will have an ever stronger institutional base in the future, thanks to efforts by a bipartisan team of congressional enthusiasts for special operations.

In August 1985, reflecting a consensus in Congress, the House Armed Services Subcommittee on Military Readiness named a Special Operations Panel. Its chairman, Rep. Earl Hutto, D-FL, declared that "the most valuable service the panel can perform is holding the services' feet to the fire and insuring that more conventional and lower priority programs do not supplant SOF requirements in service budgets."[88]

In June 1986, the House's leading SOF advocate, Rep. Dan Daniel, D-VA, introduced a bill to create a National Special Operations Agency, with a civilian director reporting to the president directly through the secretary of defense. The bill enjoyed bipartisan support, including from the House Armed Services chairman Les Aspin, D-WI.[89]

On the Senate side, William Cohen, R-ME, and Sam Nunn, D-GA, took a different approach to boosting SOF: keeping it within the military chain of command, but bringing all special operations under a unified command headed by a four-star general and reporting to a new assistant defense secretary. Like Daniel, they aimed to "greatly improve the effectiveness, funding levels, readiness, force structure, and command and control of special operations forces."[90] Ironically, in Senate debate Cohen quoted retired Maj. Gen. John Singlaub on the need for greater integration of SOF functions.[91] And in a chilling argument for a boost in special operations capabilities, Cohen noted in early 1986 that "today we face a situation in Central America which is in many respects similar to Vietnam and yet...we are not organized effectively to deal with it."[92]

The final legislation closely followed the Senate model. It mandated a unified military command for special operations forces, a new board within the National Security Council for "low intensity conflict" and an accompanying presidential adviser on the same, and a new assistant secretary position within the Pentagon to oversee SOF.[93] The bureaucratic structure is now in place for a continued expansion of special operations resources and missions.

Defense Secretary Weinberger has assured Congress of his commitment to a four-year, $8.5 billion expansion of special operations manpower, procurement and training. "Through the rest of this century," he told the Senate Armed Services Committee in January 1987, "low-intensity conflict will be the most likely challenge to U.S. national interests."[94] Defense insiders predict that Congress will appropriate the money even if Weinberger reneges.[95]

If Congress exposes a few individual wrongdoers while strengthening the very institutions that made their abuses possible, it will lay the groundwork not for a more responsible foreign policy, but for a recurrence of the sort of back-alley crimes whose revelation has left this administration paralyzed and discredited.

X.
The Deeper Malady:
From Terrorism to Covert Action

A political crisis can rend or it can heal: everything depends on whether institutional reforms follow the trauma of scandal.

Precious few deep remedies have been conceived or proposed in the months since the contra and Iran scandals began dominating the headlines. Blame has fallen to individuals, not the system: a few overzealous officials derailed White House policy while the president slept at the switch. And as in Watergate, the focus of attention has shifted rapidly away from more significant issues to the coverup: did Oliver North shred the documents? Did his secretary alter key memos?[1]

The investigations have produced enormous riches of information but a poverty of analysis. Members of Congress and media commentators have proposed limiting the number of military officers in the National Security Council and restricting the NSC's authority to conduct independent operations. Senate intelligence committee chairman David Boren (D-OK) even identifies the "underlying problem" as the "collapse of the concept of a bipartisan foreign policy" and proposes that "disarray...be replaced by bipartisan unity." Such thoughts pass for profundity in Washington.[2]

The Tower Commission, appointed by President Reagan to study the affair, has powerfully shaped the public's perception of the crisis as a simple and ultimately innocuous failure of "management style."[3] Its report portrays an inattentive and inadequately briefed president misled by a handful of overzealous NSC officers. Faulting individuals and not the system, it warns against "rearranging organizational blocks or passing new laws."[4]

Yet the Tower panel did propose one organizational reform—for Congress. "We recommend that Congress consider replacing the existing intelligence committees of the respective Houses with a new joint committee with a restricted staff to oversee the intelligence community..." Along with returning the institutional home of covert operations to the CIA from the NSC, the commission would strengthen the CIA's hand vis-à-vis Congress.[5]

That single recommendation sums up everything that is wrong with the debate over the current foreign policy crisis. The real scandal of the Iran and contra affairs is not the secret delivery of arms, nor even the lying and hypocrisy that went in tandem. The scandal—so far as Americans are concerned—is the subversion of law, congressional authority, and the will of the public in order to produce immoral and counterproductive policies. And the underlying problem is common to all covert operations: how can they be kept accountable? How can abuses be prevented in a climate of secrecy? How can secrecy and power not breed corruption? How can a democracy function effectively when vital information is kept from the American people?

These questions go to the heart of the Reagan administration's foreign policy, so often has it relied on covert intervention rather than public diplomacy. In six years, President Reagan has approved at least 50 major covert operations, more than any president since John Kennedy. "U.S. agents have armed anti-communist rebels, helped stage a successful revolution, manipulated elections, mounted propaganda campaigns, blocked supplies to leftist guerrillas and swapped weapons for American hostages," according to *Miami Herald* correspondent Alfonso Chardy. "In the United States...the administration has influenced press coverage on Central America and monitored Americans opposed to U.S. policies there."[6]

And in the name of preserving its vital secrets from exposure, the administration has made a fetish of security measures: reviving the Espionage Act against leakers, hacking away at the Freedom of Information Act, proposing polygraph tests and life-time secrecy oaths for tens of thousands of government employees and cracking down on scientific papers and commercial databases. Domestic freedoms no less than foreign governments and movements have come under assault.

The Price of Covert Operations

Congress as a whole has never admitted what both champions and critics of the CIA have long maintained: covert actions cannot be both truly accountable and effective at the same time. When closely regulated, scrutinized, debated and second-guessed, covert actions remain secret only a short time. This logic has persuaded every administration since Harry Truman's to choose secrecy over accountability, in the name of national security. And it has persuaded every Congress since then to bow to presidential authority in the final showdown. Irangate was merely the latest product of that syndrome.

The temptations of power and secrecy overcame law and constitutional authority from the CIA's founding by the National Security Act of 1947. The agency's first general counsel, Lawrence Houston, was quickly called upon to interpret the meaning of the act's phrase assigning the CIA "such other duties and functions related to intelligence affecting the national security as the National Security Council may from time to time direct." Houston concluded that "taken out of context and without knowledge of [the act's] history, these Sections could bear almost unlimited interpretation. In our opinion, however, either [propaganda or commando type] activity would be an unwarranted extension of the functions authorized by" the act. "We do not believe that there was any thought in the minds of Congress that the Central Intelligence Agency under this authority would take positive action for subversion and sabotage." Any such missions would necessitate going to Congress "for authority and funds."[7]

A mere three months later, the NSC directed the CIA to initiate psychological warfare operations against the USSR. Six months after that, the NSC added paramilitary, economic warfare and political action operations to the list. Covert action was officially born. Future administrations would justify such authority on the basis of the president's inherent powers in foreign affairs and the willingness of Congress to appropriate money for the CIA. In effect, covert operations gave successive presidents the power to legislate as well as execute foreign policy with secret resources. Not until the 1980 Intelligence Oversight Act did Congress supply clear authority for covert operations.[8]

On the other hand, Congress never showed the courage to rein in what had become a routine usurpation of authority. The closest it ever came to making fundamental reforms was in the mid-1970s, when House and Senate investigations of intelligence abuses uncovered evidence of assassination plots, illegal mail opening, illicit drug testing, massive domestic spying and sabotage of domestic political movements. The Senate committee, named after its chairman Frank Church of Idaho, also looked at several covert operations, including the destabilization of Chilean President Salvador Allende, that had blackened America's image throughout the world.

The Church Committee warned that covert operations had developed a dangerous "bureaucratic momentum." Numbering some 900 between 1960 and 1975, such operations were becoming "increasingly costly to America's interest and reputation," the committee concluded. But instead of proposing truly meaningful reforms—other than the creation of permanent oversight committees—the panel merely implored that covert operations be reserved for "grave threats to American security" and be "consistent with publicly defined U.S. foreign policy goals." *New York Times* columnist Anthony Lewis called its recommendations "a gamble that the American system of checks and balances can work even in the powerful secret world of intelligence."[9]

America is losing that gamble. It is losing because the public's sense of concern did not survive the immediate scandals uncovered by the investigations. Covert operations only dimly affect the average citizen—until they trigger a foreign or domestic crisis. General indifference finally greeted Church's report on intelligence abuses. "It all lasted too long and the media, the Congress and the people lost interest," observed Rep. Otis Pike (D-NY), who headed the House investigation. His committee's report was never officially published and its conclusions were ignored.[10]

The ascendancy of a Democratic administration changed little. President Carter still withheld from Congress advance notice of covert operations, despite the promise of his 1978 Executive Order 12036; Attorney General Griffin Bell held that guarantees of "prior" notice really meant "timely" notice.[11] Carter sought further reductions in congressional reporting requirements and a "revitalization" of the CIA in the wake of the Soviet invasion of Afghanistan and political turmoil in Iran.[12] And he asked for sweeping exemptions from the Freedom of Information Act for the CIA, FBI, National Security Agency "and other intelligence agency components."[13]

And when legislators tried to write a new CIA charter to limit presidential powers and check abuses, Carter's people fought every inch of the way. Exhausted liberals caved in. To complaints from the American Civil Liberties Union that the proposed charter was too permissive, Senator Joseph Biden (D-Del) said, "Let me tell you something, fellas. The folks don't care. The average American could care less right now about any of this...You keep talking about public concern. There ain't none."[14]

In the end, in any event, the 1980 Intelligence Oversight Act required advance reporting of covert operations except under unusual circumstances (the loophole that permitted President Reagan to conduct the Iran arms deal without notifying Congress), but cut the number of oversight committees from eight to two to satisfy complaints from the intelligence community that leaks from Capitol Hill undercut the CIA's effectiveness and access to foreign intelligence sources. That year, Congress made it illegal to reveal the names of agents.

Yet the "reforms" accomplished little because they did not touch the underlying incentives for political abuses inherent in covert operations. "When Congress collapsed from eight to two committees, many of us believed there would be a new day of openness and trust," complained Rep. Charlie Rose (D-NC), former head of House intelligence committee. "That day never came. It was foot-dragging and obfuscation as usual."[15]

The Reagan administration took such foot-dragging to new extremes. It understood "oversight" to mean Congress should overlook rather than review CIA practices. Its spirit was summed up in the declaration of the 1980 transition team report on intelligence: "Decisive action at the CIA is the keystone in achieving a reversal of the unwise policies of the past decade."[16] Congressional meddling could not be permitted to stand in the way of that reversal.

Perhaps the most blatant example of this contempt of Congress was the CIA's failure to notify the proper committees of the mining of harbors in Nicaragua, a violation of international law protested not only by the Managua regime, but by most of its Western European trading partners. (Such violations of the rights of foreigners figure nowhere in any official investigation to date of the Iran-contra connection.) The Nicaraguan government itself announced the mining on January 3, 1984, but the CIA first mentioned it in passing to the House intelligence committee on January 31. The Senate committee first heard of it in March. The CIA released major details only on March 27, to the House committee. CIA Director William Casey made it clear that what Congress didn't ask for explicitly, he would not tell them. The Republican Senator David Durenberger admitted, "We have to share, as a committee, some responsibility for the situation."[17]

Only two months later, the CIA reportedly failed to inform the House committee of its covert intervention in El Salvador's election on behalf of Jose Napoleon Duarte, the Christian Democratic candidate for president. *New York Times* reporter Martin Tolchin noted at the time that "members of Congress rotate on and off the intelligence committees, so that the intelligence community knows that it can outwait its severest critic."[18]

Surely the most significant breakdown of oversight, however, came in the fall of 1985. Reporters from Associated Press and major newspapers had broken the story that an obscure NSC official, Oliver North, was advising and raising funds for the contras in apparent violation of the Boland amendment. Rep. Lee Hamilton (D-IN), chairman of the House Intelligence Committee, vowed to hold hearings to get to the bottom of the matter. Rep. Michael Barnes (D-MD) demanded that the White House produce records of North's activities for his Western Hemisphere subcommittee. Barnes came away empty handed. Hamilton was unable even to convene a hearing; all he could get was an informal briefing by Robert McFarlane and the national security adviser's "assurance" that North and others in the NSC were respecting the law. Ultimately, Hamilton and Barnes were stymied because Congress was politically divided; those members favoring aid to the contras didn't want to know the truth. The impasse led a despondent Rep. George Brown Jr. (D-CA) to declare that the oversight law "is not working."[19]

What little information the committees did pry out of the CIA convinced some members that covert action was out of control. "The planning is being handled sloppily," Vermont Sen. Patrick Leahy said with uncanny prescience. "Sooner or later they're going to get caught with their pants down and we'll all read about it in the newspapers."[20]

As serious as the inadequacy of oversight has been the legitimacy lent to covert operations by the appearance of oversight. Congress appears to grant its stamp of approval to operations it does not halt. Knowledgeable critics on the oversight committees suffer a special handicap: they cannot speak freely about what they know. "We become the buffer for the CIA to do whatever they want," observed Rep. Norman Mineta (D-CA). "They tell us, but we can't tell anybody, and they hide behind our skirts."[21]

Even when it has the facts, Congress rarely blocks covert projects. Most members are content to let the president take the heat if something goes wrong and unwilling to face responsibility for making foreign policy.

A Blank Check for "Counterterrorism"

But that predisposition has been heavily conditioned by historical circumstances. In particular, successive presidents have manipulated popular fears to argue convincingly for centralizing power and excluding

Congress from the making of national security policy. Over time the specific "threats" have changed, but the reliance of presidents on the public's unquestioning reaction to them has not.

Since World War II, the most important ideological prop to presidential power has been anticommunism. More often than not, the charge was false and the intervention counter-productive, not to mention an exercise in imperial power. Having defined the Soviet Union as the preeminent threat to American security, Washington argued by extension that Soviet manipulation lay behind everything from turmoil in the developing world to political challenges from the left in Western Europe. Thus nearly any form of foreign intervention could be justified in the name of anticommunism. The CIA's overthrow of Iranian Prime Minister Mossadegh in 1953 installed the Shah on the throne and sowed the seeds of the radical Khomeini revolution. Its 1954 coup against the Arbenz regime in Guatemala spawned an ongoing guerrilla war there and hardened the Marxist, revolutionary left elsewhere in Central America with results that haunt the Reagan administration today. Although Washington claimed otherwise, those CIA targets—and many others—were nationalists, not Soviet surrogates.

With the advent of "detente" and the visit of arch-anticommunist Richard Nixon to the People's Republic of China, anticommunism lost much of its emotive appeal and thus its effectiveness in mobilizing Congress behind unquestioned acceptance of covert operations. The Nixon administration discovered a new and seemingly uglier menace to take its place: drugs. Nixon's "war on drugs" opened loopholes in congressional restrictions on foreign police training, provided cover for counterinsurgency campaigns from Burma to Mexico and even justified plots to assassinate foreign political leaders. All were programs picked up from the CIA in the guise of narcotics enforcement.[22]

Ronald Reagan's contribution was to fully develop the potential of the ultimate bogeyman: terrorism. His predecessors, Presidents Ford and Carter, had identified drugs and terrorism as two foreign intelligence targets of such unquestioned importance and sensitivity as to justify barring congressional supervision.[23] But the Reagan White House mastered the exploitation of public fears aroused by highly publicized terrorist acts as a means of restoring covert operations to their central role in presidential foreign policy. (The seizure of the American embassy in Tehran had dramatized the issue like no other event.) By defining terrorism sweepingly to include even guerrilla wars and insurgencies against uniformed armies— but never anything the U.S. or its allies do—the administration expanded the rationale for anti-terrorist interventions. By inventing a new category of "narco-terrorism" with which to brand certain rebel groups, the administration conjured up even more nightmarish images.[24] And by defining diverse terrorist outrages as "Soviet sponsored," the administration dealt the final blow to detente.

The terrorist threat provides the perfect rationale for secrecy and covert operations. Responding to terrorist attacks requires speedy intervention and absolute secrecy, not lengthy debate with Congress. And if anyone doubts the means, the end of stamping out terrorism justifies them as well as anything could.

Paradigm Shift

The intellectual genesis of Reagan's anti-terror revolution goes back to 1970s, when cold-war conservatives were looking for new mobilizing issues to replace detente and human rights. The concept of Soviet-sponsored international terrorism as new mode of warfare against the West was kicked off at the Jerusalem Conference on International Terrorism in July 1979. Led by a group of top Israeli intelligence officers and political leaders, the conference was also studded with those Americans most actively seeking a renewal of the clandestine approach to American foreign policy. The participants included former CIA director George Bush and former CIA deputy director Ray Cline; the hawkish former Air Force intelligence chief Major General George Keegan, who resigned from the Air Force in 1977 to protest the Carter administration's estimate of the Soviet threat; Harvard's Soviet scholar Richard Pipes, whom Bush had recruited to bring the CIA's strategic estimates of Soviet power more in line with worst-case military thinking; some prominent neoconservatives including *Commentary* magazine editor Norman Podhoretz; the newspaper columnist and Reagan's 1980 debating coach George Will; and reporter Claire Sterling, who two years later would publish this faction's bible, *The Terror Network.*[25]

At the conference, Ray Cline developed the theme that terror was not a random response of frustrated minorities, but rather "a preferred instrument" of East bloc policy adopted after 1969 "when the KGB persuaded the Politburo of the Communist Party of the Soviet Union to accept the PLO as a major political instrument in the Mideast and to subsidize its terrorist policies by freely giving money, training, arms and co-ordinated communications." Terrorism, he maintained, had "hardened into a system—an international troublemaking system." The British propagandist

Robert Moss extended the theory to Iran, where he charged that a Soviet-controlled PLO unit was functioning "as the nucleus of a secret police, a revolutionary SAVAK." And conference participants singled out the Sandinistas for their alleged international terrorist connections.[26]

This formulation was as significant for what it ignored as for what it put in. Left out of the equation was any mention of terrorist acts by CIA-trained Cuban exiles, Israeli ties to Red Brigades[27] or the function of death squads from Argentina to Guatemala. Soviet sponsorship, real or imagined, had become the defining characteristic of terrorism, not simply an explanation for its prevalence. Moreover, there was no inclination whatsoever to include under the rubric of terror bombings of civilians, for example, or any other acts carried out by government forces rather than small individual units.

The Heritage Foundation, a conservative, Washington-based think-tank that rode Ronald Reagan's coat-tails to influence, saw these themes as as a potent vehicle for reversing political reforms of the Watergate/Church committee era. Its master political blueprint, prepared before Reagan's inauguration to guide his transition team, urged "presidential emphasis on the nature of the threat, repeated speeches on the escalation of Soviet bloc intelligence activities, the nature of the terrorist threat and its international dimensions and the reality of subversion." Such tactics, the report hoped, would allow the CIA to regain authority to conduct "surreptitious entries," mail opening and other powers lost in the 1970s.[28]

The Reagan team took the report to heart. The lead item on the agenda of the its first NSC meeting on January 26, 1981 was terrorism. The next day, President Reagan declared, "Let terrorists be aware that when the rules of international behavior are violated, our policy will be one of swift and effective retribution."[29]

At his first news conference as secretary of state, on January 28, Alexander Haig gave terrorism an address. He charged that the Kremlin was seeking to "foster, support and expand" terror around world and was "training, funding and equipping" terrorist armies. And he vowed that "international terrorism will take the place of human rights" as the new administration's top priority.[31]

Jerusalem Conference alumna Claire Sterling was on hand to supply "massive proof that the Soviet Union and its surrogates, over the last decade, have provided the weapons, training and sanctuary for a worldwide terror network aimed at the destabilization of Western democratic society." Her book *The Terror Network*, excerpted that March in the *New York Times Magazine* and *New Republic*, branded the 1970s "Fright Decade I" and warned that Fright Decade II was at hand.[32]

Sterling's book, with all its evidentiary and methodological weaknesses, was all that administration polemicists could cite to justify their claims. A CIA report drafted after Haig's outburst directly rebutted his claim that most terrorism found sponsorship from the Soviet Union. CIA Director William Casey sent the report back for further review.[33] Casey also asked the more conservative Defense Intelligence Agency for a report, but found it inadequate as well. So a third report was prepared—but it, too, concluded that Soviets were not directly equipping or training terrorists, nor did they have a master plan for terrorism.[34] What little evidence there was against the Soviets came from unverifiable claims of a Czech defector, Gen. Jan Sejna, whose credibility the CIA came to doubt.[35]

"There's just no real evidence for it," one administration official said of the Haig thesis.[36] Another high administration source lamented that such charges put "the American intelligence community in a terrible political bind. The CIA has been requested to look harder. When they come back and say it isn't true, that they don't see the hand of Russia everywhere, they're told, 'Goddamn it, you are either stupid or you aren't trying.'"[37]

FBI chief William Webster threw a little cold water of his own on official claims pointing out that the number of bombings had declined steadily in the United States, from 100 in 1977 to 20 in 1980. He added, "I can say that there is no real evidence of Soviet-sponsored terrorism within the United States."[38]

The administration was on the defensive. Since the evidence wasn't good enough, officials fell back on altering the data. Statistics on terrorist incidents were changed to include not only acts but also "threats," thus at one swoop doubling the apparent numbers.[39]

A more effective and subtle counter came from the private sector. Claire Sterling impugned the CIA as "the least informed and most timid of any intelligence service on this issue."[40] Michael Ledeen, Sterling's long-time journalistic collaborator, who would later become the key emissary in the Iran arms plot, also accused the agency of incompetence. "They are scared in the [State Department and CIA] bureaucracy," Ledeen maintained, "because if Haig is right about the Russians, then they have failed in their jobs." In terms almost identical to Haig's, Ledeen called the Soviet Union "the fomenter, supporter and creator of terrorism" worldwide. In the late spring of 1981, Haig appointed him an adviser on international terrorism.[41]

The Wall Street Journal editorial writers weighed in as well. They claimed—without having seen the analysis—that the CIA document's "underlying reasoning would not survive the light of public day." The editorial dismissed appeals to the evidence: "no one should be allowed to argue successfully that because there's evidence of the Soviet influence in some places but not in others, the whole Soviet-connection theory must be thrown out." And most important, the editorial insisted on the broadest possible definition of terrorism to justify a counter-revolutionary policy abroad: "no one should be allowed to say without challenge that Soviet support for national liberation movements is by definition different from Soviet support for terrorism."[42]

The themes formulated by Sterling, Ledeen and the *Journal* served conservatives as a hammer with which to hit not only detente, but also the Carter-era CIA. Cold-war interventionists portrayed the CIA as crippled by excessive oversight, misplaced human rights concerns, a deplorable timidity toward covert action and the purge of experts in paramilitary war. The terrorism issue thus ignited demands for a sweeping bureaucratic upheaval in the intelligence community.

That February, for example, Senator Sam Nunn (D-GA) applauded Haig's speech and called for "a permanent, highly professional organization to plan and train on a continual basis" against terrorism. He stressed:

> One of the most important ingredients must be a strong, revitalized intelligence community...No antiterrorist capability can be adequate without excellent intelligence, including covert capabilities which have largely been demolished...We must... repeal some laws and executive orders which go far beyond constitutional requirements or court decisions and which have resulted from a massive overreaction to the Watergate/Vietnam era.[43]

Neo-conservative and intelligence-connected circles quickly mobilized public support for giving the administration and CIA a freer hand abroad. Writer Midge Decter (the wife of Norman Podhoretz) founded the the Committee for the Free World in February 1981 to call attention to the terrorist threat and revive America's interventionist impulse. According to the *New York Times*, Decter

> said the idea for the committee emerged almost two years ago after she and others attended a meeting in Jerusalem on international terrorism. She said she came away convinced of the need for action against those who kidnap and throw bombs, many of whom are trained in the Soviet Union and Cuba, but also concerned about a spreading practice of indulging in self-criticism to the point of condoning terrorism as being justified.[44]

The members included Michael Ledeen; former CIA deputy director of plans Ray Cline; Leo Cherne, chairman of the President's Foreign

Intelligence Advisory Board; and Paul Henze, former CIA station chief in Turkey, who would take the lead with Sterling in publicizing alleged Soviet-bloc complicity in the attempted assassination of Pope John Paul II.[45]

Lest domestic dissent at home hamstring administration plans for a tougher foreign policy, the terrorism issue served to break down barriers to surveillance and intimidation of domestic critics. The new Republican Senate formed a special subcommittee on security and terrorism in February. Senator Strom Thurmond (R-SC), chairman of the parent Judiciary Committee, predicted it would be "one of the most important subcommittees of the entire Congress."[46] The subcommittee's chief counsel, Joel Lisker, pledged that "we will do everything we can to modify and eliminate" restrictions on infiltration and surveillance of domestic groups. Members said they would strongly urge the administration to remove other restraints on the intelligence agencies. Witnesses at their first hearing included Claire Sterling and Michael Ledeen, who reiterated their warnings of the Soviet threat.[47]

In March, the Reagan administration moved on the same front. It came up with a draft executive order that would allow sweeping additions to the CIA's authority, particularly in area of domestic operations previously ruled off-limits.[48] Several months later, the administration also proposed amending the Freedom of Information Act to exempt files relating to organized crime, foreign counterintelligence and terrorism. "It isn't an accident that they picked terrorism and foreign counterintelligence," observed Jack Landau, director of Reporters Committee for Freedom of the Press. "That's the mandate that the FBI used to violate peoples' civil liberties."[49]

The proposals naturally met opposition from civil libertarians and some members of Congress. Liberals who had not abandoned the Carter-era commitment to human rights deplored Reagan's apparent double standard on terrorism. In March, for example, the administration announced its intention to lift the ban on arms sales to Argentina, imposed three years earlier by Carter because of the mass killing of civilians committed by the military.[50] And the CIA was reported to be "considering the renewal of cooperation with anti-Castro Cuban exiles as part of a general expansion of its covert operations."[51]

But Congress as a whole was in no mood to quibble over such inconsistencies. After the humiliation of the Tehran embassy crisis and the Reagan election sweep, it granted Reagan almost everything he wanted in the way of intelligence resources. The first three years of the Reagan presidency saw a 50 percent increase in CIA appropriations and a five-fold increase in the number of authorized covert operations. And after all the layoffs of the Nixon-through-Carter years, the CIA workforce grew by over a third.[52] The White House now had the tools and the incentive to go undercover with the implementation of its foreign policy agenda.

Libya Bashing

This initial vote of confidence in the CIA was not enough. The administration redoubled its domestic propaganda campaign to persuade the nation of the virulent menace of foreign terrorism. If no one could find convincing evidence of Soviet-sponsored terror, they could of Libyan support for violent European and Middle Eastern groups. And the administration could magnify the evidence until Americans felt positively threatened by what was in fact a weak and ineffectual power—and one that, far from being a surrogate of the USSR, did not even let the Soviets base ships at its ports.

The campaign against Libya started at the *New Republic*, whose line on terrorism and foreign policy in general was shaped increasingly by editor Martin Peretz's strong political commitment to Israel. The once-liberal magazine had begun publishing regular articles by Michael Ledeen and former *Newsweek* correspondent Arnaud de Borchgrave, a Jerusalem conference participant and a vociferous exponent of the theory that Soviet disinformation had duped the American media. (De Borchgrave would later become editor of the *Washington Times*, owned by the Rev. Sun Myung Moon.) Now, in March, the *New Republic* excerpted a chapter from Claire Sterling's new book on terrorism. Entitled "Qaddafi Spells Chaos," the kicker read "A murder, a maniac—and Moscow's man."[53]

On July 26, 1981 *Newsweek* reported that the administration was gearing up a major effort to topple Gadhafi, involving a "disinformation" campaign to erode the colonel's domestic support, formation of a "counter government" of Libyan exiles and a program of paramilitary and sabotage operations inside Libya to stir up discontent and expose Gadhafi's vulnerability.

The next month, provocative U.S. naval exercises off Libya's coast provoked a rash—and desired—response from Gadhafi. U.S. jets downed two Libyan fighters in a dogfight over Gulf of Sidra.

In September, columnist Jack Anderson confirmed that CIA director Casey had concocted a disinformation campaign to mislead the American press about Libya by planting false stories abroad. The stories accused

Gadhafi of supporting the slave trade in Mauritania, mismanaging his country's petrodollar accounts and stirring up terrorism.[54]

On October 19, *Newsweek* passed along a provocative leak that the administration was talking with Egypt about a possible invasion of Libya. After the August confrontation over the Gulf of Sidra, according to this account, Gadhafi hatched a scheme to kill the American ambassador in Rome, Maxwell Rabb. The plot "was aborted when Italian police deported ten suspected Libyan hit men," *Newsweek* reported. "Washington officials now believe Kaddafi has called off the assassination attempt, but they are not entirely certain." It also mentioned in passing that U.S. intelligence had "picked up evidence that Kaddafi had hatched yet another assassination plot—this time against President Reagan."

The plot continued to thicken—with numerous ominous leaks but no evidence. On October 25 the *New York Times* revived the Libyan plot to murder Rabb, reporting that he had been rushed out of the country "without even a change of clothes." (Other sources insisted he had simply left for Washington to lobby for the sale of AWACS to Saudi Arabia.[55]) Gadhafi hotly denied the charge and noted correctly that to carry out such a plot would be suicidal.[56]

November saw a positive flurry of reports linking Gadhafi to terrorist plots. *Newsweek* cited reports of Libyan plans to attack four U.S. embassies in Western Europe.[57] Secretary of State Haig blamed Gadhafi for hiring a killer to target Christian Chapman, the U.S. charge d'affaires in Paris.[58] *Time* magazine joined in with a report that National Security Advisor Richard Allen had discussed with French officials plans to assassinate Gadhafi.[59] And in late November claims surfaced that Gadhafi planned to kill the president of Niger.[60]

But the most significant theme in this strategy of tension surfaced with *Newsweek*. Its voluble U.S. intelligence sources tipped the magazine that "Kaddafi is plotting to assassinate the president and other top American officials," including Vice President Bush and Secretaries Haig and Weinberger. The average reader could sympathize with administration officials who were said to "openly admit that they would be delighted if someone else killed Kaddafi."[61]

The notorious Reagan assassination plot story hit the front pages of the *New York Times* on December 4. "The government has received detailed reports that five terrorists trained in Libya entered the United States last weekend with plans to assassinate President Reagan or other senior officials," the paper revealed. A "huge nationwide search for the potential assassins" was underway. Later reports added lurid flourishes:

no less than Carlos "the Jackal," the infamous Venezuelan terrorist, was on his way to kill the president.[62]

Fed a steady diet of Gadhafi rumors, the American public could be excused for believing President Reagan's dismissal of the Libyan's denials: "We have the evidence, and he knows it....I wouldn't believe a word he says if I were you."[63]

A few skeptics raised questions. It seemed doubtful that any one informant (as reported) could supply so much detail on each member of the hit team, that Libya would send so large a squad and that the East bloc would have risked training the assassins.[64] Government sources told the *Washington Post* that reports of the plot included "lots of speculation" based on "a plausible scenario" resting on "a limited amount of knowledge."[65]

Haynes Johnson, a veteran *Post* correspondent, noted "It's almost as if public opinion were being prepared for dramatic action—say a strike against Libya or Qaddafi himself...It is reminiscent of the talk about Castro in the days when the United States was planning the Bay of Pigs invasion, and in fact, commissioning assassination schemes against Castro."[66]

Then, as mysteriously as they had appeared, the hit teams vanished. By late December, officials decided "the hit squads have become inactive." Indeed, "the information about the hit squads has been and still is mushy," sources told the *Washington Post*. "The United States still does not know for sure whether any members of the two hit squads ever left Libya."[67]

Only in the context of the latest Iran arms scandal has the public finally learned that the source of the fanciful "hit squad" story was Manucher Ghorbanifar, a former Iranian SAVAK agent with close ties to Israeli intelligence. According to the *Washington Post*, the CIA believed he was a lying schemer who "had made up the hit-squad story in order to cause problems for one of Israel's enemies."[68]

These details confirm what the *Los Angeles Times* had learned in 1981: "Israeli intelligence, not the Reagan administration, was a major source of some of the most dramatic published reports about a Libyan assassination team allegedly sent to kill President Reagan and other top U.S. officials... Israel, which informed sources said has 'wanted an excuse to go in and bash Libya for a long time,' may be trying to build American public support for a strike against Libyan strongman Moammar Kadafi, these sources said."[69]

In short, the whole story was an intelligence provocation from start to finish. So, it would now appear, was Israel's promotion of Ghorbanifar as a reliable go-between for Washington with Iran in 1985.

But if it served Israeli interests to discredit Gadhafi, it also served the Reagan administration. The deadly threat from Libya swept aside public objections to a sweeping expansion of CIA powers. Never mind that the reality, as evidenced by the 1986 bombing attack on Tripoli, that in fact it was Reagan who planned and attempted to assassinate Gadhafi, not the reverse.

Unleashing the CIA

On the very day the *New York Times* reported the existence of the Libyan hit squad, President Reagan announced his signing of Executive Order 12333, a controversial and long-awaited blueprint for the intelligence community's resurgence.

When first drafted in March 1981 under the supervision of an interagency task force led by CIA officials, the order provoked instant controversy. "The proposed order would recast Mr. Carter's [1978] decree in terms that authorize, rather than restrict, the collection of intelligence information and the use of such techniques as searches, surveillance and infiltration," the *New York Times* had noted that spring. "The existing order says that intelligence agencies may collect, store and disseminate information about a person who is 'reasonably believed' to be acting on behalf of a foreign power or engaging in international terrorist or narcotics activities. The draft order drops the requirement for a 'reasonable' belief." Significantly, the *Times* added that the revised order had grown out of a meeting held at the outset of the administration "in which intelligence officials discussed terrorism with President Reagan. The White House asked various agencies to suggest changes in intelligence regulations to improve antiterrorism capabilities and approved a suggestion by the CIA for a study group to make specific recommendations."[70]

As Congress reviewed successive drafts, Republican Sen. David Durenberger warned the order would "give credence to many of the public's fears and worst-case scenarios of government misuse of power."[71]

But the timing of Reagan's announcement of the final order ensured a minimum of protest. Coming on the heels of so much talk of Libyan plots, his stress on the dangers of terrorism sold the plan. "The American people are well aware that the security of their country—and in an age of terrorism, their personal safety as well—is tied to the strength and efficiency of our intelligence gathering organization," Reagan maintained. "An approach that emphasizes suspicion and mistrust of our own intelligence efforts can undermine this nation's ability to confront the increasing challenge of espionage and terrorism...We need to free ourselves from the negative attitudes of the past and look to meeting the needs of the country."[72]

Aside from opening the door to a renewal of domestic espionage—a policy shift that may explain the rash of burglaries suffered by organizations critical of administration policy on Central America[73]—the order also contained an obscure loophole through which the NSC's covert operators would later slip. The order directed that "No agency except the CIA...may conduct any special activity *unless the President determines that another agency is more likely to achieve a particular objective.*"[74]

Washington Becomes Militant

Ongoing political turmoil in the Middle East ensured that terrorism would continue to occupy center stage in the administration's foreign policy agenda.

The antiterrorist fervor reached a new plateau after the April 1983 bombing of the U.S. embassy in Beirut—wiping out the entire CIA station—and the devastating bombing of the Beirut Marine barracks in October 1983. Although the latter suicide attack targeted uniformed military personnel and not civilians, administration spokesmen and the media denounced it as the most brutal act of terrorism to date. In response, the Joint Chiefs that January formed the Joint Special Operations Agency to coordinate special operations against terrorists.[75] And Congress would enthusiastically cooperate in promoting the buildup of SOF counterinsurgency forces in the name of fighting terrorism.[76]

On April 3, 1984, President Reagan signed National Security Decision Directive 138, which guided 26 government agencies in drafting counter-terrorist measures. Deputy Assistant Secretary of Defense Noel Koch said it "represents a quantum leap in countering terrorism, from the reactive mode to recognition that pro-active steps are needed." Although it did not authorize U.S. "hit squads," as reportedly recommended by senior Pentagon officials and the NSC's Oliver North, the directive was said to permit "the use of force in other forms, such as by FBI and CIA paramilitary teams and Pentagon military squads." Administration sources called the aggressive plan an "effort to give the cloak and dagger back to the Central Intelligence Agency. The campaign will include pre-emptive strikes and direct reprisals" based on Israeli models. Officials admitted that the distinction between retaliation and assassination was mainly rhetorical.[77]

Jeff McConnell observed:

> This new policy on counterterrorism could not have come at a
> better time for the Reagan administration. Its effort to end the
> so-called 'Vietnam Syndrome' had blown up in Lebanon.
> Support in congress for war in Nicaragua was at an all-time
> low...Though the 1984 directive had been drafted with more
> limited purposes in mind, administration planners now saw in it
> a way to resuscitate its foreign adventures. Yet the policy lacked
> a rationale large enough to sustain so much. It was one thing to
> make a case for commando assaults against hijacked airliners,
> quite another to sell military action all over the world as
> counterterrorism. What was needed was an ideological frame-
> work for the new policy that would spell out terrorism's threat
> in a way clear enough to enlist popular sympathy and, at the
> same time, comprehensive enough to justify action against all
> the Third World nations that Washington opposed."[78]

That framework was found in the concept of "state-sponsored
terrorism," and more particularly, the presumption of Soviet sponsorship
of terrorist cadre that Haig and other administration officials had pushed
from the opening days of the administration. Secretary of State George
Shultz recalled those old themes along with the new counterrorism stance
in late June at a Washington conference sponsored by the Jonathan
Institute. He blamed the Soviets for providing "financial, logistic and
training support for terrorists worldwide." They "use terrorist groups for
their own purposes, and their goal is always the same: to weaken liberal
democracy and undermine world stability," he charged. The threat called
for tougher countermeasures. "It is time to think long, hard and seriously
about more active means of defense—about defense through appropriate
preventive or pre-emptive actions against terrorist groups before they
strike." Shultz added, "We will need to strengthen our capabilities in the
area of intelligence and quick reaction." Those two areas encompassed the
CIA and Pentagon special operations forces.[79]

CIA Director Casey told an interviewer in the same month that "I
think you will see more...retaliation against facilities connected with the
country sponsoring the terrorists or retaliation that just hurts the interests
of countries which sponsor terrorism"—an open-ended formula for
aggression against any country that the administration labeled a sponsor of
terrorism, with or without evidence.[80]

The Road to Irangate

For many conservatives, and Americans generally, the contradiction between the administration's tough-minded fight against terrorism and its delivery of arms to the headquarters of Mideastern radicalism is the signal outrage of the whole affair. Was it not William Casey who, only four months before the first arms delivery to Tehran, said "more blood has been shed by Iranian-sponsored terrorists during the last few years than all other terrorists combined"?[81] Was it not President Reagan who declared, less than two months before approving that arms shipment, "America will never make concessions to terrorists"?[82]

The hypocrisy was, in fact, institutionalized by the fact that the very officials in charge of handling the ransom to Iran were also the ones in charge of conducting planning and directing operations for counterterror. Chief among these officials was Oliver North. Along with Central America, terrorism was his chief beat at the NSC.

This confluence of apparently contradictory roles was no accident. North's leadership in such risky and macho adventures as the 1981 dogfight over Libya's Gulf of Sidra, the 1986 bombing of Libya and the interception of the Egyptian airliner carrying the Achille Lauro hijackers gave him the prestige and authority, far beyond his rank of colonel, to circumvent the normal chain of command and lead audacious covert operations from the NSC. And the extraordinary importance of his mandate to stamp out foreign terrorism licensed his access to special intelligence resources and his demands for secrecy so tight that even the secretaries of state and defense were left in the dark.[83]

North's influence reached its apogee just as President Reagan was giving official authorization for the Iran arms deals that would ultimately cripple his presidency. In January 1986, the very month of his "finding" approving those sales, Reagan issued another finding on counterterrorism. This one he showed to Congress as the law required. According to one source cited by the *Washington Post*, "Congress 'gulped' when it saw the directive but ultimately accepted it because of widespread alarm about terrorism. Among other things, the directive allowed the CIA to abduct suspected terrorists abroad and bring them to the United States for trial."[84] It also authorized the CIA to "harass and interdict terrorists in foreign countries by sabotaging their supplies, finances, travel, recruiting and operations."[85]

Shortly afterward, Vice President Bush's task force on terrorism issued its public report on terrorism. Among other recommendations, the task force proposed creating a new National Security Council position to strengthen coordination of counterterrorist programs. To that report, North (who was a task force member) added a classified annex that led to the creation of a secret interagency committee, the Operations Sub-Group, to oversee covert operations against terrorism. North chaired the committee with Duane Clarridge, the former manager of the CIA's war against Nicaragua whom Casey now put in charge of counterterrorism.[86] In April 1986, the OSG received a boost from a new pesidential finding giving more specific authorization to aggressive measures against foreign terrorists.[87] "The North group became the focal point within the government for devising tactics for penetrating and disrupting terrorist networks and for planning preventive or retaliatory strikes against them," according to the *Washington Post*.[88]

As its political momentum grew, so did this group's political reach. From counterterrorism it branched far afield from its given mission. "The group did start out just on terrorism," one source told *Newsweek*, "but because it was meeting so regularly it became the clearinghouse for all sorts of covert operations."[89]

The members of this secret and select committee also supplied much of the impetus for the Iran and contra operations. "At least two members of North's counterterrorism group had detailed knowledge of [the Iran arms] program," the *Post* reported. "One was Duane "Dewey" Clarridge, head of the counterterrorism section of the CIA. The other was Noel Koch, then-deputy assistant secretary of defense, who represented the Pentagon on the North group until May 1986."[90] Clarridge helped North establish the Ilopango air base in El Salvador as a staging point for contra supply operations and supplied the logistics help in November 1985 to deliver a load of U.S. arms to Tehran without the knowledge of Congress or some of his superiors at the CIA.[91]

Other U.S. counterterror specialists played a similarly prominent if ironic role in the Iran arms deals. These included Clarridge's assistant Charles Allen, who handled day-to-day contact with the chief Israeli representative (Amiram Nir, himself the counterterror adviser to Israel's prime minister), and the NSC's consultant on terrorism, Michael Ledeen, who acted as the go-between with Israel and Iranian arms broker Manucher Ghorbanifar on deals with Tehran.[92] Richard Secord, North's favorite private operator and arms logistics agent, reportedly ran a secret anti-terror unit set up in 1984 after his official retirement from the Pentagon. One Secord associate described Secord's operation as "a small group of government employees and consultants...experienced people from the

Middle East and Southeast Asia...absolutely trustworthy, low profile people who won't talk."[93]

The decision to entrust the Iran operation to the terror specialists in the NSC and CIA—rather than the area experts—contributed to the foreign policy disaster. A deep internal split within the administration wreaked havoc: "CIA activists in the agency's counterterrorism program [headed by Clarridge] supported the use of [Iranian arms dealer Manucher] Ghorbanifar but eventually were outmaneuvered by the agency's Middle East operations officers, who waged a campaign to discredit the Iranian," according to *Time* magazine. "...Infuriated, Ghorbanifar then urged an Iranian faction to leak the story of the whole sorry affair."[94]

Evidence from the Tower Report bears out this analysis. The CIA counterterror expert Charles Allen wrote on February 20, 1986, "I believe we should move quickly to consolidate our relations with" Ghorbanifar.[95] The chief CIA operations officer for the Near East said of Ghorbanifar, "This is a guy who lies with zest."[96] Ghorbanifar may have won the trust of these counterterror officers in part by planting juicy, if almost certainly untrue, stories about Libyan and Iranian hit teams in the United States and Europe.[97] No doubt these anti-terror officers were swayed by the unstinting support of Ghorbanifar from Israel's top counterterror specialist, Amiram Nir. But judging by Ghorbanifar's hopeless performance on CIA lie detector tests, the CIA's Middle East area officers would seem to have the better case.

Looking to the Future

The continued use of terrorism as an ideological rationale for expanded covert operations, foreign intervention and government secrecy still goes largely unchallenged in the wake of the Iran and contra scandals. Frank Carlucci, the former CIA deputy director brought to replace Admiral Poindexter as national security advisor and clean house on the NSC, has chosen to place reponsibility for counterterrorism

> under an expanded intelligence unit, as yet unnamed. 'Terrorism and intelligence are very closely related,' says Carlucci. 'The best way to stop a terrorist act is to know it's going to happen.' The head of the new section...will be Barry Kelly, who...had previously served in the CIA's clandestine service during Carlucci's tour as deputy director.

The new intelligence unit, according to James Bamford, will handle not only counterterrorism and all covert actions, but narcotics control as well—significantly the one other area where Congress has abdicated its oversight responsibilities.[98] New officials have replaced old and discredited ones, but the potential for abuses may be greater than ever.

Accompanying this centralization of secret authority for covert operations is a massive expansion of the president's ability to intervene abroad. A new Special Operations command at the Pentagon will coordinate covert terrorism and insurgency, grouping together some 30,000 men from the Army Special Operations Command, the Rangers, SEALS, Delta Force and others. The command reportedly will be "very tightly controlled by the White House," so that it can carry out operations "closely tied to the national interest."[99]

Finally, following the Tower Commission's recommendation, congressional conservatives are pushing for a merger of the House and Senate intelligence committees to further limit oversight of covert operations. Rep. Henry Hyde (R-IL) seeks a "lean, mean, small, very active committee with as few malcontents as possible."[100] It would be ironic, but far from unprecedented, if a "reform" commission ended up grossly aggravating the problem by so fundamentally misidentifying the cause.

Covert action embodies in its purest form the philosophy that ends (anticommunism, counterterrorism, democracy, economic gain) justify the means (political manipulation, disinformation, even support for death squads). Where such tools exist, abuses will follow whether the ends are good or not. The fact that the ends are so often verbal rationales themselves only makes the situation that much worse. Power corrupts, and secrecy is an essential element of unchecked power. Where secrecy is allowed to flourish, under the guise of protecting national security, fighting terrorism or combating narcotics traffickers, the conditions are ripe for presidential usurpation of power from the Congress and the cynical manipulation of public opinion.

Secrecy and covert policy making are not only undemocratic, they inevitably lead to bad policy. Secrecy breeds arrogance among policy makers who consider themselves uniquely "in the know" and thus less fallible in their judgments; at the same time it motivates the elite of "cleared" individuals to elevate their status by confining secrets (and thus policy advice) to an ever tighter circle. The consequences can be disastrous; the administration's failure to consult a wider group of experts or members of Congress surely contributed to its extraordinary blunders in Iran. Ignorant errors are compounded by the temptation to adopt covert means—to avoid messy public debates—where policy objectives are unclear and public support is lacking. Most damaging of all, covert operations usually become overt, discrediting not only the particular administration but the United States as a whole.

If the immorality of covert policies like the Iran and contra operations doesn't decide the case, these practical considerations should. Failure to curb the extraordinary power of presidents to wage covert foreign and military campaigns can only ensure a succession of similar policy disasters in the future.

XI.
Conclusion

Every crisis is also an opportunity. The Iran-Contra crisis is not one accidentally or gratuitously engaged upon, not the result of inadequate presidential attention or someone's misjudgments in the recruitment of White House personnel. It is deeply rooted in tensions which go back at least to the beginning of this century, if not earlier.

It would appear that, time after time, vanguard experiments in liberal democracy (Athens, Rome, Spain, England), have become, from the resultant liberation of expansive social energy, vanguard experiments in imperial expansion. Leaving aside the debatable example of Rome (which had no imperial competitors), one is struck by how brief has been the period of vanguard imperial hegemony (usually not more than a century), and how costly to the economic base of the mother country. Especially when set against the examples of Germany and Japan (two nations frustrated in their early drift towards empire), the depressing examples of modern England and Spain are memorials to empire's appalling erosion of both cultural dynamism and parliamentary institutions. They illustrate not only the crippling costs of maintaining a military hegemony, but also the ensuing flight of capital and entrepreneurship (and hence power) out of the home political economy.[1] This calculus is unfavorable even before we take into account the overwhelming cost to the colonized peoples.

Crudely put, this is the background of the Iran-Contra affair: the unresolved conflict between the needs of hegemony and the needs of an open society. The strong executive essential to the pursuit of hegemony is fundamentally at odds with the constitutional system of checks and balances and the restraints afforded by public opinion. Covert operations inevitably shield activist administrations from public accountability and the law.

The striving for unilateral hegemony in a multi-polar world is, moreover, inevitably destabilizing, and dangerous to peace, world order, and international law. Indeed the sequence of illegal American covert and paramilitary interventions for at least the last three decades (by which even our closest allies have been increasingly alienated) has been a prime cause for the progressive erosion of America's professed commitment to international order. One does not have to romanticize that order to find it a more promising arena for global security, and our own, than the arena of the great-power adventurism we have long endured.

The mining of Nicaragua's harbors in 1984 by the CIA (without even involving the contras) triggered the immediate conflict between the Administration and Congress; on the international level, it also showed how the cost of hegemonic intrigue is a decline in international influence. The United States has isolated itself in world opinion to a degree unthinkable even a decade ago, to a low comparable to that of Britain, France and Israel after their futile Suez Canal attack of 1956.

Nicaragua's complaint to the World Court about the mining was sustained by that court by votes of twelve to three (On one issue the sole dissenting vote was cast by the judge from the United States.) After Washington announced that it would not consider itself bound by that court's ruling, Nicaragua appealed to the United Nations, where it won again. In the United Nations General Assembly the United States garnered a total of three votes, being supported by only its two client states, Israel and El Salvador. Even Canada, whose Conservative government had been elected on a Reaganite domestic platform, did not abstain, but voted against the United States.

The adventurism of Britain and France in the 1956 Suez fiasco was in part an effort at self-prolongation and self-justification by threatened hegemonic bureaucracies—the obsolete armies and navies of two post-imperial powers. To their credit, the Joint Chiefs of the U.S. armed forces have so far shown no appetite to risk the political future of the Pentagon on a similar venture in Central America, without Congressional or popular support. They know very well that Nicaragua, with its army of 75,000 troops, will not be another Grenada.

That the United States, in pursuit of its contra policy, should nonetheless show similar disregard for international law and global public opinion, is symptomatic of the way one small losing policy, essential to the survival of one small bureaucratic subset, can become a neurotic obsession when power is undemocratic.

In the eyes of its allies, the United States' role as a residual guarantor of world order and process has been superseded, even more than before, by its eagerness to display its capacity for unilateral intervention and violence.

Europeans, above all, find our preoccupation with violence and unilateralism especially unfortunate, at a time when a change of leadership in the Soviet Union has raised new hopes for a restoration of international understanding and possible breakthroughs in checking the arms race. As our country grows increasingly dependent on international support for its economy and currency, the mood in Washington for solipsistic defiance of global political opinion seems particularly short-sighted.

It is important however to remember that this conflict between the needs of hegemony and the needs of an open society cannot be blamed on any single U.S. administration or party. It had been building for decades before it burst open in the Watergate crisis. Unfortunately, in the ensuing debate over Nixon's impeachment, about which press, politicians, and pundits have been so self-congratulatory ("The system worked!"), the deep issues about the imperial presidency in an open society were almost entirely replaced by discussions of personal responsibilities. Questions of constitutional infractions (such as, for example, the undeclared "secret" wars in Laos and Cambodia) were replaced by questions of cover-ups.

We are not suggesting that the Watergate discussions and hearings were of no worth. Calling as they did for new levels of investigative journalism and Congressional inquiry, as well as of statesmanship and balanced citizen concern, the Watergate debate did perhaps as much as could be done at that time to rectify executive excess by democratic process as traditionally practiced in the United States.

But when Congress failed to resolve the deeper questions, especially those relating to the desirability or undesirability of the so-called "Vietnam syndrome," the re-emergence of a new crisis like the present one was virtually guaranteed. The present crisis is not only deeper than Watergate, it is more directly related to the on-going debate over a hegemony for which no one ever voted. At the center is not a break-in, a "third-rate burglary" (with its consequent flurry of shredded memos), but a well-elaborated scheme to deceive Congress and responsible parts of the national security bureaucracy, as well as the public, by using a secret network of parallel institutions to circumvent the law (see Chapter II).

To understand the inevitability of this confrontation, we have to put ourselves in the position of those responsible for forcing it to happen. CIA Director Casey had a point: it is just not possible to run a lot of covert operations abroad, and also report on them (as the law now requires) to a gallery of Congressional critics and their staffs. In his own way Casey was verbalizing the dilemma of the need to choose between hegemony and democracy.

So, in a more theoretical way, was Michael Ledeen, one of the first architects of the Irangate arms deals, when he argued that we must learn to understand the need for occasional law-breaking and assassination.[2] We should be grateful for his candor. Failure this time to respond to such arguments, with equal energy and conviction, would be tacitly to concede by default that the time for an open society has passed.

Thus the Iran-contra affair is an urgent challenge for all those who see hegemony, and not our open society, as the curse to be mitigated. A simple re-run of Watergate, in which the public are essentially spectators to a succession of sensationalist headlines and televised hearings, would almost surely degenerate, as the Watergate hearings did, into an elaborate public relations exercise in damage control: one in which the focus is transferred from systemic irregularities and basic policy questions to personal shortcomings.

There is no doubt that Nixon, as a person, was responsible for Watergate, in a way that Reagan with his Teflon, or remoteness from decision-making, could never be. Many commentators have turned this, remarkably, into an argument that Iran-Contragate is less important than its predecessor—as if we should think of Ollie North or of Albert Hakim as the problems, rather than the system of illegal covert intervention which needed them, and the hegemonic system which in turn depended on covert intervention.[3]

Such punditry is not encouraging. It should remind us that the media and Congress, necessarily, are part of and beholden to the systemic process which they must now criticize. The press, for example, is not likely to expose the elaborate disinformation programs, such as Ghorbanifar's fictitious "Libyan hit-squads" in 1981, which played such an important role in re-mounting domestic CIA covert operations (see Chapter XI). Some of the media, to put it bluntly, were themselves too willing and active partners in such disinformation scenarios.[4] Nor will Congress raise the even more sensitive and complex issues of pro-Israeli lobbying and the incorporation of Israel as an adjunct to unauthorized foreign operations— even though Israel is now clearly and unambiguously defined as a prominent player at both the Iran and the Contra end of the current

Iran-contra controversy (see Chapter V, VIII).[5]

The power of the intelligence apparatus and its corporate allies seems to have virtually silenced genuine Congressional opposition on the deep issues of covert operations. The Democrats in particular have flocked to show their support of the CIA and Pentagon, and for the most part have confined their criticisms to the behavior of members of the Reagan White House staff. As the *New Yorker* has observed,

> The buzzwords the Democrats have put forth—"competitive-ness," "excellence,"—are of singularly low voltage. They hardly buzz at all. Even in decline, Reagan seems more commanding than these opponents. His absence from the scene is larger than their presence on it. Reagan rose. Reagan fell. The Democrats seem to have had little to do with it.[6]

In the last few years, unfortunately, members of Congress, much like Weinberger and Shultz, merely "distanced themselves" (to use the tactful rebuke of the Tower Report) from what was going on. In the fall of 1985, when the *New York Times* reported on the support of North and the National Security Council, both the House and the Senate Intelligence Committees received assurances from McFarlane that no one on the NSC staff had broken the law; and declined to investigate further.[7] Press stories the same year that aid was reaching the contras from third countries, including Israel, led to initial legislative efforts to close any possible loopholes. After White House lobbying, however, the final language had the opposite effect—to legitimize the administration's collection of "dona-tions" (including kickbacks) from third countries.

It remains to be seen whether the isolated voices of Congressional opposition in both parties can now begin belatedly to articulate the mood of alienation and activism that is beginning to be heard on the nation's campuses, and enlist the corrective participation of a citizenry grown cynical.

Opponents of the Iran-Contra system must first identify which parts of that system must be most urgently changed, and then not hesitate to work with some parts of the status quo against others, by working with, and hopefully influencing, existing currents for change.

A viable politics must bring the values of an alternative system into engagement with those institutions which exist now, in all their defects and limitations. Thus for example it may be important to encourage and support Senator John Kerry and the Senate Foreign Relations Committee in their announced plans to investigate the contra involvement in earlier smuggling and assassination conspiracies, even though Senator Kerry, to our dismay, has already declared Israel to be clean in the Iran-contra affair.

One can and must make choices that are discriminating rather than absolute. Just as compassion without criticism changes nothing, so criticism without compassion is condemned to sterile fault-finding. Merely to reject the system, to pronounce it incorrigibly corrupt, may be rhetorically cogent and psychologically gratifying. As matters now stand, however, such studied contempt for our existing democratic processes is more likely to favor the political fortunes of the extreme right, than of the left.

In much of the world today, the current political situation is one in which, as in the economic stagnation of the 1930s, there is danger of fascism of the WACL and P-2 varieties (see Chapter IV), and ultimately of war. Those forces abroad, unfortunately supported by too many states and multinational corporations, have over the decades been developing their alliances with forces of the right in this country. In the resulting crisis we can no more be defeatist than complacent about our institutions, which we should not be prepared to abandon unless we have within our power the ability to create better alternatives.

In our criticisms of Washington, we must not lose the ability to make discriminations. Even the present administration, for all its faults, is far more remote from the authoritarianism of a Ledeen, a Singlaub, or a Sandoval, than are some of the right-wing political forces hoping to replace it. This was demonstrated by Reagan's appointment of Frank Carlucci to succeed Admiral Poindexter as national security adviser, for Carlucci has enemies on the right as well as on the left.

To say this, of course, does not mean that we can expect Carlucci to change the drift of the whole national security apparatus. On the contrary, Carlucci has already a new national security threat—"narco-terrorism"— to succeed past threats (the Red menace, Qaddafi's hit squads) as a pretext for further covert operations. More significantly, he has already placed the NSC response to this threat in the hands of yet another veteran of the CIA's clandestine service.

What this does mean is that critics of hegemonic intervention must, more rigorously than in the 1970s, continue to do their homework. The details of the current crisis are difficult to master, and the lists of shady characters are hard to retain. No doubt in the months ahead we will again, as in Watergate, be inundated in floods of detail; and excesses of information, just as securely as secrecy, can become a means whereby the issues are concealed. But in our view a coherent interpretation of these facts, however abstruse and remote from the usual concerns of press and Congress, are necessary for understanding and articulating the real issues of the Iran-Contra crisis. And to keep these issues clear, as they develop, is an important part of the task ahead: for ourselves and for the North American people.

Footnotes

Footnotes to Chapter I

1. *San Francisco Chronicle*, 11-26-86.
2. Gregory Fossedal, "Strategic Defense Indecision," *Washington Times*, 2-9-87.
3. Cited in *Washington Post*, 7-9-84.
4. *San Francisco Examiner*, 7-27-86.
5. *Los Angeles Times*, 10-8-86.
6. On October 13, 1986 the *Los Angeles Times* referred to "a secret network of ex-CIA officials, foreign governments and arms dealers that has operated with the knowledge and approval of the White House but out of public view."
7. *Wall Street Journal*, 12-24-86.
8. The reluctance of those probers to cast their net too widely should be clear from a comparison of standard press accounts with the material in this book. To take a central example: over the last forty years the *New York Times* has given only the most cautious and limited references to those U.S. covert operations that have continuously, without interruption, intersected with and been enhanced by the international drug traffic. The sordid story of the drug-linked Nugan Hand Bank in Australia, and its connections to at least four members of the contra secret team, made front-page stories in the Australian press and were the subject of intensive investigation by two separate Australian government commissions. Yet despite the fact that the key figures were American intelligence veterans based mostly in the United States, the *New York Times* never reported the story until after the relevant pages in this book had (in slightly different form) already been published (see Peter Dale Scott, "Contragate and the CIA's 'Off-loaded Operations'," Pacific News Service, January 28, 1987; *New York Times*, March 8, 1987. Cf. Jonathan Marshall, *Inquiry*, November 24, 1980; *Parapolitics/USA*, March 1, 1983).
9. Quoted in *San Francisco Chronicle*, 2-27-87.
10. South End Press, 1985.

Footnotes to Chapter II

1. Cf. *Newsweek*, 12-15-86 on Poindexter's concern for "insulation" for Reagan.

2. Michael Ledeen, a key private operator in the Iran arms-for-hostages deals, "made the point that any serious covert action operation directed against Iran using Manucher Ghorbanifar should be run out of the White House not CIA because 'it will leak from Congress.'" *TCR*, p. 204, citing undated CIA memorandum.

3. James Bamford, "Carlucci and the NSC," *New York Times Magazine*, 1-18-87, p. 76.

4. *Washington Post*, 11-30-86. Vice President George Bush came to much to same conclusion: "There has got to be a chance for the president and his NSC adviser to undertake certain things and do certain things for him that the State Department and the Defense Department can't do because of the bureaucracy or because of the ability of any individual who does not like the policy to abort the policy" (*New York Times*, 2-27-87).

5. *U.S. News and World Report*, 12-15-86.

6. Angelo Codevilla, "The Reagan Doctrine—(As Yet) A Declaratory Policy," *Strategic Review*, XIV (Summer 1986), 19. Codevilla may well be referring to former CIA deputy director John McMahon, who allegedly left the agency after conservatives complained of his lukewarm support for the Afghan rebels. It was McMahon—an opponent of Iran arms deals from the start—who insisted that the CIA demand a presidential finding before aiding Oliver North's back-channel arms deals with Iran (*New York Times*, 1-17-87; *Washington Post*, 1-22-87; *Mideast Markets*, 12-8-86).

7. *Washington Times*, 12-8-86; *Newsweek*, 12-22-86; *Washington Post*, 12-19-86; *Washington Times*, 12-23-86; *Los Angeles Times*, 12-21-86; *Boston Globe*, 12-28-86; *Village Voice* 12-9-86. Besides North, the 208 Committee included CIA veteran Vincent Cannistraro, who helped direct the contra operation until moved aside in the wake of the scandal over the CIA-produced assassination manual; Clair George, the head of the CIA's clandestine service; Michael Armacost, Undersecretary of State; Fred Ikle, Undersecretary of

Defense for Policy; Morton Abramowitz, head of the State Department's Bureau of Intelligence and Research; Navy Captain James Stark and the late NSC Deputy Director Donald Fortier.

8. *Newsweek*, 3-2-87. Some of this smaller group's operations were later handled out of Room 302, right next to the NSC intelligence directorate on one side and the Crisis Management Center (moved to room 304) on the other.

9. *Washington Post*, 3-9-86.

10. *New York Times*, 2-15-87.

11. Christopher Dickey, *With the Contras* (NY: Simon and Schuster, 1986), p. 107.

12. *Washington Post*, 2-24-85, quoted in *NACLA Report on the Americas*, July/August 1986, 23.

13. *New York Times*, 4-8-83.

14. *Miami Herald*, 12-19-82.

15. *New York Times*, 4-8-83; Christopher Dickey, *With the Contras*, 112.

16. The cooperation continued up to, and to some extend beyond, the Falklands war. On March 9, 1982, Assistant Secretary of State for Latin American affairs Thomas Enders, on an official visit to Buenos Aires, said he expected Argentina to be "active in whatever action is taken in Central America" by other Latin powers. One month earlier, Argentina had made public its commitment of military aid to El Salvador (*Washington Post*, 3-10-82).

17. *Washington Post*, 1-2-87.

18. *Tribune* (Oakland) 11-7-82; *Washington Post*, 12-18-82; *Miami Herald*, 12-19-82; *New York Times*, 12-6-82; *Wall Street Journal*, 3-5-85; Dickey, *With the Contras*, 54, 117, 123; Edgar Chamorro testimony before the World Court, reprinted in Peter Rosset and John Vandermeer, eds., *Nicaragua: Unfinished Revolution* (Grove Press, 1986), 236-237; Shirley Christian, *Nicaragua: Revolution in the Family* (NY: Random House, 1986), 197-202. Vernon Walters himself handled these negotiations, according to Chamorro. Several accounts note that Chilean officials supplemented the Argentinians' role in Honduras and El Salvador; cf. *Latin America Regional Reports*, Mexico & Central America, RM-81-10, 11-27-81; *New York Times*, 12-9-81.

19. *Washington Post*, 9-15-84; *U.S. News and World Report*, 12-15-86 (Operation Elephant Herd).

20. *New York Times*, 1-3-87. The CIA officer was Duane Clarridge. In May 1984, according to former contra leader Edgar Chamorro, Clarridge showed up with North in Tegucigalpa and reassured the rebels that "If something happens in Congress, we will have an alternative way, and to assure that, here is Colonel North. You will never be abandoned" (*New York Times*, 1-21-87).

21. *Washington Post*, 12-7-86.

22. Ibid; *Miami Herald*, 11-27-86. The process of "contracting out" to private individuals accelerated after the Boland Amendment in 1984. As one special operations veteran told *U.S. News and World Report*, "In Central

America, there is no such thing as a private mercenary. But after the mining of the harbors in 1984, we needed deniability. So these guys now work on contract" (*U.S. News and World Report*, 10-20-86).

23. *Washington Post*, 12-7-86.

24. *Washington Post*, 11-30-86.

25. *Los Angeles Times*, 1-8-87 (Robert Owen to John Hull in Costa Rica). With the money taken care of, the White House also saw to it that the contras had access to private arms sources regardless of congressional will. As early as 1981, CIA officials began advising the Nicaraguan exiles on how to smuggle weapons out of Miami under the nose of U.S. Customs (*Miami Herald*, 12-19-82). The FBI is now investigating a March 1985 shipment of mortars, rifles and ammunition from Fort Lauderdale to El Salvador, for transshipment to the rebels.

26. Senate Select Committee on Intelligence, *Report on Preliminary Inquiry into the Sale of Arms and Possible Diversion of Funds to the Contras* (January 29, 1977), p. 45.

27. *Legal Times*, 12-8-86. The major countries approached were Israel, Saudi Arabia, Brunei, Singapore, South Korea and Taiwan; *San Francisco Chronicle*, 1-23-87.

28. *Israeli Foreign Affairs, (IFA)*, March 1986.

29. *Dallas Morning News*, 10-18-86.

30. ABC News, 2-25-87; *San Francisco Examiner*, 3-12-87. At least 15 South African pilots and cargo handlers were based in Honduras to deliver supplies to the Contras.

31. *San Francisco Examiner*, 10-21-86.

32. The sultan had earlier been turned into a CIA "asset" by Ronald Ray Rewald, a Honolulu investment counselor convicted of fraud following the collapse of what he says was a CIA front company (*San Francisco Chronicle*, 11-8-84; *Counterspy*, June-August 1984).

33. *Los Angeles Times*, 12-6-86; *New York Times*, 12-7-86, 12-25-86; *San Francisco Chronicle*, 1-16-87 (Jack Anderson).

34. *Los Angeles Times*, 12-16-86.

35. *Los Angeles Times*, 1-7-87; cf. *MidEast Report*, February 1, 1987.

36. *San Francisco Examiner*, 10-21-86; *New York Times*, 10-22-86, 11-30-86.

37. *San Francisco Chronicle*, 10-28-86; *San Francisco Examiner*, 1-12-87; *New York Times*, 2-4-87, 2-27-87, 3-15-87.

38. *New York Times*, 10-22-86.

39. *San Francisco Chronicle*, 11-27-86.

40. *San Francisco Chronicle*, 11-26-86.

41. *Miami Herald*, 10-12-86.

42. *San Francisco Examiner*, 12-3-86.

43. NBC 11-25-86; *Wall Street Journal*, 11-6-86, 5-2-84; *Time*, 7-25-83.

44. Some of the relevant individuals with ties to South Korea are:
* Michael Deaver, the Reagans' trusted friend and a registered lobbyist for

both South Korea and Saudi Arabia. He got his $500,000 a year contract to represent Riyadh from Prince Bandar bin Sultan, the Saudi Ambassador to the United States who coordinated covert Saudi aid to Afghanistan, Angola and the Nicaraguan contras (*Washington Times*, 12-8-86.) Deaver steered Robert McFarlane into the slot as national security adviser where he organized the contra supply operation and the Iran arms route (*New York Times*, 11-17-86 [Safire]). A California businessman, Sam Bamieh, alleges that King Fahd endorsed using Deaver to promote a U.S.-Iran rapprochement (*Los Angeles Times*, 2-25-87).

* Robert Owen, a registered lobbyist for South Korea, Taiwan and the League of Arab States. He acted as the NSC's chief field liaison to the contras (*Miami Herald*, 6-8-86; NBC 6-13-86; AP 6-10-86; CBS 6-25-86; *New York Times*, 10-16-86).

* Donald Gregg, George Bush's top national security aide, and former CIA station chief in South Korea. He served as a key White House contact of the veteran CIA Cuban exiles who organized the contra supply flights (*Miami Herald*, 10-11-86, *Miami Herald*, 10-12-86, *Washington Post*, 10-24-86).

* Albert Hakim, chief executive of Stanford Technology Trading Group. He played a key role with retired Air Force major general Richard Secord in establishing the Swiss financial conduits through which Iranian arms money was transferred to the contras. The Iranian-born Hakim sold electronic security and monitoring systems to both South Korea and Saudi Arabia (*Wall Street Journal*, 12-5-86; *San Jose Mercury*, 7-18-86; *Tribune*, 12-4-86).

* Retired Gen. John Singlaub, who served in South Korea with the CIA and later as commander of U.S. forces there in the mid-1970s. As a private citizen and Pentagon counterinsurgency adviser in the Reagan period, he was assigned the task of raising funds in the United States and oversees for the contras and similar anti-communist resistance groups (*Washington Post*, 12-10-84; *Boston Globe*, 12-30-84; *Village Voice*, 10-22-85).

* The World Anti-Communist League, an umbrella group for right-wing extremists including European nazis and Latin death squad leaders. It operated under Singlaub's direction as a prime conduit for funds and arms to the contras. Much of this support came from WACL's two founder countries, South Korea and Taiwan (*Miami Herald*, 10-28-86). WACL member organization Alpha 66, a group of Cuban exile extremists, reportedly trained former Nicaraguan National Guard members in the Florida Everglades for service against the Sandinistas.

* CAUSA, the political wing of the Rev. Sun Myung Moon's Unification Church. It has taken a leading role in organizing political and material support for the contras in the United States and Latin America. Like its parent church, it is assumed to have close Korean CIA connections (*Nation*, 10-6-84; *Washington Post*, 1-4-86 [Jack Anderson]).

45. Quoted in *Honduras Update*, #5 (early 1983).

46. *Los Angeles Times, San Francisco Chronicle*, 12-3-86; *New York Times*, 12-3-86; *San Francisco Chronicle*, 11-26-86, 12-5-86; *Washington Post*, 11-28-

86, 12-12-86.

47. *San Francisco Examiner*, 1-12-87.

48. Benjamin Beit-Hallahmi, "U.S.-Israeli-Central American Connection," *The Link*, XVIII (November 1985).

49. Bishara Bahbah, *Israel and Latin America: The Military Connection* (New York: St. Martin's Press, 1986), 123-134; *New York Times*, 12-5-86.

50. During the period of its military dictatorship Argentina ranked behind only South Africa as a customer for Israeli arms; Argentina and Israel also collaborated on aid to right wing security forces in Central America (*Washington Post*, 12-16-84, 6-16-84; *The Middle East*, September 1981; *NACLA Report*, May/June 1983).

51. *U.S. News and World Report*, 12-15-86.

52. *Time*, 5-7-84.

53. *San Francisco Chronicle*, 11-26-86.

54. Ironically, the chief Israeli intermediary on the Iran arms deal in 1986 admitted that summer that "we are dealing with the most radical elements" in Iran, not the moderates (*San Jose Mercury*, 2-8-87).

55. *Monitin*, April 83 [Shahak]; *San Francisco Chronicle*, 11-12-86 (Sharon interview).

56. *Wall Street Journal*, 12-5-86.

57. *Miami Herald*, 4-30-86, 6-8-86; *Washington Times*, 10-8-85; *New York Times*, 11-9-86.

58. *Los Angeles Times*, 12-7-86.

59. *New York Times* 10-24-86; *Los Angeles Times*, 7-27-86; *San Francisco Examiner*, 7-27-86, 10-21-86; *San Francisco Chronicle*, 11-27-86; Joseph Goulden, *The Death Merchant* (NY: Simon and Schuster, 1984), 47-8.

60. *San Francisco Chronicle*, 11-24-86 (Jack Anderson); *New York Times*, 1-17-87.

61. *Boston Globe*, 12-14-86; *TCR*, p. 55.

62. *Wall Street Jouirnal* 1-2-87; *New York Times*, 12-6-86; *San Francisco Examiner*, 2-12-82.

63. Peter Maas, *Manhunt*, 138, 231; Maas, "Oliver North's Strange Recruits," *New York Times Magazine*, 1-18-87, p. 22; *San Francisco Examiner*, 2-12-87; *Dallas Morning News*, 12-21-86.

64. *Los Angeles Times*, 10-16-86.

65. *Miami Herald*, 10-23-86. Oliver North urged the State and Justice Departments to go easy on Latchinian (*New York Times*, 2-23-87).

66. *New York Times*, 12-13-86.

67. Senate Select Committee to Study Governmental Operations with Respect to Intelligence Activities, Final Report, *Foreign and Military Intelligence*, Book I, (Washington: USGPO, 1976), p. 239.

68. *New York Times*, 12-4-86; *San Jose Mercury*, 11-26-86; *Miami Herald*, 12-9-86.

69. *Washington Post*, 12-7-86. A more obscure firm, Race Aviation, reportedly made one U.S.-sponsored arms delivery to Tehran on July 4, 1986.

Its predecessor, Global International Airways, previously flew arms to the Afghan rebels (presumably on behalf of the CIA) and, most significantly, delivered arms for EATSCO, the consortium associated with the Wilson-Clines group (*Kansas City Star*, 6-10-84, 11-13-86; *Wall Street Journal*, 1-2-87).

Footnotes to Chapter III

1. Christopher Dickey, *With the Contras: A Reporter in the Wilds of Nicaragua* (New York: Simon and Schuster, 1983), passim.

2. U.S. Congress, Senate, Committee on Foreign Relations, *Activities of Nondiplomatic Representatives of Foreign Principals in the United States, Hearings*, 88th Cong., 1st Sess. (Washington, Government Printing Office, 1963), pp. 1587, 1626; cf. Peter Dale Scott, *Crime and Cover-Up* (Berkeley: Westworks, 1977), pp. 26-28, etc.

3. Scott Anderson and Jon Lee Anderson, *Inside the League: the Shocking Expose of How Terrorists, Nazis, and Latin American Death Squads Have Infiltrated the World Anti-Communist League* (New York: Dodd, Mead, 1986), pp. 10-45. The European regional secretary of the original steering committee in 1958 to convene a World Anti-Communist Congress for Freedom and Liberation was Alfred Gielen, a former Nazi publicist for Goebbels' Anti-Komintern.

4. James Ridgeway, *Village Voice*, December 9, 1986.

5. Jenny Pearce, *Under the Eagle: U.S. Intervention in Central America and the Caribbean* (Boston: South End Press, 1981), pp. 178, 180. Officially Deaver's firm did not register as agent for the group until August 27, 1980. However it did so after coming under Justice Department scrutiny for possible violation of the Foreign Agents Registration Act, for failure to register the contract within the required ten days (Washington Post, September 8, 1980). A former Vice-President of Guatemala told the BBC in 1981 that the contributions to Reagan's victory, "all in all...went up to 10 million dollars" (Pearce, p. 180; cf. Marlene Simons, "Guatemala: The Coming Danger," *Foreign Policy* [Summer 1981], p. 101; Anderson, p. 175).

6. Simons, p. 101; Anderson, p. 200. According to Simons, Sandoval "mixed with the Reagan inner circle during inauguration week."

7. *Washington Post*, February 22, 1981.

8. Alan Nairn, "Controversial Reagan Campaign Links with Guatemalan Government and Private Sector Leaders," Research Memorandum for Council on Hemispheric Affairs, October 30, 1980, p. 11.

9. Shirley Christian, *Nicaragua: Revolution in the Family* (New York: Random House, 1985), p. 197; Anderson, p. 176.

10. Dickey, p. 87.

11. Dickey, p. 88.

12. Dickey, p. 88; Anderson, p.202. According to Dickey, "the CIA took more than two years to begin seriously analyzing these papers." By this time the Reagan administration had backed away from d'Aubuisson, who once told German reporters, "You Europeans had the right idea. You saw the Jews behind Communism and you started to kill them" (*Oakland Tribune*, August 15, 1986).

13. Anderson, pp. 202, 207-08; citing White's testimony to Senate Foreign Relations Committee, April 1981, and to House Foreign Relations Committee, 1984.

14. Ronnie Dugger, *On Reagan: The Man and His Presidency* (New York: McGraw Hill), p. 273; Anderson, p. 208. The Andersons charge categorically that the documents supplied by d'Aubuisson were forged.

15. Cf. e.g. "Is There a Contra Drug Connection?" *Newsweek*, January 26, 1987. South Africa, the other most prominent example of Reagan's inflexibility, was like Deaver's three international clients in 1980 one of the hard core members of WACL.

16. Stephen Schlesinger and Stephen Kinzer, *Bitter Fruit: The Untold Story of the American Coup in Guatemala* (Garden City, N.Y.: Doubleday, 1982), p. 11

17. Anderson, p. 140.

18. Magnus Linklater et al., *The Nazi Legacy* (New York: Holt, Rinehart, and Winston, 1984), pp. 278-85 (see Chapter IV).

19. Penny Lernoux, *In Banks We Trust* (Garden City, N.Y.: Anchor/Doubleday 1984), p. 217.

20. Thomas Ferguson and Joel Rogers, *Right Turn: The Decline of the Democrats and the Future of American Politics* (New York: Hill and Wang, 1986), pp. 89-100.

21. John Ranelagh, *The Agency: The Rise and Decline of the CIA* (New York: Simon and Schuster, 1986), pp. 549, 644.

22. Ranelagh, p. 644. Under Schlesinger a total of 1500 are said to have left the CIA; under Turner, 2800. Cf. Theodore Shackley, *The Third Option* (New York: Reader's Digest Press/McGraw Hill, 1981), p. ix.

23. *San Francisco Examiner*, July 27, 1986; *Newsweek*, December 15, 1986, *U.S. News and World Report*, December 15, 1986.

24. Ranelagh, pp. 644-65.

25. John Prados, *Presidents' Secret Wars: CIA and Pentagon Covert Operations Since World War II* (New York: William Morrow, 1986), pp. 351-54, 377.

26. One of these men is Robert K. Brown, today the publisher of the mercenary magazine *Soldier of Fortune*. Cf. *Search-light* (London), May 17, 1985; reprinted in *Intelligence/Parapolitics* (July 1985), pp. 25-26.

27. According to *Newsweek* (December 15, 1986), "in the late 1960s Secord directed air operations in support of the CIA's secret war in Laos."

28. *Los Angeles Times*, October 10, 1986.

29. Prados, p. 275.

30. *Miami Herald*, October 23, 1986; *Washington Post*, October 24, 1986.

31. Peter Maas, *New York Times Magazine*, January 18, 1987.

32. *Newsweek*, December 15, 1986; Peter Maas, *Manhunt* (New York: Random House, 1986), pp. 279-80: "Although he had taken out at least two and a half million from EATSCO before being forced to depart...Clines in his own plea bargain...was let off with a corporate fine [and] paid $10,000" (p. 280).

33. Peter Maas, *Manhunt* (New York: Random House, 1986), pp. 138-40.

34. *New York Times*, November 27, 1986.

35. Ibid. Shackley has denied any involvement in the Contra supply operation and we know of no contrary evidence.

36. Peter Maas, p. 138; cf. p. 231.

37. Daniel Sheehan, *Affidavit*, (Washington: Christic Institute, 1324 North Capitol St., Washington DC 20002, 1986), Para. 70.33.

38. U.S. Cong., Senate, Select Committee to Study Governmental Operations with Respect to Intelligence Activities, Final Report, Book I *Foreign and Military Intelligence*, 94th Cong., 2nd Sess., Report No. 94-755 (April 26, 1976), p. 1.

39. John Prados, *Presidents' Secret Wars* (New York: Morrow, 1986), pp. 119-21.

40. William R. Corson, *The Armies of Ignorance: The Rise of the American Intelligence Empire* (New York: Dial Press/ James Wade, 1977), pp. 322-23.

41. Alfred W. McCoy, with Cathleen B. Read and Leonard P. Adams II, *The Politics of Heroin in Southeast Asia* (New York: Harper and Row, 1972), pp. 126-35. Cf. Peter Dale Scott, *The War Conspiracy* (New York: Bobbs Merrill, 1972), pp. 194, 199-212. At the time Washington officials countered the charge that the white advisers were American with the speculation that "the men may have been German deserters from the French Foreign Legion" (*Time*, August 13, 1953, p. 38).

42. Scott, pp. 210-11.

43. Henrik Kruger, *The Great Heroin Coup: Drugs, Intelligence, and International Fascism* (Boston: South End Press, 1980), pp. 16, 20, 129-31, 181-82.

44. Prados, p. 77. A vivid eyewitness description of Stilwell's departure will be found in Ranelagh, p. 221; cf. p. 223.

45. Thomas Powers, *The Man Who Kept the Secrets: Richard Helms and the CIA* (New York: Knopf, 1979), pp. 48-49; cf. Ranelagh, p. 199.

46. Scott, *War Conspiracy*, p. 199.

47. Technically, what happened was as follows: the CIA's American proprietary CAT Inc. (renamed Air America in 1959) had been supplying planes and pilots to a Taiwan airline, CATCL, which was controlled chiefly by

KMT interests in Taiwan (with a 40% CIA minority interest). Thus it was not surprising that, despite the official CIA termination, the planes of Civil Air Transport (i.e. CATCL) continued to fly into Burma. See Scott, *War Conspiracy*, p. 197.

48. *New York Times*, February 16, 1961; *Singapore Straits-Times*, February 20, 1961, p. 1; Scott, *War Conspiracy*, p. 204.

49. Scott Anderson and Jon Lee Anderson, *Inside the League* (New York: Dodd, Mead, 1986), pp. 10-45.

50. McCoy, p. 315; *New York Times*, February 23, 1961.

51. Scott, *War Conspiracy*, passim; especially pp. 8-24, 199-206.

52. McCoy, p. 259.

53. McCoy, p. 263.

54. McCoy, pp. 186-87, 242-44.

55. Prados, pp. 171, 176.

56. Peter Dale Scott has speculated about DePuy's and SOG's possible responsibility for the South Vietnamese-U.S. provocations which preceded and possibly led to the Tonkin Gulf incidents of 1964: *New York Review of Books*, January 29, 1970; reprinted in Scott, *War Conspiracy*, p. 64.

57. Ranelagh, pp. 223, 457 (FitzGerald).

58. Ranelagh, p. 221.

59. For example Jesus Garcia, a former contra supporter in Miami, told freelance reporters Vince Bielski and Dennis Bernstein in a telephone interview that "it is common knowledge here in Miami that this whole contra operation in Costa Rica was paid for with cocaine" (*In These Times*, December 10, 1986).

60. *Newsweek*, January 26, 1987.

61. *Washington Post*, October 19, 1986.

62. Anderson, p. 141 (Paraguay). The Korean CIA is closely linked to the Unification Church of the Reverend Sun Myung Moon, some of whose business enterprises are believed by some Moonie-watchers to be "actually covers for drug-trafficking" (Anderson, p. 129). The church's political arm, CAUSA, collaborated with WACL members in the 1980 "Cocaine coup" in Bolivia (ibid.; *Le Monde Diplomatique* (February 1985); *Covert Action Information Bulletin*, 25 [Winter 1986], pp. 18-19); and since the cutoff of CIA aid in 1984 has supported the Miskito Indian anti-Sandinista guerrilla force Misura of Steadman Fagoth (Anderson, p. 23).

63. Ross Y. Koen, *The China Lobby in American Politics* (New York: Macmillan, 1960), p. ix; Scott, *War Conspiracy*, pp. 203-04; cf. Kruger, pp. 15-16.

64. For this continuity in the 1950s and 1960s, and its connections to organized crime, cf. Peter Dale Scott, *Crime and Cover-Up: The CIA, the Mafia, and the Dallas-Watergate Connection* (Berkeley: Westworks, 1977), pp. 8-11. For Koreagate, cf. Robert Boettcher, *Gifts of Deceit: Sun Myung Moon, Tongsun Park, and the Korean Scandal* (New York: Holt, Rinehart and Winston, 1980).

65. For Mafia involvement in KMT drug activities in the United States, cf. Scott, *War Conspiracy*, p. 203. For Mafia involvement in the Caribbean and

ex-CIA drug traffic, cf. Kruger, pp. 7, 105, 223-24.

66. U.S. Cong., Senate, Select Committee to Study Governmental Operations with Respect to Intelligence Activities, *Alleged Assassination Plots Involving Foreign Leaders*, Interim Report, 94th Cong., 1st Sess., Report No. 94-465 (November 20, 1975, henceforth cited as Assassination Report), p. 132.

67. Assassination Report, p. 84.

68. Assassination Report, p. 84.

69. United States District Court for the Southern District of Florida, Avirgan v. Hull, et al., Case No. 86-1146-CIV-KING, Amended Complaint, October 3, 1986, pp. 25-26.

70. *New York Times*, September 6, 1981; Maas, *Manhunt*, p. 223.

71. *Business Week*, December 29, 1986, p. 45; cf. Maas, p. 65.

72. *Wall Street Journal*, January 2, 1987, p. 2.

73. *New York Times*, January 4, 1975, p. 9; Kruger, p. 16.

74. Maas, pp. 24-27, 37, 54-56, 77.

75. In 1976 Wilson's company Consultants International was shipping riot-control equipment to the new military junta of Argentina (see Chapter IV): Maas, p. 60.

76. Maas, pp. 58-59; *Newsweek*, December 15, 1986.

77. *Wall Street Journal*, January 2, 1987, p. 2.

78. *Wall Street Journal*, January 2, 1987, p. 2.

79. Maas, p. 223.

80. James A. Nathan, "Dateline Australia: America's Foreign Watergate?" *Foreign Policy* (Winter 1982-83), pp. 168-85 (p. 183).

81. Nathan, p. 182.

82. Nathan, pp. 182-83; Commonwealth-New South Wales Joint Task on Drug Trafficking, 1983 Report, pp. 697-703.

83. Jonathan Marshall, "The Friends of Michael Hand," *Inquiry*, November 24, 1980, pp. 9-12; *Wall Street Journal*, August 24, 1982; *National Times*, September 12, 1982; Penny Lernoux, *In Banks We Trust* (Garden City, N.Y.: Anchor/Doubleday, 1984), p. 75.

84. Nathan, p. 170.

85. Lernoux, p. 72, *Mother Jones*, March 1984).

86. Commonwealth-New South Wales Joint Task Force on Drug Trafficking, *Report* (March 1983), IV, "Nugan Hand," p. 744.

87. Joint Task Force Report, p. 763; Lernoux, p. 75n; *National Times*, September 12, 1982; *Parapolitics/U.S.A*, March 1, 1983.

88. Ranelagh, p. 636; Joseph C. Goulden, with Alexander Raffio, *The Death Merchant: The Rise and Fall of Edwin P. Wilson* (New York: Simon and Schuster, 1984), pp. 15, 176.

89. Peter Maas, *Manhunt: The Incredible Pursuit of a CIA Agent Turned Terrorist* (New York: Random House, 1986), p. 247; Michael Ledeen, *New York*, March 3, 1980.

90. Maas, p. 247.

91. Maas, p. 279.

92. Maas, pp. 139, 278.

93. Maas, pp. 8, 233.

94. Maas, pp. 247, 280.

95. *San Francisco Examiner*, July 27, 1986.

96. Ibid. Von Marbod by 1986 was also in the private arms sales business, having been hired by his former boss Frank Carlucci, who once ordered the reinstatement of Secord. The two men worked for a subsidiary of Sears Roebuck, perhaps the largest corporate backer of the American Security Council (Maas, p. 288).

97. Affidavit of Daniel P. Sheehan (Washington: Christic Institute, 1324 North Capitol St., DC 20002, 1986), p. 22.

98. According to John Dinges and Saul Landau, Manuel Contreras, the chief of the Chilean Intelligence Service DINA "set up his own men in...cocaine factories and shipping points. The anti-Castro Cubans had a piece of the action. The enormous profits went to supplement DINA's clandestine budget. The Cubans' share went into individual pockets and to the anti-Castro cause:" John Dinges and Saul Landau, *Assassination on Embassy Row* (New York: Pantheon, 1980), p. 264n. For the drug involvement of Argentine intelligence under Lopez Rega in 1973-75, cf. e.g. Lernoux, p. 177.

99. *Wall Street Journal*, January 16, 1987, p. 11. Luis Posada, who once allegedly helped blow up a Cuban civilian airline for CORU, has also been linked by a Congressional staff investigation to CORU assassination plots against Cuban officials, including two who were murdered in Argentina on August 9, 1976, with the aid of Argentine intelligence (House Assassinations Committee, X, 44).

100. *Wall Street Journal*, January 16, 1987, p. 1.

101. Lernoux, pp. 147, 152.

102. Lernoux, pp. 153-54. In 1977 the daughter of Orlando Bosch, CORU's most famous terrorist and spokesman, was arrested for allegedly attempting to import seven pounds of cocaine. In her address book was the name and address of WFC. Local police also learned that WFC had been printing and selling "bonds" to raise funds for CORU.

103. Lernoux, pp. 147-48; 160. At one point a WFC-linked firm at the same Coral Gables address, Dominion Mortgage Corporation, was negotiating to buy the Las Vegas casino Caesar's Palace.

104. *Wall Street Journal*, January 16, 1987, p. 11.

105. The three-man team included Tom Clines' business partner Rafael Quintero and Hernandez Cartaya's close friend Rafael Villaverde.

106. Hinckle and Turner, p. 53. The funds were handled by Norman "Roughhouse" Rothman, who had served as manager of the Sans Souci and Copacabana Clubs in Havana, representing the interests of the Mannarino brothers of Pittsburgh (Assassination Hearings, X, 183).

107. Lukas, p. 95

108. New York Times, January 4, 1975; Hinckle and Turner, p. 314.

109. Hinckle and Turner, p. 308; Warren Hinckle, *San Francisco Examiner*, October 12, 1986.

110. *San Francisco Chronicle*, June 23, 1972; *New York Times*, June 23, 1972; Watergate Hearings, I, 375.

111. *Miami Herald*, October 23, 1986.

112. *Business Week*, December 29, 1986, p. 45. The 1961 mission of Felix Rodriguez and his companion Edgar Sopo was to establish contact with resistance leaders in Las Villas and Havana, and to seize the Havana radio station. It has also been alleged that Quintero was a member of Rodriguez' four-man team. Compare the piecemeal accounts in Hinckle and Turner, pp. 71-73 (assassination plot); *Miami Herald*, October 23, 1986 (Rodriguez and Sopo); Wyden, pp. 76, 112-13, 246-48 (Sopo). Sopo was subsequently a source of information on the CIA's AMLASH assassination plot of 1963-65, involving Manuel Artime and Rolando Cubela: cf. Jaime Suchlicki, in Donald K. Emmerson (ed.), *Students and Politics in Developing Nations* (New York: Praeger, 1968), p. 349.

113. Maas, p. 223; *New York Times*, September 6, 1981.

114. Hinckle and Turner, p. 320.

115. *Washington Post*, November 7, 1976.

116. *Miami Herald*, April 9, 1976. Perez said he had "no official knowledge of the attack. These are individual efforts of some of our members, but we congratulate them for carrying out operations of this type." Earlier a caller had taken credit for the action in the name of both the FNLC and Brigade 2506.

117. U.S. Senate, Office of Senator John Kerry, *"Private Assistance" and the Contras: A Staff Report* (October 14, 1986), p. 9.

118. Scott Anderson and Jon Lee Anderson, *Inside the League* (New York: Dodd Mead, 1986), pp. 76, 280, 298. The three foreign guests at the July 1976 Congress of Alpha 66, one month after the CORU meeting, were Sandoval's nephew and personal representative Carlos Midence Pivaral, as well as another Guatemalan MLN representative and Dr. German Dominguez from the Chilean junta.

119. Hinckle and Turner, p. 322.

120. Henrik Kruger, *The Great Heroin Coup* (Boston: South End Press, 1980), p. 209; citing *Information*, February 22, 1977.

121. Kruger, pp. 10-11, 204, 213; *New York Times*, Feb. 1, 1977, p. 8.

122. *CounterSpy* (Spring 1976), p. 41; citing *Temoignage Chretien*, August 21, 1975.

123. James Mills, *The Underground Empire* (Garden City, New York: Doubleday, 1986), pp. 361-64.

124. Hinckle and Turner, pp. 321-22.

125. Anderson, p. 101; Laurent, p. 308. In the mid-1970s, a time of great international economic and political upheaval, European fascists were supported by some Americans as well as CORU Cubans. In 1975 Ray Cline, a key supporter of the contras and of WACL today, called upon the United States to rally behind Spinola.

Footnotes to Chapter IV

1. Christopher Dickey, *With the Contras* (New York: Simon and Schuster, 1985), p. 289, emphasis added; citing *Miami Herald*, June 5, 1983.

2. Dickey, pp. 102, 107, 289; *Los Angeles Times*, March 3, 1985.

3. Dickey, pp. 60, 102-03.

4. Pearce, pp. 178-80. Cf. Chapter III, pp. 1-2.

5. Pearce, p. 180.

6. Pearce, p. 176; *Atlantic Monthly*, January 1980. Coca-Cola conducted its own investigation, which confirmed Trotter's involvement in the persecution (*Congressional Record*, February 25, 1980, p. 3627).

7. *Congressional Record*, December 4, 1979, p. 34551; Pearce, pp. 178-79. According to Nairn, Ayau is "considered to be the ideologue of the more extremist sector of the [Guatemalan] business community" (p. 7).

8. Nairn, p. 5.

9. Pearce, p. 180.

10. Nairn, p. 12: "Reagan himself was reportedly aware of the potential of the Guatemalan connection. One businessman tells the story of the wife of an Amigos del Pais board member who attended a Californian fund-raising party with Reagan. 'He was standing there....She said, "I represent 14,000 Americans in Guatemala," and Reagan turned around and said, "Get that woman's name!"'"

11. Pearce, pp. 177, 180.

12. On his first ASC trip, Singlaub was accompanied by former Defense Intelligence Agency director General Daniel O. Graham, later the Vice-Chairman under Singlaub of WACL's U.S. chapter, as well as a director of the political arm CAUSA of Sun Myung Moon's Unification Church and a leading lobbyist for the ASC's Strategic Defense Initiative (Anderson, pp. 126, 152). Trotter himself linked his ASC fundraising to the Singlaub-Graham visit (Pearce, pp. 177-78).

13. Nairn, p. 9; Anderson, p. 174. In another interview, Villagran "recalled that among recent Amigos efforts was the invitation of retired U.S. military opponents of Carter's human rights policies to Guatemala" (*Washington Post*, September 8, 1980).

14. Pearce, p. 178.

15. Anderson, p. 158. How Singlaub became empowered to convey such sensitive messages is unclear, but there is no doubt that his predictions were correct. Carter's Central American team was sacked, and in May 1981 Vernon Walters, another veteran of CIA covert operations, was sent to repeat publicly that there would be "no more Irans," and that it was "essential" that Lucas "get rid of the guerrillas" (*Washington Post*, May 14, 1981). A *New York Times* editorial on May 18 criticized Walters' "peculiar" words.

16. Ibid.

17. *Miami Herald*, October 28, 1986; *Washington Post*, October 19, 1986.

18. Lou Cannon, *Reagan* (New York: Putnam's, 1982), pp. 192, 196.

19. By "WACL countries" we mean those nations whose WACL delegations included persons exercising public or covert power, and which used WACL as a prominent instrument of their foreign policy. In 1980 the hard core of WACL countries included Argentina, Taiwan, South Korea, Paraguay, Bolivia, Guatemala, and South Africa.

20. Dugger, p. 272; cf. *Washington Post*, June 6, 1980.

21. *Los Angeles Times*, July 11, 1980, quoted in Cannon, p. 272.

22. *Time*, September 8, 1980; reprinted in Data Center, *The Reagan File*, pp. 558-59.

23. Ibid.

24. J. Anthony Lukas, *Nightmare* (New York: Viking, 1976), pp. 283-84.

25. Lou Cannon would later claim that Deaver "took a leave of absence from the firm for the campaign" (p. 272), but as late as July 15, 1980, Jack Anderson reported that "Deaver and Hannaford confirmed their status as foreign agents." Deaver formally left his firm when he joined Reagan's White House staff in January 1981.

26. Laurence I. Barrett, *Gambling with History: Ronald Reagan in the White House* (Garden City, N.Y.: 1983), p. 233; Cannon, p. 399.

27. Ronald Reagan, "Common Sense from a Neighbor," (August 1979); in Dugger, pp. 520-21.

28. Ranelagh, p. 681.

29. Alejandro Dabat and Luis Lorenzano, *Argentina: the Malvinas and the End of Military Rule* (London: Verso, 1984), pp. 80-81.

30. Barrett, p. 238.

31. Barrett, p. 239. Haig and Deaver had also clashed over a minor State Department appointment, and the President ruled in Deaver's favor (p. 235).

32. Barrett, p. 236.

33. Ranelagh, p. 680.

34. Christian, pp. 202, 286.

35. Anderson, p. 177.

36. *New York Times*, February 18, 1981; Pearce, p. 178.

37. Anderson, p. 178.

38. Quoted in Barrett, p. 290.

39. Banning Garrett, "China Policy and the Constraints of Triangular

Logic," in Kenneth A. Oye et al., *Eagle Defiant: United States Foreign Policy in the 1980s* (Boston: Little Brown, 1983), p. 265.

40. Dugger, p. 373, citing *New York Times*, March 18, 1983, etc.

41. Barrett, pp. 289-91, 333.

42. Cannon, p. 103. By 1980 Reagan's "kitchen cabinet" of L.A. millionaires included other ASC backers, such as Earle M. Jorgenson, Jack Wrather, and Lockheed investor William Wilson.

43. Back in 1960 the ASC Washington Report had called for unleashing Chiang Kai-shek's soldiers in Vietnam, as a way of "assisting the Chinese Nationalists to regain their homeland and to overthrow on the way home the bloody Communist tyranny which holds much of Vietnam in its grip" (Turner, p. 205).

44. Anderson, pp. 93-102: "Pearson...once bragged to an associate about his alleged role in hiding Nazi doctor Josef Mengele, the infamous 'Angel of Death' of the Auschwitz extermination camp. He is also the man who, as world chairman of the World Anti-Communist League in 1978, was responsible for flooding the European League chapters with Nazi sympathizers and former officers of the Nazi SS" (p. 93).

45. Anderson, p. 150.

46. Dugger, p. 529; quoting broadcast of 2/3/78.

47. Hank Messick, *Of Grass and Snow: The Secret Criminal Elite* (Englewood Cliffs, N.J.: Prentice-Hall, 1979), p. 84.

48. Anderson, pp. 181-82; personal communication.

49. Dickey, pp. 62-63.

50. Anderson, pp. 150-52; Dickey, p.112.

51. *Boston Globe*, August 3, 1986, A20 (see Chapter VI).

52. Christopher Buckley, *Violent Neighbors* (New York: Times Books, 1984), p. 103. Congressional aides of Helms and of Congressman Jack Kemp, as well as Reagan advisors such as Richard Allen and Roger Fontaine, visited Guatemala through 1980 and spoke to right-wingers there (Pearce, p. 178, citing Nairn).

53. *Asian Outlook*, November 1980, p. 19. Another Reagan supporter at the Conference, Congressman Daniel Crane, said that Carter's Nicaraguan policy had been, in General Sumner's word, "treason"; he promised that Reagan would strive to ensure that the "State department will be swept clean of communists and fellow travelers" (p. 15).

54. *Asian Outlook*, November 1980, p. 45. The role of Ray Cline in generating the Reagan-WACL-contra alliance was considerable. So was that of Cline's two son-in-laws, Roger Fontaine and Stefan Halper. Roger Fontaine made at least two visits to Guatemala in 1980, as well as (with General Sumner) drafting the May 1980 Santa Fe Statement, which said that World War III was already underway in Central America against the Soviets, and that Nicaragua was the enemy (Pearce, p. 178; Dickey, p. 72). Halper was coincidentally a member of the Reagan campaign who became a principal suspect in the later Congressional investigation of "Debategate," the illegal transmission of

documents from the campaign of President Carter (U.S. Cong., House, Committee on Post Office and Civil Service, *Unauthorized Transfers of Nonpublic Information During the 1980 Presidential Election*, Report, 98th Cong., 2nd Sess., May 17, 1984, pp. 36-40). According to Elizabeth Drew, some former Reagan aides told her that, in his intelligence-gathering operation for the campaign, Halper "was receiving information from the C.I.A." Halper vigorously denied this; and so, for good measure, did Cline. (Elizabeth Drew, *Campaign Journal: The Political Events of 1983-1984* [New York: Macmillan, 1985], pp. 130-31; cf. pp. 133-34).

55. *Wall Street Journal*, April 18, 1980; Lernoux, p. 79.

56. Scott, *War Conspiracy*, pp. 194, 208, 210; Hinckle and Turner, p. 47.

57. McCoy, p. 212. Conein is also said to have handled cross-border operations into North Vietnam for the so-called Studies and Operations group in Vietnam (SOG, cf. Chapters III, IX): Scott, *War Conspiracy*, p. 162n.

58. Tad Szulc, *Compulsive Spy* (New York: Viking, 1974), p. 72.

59. Anderson, pp. 56, 135, 194, etc.

60. "Training Under the Mutual Security Program (with emphasis on development of leaders), May 15, 1959"; reprinted in L. Fletcher Prouty, *The Secret Team: The CIA and Its Allies in Control of the United States and the World* (Englewood Cliffs, N.J.: Prentice Hall, 1973), pp. 444-79; cf. especially pp. 463, 477. Colonel Prouty, who observed the "secret team" from his vantage as Focal Point Officer for Pentagon-CIA liaison calls this document "one of the most influential documents of the past quarter-century...When highest officials of this Government assert that the majority of the nations of the uncommitted 'Third World' would be better off under the control of their military elite, an elite to be selected by Americans, it is time for other Americans to...sound the warning on the possibility that this same American elite may not [sic] become persuaded of its own role in this country" (pp. 442-43). Peter Dale Scott has argued independently for the importance of this document, and of the planning process it represents, in helping to engender the Indonesian military coup of 1965. Cf. his articles in Malcolm Caldwell (ed.), *Ten Years' Military Terror in Indonesia* (Nottingham: Spokesman Books, 1975), pp. 218-21, 252-53; and in *Pacific Affairs* (Summer 1985), pp. 246-51.

61. Anderson, pp. 54-55.

62. Personal communication. Singlaub's and Stilwell's careers were closely intertwined at this point, first in 1949 in establishing the special warfare training center at Fort Benning, then when both men were battalion commanders in South Korea, 1952-53 (Anderson, p. 151; Prados, p. 36; Ranelagh, pp. 221-23). The French intelligence liaison with CIA in the Korean War was Yves Guerinerac, later a key figure in the private intelligence group Aginter-Presse, melding the alliance between WACL in Latin America and European neofascists (see Chapter III, also below). In 1976 Singlaub succeeded Stilwell as U.S. Commander in South Korea.

63. Personal communication from former CIA officer; Asian Peoples' Anti-Communist League, Twelfth Conference, Proceedings (Seoul, Oct. 31-

Nov. 8, 1966), pp. 389-92 (CIADC Report): "In March 1964 a military 'coup d'etat' delivered Brazil of a corrupt and leftist government... The Confederation and the Brazilian Anti-Communist Crusade were instrumental in pushing the Armed Forces into taking that drastic liberating decision" (p. 392).

64. David Atlee Phillips, *The Night Watch* (New York: Atheneum, 1977), p. 38; U.S. Cong., House, Select Committee on Communist Aggression, Ninth Interim Report, 83rd Cong., 2nd Sess. (Washington, 1954), pp. 92, 101 (Sisniega-Phillips); p. 110 (Sisniega-Sandoval). When Sandoval and Sisniega tried to launch a coup against Guatemalan President Rios Montt in 1982, Mitchell WerBell III (another veteran of the Cline/Hunt/Singlaub OSS team) flew down to neighboring Belize to assist them (Anderson, pp. 181-82). Cline was later an official in the Association of Former Intelligence Officers which Phillips formed on his retirement from CIA.

65. Anderson, p. 83; William Turner, *Power on the Right* (Berkeley: Ramparts Press, 1971), p. 213.

66. Alfred W. McCoy, *The Politics of Heroin in Southeast Asia* (New York: Harper and Row, 1972), pp. 215-16. See Chapter III.

67. Personal communication from friend of Martino, 1980. John Martino claimed to have inside knowledge about the John F. Kennedy assassination, and was the first to offer the hypothesis (later given wide circulation by mafioso John Roselli and columnist Jack Anderson), that the President had been killed by an assassination team originally recruited (possibly, though Martino did not say this, by himself) to kill Castro: cf. U.S. Cong., House, Select Committee on Assassinations, *Investigation of the Assassination of President John F. Kennedy, Hearings*, 95th Cong., 2nd Sess., XI, 438-41; Hinckle and Turner, pp. 349-50; Anthony Summers, *Conspiracy* (New York: McGraw-Hill, 1980), pp. 126, 449-52.

68. *New York Times*, October 7, 1979, B16.

69. Hank Messick, *Of Grass and Snow: The Secret Criminal Elite* (Englewood Cliffs, N.J.: Prentice-Hall, 1979), p. 84; Anderson, pp. 181-82.

70. *Washington Post*, August 16, 1977, A8; Hinckle and Turner, pp. 250-59. The *New York Times* obituary for WerBell reported that his "anti-communist activities were often said to be linked with the Central Intelligence Agency" (December 18, 1983).

71. Kruger, p. 8; Hougan, *Spooks*, p. 99; Messick, pp. 81-84. Hougan links WerBell's arms indictment in 1974 to his alleged dealings with the fugitive financier Robert Vesco and also with his old Kunming OSS friend Lucien Conein, who in 1976 appeared at WerBell's drug trial to testify for the defense. (He did not have to testify, the case having been thrown out after the mysterious death of the key witness.)

72. *National Times* [of Australia], September 12, 1982 (reprinted in Lernoux, p. 158); quoting an unnamed former deputy director of the CIA.

73. Propper, p. 182. WerBell was also alleged to have been involved in a potential arms deal with the ex-CIA Cuban drug king of Mexico, Alberto Sicilia Falcon, (who may have been installed there with the aid of Conein's

DEA hit squad of ex-CIA Cubans: see Chapter III): Kruger, pp. 182-83.

74. *Washington Post*, August 16, 1977; Anderson, pp. 155-56.

75. *Miami Herald*, December 14, 1986; *Guardian*, December 24, 1986; *San Francisco Bay Guardian*, December 24, 1986; see Chapter X.

76. *New York Times*, October 7, 1979, B16.

77. Anderson, pp. 181-82.

78. Magnus Linklater et al., *The Nazi Legacy* (New York: Holt Rinehart and Winston, 1984), pp. 266-84.

79. Linklater, pp. 269-70; 288-89; Anderson, pp. 144-45, 204.

80. Lernoux, p. 178: "What had all this plotting to do with the Vatican Bank? The bank's two principal financial advisers and partners, Michele Sindona and Roberto Calvi, were members of P-2, a neofascist Masonic lodge in Milan headed by the Italian fascist financier Licio Gelli, who had dropped from public sight. Gelli was wanted in Italy for, among other things, his connection with the Pagliai and delle Chiaie bombing of the Bologna railroad station...As shown by Italian authorities, P-2 was 'a state within the state,' its aim being to restore fascism in Italy and buttress its hold on Latin America... That Archbishop Paul Marcinkus, the American-born head of the Vatican Bank, knew of such connections is considered unlikely, although the Vatican Bank was perhaps the largest shareholder in Ambrosiano and Calvi [who was murdered when his Banco Ambrosiano failed] worked closely with Marcinkus on financial matters. More to the point, the Vatican's own investigation of the Calvi connection disclosed that the Vatican Bank owned ten Panamanian shell companies that were used to advance the political ambitions of Calvi and Gelli in Latin America and, through them, the P-2." In February 1987 Archbishop Marcinkus was finally indicted by an Italian court for his role in the Banco Ambrosiano failure.

81. Frederic Laurent, *L'Orchestre noir* (Paris: Stock, 1978), passim.

82. Anderson, p. 298; Kruger, p. 211.

83. Quoted in Edward S. Herman and Frank Brodhead, *The Rise and Fall of the Bulgarian Connection* (New York: Sheridan Square Publications, 1986), pp. 85-86.

84. Herman and Brodhead, p. 93.

85. Laurent, pp. 7-14; Herman and Brodhead, pp. 88-89, Linklater et al., p. 207.

86. Propper, pp. 305-14. See Chapter III.

87. Herman and Brodhead, p. 90; citing Martin A. Lee and Kevin Coogan, *Village Voice*, December 24, 1985.

88. Dickey, pp. 88, ; Anderson, p. 144. "While Sandoval danced and chatted with the elite of Reagan's inner circle [in 1981], his minions back home were busy; the Secret Anti-Communist Army (ESA), which was believed to be an extension of Sandoval's MLN, had just threatened to exterminate the entire Jesuit order in Guatemala" (Anderson, p. 177).

89. Anderson, pp. 145-56.

90. *Oakland Tribune*, February 12, 1987, B6.

91. Kruger, p. 114. When Lopez-Rega was Argentina's Minister of the Interior, Ed Wilson's company Consultants International was shipping "an array of riot-control equipment to Brazil and Argentina" (Maas, p. 60).

92. Kruger, p. 11.

93. Anderson, pp. 141-42; Henrik Kruger, *The Great Heroin Coup* (Boston: South End Press, 1980), pp. 85, 106, 110.

94. Penny Lernoux, *In Banks We Trust* (Garden City, N.Y.: Anchor/Doubleday, 1984), p. 179; Kruger, p. 224.

95. Lernoux, p. 189. Italian investigators traced the neofascist-Anonima Sequestri connection to a May 1972 Mafia meeting of Italian *mafiosi* involved in the trans-Atlantic narcotics traffic, including Tomasso Buscetta, the go-between between the Ricord drug network and the Gambino family in New York. Cf. Gaia Servadio, *Mafioso* (New York: Delta, 1976), pp. 259-60; Kruger, pp. 105-06.

96. Anderson, p. 172: "Now [in 1978] in the opposition, Sandoval turned to Mafialike tactics to get financing. 'He authorized the leaders of his bands to obtain funds by robbery and kidnappings,' says a wealthy Guatemalan politician who knows the MLN chief [Sandoval] well. 'He would send death threats, supposedly from the guerrillas, to the rich *finqueros* [coffee growers] and the next day, either Leonel [Sisniega] or Raul [Midence Pivaral, Sandoval's brother-in-law] would collect the money." In the CIA's 1954 Guatemala coup, Sisniega worked directly under David Phillips.

97. Lernoux, pp. 188-89; Herman and Brodhead, pp. 73-75. Lernoux claims that "both men belonged to the P-2" (p. 188); others point to Sindona as P-2's original financier (Cornwell, p. 47), and Miceli as a "close friend" of Gelli and source of his military intelligence connections (Gurwin, p. 187). John McCaffery, a veteran of British intelligence and of the wartime Allen Dulles OSS-SS deal known as "Operation Sunrise," prepared an affidavit in 1981 for his friend and banking associate Sindona. In it he stated that he helped Sindona plan the 1970 coup attempt and that he was "sure to a moral certainty" that the CIA was aware of the plot. The CIA-Miceli connection grew directly out of the World War II OSS-SS connection; and Prince Borghese, the nominal head of the 1970 coup attempt, was saved by then OSS-officer James Angleton from a Resistance death sentence in April 1945. In 1974 Borghese introduced the fugitive delle Chiaie to officers of the Pinochet Chilean Secret Service DINA, a connection which led to the attempted murder of a Chilean exile in Rome by delle Chiaie and Letelier's nemesis Michael Townley. A CORU Cuban group took credit publicly for this attack.

98. Kruger, p. 225.

99. Laurent, *L'Orchestre noir*, p. 254; Lernoux, p. 201. In the 1976 Italian election Guarino chaired a group, "Americans for a Democratic Italy," organized by Sindona, which channeled U.S. funds to the Italian neofascist party, the M.S.I.

100. Peter Maas, *Manhunt: The Incredible Pursuit of a CIA Agent Turned Terrorist* (New York: Random House, 1986), p. 247; Michael Ledeen, *New York*, March 3, 1980.

101. Maas, p. 247.

102. Herman and Brodhead, pp. 94-96; quoting the Italian journal *La Repubblica*, in Diana Johnstone, *In These Times*, July 10-23, 1985.

103. Gurwin, p. 191; *New York Times*, February 15, 1987.

104. Herman and Brodhead, pp. 97, 135-36, 237; citing *New York Daily News*, June 24, 1984.

105. A third collaborator with Ledeen and Sterling, Paul Henze (former CIA Station Chief in Turkey), transmitted similarly belated "information" from a 1971 Bulgarian defector (Stefan Sverdlev), about a purported Warsaw Pact plan to flood the western world with narcotics. The story was published in the November 1983 *Reader's Digest* in a story by Nathan Adams, who earlier had written about a flood of drugs from Cuba and Nicaragua (Herman and Brodhead, pp. 225-33, 238-40; *Reader's Digest*, July 1982). The 1985 judgment against Pazienza found that SISMI had prepared two diversionary reports of a Bulgarian drug connection, from information provided by Pazienza and an "external collaborator," whom Herman and Brodhead speculate may have been Ledeen (p. 93). Ledeen also took up the line that the Sandinistas had organized "a vast drug and arms-smuggling network to finance their terrorists and guerrillas, flooding our country with narcotics" (*New York Times*, April 16, 1984, quoted in *Boston Globe*, November 17, 1984).

106. Herman and Brodhead, pp. 105-09. Herman and Brodhead accuse the *New York Times* for the paper's "alliance with and protection of Michael Ledeen. Ledeen was given Op-Ed column space twice in 1984-85, allowing him to issue a call for the greater application of force in Lebanon and to stress the greater importance of National Security than individual liberty—themes that would delight the heart of Licio Gelli. Ledeen's book *Grave New World* was given a substantial and favorable notice in the Sunday *New York Times Book Review*. Perhaps more serious has been the *New York Times*'s cover-up of Ledeen's role in Italy and his unsavory linkages to Italian intelligence and the Italian Right. [With one exception] the *Times* has never mentioned his connections with Santovito, Gelli, and Pazienza [all P-2], his controversial sale of documents to SISMI, or the fact that the head of Italian military intelligence stated before the Italian Parliament that Ledeen was an 'intriguer' and unwelcome in Italy. Actually, the *Times*'s suppressions on Ledeen have been part of a larger package of suppressions that excluded any information that would disturb the hegemony of the Sterling-Henze line [that Agca and the Bulgarians conspired to kill the Pope]. Thus, just as Sterling and Henze never mention P-2 in their writings, so the *Times* failed even to mention the Italian Parliamentary Report on P-2 of July 12, 1984, which raised so many inconvenient questions about the quality of Italian society and the intelligence services" (Herman and Brodhead, pp. 197-98).

107. Herman and Brodhead, pp. 94-96. Ledeen has denied most of these allegations.

108. Lernoux, p. 216. Pazienza allegedly supplied his private yacht to help Gelli flee Italy after his escape from prison.

109. "In addition to drugs, Nugan Hand...also did business with Edwin Wilson...Memos and testimony by Nugan Hand employees show that Hand met with Wilson in Bangkok, and that Houghton held discussions with him in Switzerland. Intelligence sources also claimed that Houghton used Nugan Hand's Saudi Arabian branch to finance Wilson's arms-smuggling operations" (Lernoux, pp. 72-73; see Chapter III). Sindona's later career became dramatically intertwined with Wilson's and Terpil's. In January 1984 hearings began for the extradition of Sindona from a medium security New York jail to Italy, "to face the charge of ordering the assassination of Giorgio Ambrosoli, liquidator of Sindona's Italian bank" (Gurwin, p. 208). A key witness was William Arico, an American gangster accused of murdering Ambrosoli. Arico was awaiting extradition in the Metropolitan Correctional Center in New York, where a fellow-detainee was Edwin Wilson. Arico was planning an escape, and Wilson, whose rage against his federal prosecutor Larry Barcella was at a peak, arranged for $50,000 to be passed to Arico in London. During the attempted escape down a rope of knotted sheets, Arico was crushed to death by a falling accomplice, "an overweight Cuban drug dealer...Wilson, when confronted by these facts, denied that Barcella had been the intended target" (Maas, p. 289). Arico's death helped delay Sindona's extradition until 1986, as did an affidavit from Gregory Korkola, a former business partner of Wilson's partner Frank Terpil. (According to Korkola's affidavit, he heard Arico insist "that Michele did not have anything to do with the [Ambrosoli] murder; Nick Tosches, *Power on Earth: Michele Sindona's Explosive Story* [New York: Arbor House, 1986], p. 273.) In 1986 Sindona was finally extradited to Italy, following which he soon died by poisoning in an Italian prison.

110. It is no coincidence that Edwin Wilson's two closest friends in the House, Congressmen John Murphy and Charles Wilson, were also the key figures in the House Somoza lobby (Maas, p. 52; Christian, p. 87). After Somoza's departure from Nicaragua, on August 1, 1979, Murphy presented Enrique Bermudez and other future contra leaders at their first public press conference (Dickey, pp. 62-63).

111. Lernoux, p. 217. Miguel Angel Napout, reputedly Paraguay's biggest smuggler, with links to Nixon's confidant, Bebe Rebozo, and South American heroin traffickers, allegedly received an invitation to attend the Republican convention, where he interviewed presidential candidate Reagan (Lernoux, p. 217, citing *Latin American Regional Report—Southern Cone*, July 31, 1981).

112. Gurwin, pp. 56-57; Rupert Cornwell, *God's Banker* (London: Victor Gollancz, 1983), pp. 94-95.

113. Cornwell, p. 95.

114. P-2 political influence, as opposed to CAL's, was marked by this double opening to both neofascists and social democrats. Robelo and Cruz owed some of their influence to their backing by European socialist parties such as Italy's, which had benefited from the CIA/P-2 handouts and "privileged financial treatment at Banco Ambrosiano" (Gurwin, p. 75).

115. David A. Yallop, *In God's Name: An Investigation into the Murder of Pope John Paul I* (New York: Bantam, 1985), p. 320.

116. Gurwin, p. 56; cf. pp. 59-60.

117. Yallop, p. 326; cf. Gurwin, pp. 56-57; Cornwell, p. 95.

118. Yallop, pp. 333-34.

119. Yallop, p. 327.

120. Yallop, pp. 359-60.

121. Testimony of former contra leader Edgar Chamorro before the International Court of Justice, quoted in Ellen Ray and William Schaap, "Vernon Walters: Crypto-diplomat and Terrorist," *Covert Action Information Bulletin* 26 (Summer 1986), p. 8.

122. Gurwin, p. 194.

123. KRON-TV News Release, August 7, 1986.

124. Kruger, p. 20; Fred Strasser and Brian McTigue, "The Fall River Conspiracy," *Boston* (November 1978), pp. 124, 180, 182.

125. U.S. Ambassador Robert Hill, who personally received Helms and his aides, was part of the CIA-State "team" on the 1954 Guatemalan Operation. A former employee of Grace Shipping Lines, which had interests in Guatemala, he became in 1960 a director of United Fruit: Stephen Schlesinger and Stephen Kinzer, *Bitter Fruit: The Untold Story of the American Coup in Guatemala* (Garden City, N.Y.: Doubleday, 1982), p. 107.

126. Anderson, p. 175.

127. Buckley, p. 103.

128. Anderson, pp. 147, 207, 209. Carlos Midence Pivaral has also attended Miami meetings of Alpha-66, the leading Cuban exile connection to WACL.

129. Buckley, pp. 311, 318.

130. Anderson, p. 246.

131. Molina was associated with the American Nicaraguan Council and in 1976 brought Fediay and a group of international anti-Communist journalists to Nicaragua; cf. *Latin American Political Report*, August 26, 1977. Meanwhile for years Molina, like Fediay, has been paid by a so-called news service, Capitol Information Services, run by James Lucier, an aide of Jesse Helms (*Oakland Tribune*, August 15, 1986, B-4).

132. John Dinges and Saul Landau, *Assassination on Embassy Row* (New York: Pantheon, 1980), p. 252. Another Molina associate, Somoza employee, and Bay of Pigs Veteran, Fernando Penabaz, graduated from his position as "special assistant" to the Republican Party in 1964 to "a twenty-year sentence in the Atlanta penitentiary for smuggling nine and a half pounds of cocaine" (Hinckle and Turner, p. 315).

133. This parallel may be more than superficial, as Watergate burglar Frank Sturgis is said to have collaborated with Howard Hunt's and David Phillips' Guatemalan proteges, Mario Sandoval Alarcon and Lionel Sisniega Otero, in the liberation from a Guatemalan jail of the CIA-Somoza coup candidate, Carlos Castillo Armas. Cf. Donald Freed with Fred Landis, *Death in*

Washington (Westport, Conn.: Lawrence Hill, p. 1980), p. 41.

134. Nairn, p. 3; Albosta Report, p. 60.

135. Kruger, p. 217.

136. Delle Chiaie, the more seasoned and sophisticated of the two terrorists, somehow eluded capture. He "was later to claim that, through infiltration of both the American and Italian intelligence services, he knew in advance of the plans" to seize him (Linklater, p. 300).

137. Dickey, pp. 152, 156.

138. Dickey, pp. 259-61.

139. Anderson, p. 230; Dickey, p. 261.

140. Anderson, p. 232; Dickey, p. 262.

141. *Oakland Tribune*, August 17, 1986 (for further examples see Chapter VI).

142. *New York Times*, April 11, 1986.

143. Renata Adler, "Searching for the Real Nixon Scandal," *Atlantic* (December 1976), pp. 76ff.

144. Adler, pp. 77, 90; Peter Dale Scott, *The War Conspiracy* (New York: Bobbs Merrill, 1972), pp. 204, 206.

145. Kissinger left Washington for Peking in late June 1971; Hunt was hired as a White House consultant on July 6.

146. Adler, pp. 92-93.

147. Adler, p. 91.

148. Adler, pp. 91, 94.

149. Lukas, p. 283.

150. *San Francisco Chronicle*, August 11, 1981, p. 6.

151. To facilitate the Chun visit, and the resumption of normalized relations with South Korea which followed, the Reagan adminstration delayed publication of the State Department's statutorily required report on international human rights, which noted a "deterioration" of human rights in South Korea in 1980 (*New York Times*, February 2, 1980, p. 8; February 10, 1980, p. 10). On his return to Seoul, Chun announced harsh new labor laws banning strikes (*New York Times*, March 1, 1980, IV, 4). The United States followed with an announcement it would sell $900 million in arms to South Korea, including 36 F-16 fighters (*New York Times*, March 27, 1980, p. 9).

152. Anderson, pp. 66-70. The church was also promoted with assistance from Sasakawa Ryoichi and Kodama Yoshio, two of the CIA's most notorious contacts in Japan.

153. Anderson, p. 302; quoting *Le Monde Diplomatique*, February 1985.

154. Anderson, p. 129; *Washington Times*, Oct. 8, 1985, p. 5A.

155. *Miami Herald*, June 8, 1986, p. 26A; NBC Nightly News, June 13, 1986.

Footnotes to Chapter V

1. Ehud Avriel, "Israel's Beginnings in Africa," Michael Curtis and Susan Aurelia Gitelson, Eds. *Israel in the Third World,* Transaction Books, New Brunswick, NJ, 1976, pp. 69-74. The introduction was made by President Tubman of Liberia.

2. This was more than a little ironic, as Zionist leader Chaim Weizmann wrote many times to British leaders trying to sell them on the merits of using an independent Jewish state (white and Western-educated in a darker sea of uncivilized humanity) as an outpost of the British Empire.

3. Curtis & Gitelson, op. cit., Appendix, pp. 393-397 and passim. Dahomey (now Benin) even received help setting up a state lottery.

4. D. V. Segre, "The Philosophy and Practice of Israel's International Cooperation," Curtis & Gitelson, op. cit., p. 10.

5. *Washington Post*, June 15, 1986.

6. *Latin America Weekly Report,* May 4, 1984 The FRG also has recently been funding Israeli activities, see IFA October 1985.

7. *Africa Report,* November-December 1983 and *L'Express* (Paris) October 7, 1983.

8. Hilmi S. Yousuf, *African-Arab Relations,* Amana Books, Brattleboro VT, 1986, p. 55.

9. Edy Kaufman, Yoram Shapira and Joel Barromi, *Israel-Latin American Relations,* Transaction Books, New Brunswick, NJ, 1979 has a full account of Israeli development programs and political relations in Latin America.

10. Yousuf, op. cit., pp. 90-94; Arye Oded, "Africa, Israel and the Arabs: On the Restoration of Israeli-African Diplomatic Relations," *The Jerusalem Journal of International Relations,* Vol. 6, No. 3, 1982-1983, among many others dealing with this issue.

11. Aaron Klieman, *Israel's Global Reach: Arms Sales as Diplomacy,* Pergamon-Brassey's, Washington, London, N.Y., 1985, pp. 16 and 26 (footnote 7).

12. Leonard Slater, *The Pledge,* Simon & Schuster, New York, 1970 celebrates the whole panoply of scams run by the pre-state arms smugglers.

Actually the borders established after the fighting created a state one third larger than that contemplated by the UN partition plan. And of course, there was no Palestinian state as provided for in the plan. Al Schwimmer, the Israeli arms dealer involved in the Iran-contra affair figures largely in *The Pledge* as the main organizer of aircraft for the Haganah, the pre-state army.

13. Bernard Reich, *Israel: Land of Tradition and Conflict,* Westview Press, Boulder, CO, 1985, p.151.

14. Robert E. Harkavy, *Spectre of a Middle Eastern Holocaust: The Strategic and Diplomatic Implications of the Israeli Nuclear Weapons Program,* University of Denver Monograph Series in World Affairs, 1977 p. 5. Israel is now ranked as the world's sixth greatest nuclear weapons state, with an arsenal thought to include sophisticated thermonuclear weapons.

15. Andrew J. Pierre, *The Global Politics of Arms Sales,* Council on Foreign Relations, Princeton University Press, 1982, p. 161.

16. Klieman, *Israel's Global Reach,* p. 23.

17. Ibid. pp. 17-19 and passim.

18. Bishara Bahbah, *Israel and Latin America: The Military Connection,* St. Martin's Press, New York, & Institute for Palestine Studies, Washington, 1986, pp. 38-53. Some well known recent cases of theft are the technology for plating the inside of cannon barrels, for a sophisticated aerial photographic system, and cluster bomb packing machinery. (*Israeli Foreign Affairs,* October 1986) Israel's thefts of enriched uranium and spent nuclear fuel from the U.S. and Europe are legend.

19. Jane Hunter, *Israeli-Foreign Policy: South Africa & Central America,* South End Press, Boston 1987 pp. 31-45.

20. *U.S. Assistance to the State of Israel,* Report prepared by the General Accounting Office, June 24, 1983 (and released in its uncensored version by the American-Arab Anti-Discrimination Committee) p. 43.

21. Aharon Klieman, *Israeli Arms Sales: Perspectives and Prospects,* Jaffee Center for Strategic Studies, Tel Aviv University, February 1984, pp. 40-41.

22. The figure 40% was cited for the late 1970s. Pierre, op. cit., p. 161.

23. Klieman, *Israel's Global Reach,* p. 22.

24. Neubach and Peri, *The Military Industrial Complex in Israel,* International Center for Peace in the Middle East, Tel Aviv, January 1985 p. 68.

25. Klieman, op. cit., p. 57.

26. Pierre, op. cit., p. 125.

27. Neubach & Peri, op. cit., p. 81.

28. Dan Fisher, *Los Angeles Times,* September 18, 1986.

29. Ibid.

30. Klieman, *Israel's Global Reach,* p. 93; Neubach and Peri, op. cit., p. 4 and passim.

31. Ze'ev Schiff, *Ha'aretz,* December 17, 1986, translated in *News From Within* (Alternative Information Centre, 14/E Koresh Street, West Jerusalem Israel), January 10, 1987.

32. Klieman, *Israel's Global Reach,* p. 99.

33. *Washington Report on Middle East Affairs,* March 1987.

34. In 1981 an Israeli cabinet minister, Ya'acov Meridor laid this out: "Don't compete with us in South Africa. Don't compete with us in the Caribbean area or in any other country where you can't operate in the open. Let us do it. I even use the expression, "You sell the ammunition and equipment by proxy. Israel will be your proxy." And this would be worked out with a certain agreement with the United States where we will have certain markets ... which will be left for us." *Ha'aretz*, August 25, 1981.

35. *U.S. Assistance to the State of Israel*, pp. 36-45 (much of this material was censored out of the report originally released by GAO.) Also see *Wall Street Journal*, June 22, 1984.

36. Bahbah, op. cit., table pp. 78-85. A recent report (ACAN (Panama City, 1959 GMT, April 5, 1986 in *FBIS Latin America*) said that Israeli military sales to Honduras, second poorest nation in the hemisphere, were barter agreements, with Honduras paying in agricultural products.

37. Hunter, *Israeli Foreign Policy*, pp. 95-143.

38. Ibid. p. 128. Distribution of food aid in both El Salvador and Guatemala is often contingent upon moving into one of these fortified hamlets.

39. Interview with Lucas, *HaAretz Weekly Supplement*, February 7, 1986, translated in *News From Within*, January 10, 1987.

40. *Time*, March 28, 1983.

41. *SIPRI Yearbook 1980*, p. 96.

42. *Miami Herald*, September 17, 1978.

43. op. cit., November 18, 1978.

44. *Latin America Political Report*, June 29, 1979.

45. Ibid., July 6, 1979.

46. *Miami Herald*, Nov. 18, 1978. The "permission" was supposedly for "small arms," but Israel no doubt interpreted that to mean a Cessna rather than a Phantom.

47. *Washington Post*, July 1, 1979.

48. Anastasio Somoza Debayle, *Nicaragua Betrayed*, Western Islands, Belmont, Ma. 1980, pp. 239-240.

49. Slater, *The Pledge*, pp. 257-259.

50. Estimate based on knowledge of the remaining 2 percent, an Argentine sale worth $7 million (documented by a bill found after Somoza fled, it is not clear whether the weapons were ever delivered) and a few known shipments from a private dealer, worth perhaps $5 million. The final figure is arrived at after subtracting $100 million, in order to err on the conservative side.

51. *U.S. Asistence to the State of Israel*, p. 38; *Jerusalem Post*, December 4, 1981 in Shahak, *Israel's Global Role*, pp. 46-47; an Israeli official was quick to point out that the pact did not limit Israel's independence of action in attacking its neighbors.

52. *Ha'aretz*, May 20, 1982 in FBIS Middle East & Africa, May 21, 1982, p. I-1.

53. *Jerusalem Post*, Dec. 4, 1981.

54. Africa was Kimche's special purview. He had done his Mossad service there and became known as "Mr. Africa" for his unflagging efforts as head of

the foreign ministry to persuade various governments to renew ties. Only four ever did: Zaire, Liberia, Cote d'Ivoire, and Cameroon. After Kimche left the ministry a change in policy was announced limiting Israeli attempts to establish diplomacy to a few "key" nations.

55. *Ha'aretz*, May 20, 1982 in FBIS Middle East & Africa, May 21, 1982, p. I-1.

56. *New York Times*, December 14, 1981.

57. *New York Times*, November 27, 1986.

58. Tel Aviv IDF Radio, 0605 GMT, October 25, 1983 in FBIS Middle East & Africa, October 25, 1983, p. I-2.

59. *Washington Post*, August 5, 1986. Weinberger and Casey were afraid that the Arab governments in the Middle East would construe the pact as aimed against them (they have), while Israel has always taken pains to assure the Soviet Union, which it does not wish to alienate, that of course the agreement is aimed at "the Arabs.".

60. Interview in *Hatzofe*, December 16, 1983 in FBIS Middle East & Africa.

61. *Ma'ariv*, April 10, 1984 in FBIS, Middle East and Africa, April 10, 1984, p. I-2. The UN condemned it.

62. *Ma'ariv* (Tel Aviv) November 11, 1983 in FBIS Middle East & Africa, November 15, 1983, p. I-5.

63. *Yediot Aharonot*, December 4, 1983, FBIS Middle East & Africa, December 6, 1983, p. I-5.

64. Ibid.; *Aviation Week and Space Technology*, Nov. 5, 1984.

65. *San Francisco Sunday Examiner & Chronicle*, December 4, 1983.

66. *Los Angeles Times*, January 11, 1987. Haig wanted to forge an alliance with conservative Middle East countries. Kimche urged the U.S. to do what Israel wanted: create an alliance with Ethiopia, Turkey, and Iran. There is also a military-political committee which discusses military cooperation.

67. *Ha'aretz*, November 11, 1983 in *Israel Mirror* (nd). Kimche also asked that the U.S. authorize third world recipients of U.S. foreign military sales credits (the form in which military assistance is given) to spend their credits in Israel and that the U.S. buy Israel's obsolete and surplus military equipment and resell it to third countries. Serious discussion of this proposal did not take place until the Reagan-Shamir summit of November 1983. *Latin America Weekly Report*, May 4, 1984.

68. *New York Times*, July 21, 1983.

69. *Ha'aretz*, November 11, 1983.

70. *Davar*, January 3, 1982. The loan was confirmed by Danny Halperin, economic consul at the Israeli embassy. It was repaid in Israel's aid the following year.

71. *The Times* (London), September 19, 1983.

72. *San Francisco Chronicle*, December 5, 1986.

73. *Boston Globe*, January 25, 1987.

74. *Boston Globe*, November 30, 1986. According to this article, Daniel Sheehan of the Christic Institute said that his sources said the Shackley-Clines

connection began right after Congress passed the Harken Amendment forbidding military aid to Somoza.

75. *New York Times,* February 8, 1987.

76. *Newsweek,* October 10, 1983.

77. Ibid., December 6, 1986. Reminiscent of paying the staff of a brothel in drugs.

78. *Boston Sunday Globe,* January 18, 1987.

79. *Le Monde* (Manchester Guardian English Section) May 6, 1984.

80. *Le Monde Diplomatique,* October 1984.

81. *Washington Post,* December 7, 1982; *Le Monde Diplomatique,* February 1983. Ultimately the bulk of the war booty was sold to Iran. Israel has always had a huge stock of East bloc arms, however, only some of which are thought to have been captured in its wars.

82. *Latin America Weekly Report,* December 17, 1982.

83. *SIPRI Yearbook 1984,* p. 238.

84. *Miami Herald,* December 13, 1982.

85. *Boletin Informativo? Honduras,* Centro de Documentacion de Honduras, Tegucigalpa, March 16, 1985.

86. *Ha'aretz,* December 3, 1986, in FBIS Middle East & Africa, pp. I-3-4.

87. *Israeli Foreign Affairs,* November 1986 and December 1986.

88. *AfriqueAsie,* Paris, April 25, 1983.

89. Quoting Washington intelligence sources, ANN, ANSA, AP and EFE, *unomasuno,* (Mexico City) July 1, 1983. These sources also spoke of support from Brazil and Venezuela.

90. *Sh'ma,* November 2, 1984. Nicaragua has thoroughly infiltrated the contras.

91. *Davar,* cited by *Latin America Regional Reports Mexico and Central America,* March 23, 1984.

92. (*Davar*), *Guardian* (London), October 11, 1985.

93. *Latin America Regional Report Mexico and Central America,* February 14, 1986.

94. *Der Spiegel,* July 26, 1983 in Jesus Guevara Morin/Notimex, *unomasuno,* April 23, 1984.

95. *Counterspy,* Sept. - Nov., 1983.

96. *Miami Herald,* September 9, 1983. 5 or 6 donations to ARDE in the "tens of thousands of dollars" from "mysterious" sources might have come from the CIA. "The Most Dangerous Game," *Time,* October 17, 1983.

97. Panama City ACAN, 0045 GMT, April 24, 1984 in FBIS Latin America, April 25, 1984, p. P-12.

98. Sonia Vargas L., Alfonso Robelo, "Pastora debe aceptar union de ARDE y FDN," *La Nacion Internacional,* (San Jose, Costa Rica) June 7-13, 1984.

99. Madrid EFE, 022 GMT, September 25, 1984 in FBIS Latin America, September 27, 1984, p. P-15.

100. *Sunday Times* (London) August 30, 1983, in Jesus Guevara Morin/Notimex, *unomasuno,* April 23, 1984.

101. *Diario La Hora* (Guatemala) March 19, 1985 in *Inforpress Centro-americana*, March 28, 1985. *New York Times*, December 1982.

102. Testimony of Hector Francis, a defecting Argentine contra trainer, to Latin American Federation of Journalists, Mexico City, published in *Barricada*, (Managua) December 2, 1982, translated by Carmen Alegria in *Black Scholar*, March-April, 1982.

103. Author's source.

104. *Ha'aretz*, November 1, 1982, transl. in *Israeli Mirror*, n.d.; *Defense Latin America*, August 1983 and *Pittsburgh Press*, March 1, 1983 in *Counterspy*, September-November 1983; *Libertad*, (San Jose) May 4-10, 1984 in FBIS Latin America, May 22, 1984; *Los Angeles Times*, May 23, 1983; *Washington Post*, February 14, 1983; *Inforpress Centroamericana*, April 11, 1985.

105. *Davar*, July 25, 1986, FBIS Middle East & Africa.

106. *Rumbo Centroamericano*, (San Jose, Costa Rica) September 26-October 2, 1985.

107. *Time*, May 7, 1984.

108. *Philadelphia Inquirer*, May 31, 1984.

109. *New York Times*, February 8, 1987; Congressional investigators "suspected" the "basic outline" of Terrell's account "to be accurate."

110. Ibid., July, 21, 1983.

111. Interview with Michael Saba, 1985.

112. *Ha'aretz*, Nov. 11, 1983 in *Israel Mirror*, nd.

113. *Miami Herald*, June 4, 1983.

114. *Latin America Regional Report, Mexico and Central America*, May 4, 1984.

115. Ibid.

116. *Los Angeles Times*, March 14, 1985.

117. Author's source.

118. *Boston Sunday Globe*, January 18, 1987.

119. Ibid.

120. *Washington Post, January 27, 1985, Jewish Currents*, June 1986.

121. *Yediot Aharonot*,, April 19, 1984, in FBIS Middle East and Africa. Eagleburger was replaced by Michael Armacost in mid-1984.

122. *San Jose Mercury News*, October 28, 1986.

123. *Latin America Weekly Report*, January 13, 1984.

124. *Ha'aretz*, April 4, 1984, transl. in Israleft No. 244, May 4, 1984.

125. *Boston Sunday Globe*, January 18, 1987.

126. *San Jose Mercury News*, October 28, 1986.

127. *Washington Post* in *San Francisco Chronicle*, December 3, 1986.

128. *New York Times*, November 26, 1986.

129. *New York Times*, November 27, 1986.

130. *Los Angeles Times*, December 5, 1986.

131. *Ha'aretz*, April 4, 1984, excerpt transl. in *Israleft* No. 244, May 4, 1984; other parts of article cited in *Latin America Weekly Report*, May 4, 1984.

132. *Ha'aretz*, nd, presumably another fragment of the April 4 report, cited

in *New York Times,* April 22, 1984.

133. *Jerusalem Post,* April 22, 1984.

134. *New York Times,* April 22, 1984.

135. *New York Times,* April 22, 1984.

136. *Washington Post,* April 13, 1984.

137. *Washington Post,* May 19, 1984; The Saudis refused, according to the "sources" who provided the details of this report, which would be contradicted when the contra supply network was exposed in October 1986.

138. *Los Angeles Times,* (in *San Francisco Chronicle*) April 16, 1984.

139. Pastora Interviewed on Voice of Sandino (clandestine to Nicaragua) 2300 GMT, April 16, 1984 in FBIS Latin America, April 17, 1984, pp. P-20-21.

140. *Davar,* April 27, 1984 [excerpt] in FBIS Middle East & Africa, April 27, 1984, pp. I-4-5. Matamoros' name translates as "he kills Moors.".

141. Jose Quintero De Leon, "La Fuerza Democratica Nicaraguense y Su Lucha contra el Sandinismo," *La Prensa* (Panama), June 13, 1983.

142. Fred Francis, NBC Nightly News, 5:30 p.m. (PDT), April 23, 1984. Transcript courtesy of November 29th Committee for Palestine, (P.O. Box 27462, San Francisco, CA 94127.

143. Jerusalem Domestic Service in English, 1800 GMT, April 25, 1984 in FBIS Middle East & Africa, April 26, 1984, p. I-5.

144. *Los Angeles Times,* (in *San Francisco Chronicle*) April 16, 1984.

145. *Boston Sunday Globe,* January 18, 1987.

146. *Washington Post,* April 28, 1984.

147. *New York Times,* April 28, 1984.

148. *Washington Post,* April 27, 1984.

149. Kathryn Ferguson report on "All Things Considered," National Public Radio, April 27, 1984.

150. *Washington Post,* April 28, 1984 Another of the numerous flat-out lies told by Kimche was that Israel had sold arms in Central America, but not to El Salvador.

151. *New York Times,* April 28, 1984.

152. *Washington Post* in *San Francisco Chronicle,* December 3, 1986.

153. *Los Angeles Times,* April 28, 1984.

154. Kathryn Ferguson report on "All Things Considered," National Public Radio, April 27, 1984.

155. *Jerusalem Post,* April 22, 1984.

156. *Yediot Aharonot,* April 19, 1984 in FBIS Middle East & Africa, April 19, 1984, p. I-3.

157. *Los Angeles Times,* April 28, 1984.

158. *Los Angeles Times,* April 28, 1984.

159. *Los Angeles Times,* April 28, 1984.

160. Two glossy 9" x 12" books *The Private Enterprise Guide Book* and *The President's Task Force on International Private Enterprise: Report to the President,* both Washington DC, December 1984, reveal very little other than a string of names from corporations, none of which is well known except for the Hearst

Corporation.

161. *Jerusalem Post*, International Edition, week ending October 13, 1984.

162. *Ma'ariv*, October 5, 1984 FBIS Middle East & Africa, October 5, 1984.

163. At around the same time, Fred Ikle (whose Israeli contacts were the hard line Defense Minister Arens and embassy minister Benyamin Netanyahu) at the Defense Department is said to have asked Israel to send advisers to El Salvador "openly, as a demonstration of Israeli participation in the load the United States bears in Central America." It was considered that Israel owed a debt to El Salvador because of that country's agreement in August 1983 to move its embassy from Tel Aviv to Jerusalem. Obviously, it would have been helpful to the U.S. if Israeli advisers helped them exceed the 55-man limit Congress had placed on U.S. advisers. *Davar*, May 3, 1984, in FBIS Middle East & Africa, May 4, 1984, pp. I 6-7.

164. *New York Times*, December 29, 1986. While Israeli embassy officials and some Zionist activists did support the contras, they warned Israel "to maintain its more discreet stance" so as not to alienate congressional Democrats, many of whom were staunch supporters of Israel and ardent foes of U.S. intervention in Nicaragua. See, Wolf Blitzer, "U.S. wants Israeli aid in Central America," Jerusalem Post, April 22, 1984.

165. Oswald Johnston, "Israel Denies That It's Aiding Nicaragua Rebels," *Los Angeles Times*, April 28, 1984.

166. *Inforpress Centroamericana*, June 14, 1984.

167. *Los Angeles Times* Syndicate, May 10, 1984.

168. *Washington Post*, May 19, 1984. When asked by House and Senate Intelligence committees if they knew of third country aid to the contras, Casey and other CIA officials said they did not.

169. *Philadelphia Inquirer*, May 31, 1984.

170. *This Week Central America and Panama*, September 17, 1984. *New York Times*, September 4, 1984. Venezuela's relationship was with ARDE; the Argentine military prevailed upon Alfonsin to complete earlier commitments.

171. *Miami Herald*, September 9, 1984.

172. *Jerusalem Post*, September 10, 1984 [excerpts in FBIS Sept. 11, 1984].

173. *New York Times*, January 13, 1985.

174. At the time, Taiwan had good relations with Nicaragua. Subsequently Nicaragua decided to recognize the Peoples Republic of China.

175. *New York Times*, March 6, 1985.

176. Ibid., March 13, 1985.

177. *New York Times*, July 12, 1985 The bill repealed the Clark Amendment which had forbid the CIA to support UNITA mercenaries waging war on Angola. The bill also carried an amendment forbidding the sale of advanced weapons to Jordan until it recognized Israel and entered into peace talks with it and reaffirmed a ban on recognition of the PLO.

178. An exhaustive investigation found opinion divided and few willing to discuss the issue.

179. *Oakland Tribune*, August 9, 1985.

180. *Washington Post*, September 15, 1985; *The Nation*, September 28, 1985.

181. *New York Times*, August 13, 1985.

182. *All Things Considered* April 23, 1985.

183. *Guardian*, (NY) October 2, 1985.

184. *San Jose Mercury News*, October 28, 1986.

185. Ibid.

186. *Washington Post*, November 28, 1986.

187. *Guardian*, (NY) October 2, 1985.

188. Report on Preliminary Inquiry, p. 43.

189. *Los Angeles Times*, January 11, 1987.

190. *New York Times*, December 30, 1986.

191. *Jerusalem Post* January 4, 1987.

192. *Report on Preliminary Inquiry*, p. 43.

193. *London Times* January 12, 1987.

194. *Washington Times*, December 8, 1986.

195. This hadn't happened with any of Israel's previous misadventures: the attacks on Iraq and Tunisia, the gift of nuclear weapons capability to South Africa, but with $3 billion or so a year at stake, the risk was definitely there.

196. *Dallas Morning News,* December 10, 1986.

197. *New York Times*, October 21, 1985.

198. *Milwaukee Journal*, January 19, 1987.

199. *Newsday,* January 18, 1987 cited in Jack Colhoun, "Congress deflects gaze from contra side of scandal," *Guardian*, February 4, 1987.

200. *Newsweek*, December 15, 1986.

201. *New York Times*, February 8, 1987.

202. *Report on Preliminary Inquiry*, p. 50.

203. *Washington Post*, December 12, 1986.

204. *Miami Herald*, December 1, 1986.

205. *Ma'ariv,* November 27, 1986 in FBIS Middle East & Africa, December 1, 1986, p. I-7. The original *Ma'ariv* article December 13, 1985, translated by Israel Shahak in *Collection: More about Israeli weapons trade, and the way it influences Israeli politics,* which this one updates, focused primarily on Ben Or's activities in Guatemala.

206. *Washington Post*, December 12, 1986. Another company with Israeli links is Sherwood International Export Corp. Former U.S. Diplomat Wayne Smith said the administration had "used Sherwood before for weapons sales to the FDN" and that the CIA had frequently used it so that Israel wasn't directly supplying the contras. Smith said he had been told by an administration official that a shipment of weapons Sherwood sold the contras had come from Israel's East bloc stocks. *Guardian,* April 16, 1986.

207. *New York Times*, August 10, 1985. Some were purchased by Gen. Singlaub, others came from Israel. *Guardian*, October 11, 1985.

208. *Guardian*, April 16, 1986.

209. *Latin America Regional Report Mexico and Central America,* February 14, 1986. Contra sources said that when they had trouble operating the SAM-

7s, Gen. Singlaub arranged for a technician to fix them and train the contras to maintain them. Singlaub acknowledged the story but "refused to identify the technician or his nationality, saying, 'It would put too many people in jeopardy.'" *Los Angeles Times,* December 7, 1985.

210. *Ma'ariv,* November 27, 1986 in FBIS Middle East & Africa, December 1, 1986, p. I-7.

211. *Guardian,* April 16, 1986. Dagan and Gil'ad were friends of Ben Or. Dagan, who had once represented IAI in territory stretching between Mexico and Columbia, had lived in Ben-Or's Miami house.

212. *Ma'ariv,* November 27, 1986 in FBIS Middle East & Africa, December 1, 1986, p. I-7.

213. Author's source.

214. *Jerusalem Post,* January 19, 1987.

215. *Washington Post,* December 12, 1986.

216. *Middle East International,* (London) April 3, 1987.

217. *Los Angeles Times,* September. 18, 1986.

218. *New York Times,* February 8, 1987.

219. *Washington Post,* December 12, 1986.

220. *Milwaukee Journal,* January 19, 1987.

221. *Dallas Morning News,* December 10, 1986.

222. *All Things Considered,* National Public Radio, December 6, 1986.

223. *Newsweek, December 15, 1986.*

224. *All Things Considered,* National Public Radio, December 6, 1986.

225. *Dallas Morning News,* December 10, 1986.

226. *All Things Considered,* National Public Radio, December 6, 1986.

227. *Dallas Morning News,* December 10, 1986.

228. Tel Aviv IDF Radio, 0600 GMT, December 10, 1986 in FBIS Latin America, December 10, 1986, p. P-16.

222. Reuters European Service, August 2, 1986.

230. *Dallas Morning News,* December 7, 1986.

231. *Ha'aretz,* cited in "Israeli contra training reported," *Christian Science Monitor,* January 13, 1987.

232. *Mideast Observer,* March 15, 1986; *New York Times,* March 6, 1986.

233. *New York Times,* March 7, 1986.

234. JTA, *Washington Jewish Week,* March 20, 1986.

235. *New York Times,* March 6, 1986.

236. *Israeli Foreign Affairs,* April 1986.

237. *Mideast Observer,* April 1, 1986.

238. Author's source.

239. *Jewish Currents,* June 1986.

240. *Jerusalem Post,* November 11, 1986.

241. Panama City ACAN, 1959 GMT, May 5, 1986 in FBIS Latin America, May 6, 1986, p. P 11.

242. *Ha'aretz,* June 18, 1986 in FBIS Middle East & Africa, June 19, 1986, p. I-2. Another version has Shamir saying that the Nicaraguan government is assisting the PLO, which maintains training bases and propaganda offices in

Nicaragua. *La Jornada,* (Mexico City) June 19, 1986.

243. *Dallas Morning News,* December 7, 1986. This claim was doubly suspect in that soon after President Reagan told *Time* magazine that Israel had transferred the profits from Iranian arms sales to the contras, Henry Kamm, who usually reports from Athens (and from a rightist perspective) wrote a single article from Jerusalem, saying that Israel had been trying from 1982 "until last year" to establish diplomatic ties with Nicaragua. To this end, Kamm wrote, Israel had offered Nicaragua "various forms of development assistance." *New York Times,* December 12, 1986. Nicaraguan sources said that those claims were overblown, that Israel had played a very negative role in Central America—the week before Kamm's article, it had voted with Washington against a resolution endorsing a World Court judgment against the U.S. war on Nicaragua. In fact, although Israel has asserted its good intentions from time to time—it has also ritualistically endorsed the Contadora peace process and denounced apartheid—the most concrete gesture of reconciliation on record is a Nicaraguan offer conveyed to the New Jewish Agenda in 1984 to normalize relations. *Israeli Foreign Affairs,* January 1987.

244. News Conference, November 25, 1985, CBS Radio News.

245. *Report on Preliminary Inquiry,* pp. 44-45.

246. *New York Times,* November 26, 1986.

247. *Washington Times,* December 16, 1986.

248. *Report on Preliminary Inquiry,* p. 54.

249. Ibid., p. 45.

250. *MidEast,* a twice-monthly New York report cited in *Washington Times,* February 3, 1987.

251. Ibid.

252. *Report on Preliminary Inquiry,* p. 44.

253. Ibid., p. 46.

254. *Washington Post,* November 28, 1986; if counterpart means Ghorbanifar, that is almost the same as Israeli.

255. *Report on Preliminary Inquiry,* pp. 50, 63.

256. *Ha'aretz,* November 30, 1986 in FBIS Middle East and Africa.

257. *Los Angeles Times,* December 28, 1986.

258. *Yediot Aharonot,* December 5, 1986 in FBIS Middle East and Africa.

259. *Washington Times,* December 16, 1986.

260. *Israeli Foreign Affairs,* July 1986.

261. *Report on Preliminary Inquiry,* p. 45.

262. Ibid., p. 46.

263. Ibid., p. 53.

Footnotes to Chapter VI

1. *Washington Post*, 4-6-86.
2. Tad Szulc and Karl Meyer, *The Cuban Invasion*, (N.Y.: Ballantine Books, 1962) p. 96.
3. *Washington Post*, 10-27-86.
4. Quoted by Bill Moyers, CBS 6-10-77.
5. Ibid.
6. *Wall Street Journal*, 1-16-87, quoting Jose Basulto.
7. House Select Committee on Assassinations, (HSCA), appendix to hearings on the Assassination of President John F. Kennedy, v. 10 (Washington: USGPO, 1979) p. 67.
8. HSCA, v. 10, p. 15..
9. Interview with David Atlee Phillips, 11-4-86.
10. Newsday, *The Heroin Trail* (London: Souvenir Press, 1975), p. 169.
11. Warren Hinckle and William Turner, *Fish is Red*, 319.
12. *New Times*, 5-13-77.
13. These CORU-contra Cubans are Armando Lopez Estrada, Luis Posada, Juan Perez Franco and Dionisio Suarez (*Wall Street Journal*, 1-16-87; and see below on Suarez).
14. *New York Times*, 11-15-76.
15. *Miami News*, 7-2-77.
16. Ibid.
17. Hinckle and Turner, *Fish is Red*, 316.
18. Szulc and Meyer, *The Cuban Invasion*, 90.
19. Anderson, *Inside the League*, 249. For the record, the terror wave began earlier under President Ford, who first explored the possibility of detente with Castro. Vidal "has been arrested at least seen times in Miami on narcotics and weapons charges." *Miami Herald*, 2-16-87.
20. *New York Times*, 12-23-81; *Miami Herald*, 12-28-81. The camp organizer was Hector Fabian, possibly an alias for Hector Alfonso-Ruiz, head of Movimento Insurreccional Martian.
21. *Los Angeles Times*, 12-19-83; *Washington Post*, 12-18-82.

22. Anderson, *Inside the League*, 177.

23. *Wall Street Journal*, 3-5-85.

24. These commanders include Colonels Enrique Bermudez, military chief of the FDN; Ricardo Lau, former head of intelligence for the contras; and Emilio Echeverry. Hector Frances, "The War of Terror Against Nicaragua," *Black Scholar*, March-April 1983, p. 4; Christopher Dickey, *With the Contras* (Simon and Schuster, 1986), 55, 115-116.

25. *Los Angeles Times*, 10-16-86.

26. HSCA v. 10, p. 44.

27. *New Times*, 5-13-77; *Washington Post*, 10-17-86, 11-3-86; Vicky Bergerson memo; *Miami Herald*, 12-30-81.

28. Larry Barcella interview, 11-6-86.

29. Peter Maas, *Manhunt*, 202; Eduardo Arocena telephone conversation, 12-30-82.

30. John Cummings, "Omega 7," *Gallery*, November 1981; cf. *Miami Herald*, 3-27-79.

31. Edgar Chamorro testimony to World Court, reprinted in Peter Rosset and John Vandermeer, eds., *Nicaragua: Unfinished Revolution* (Grove Press, 1986), 237.

32. Defense Intelligence Agency, Weekly Intelligence Summary, 7-16-82.

33. *Philadelphia Inquirer*, 10-20-84.

34. Reed Brody, *Contra Terror in Nicaragua* (Boston: South End Press), 1985. The manual was put together by a CIA contract agent who went as "John Kirkpatrick." A former Green Beret, "Kirkpatrick" was reportedly a veteran of the Phoenix program, a Vietnam-era, CIA-directed operation to assassinate civilians suspected of collaborating with the Vietcong. See Chapter IX below; Christopher Dickey, *With the Contras*, 226.

35. *Tribune* (Oakland), 10-21-84.

36. Testimony to World Court, reprinted in *Nicaragua: Unfinished Revolution*, 238.

37. *Boston Globe*, 6-12-86.

38. *Los Angeles Times*, 2-10-87.

39. Brody, op. cit. Joseph Adams, an American mercenary who served as chief of security to Adolfo Calero, head of the Nicaraguan Democratic Front, told a reporter that "he helped maintain a list of Managua civilians—including members of the clergy as well as Sandinista politicians—who would be marked for assassination when the FDN forces entered the Nicaraguan capital. Adams also acknowledged participating in discussions at Calero's Miami home regarding plans to assassinate rival contra leader Eden Pastora. Calero knew and approved of the scheme, he said." (Allan Nairn, "The Contras' Little List," *Progressive*, March 1987, 24).

40. *San Francisco Chronicle*), 3-22-85; Dickey, 88.

41. *Los Angeles Times*, 12-19-83 (Argentinians); *Christian Science Monitor* 5-8-84 (Cubans).

42. *New York Times*, 2-14-86; *Washington Post*, 12-16-84, 3-21-85; *Miami*

Herald, 1-15-85; Dickey, *With the Contras*, 115-116. One of the victims was a pro-Marxist Argentine travelling on an Ecuadoran passport, who may have been targeted to suit the Argentine military (*Washington Post*, 1-15-85). Alvarez, the CIA's favorite, "was implicated in the Standard Fruit Company bribe scandal in 1975" and was held responsible for the alleged embezzlement of $30 million in public money by members of his deposed high command (*Central America Report*, 4-6-84). He may also have made illicit profits through his stock ownership in the Union Star company, which "supplies the Army with arms, liquor and other goods" (*Central America Report*, 4-27-84).

43. *Central America Report*, 10-18-85. His name was Ricardo Zuniga.

44. *Christian Science Monitor*, 11-19-85, 12-18-85; *New York Times*, 2-14-86.

45. *Central America Report*, 10-4-85. The alleged head of the plot was a Cuban exile (*Christian Science Monitor*, 11-19-85). In March 1986, two contras murdered the Canadian head of CARETAS, a Catholic relief organization, apparently also for political reason (Larry Birns, Colin Danby, and David MacMichael, "Getting in Deeper," *Democratic Left*, May-August 1986). And on January 14, 1987, a bomb exploded near the home of Honduras' top woman union leader, who is also a leading critic of the contras. Her union federation believes the contras targeted her (*Guardian*, 1-28-87).

46. George Black, *Garrison Guatemala* (London: Zed Books, 1984), 164-166; *Ha'aretz*, 11-25-85; Cheryl Rubenberg, "Israel and Guatemala: Arms, Advice and Counterinsurgency," *Middle East Report*, May-June 1986. Another report notes "European diplomats in Guatemala say Israeli NCOs have also been used by private landowners to train their squads of security guards. Private security guards and off-duty military officers formed the fearsome ¢death squads' which later spread to neighbouring El Salvador..." (*Financial Times*, 11-27-86).

47. Dickey, 82-84; Shirley Christian, *Nicaragua: Revolution in the Family* (NY: Random House, 1986), 196-200 (financing from Argentina and Luis Pallais Debayle).

48. National Public Radio, 6-21-86; Sen. Kerry memorandum, 10-14-86.

49. *In These Times*, 12-10-86. More evidence on the Pastora plot has come to light from the American mercenary Joseph Adams. See Allan Nairn, "The Contras' Little List," *Progressive*, March 1987, 24-26.

50. *Miami Herald*, 1-23-76.

51. Interview, 11-6-86.

52. *Reno Evening Gazette*, 1-8-75.

53. Hinckle and Turner, *Fish Is Red*, 314.

54. This drug kingpin was Juan Restoy. See Hank Messick, *Of Grass and Snow*, (NJ: Prentice Hall, 1979), 6; *New York Times*, 1-4-75; Szulc and Meyer, *The Cuban Invasion*, 95; Hinckle and Turner, 308.

55. *New York Times*, 1-4-75.

56. John Cummings, "Omega 7," *Gallery*, November, 1981.

57. Kerry report, October 14, 1986.

58. *Miami Herald*, 8-6-81, 7-26-83.

59. *Nation*, 3-19-77; *Miami Herald*, 12-30-83.

60. *Los Angeles Times*, 12-21-85.

61. *San Francisco Examiner*, 3-18-86; *Washington Post*, 4-11-86, 4-17-86; *Christian Science Monitor*, 5-9-86; *San Francisco Chronicle*, 4-27-86.

62. *San Francisco Examiner*, 4-24-86.

63. AP 1-20-87; *Newsweek*, 1-26-87; cf. *San Francisco Chronicle*, 1-27-87 (Morales pleads guilty); Chris Davis, "How the Feds Busted George Morales," *Motor Boating and Sailing*, October 1986, pp. 68ff. His partner was Gary Betzner.

64. *San Francisco Examiner*, 3-16-86; characterization from Dickey, 117. The initials stand for Nicaraguan Democratic Union-Nicaraguan Revolutionary Armed Forces.

65. *San Francisco Examiner*, 6-23-86.

66. CBS 6-12-86.

67. *San Francisco Examiner*, 3-16-86, 6-23-86.

68. *Central America Report*, 8-8-86.

69. UPI 4-26-86.

70. CBS "West 57th St." 6-25-86. Working those "secret routes" on the arms side were the cargo planes hired by the CIA or agents of the National Security Council to serve the rebel army. The preeminent airline in the contra supply business was the former CIA-controlled firm Southern Air Transport. One witness, whose account has not been verified, told the Justice Department of seeing cocaine unloaded from a Southern Air Transport plane in Colombia. The airline denies any link to drug smuggling (*San Jose Mercury*, 10-31-86; AP 1-20-87; *Washington Post*, 1-20-87; *Newsweek*, 3-2-87).

71. *Miami Herald*, 12-20-85.

72. *Miami Herald*, 8-4-86 (Jose Coutin, Miami gun dealer); *Dallas Morning News*, 8-17-86 (Ochoa as unindicted co-conspirator in Seal's murder).

73. *New York Times*, 7-3-72. "Seal was supposed to fly seven tons of plastic explosives to anti-Castro forces in Mexico" (*Miami Herald*, 10-12-86).

74. *Miami Herald*, 10-16-86.

75. Joel Millman, "Who Killed Barry Seal?" *Village Voice*, 7-1-86.

76. *Miami Herald*, 10-9-86.

77. *In These Times*, 12-10-86.

78. *In These Times*, 12-10-86. Jesus Garcia, the informant, says he saw the cocaine in the house of Francisco Chanes, a Miami-based seafood importer who helps the contra cause. Chanes, in turn, was named in an October 14, 1986 staff report from the office of Sen. John Kerry as a business associate of exile terrorist and drug trafficker Frank Castro.

79. *Miami Herald*, 4-14-83.

80. *Washington Post*, 3-14-65.

81. The owner of the properties on which Artime established his camps, Colonel Ludwig "Vico" Starke Jimenez, was a key figure in MCRL (Hinckle and Turner, *Fish is Red*, 149; Charles Ameringer, *Don Pepe: A Political*

Biography of Jose Figueres of Costa Rica (Albuquerque: University of New Mexico Press), p. 258). Starke had previously lent his farm to the CIA for military training prior to the Bay of Pigs invasion (Jean Hopfensperger, "Costa Rica: Seeds of Terror," *Progressive*, September 1986). She notes further that the MCRL includes "former pro-Nazi Germans and their children."

82. *Latin America*, 2-13-70; Ameringer, *Don Pepe*, 259-60. Starke was named in connection with both episodes as well.

83. *Latin America*, 1-21-72; Guatemala and *Central America Report*, December 1974. Among those linked to the plotting were the pro-Chilean Cuban Evarista Garcia Sarmiento and Patria y Libertad leader Benjamin Matte. Costa Rica's foreign minister, Gonzalo Facio, was the target of death threats for lifting sanctions against Cuba.

84. Hopfensperger, op. cit.

85. *Central America Report*, 6-27-81.

86. Anderson, *Inside the League* (NY: Dodd, Mead & Co., 1986), 245.

87. *Washington Post*, 12-2-82. Precisely such an assassination attempt took place in 1984 at La Penca. Two journalists injured in the bomb attack, Tony Avirgan and Martha Honey, have since charged in a lawsuit that Americans and CIA agents close to the contra cause directed the plot.

88. *Nation*, 10-5-85; *Central America Report*, 6-14-85; Central America Update, January-February 1986. The December 1985 peace march was disrupted after the U.S. Embassy in San Jose distributed to MCRL members a document purporting to show that the KGB was behind the march (Hopfensperger, op. cit.).

89. *Los Angeles Times*, 4-27-86; *Central America Update*, September-October 1984.

90. *San Francisco Examiner*, 8-25-85, quoting Juan Jose Echeverria.

91. *Central America Report*, 7-19-85. One might also note the fact that the Security and Intelligence Directorate under his control was caught wiretapping public officials and members of the ruling PLN (*Central America Report*, 6-14-85).

92. Dickey, *With the Contras*, 90-92; *Central America Update*, March 1981.

93. *Central America Report*, 2-21-81.

94. *Central America Report*, 11-7-81.

95. Defense Intelligence Agency, Weekly Intelligence Summary, 7-16-82.

96. *Central America Report*, 11-1-85.

97. Tony Avirgan and Martha Honey, "The CIA's War in Costa Rica," *Nation*, January 31, 1987, 105-107.

98. Monge sent a message of support to the World Anti-Communist League in 1984—read to the annual conference by Urbina Pinto (Anderson, *Inside the League*, 250-251).

99. *Central America Report*, 7-19-85. Perhaps not coincidentally, Monge sought foreign aid and investment from three of the contras' major foreign backers: Israel, Taiwan and South Korea (*Central America Report*, 6-14-85).

100. *Central America Update*, September-October 1984; *Central America*

Report, 10-5-84.

101. *Central America Report*, 8-8-86.

102. *Central America Report*, 4-12-85.

103. *Central America Report*, 5-31-85. The training, took place on a ranch formerly owned by Nicaraguan dictator Anastasio Somoza, skirted Costa Rican prohibitions on foreign military advisers (Central American Historical Institute newsletter, 7-11-85).

104. *Central America Report*, 4-12-85.

105. *Central America Update*, July-August 1985.

106. Central American Historical Institute newsletter, 7-11-85.

107. Alan Hruska, "The Road from Switzerland to Honduras: The Militarization of Costa Rica," in *Nicaragua: Unfinished Revolution*, 283-286.

108. *Mediafile Central America Report*, no. 3. How long Arias can maintain this neutrality remains to be seen, given the presence of at least six MCRL members in his administration (Hopfensperger, op. cit.).

109. *New York Times*, 9-29-86; *Wall Street Journal*, 12-5-86.

110. *Miami Herald*, 8-16-77; *Wall Street Journal*, 1-16-87.

111. *Central America Report*, 8-22-86; *New York Times*, 9-14-86.

112. *San Francisco Examiner*, 3-29-81.

113. *Washington Post*, 10-19-86; *Miami Herald*, 10-11-86; *Los Angeles Times*, 10-21-86.

114. *Christian Science Monitor*, 5-8-84.

115. *New York Times*, 10-15-86.

116. NACLA, *Guatemala*, (New York: 1974) p. 119.

117. *Latin America Weekly Report*, 4-7-78, 6-30-78. In 1969, Miami-based Cuban exiles crowed about "our first coup" after they arranged with the MLN and the death squad MANO to oust a moderate interior minister under President Julio Cesar Mendez Montenegro (Thomas and Marjorie Melville, *Guatemala—Another Vietnam?* (Penguin Books, 1971), 284).

118. *Central America Report*, 5-6-83, 1-13-84; Peter Calvert, Guatemala: *A Nation in Turmoil* (Boulder, CO: Westview Press, 1985), 110; Anderson, *Inside the League*, 179-181, notes that the American arms dealer and special warfare expert Mitchell WerBell III plotted with Sisniega. On Israel's role, see George Black, *Garrison Guatemala* (London: Zed Books, 1984), 166).

119. *Washington Post*, 2-22-81.

120. The proper name for the MLN-sponsored terror organization was Movimiento Anticommunista Nacional Organizado, or MANO. Richard Nyrop, ed. *Guatemala: A Country Study* (Dept. of the Army, 1983), 31, 163; Black, 50.

121. Latin America Political Report, 6-1-79; Anderson, 172.

122. Dickey, 87.

123. Ameringer, 261.

124. *Foreign Policy*, Summer 1981; Black, 23.

125. Dickey, 86ff; *Miami Herald*, 12-19-82.

126. *San Francisco Examiner*, 12-18-86.

127. *Washington Post*, 6-2-85. Thus Orlando Bosch claims to have arranged the murder of two Cuban diplomats in Argentina with the help of AAA (*New Times*, 5-13-77).

128. HSCA, v. 10, p. 44.

129. *New York Times*, 10-31-86.

130. *Wall Street Journal*, 12-8-86.

131. *Washington Post*, 7-24-86.

132. *Washington Post*, 5-29-86; cf. *Tribune* (Oakland), 12-14-84.

133. *San Francisco Chronicle*, 2-14-86. See above on terrorism.

134. *People's Daily World*, 9-12-86.

135. *Central America Report*, 8-29-86; *Guardian*, 10-15-86; *Los Angeles Times*, 5-9-86.

136. *Central America Report*, 11-7-86; cf. *Washington Post*, 11-17-86.

137. *Washington Post*, 7-24-86.

138. *Central America Report*, 11-7-86.

139. *Washington Post*, 11-17-86.

140. *Central America Update*, VIII (November-December 1986).

141. *Wall Street Journal*, 12-8-86.

142. Jonathan Marshall, "The White House Death Squad," *Inquiry*, March 5, 1979.

Footnotes to Chapter VII

1. *San Francisco Chronicle*, 3-29-74; *Washington Post*, 1-9-75.
2. Michael Klare, "Arms and the Shah," *Progressive*, August 1979, 15-21.
3. *Washington Post*, 1-13-80. Joseph Sisco, Undersecretary of State for Political Affairs, told a House subcommittee in 1975 that "the major burden for assuring security: in the Persian Gulf region "must be borne by the gulf states themselves, and in particular by the major nations of the region, Iran and Saudi Arabia" (*New York Times*, 6-11-75).
4. Rene Theberge, "Iran: Ten Years After the 'White Revolution'," *MERIP Reports*, no. 18 (June 1973), 18.
5. *San Francisco Chronicle*, 3-20-75.
6. As a byproduct of this commitment, the CIA shifted its main Mideast station from Cyprus to Iran (*Nation*, 2-22-75, p. 195).
7. *Washington Post*, 2-26-79 (George Ball).
8. *New York Times*, 9-28-76.
9. *Forbes*, 4-15-76.
10. *Washington Post*, 5-31-79 (Jack Anderson).
11. *Washington Post*, 1-18-79.
12. *Forbes*, 4-15-76.
13. Claudia Wright, "Buried Treasure at Chase Manhattan?" *Inquiry*, April 7, 1980, p. 13.
14. *New York Review of Books* 5-14-81.
15. *Washington Post*, 11-29-79.
16. *Washington Post*, 10-25-80; *New York Times*, 7-9-78; Michael Ledeen and William Lewis, *Debacle* (Knopf, 1981), 125.
17. *New York Times*, 11-16-79.
18. Ibid.
19. (*Washington Post*, 11-16-79).
20. *Washington Post*, 1-13-80.
21. *No Hiding Place*, 153.
22. The American taxpayer, on the other hand, seems to have lost out. In a confidential report to Congress, the General Accounting Office determined

that the Pentagon was not recouping its full administrative costs on arms sales, and that Iran was enjoying further subsidies through low-interest loans offered by the Export-Import Bank (*New York Times*, 1-2-75).

23. *New York Times*, 5-18-75. Kissinger defended these purchases—which he noted were in cash—as helping Iran play a stabilizing role in the Middle East and South Asia, missions he said were in the "national interest of the United States" (*New York Times*, 8-8-76).

24. *Washington Post*, 1-13-75.

25. *Sunday Times*, 12-2-79.

26. *Los Angeles Times*, 12-7-86.

27. "Strong pressure also came from defense companies anxious to find a new market to replace the one lost through the winding down of U.S. procurement for the Vietnam war. For example, Bell Helicopter officials saw a need in October 1971 to obtain Iranian military and civilian business for the company's U.S. plants, where 'sustaining work loads are increasingly needed,' according to documents published by the Senate Banking Committee. A Pentagon official knowledgeable about the overseas arms business describes how representatives of U.S. defense companies have moved from one lucrative market to another. 'The same men who were in Saigon and later Tehran, are now in Saudi Arabia, Egypt and Morocco,' he said." (*Washington Post*, 1-20-80). The Iran market literally saved Grumman Corp., manufacturer of the F-14 fighter, from possibly financial collapse (*New York Times*, 1-21-75).

28. For example, Bell Helicopter International, headed by retired U.S. Maj. Gen. Delk Oden, put together a 500-man force of American civilians, many of them fresh from Vietnam, to set up Iran's Sky Cavalry Brigade modeled on the U.S. 1st Cavalry Division (*New York Times*, 2-12-75).

29. *Washington Post*, 1-13-80; *New York Times*, 6-10-75, 8-26-75; Barry Rubin, *Paved With Good Intentions* (NY: Oxford U. Press, 1980), 129. The jailed navy commander was Admiral Ramzi Attaei (*New York Times*, 2-25-76). Note that a future commander of the Shah's navy, Rear Adm. Ahmad Madani, would later appear on the CIA's payroll (*New York Times*, 3-7-82).

30. *Washington Post*, 1-13-80; *Washington Post*, 1-2-77; Defense Electronics, February 1979. The lead contractor on IBEX was Rockwell; other contractors included E-systems, GTE Sylvania, Martin Marietta, Stanford Technology, Watkins-Johnson and ARGOS Systems. Later Ford Aerospace replaced Martin Marietta and GTE Sylvania in the project.

31. *Washington Post*, 1-27-80. Later, Rockwell lost its lead role in the project—a casualty of politics and bureaucratic delays in Iran and the United States. "In the last year the CIA reorganization (under Carter) has brought an entirely new program staff on the project," reported *Electronics News* [8-8-77], "which brought the procurement to a virtual halt...Sources said the delay allowed Rockwell competitors to market aggressively in Iran to share portions of the program that Rockwell felt it would handle as major contractor." The CIA reportedly was the procuring agency on the project.

32. Grumman, for example, admitted that it arranged to pay more than $20

million in commissions on its $2 billion fighter plane deal with the Shah's air force (*New York Times*, 12-15-75). Bell Helicopter paid Gen. Khatemi and others $2.9 million in commissions (*New York Times*, 3-3-78).

33. One former head of the U.S. Military Assistance Advisory Group in Tehran reportedly helped Northrop set up a slush fund in Switzerland to "pay off some mid-level Iranian officials," in the words of one company official (*New York Times*, 6-26-75).

34. Jonathan Kwitny, *Endless Enemies* (NY: Congdon and Weed, 1984), 183.

35. *Washington Post*, 1-2-77; Barry Rubin, *Paved With Good Intentions*, 163. A Pentagon investigation of the activities of the U.S. Military Assistance Advisory Group was thwarted by the destruction of records (*New York Times*, 9-16-76).

36. As far back as 1952, Washington's ambassador to Tehran, Loy Henderson, had warned of the danger of triggering a xenophobic reaction in Iran: "The more attention that is attracted to the activities of these American nationals the more susceptible the Iranian people in general are likely to be to appeals to throw the Americans out of the country" (Rubin, *Paved With Good Intentions*, 136).

37. Gary Sick, *All Fall Down* (NY: Random House, 1985), 17.

38. Quoted in Barry Rubin, 174.

39. Michael Klare, "Arms and the Shah," *Progressive*, August 1979, 18.

40. *Washington Post*, 10-25-80.

41. Gary Sick, 92.

42. Joseph Goulden, *The Death Merchant*, 61. The CIA had at least 50 agents in Tehran, and another 100 "retired" U.S. intelligence specialists worked for American corporations in the country, some of them certainly undercover for the Agency (*New York Times*, 7-9-78).

43. Barry Rubin, 165.

44. Christopher Payne, unpublished ms.

45. Barry Rubin, 164-5. These included General Hamilton Howe, hired to represent Bell Helicopter; former MAAG commander Major Gen. Harvey Jablonsky who flogged Northrop's telecommunications systems; former Air Force MAAG boss Major Gen. Harold L. Price who promoted Philco-Ford's aircraft warnings systems; and former Navy MAAG chief Captain R.S. Harward who represented TRACOR and then Rockwell International.

46. *Washington Post*, 1-20-80.

47. Ledeen and Lewis, *Debacle*, 59. After the Shah's fall, Moorer proposed that the U.S. convert the port of Gwadar, in the sensitive Baluchistan region of Pakistan, as a naval facility to replace Chah Bahar (*New Yorker*, 10-1-84). Pakistan has, indeed, become a mini-Iran: led by the unpopular Gen. Zia, it has become the third largest recipient of U.S. foreign aid, a platform for opposing the Soviet presence in Afghanistan (as was the Shah's Iran) and a would-be bastion of American influence in southern Asia.

48. Indeed, he opposed abolishing it (*International Herald Tribune* 5-19-77).

49. Goulden, 57; *Washington Post*, 2-1-83.

50. *Washington Post*, 2-1-83; Maas, 54; Goulden, 47.

51. *Los Angeles Times*, 12-7-86.

52. *Insight*, 1-12-87.

53. *New York Times*, 11-26-76, 2-9-77; *Washington Post*, 1-20-80.

54. *Baltimore News American*, 10-7-82.

55. Von Marbod's career was slowed neither by the Shah's dissatisfaction, nor by the formal reprimand he received in 1975 for vacationing at Northrop's luxury hunting lodge (*Washington Post*, 1-2-77). After that article appeared, Deputy War Minister Hassan Toufanian said it was "erroneous and misleading" and that Von Marbod was held in esteem (*New York Times*, 2-10-77).

56. *New York Times*, 7-16-77, 7-21-77, 7-23-77, 7-26-77. As noted in previous chapters, the sales of AWACS planes to Saudi Arabia in 1981 served to induce Saudi contributions to the contras.

57. *New York Times*, 12-11-86. See also Chapter VIII.

58. *Defense Electronics*, February 1979; interview with Shackley, 3-31-87. As the Shah was falling, SAVAK agents reportedly bartered some of Stanford Technology's equipment to South Africa and possibly Israel in exchange for asylum (*Defense Electronics*, June 1979).

59. *Los Angeles Times*, 12-4-86; *New York Times*, 12-6-86. Hakim was in turn introduced to Wilson by Wilson's fellow CIA renegade, Frank Terpil (*Los Angeles Times*, 2-14-87).

60. Christopher Simpson, "The Middle East Connection," *Computerworld*, November 23, 1981, p. 8, citing former Wilson employee Kevin Mulcahy.

61. *San Francisco Examiner*, 12-9-86. Rockwell International reportedly paid a $4.5 million commission for the IBEX contract to a Bermuda company controlled by a multimillionaire friend of the Shah, Abolfath Mahvi. Mahvi was also the agent for huge computer contracts obtained by Electronic Data Systems, the Texas firm of H. Ross Perot. Perot and Mahvi set up a joint venture to program computers for the Iranian navy, which fell apart when Mahvi was placed on the blacklist by Gen. Hassan Toufanian (*Washington Post*, 3-10-80). Perot would become famous for springing imprisoned employees from a Tehran jail in a private commando raid, and later for supplying Oliver North with cash in a failed attempt to ransom U.S. hostages in Italy (Gen. Dozier) and Lebanon (William Buckley).

62. *Los Angeles Times*, 12-7-86, 2-14-87; *New York Times*, 10-13-81.

63. *Defense Electronics*, February 1979.

64. *Wall Steet Journal* 12-5-86; *Washington Post*, 1-27-80; *Defense Electronics*, February 1979.

65. *San Jose Mercury* 1-18-87.

66. *Los Angeles Times*, 2-14-87.

67. *Los Angeles Times*, 2-14-87.

68. *San Francisco Examiner*, 12-9-86. Hakim's role in the Iran arms deal may explain Shackley's involvement in 1984; Hakim had already discussed arms-for-hostage deals with Manucher Ghorbanifar earlier that year (*New*

York Times, 12-16-87).

69. Ironically, this assessment is shared even by Kermit Roosevelt, the CIA agent who helped bring the Shah to power in 1953, then went on to represent Northrop Corp. In the Middle East and the Shah's government in Washington. He told Robert Scheer that the Shah had been ill-advised to squander so much money on military hardware, having been "encouraged by some Americans, including President Nixon, that he could become the bulwark of the West in the Middle East and that he could carry the flag against the Soviet Union, against any other enemies. And I think that it was a very misplaced notion, but certainly the Shah believed it, and apparently Nixon believed it and I guess Henry Kissinger believed it. And by the time it was made clear that it wouldn't quite work, it was too late" (Los Angeles Times, 3-29-79).

70. San Francisco Chronicle, 8-11-79. Sadegh Tabatabai and Khomeini's son Ahmed have both been linked to the 1985 U.S.-Iran talks (San Francisco Examiner, 11-15-86; ABC, 11-21-86).

71. Washington Post, 11-19-79 (Jack Anderson).

72 No Hiding Place, 157

73. Ibid., 150; Los Angeles Times, 12-20-79; Miami Herald, 12-25-79; Washington Post, 12-29-79; Claudia Wright, "Buried Treasure at Chase Manhattan?" op. cit. Chase froze Iran's assets on a blatantly false pretext and thus managed to stave off a potentially crippling outflow of deposits (see Rep. George Hansen statement, March 26, 1980, Congressional Record H2249).

74. Clearly at some point, opportunism about the hostages also took hold.

75. Remarks to Nation, 11-13-86.

76. Cf. Washington Times, 12-1-86, on Afghanistan.

77. Washington Post, 11-5-86.

78. New York Times, 11-23-86.

79. New York Times, 4-3-86; Wall Street Journal, 4-7-86.

80. Oil and gas interests are reportedly major contributors to Bush's political action committee, Fund for America's Future (New York Times, 4-3-86). Texas bankers are no less happy at the prospect of an oil rise, it should be emphasized. The U.S. Comptroller of the Currency notes that the $18-a-barrel price "could generate enough cash flow where some of the currently non-performing loans will begin to perform" (Los Angeles Times, 12-24-86). Some Texas banks have as much as 20 percent of their loan portfolio in the energy sector (New York Times, 4-3-86).

81. New York Times, 11-23-86, 4-3-86.

82. San Francisco Examiner, 12-7-86.

83. Cf. San Francisco Chronicle, 11-29-86, re: allegations against Bush by Richard Brenneke.

84. Los Angeles Times, 11-14-86.

85. The Saudis had already opened modest lines of communications by sending their foreign minister, Prince Saud Faisal, to Tehran in May 1985. That December, the Iranians reciprocated by sending Foreign Minister Ali

Akbar Velayati to Riyadh (*Washington Post*, 12-5-86).

86. *Washington Post*, 11-5-86; *New York Times*, 11-23-86; *Los Angeles Times*, 11-27-86; *Wall Street Journal*, 12-29-86.

87. *San Francisco Chronicle*, 11-19-86; *San Francisco Chronicle*, 4-3-85; *Economist*, 6-25-83.

88. Quoted in Sheldon Richman, "The United States and the Persian Gulf," Cato Policy Analysis, No. 46 (Washington DC: Cato Institute, 1985).

89. Dennis Ross, "Soviet Views Toward the Gulf War," *Orbis* XXVIII (Fall 1984), 438.

90. *New York City Tribune*, 5-1-85; *Washington Times*, 11-25-86.

91. *Los Angeles Times*, 12-21-86.

92. *New York City Tribune*, 5-1-85.

93. *New York Times*, 11-25-86.

94. *Los Angeles Times*, 12-21-86.

95. *New York City Tribune*, 5-1-85; *Washington Times*, 11-25-86.

96. *Washington Post*, 11-18-86; *Los Angeles Times*, 12-13-86; *New York Times*, 12-23-86.

97. *Ta Nea*, 12-2-86.

98. *New York City Tribune*, 5-1-85; *Washington Times*, 11-25-86.

99. *Los Angeles Times*, 12-13-86; *Washington Times*, 12-15-86.

100. At most, 100 of the 2008 TOW missiles shipped to Iran were transferred to the mujaheddin (*Wall Street Journal*, 11-24-86).

101. *Los Angeles Times*, 12-2-86.

102. Among others directing this intelligence net was Max Hugel, who Casey put in charge of covert operations at the CIA in 1981 (*San Jose Mercury*, 8-16-83).

103. *San Francisco Chronicle*, 7-22-80.

104. Ed Meese received one memo indicating that the commander of the Strategic Air Command wanted to "blow Jimmy Carter out of the water" (*Washington Post*, 3-17-84).

105. *Power Peddlers*, 46-49.

106. Referring here to a network organized by Reagan campaign aide Adm. Robert Garrick (Ret.).

107. *Time*, 7-25-83.

108. *New Yorker*, 8-1-83.

109. *Rebel*, 11-22-83. Certain facts could suggest that the Soviets, at least, believed those leaks. In August, the Soviets mounted a major military exercise aimed at simulating an invasion of Iran, of the sort permitted by the Iran-USSR friendship treaty in case an outside force (such as the United States) violates Iran's sovereignty (*New York Times*, 12-15-86).

110. *Washington Post*, 6-10-84.

111. *Rebel*, 11-22-83.

112. Ibid.

113. *Washington Post*, 10-24-86; *Miami Herald*, 10-11-86.

114. *New York Times*, 1-16-87; *MidEast Report*, 12-19-86.

115. *New York Times*, 11-17-86.

116. *San Francisco Chronicle*, 11-29-86. For indications that the plan may have been put into effect, see *People's Daily World*, 2-13-87.

117. *New York Times*, 11-9-86.

118. *Rebel*, 11-22-83.

119. *Washington Post*, 12-2-86.

120. *Washington Post,* 11-8-86; *New York Times* 12-6-86.

121. *San Jose Mercury*, 12-12-86.

122. Col Charlie Beckwith and Donald Knox, *Delta Force*, 193.

123. AP, 11-11-86.

Footnotes to Chapter VIII

1. *The Tower Commission Report* (hereafter *TCR*) (NY: Bantam Books, 1987), p. 98.

2. The evidence is limited by the failure of the Israeli government to cooperate with U.S. investigations to date. The Tower Commission reported, "The government of Israel was asked to make certain individuals available in any way that would be convenient to them. They declined to do so. They agreed to answer written interrogatories. We dispatched those to the government of Israel but no response has, as yet, been received." *TCR*, p. 18.

3. *New York Times*, 11-22-86.

4. *New York Times*, 1-18-87.

5. *Ha'aretz*, 11-18-86.

6. *New York Times*, 11-8-86.

7. Amiram Nir, quoted in memorandum by Craig Fuller, an aide to George Bush (*San Jose Mercury*, 2-8-87).

8. "Israel: Foreign Intelligence and Security Services," March 1979 CIA report reprinted in *Counterspy*, May-June 1982.

9. Bishara Bahbah, "Arms Sales: Israel's Link to the Khomeini Regime," *Washington Report on Middle East Affairs*, January 1987, p. 10.

10. Rene Theberge, "Iran: Ten Years After the 'White Revolution'," *MERIP Reports*, no. 18 (June 1973), 19.

11. *Observer*, 2-2-86; *New York Times*, 4-1-86.

12. Thus Iran's air force commander, Gen. Mohammed Khatemi, deposited some of his commission payments—really bribes—in the Swiss Israel Trade Bank of Geneva (*Washington Post*, 1-27-80).

13. Christopher Payne, unpublished ms.

14. *Davar*, 11-29-85.

15. *London Times*, 12-1-86.

16. *Observer*, 11-30-86.

17. *Davar* 11-29-85; *Washington Post*, 12-14-86. Although Nimrodi was a high-ranking Mossad agent, the head of the Mossad mission in the last days of the Shah was apparently Uri Lubrani, former Israeli ambassador to Ethiopia

(Ledeen and Lewis, *Debacle*, 125).

18. *Israel & Palestine*, June 1986, 16-17; *San Francisco Examiner*, 11-28-86; *San Francisco Chronicle*, 11-12-86.

19. *Ha'aretz*, 11-21-86.

20. *Ha'aretz*, 12-5-86.

21. *Los Angeles Times*, 1-25-87.

22. *Ha'aretz*, 11-28-86.

23. *New York Times*, 2-1-87, referring to a 1985 deal.

24. Former Israeli air force commander, Gen. Mordechai Hod, gave a public hint of official policy in an interview with the Israeli newspaper Ma'ariv on September 25, 1980. After raising the possibility that Iran's air force would collapse, he suggested "an Israeli initiative toward a rapprochement with (Iranian President) Bani-Sadr to offer him the aid which we alone are capable of furnishing him" (quoted in *Executive Intelligence Review*, 10-14-80).

25. *Los Angeles Times*, 1-25-87.

26. *Time*, 7-25-83; *Middle East*, January 1982.

27. "Israel's Foreign Policy: The End of an Illusion," reprinted in *Al Fajr*.

28. *New York Times*, 11-22-86.

29. Contract reproduced in "Documents on Israeli Arms Supplement for Ayatollah Khomeini," extracted from *Mujahed*, issue no. 159, July 7, 1983. Nimrodi claims to have had no dealings with the Khomeini regime, and "informed observers" say Nimrodi believes the above cited contract "was forged by pro-Iranian groups bent on incriminating Israel and himself in illicit arms dealings" (*Jerusalem Post*, 12-1-86).

30. *Observer*, 11-30-86.

31. *Washington Post*, 12-21-86.

32. *Sunday Times*, (London), 7-26-81; *Middle East*, January 1982.

33. *San Francisco Chronicle*, 11-29-86; cf. *Washington Post*, 12-1-86.

34. *San Francisco Chronicle*, 11-29-86.

35. *Washington Post*, 5-28-82.

36. *Wall Street Journal*, 11-28-86. Note the similarity to the CIA's false "admission" to Robert Kennedy that Mafia-backed plots to assassinate Fidel Castro had been initiated in the past but were no longer underway. Likewise, the CIA took the Kennedy's failure to complain about plots of which they had no knowledge as evidence of approval.

37. Ibid., (including the Paul Cutter and Gen. Bar Am cases).

38. Besides the air shipments, Israel made good use of sea routes for heavy loads. The Danish Sailors Union handled at least 3,600 tons of Israeli arms bound for Iran (*Los Angeles Times*, 11-17-86; *New York Times*, 11-9-86). Washington was not informed of these shipments, nor of Jonathan Jay Pollard's espionage mission for Israel to turn up U.S. studies of foreign missile systems that "might be available for sale to Iran" (*Newsday*, 8-21-86). Pollard focused on Cactus, the South African version of the French Crotale missile (*Israeli Foreign Affairs*, October 1986). The sensitivity of this assignment was shown by the fact that Pollard called his wife soon after his arrest, asking her to destroy

the "cactus."

39. *Boston Globe*, 10-21-82.

40. *Washington Post*, 5-28-82; *Boston Globe*, 10-23-82.

41. *Jerusalem Post*, 11-25-86.

42. *Observer*, 9-29-85.

43. *New York Times*, 3-8-82, 11-23-86.

44. *Aerospace Daily*, 8-18-82.

45. *Israel and Palestine*, June 1986, 16-17.

46. *Newsweek*, 12-8-86.

47. *Newsweek*, 1-28-85.

48. *Dagens Nyheter* (Stockholm), 6-16-86. There is a South African connection here. Schmitz also reportedly arranged the sale of South African explosives to Iran, and used Danish shipping companies that had previously been implicated in smuggling arms to South Africa.

49. *World Press Review*, October 1985.

50. *Washington Post*, 1-12-87.

51. *Time*, 12-22-86.

52. *New York Times*, 12-6-86.

53. On his escapades with Italian intelligence see Chapter IV. "Secrecy is often required," he has argued, "not because we have anything to be ashamed of, but because those who are actually doing the fighting wish for reasons of their own to keep our relationship secret" (Michael Ledeen, "Fighting Back," *Commentary*, August, 1985).

54. *New Statesman*, 12-6-86.

55. *Washington Post*, 2-2-87; *Washington Report on Middle East Affairs*, March 1987.

56. Senate Select Committee on Intelligence, Report on Preliminary Inquiry Into the Sale of Arms to Iran and Possible Diversion of Funds to the Contras (January 29, 1987), 3. Hereafter cited as SSCI.

57. *Chicago Tribune*, 11-16-86.

58. Ledeen denies that he brought up the question of hostages.

59. McFarlane described Schwimmer as "a Jewish American who provides lots of money to Peres" (*TCR*, p. 526). Schwimmer's expertise in using offshore dummy companies and friendly foreign governments (Somoza's Nicaragua) for arms smuggling dated back to 1948 (Leonard Slater, *The Pledge* (Simon and Schuster, 1970), p. 223.

60. *Ha'aretz*, 12-5-86.

61. *London Times*, 12-1-86.

62. *TCR*, p. 111. Gazit was a participant at the 1979 Jerusalem Conference on International Terrorism (see Chapter X).

63. *TCR*, p. 24

64. *Ha'aretz*, 12-5-86; *Los Angeles Times*, 12-6-86.

65. Ibid.; *TCR*, p. 529.

66. *New York Times*, 12-11-86.

67. *Wall Street Journal*, 11-13-86.

68. *Los Angeles Times*, 12-28-86; *New York Times*, 1-17-87; *TCR*, p. 24. Deputy CIA Director John McMahon cabled Casey in January 1986: "Everyone at HQ is opposed to weapons support and intelligence transfer because the Principal (Ghorbanifar) is a liar and we will be aiding and abetting the wrong people" (*Wall Street Journal*, 2-26-87).

69. *New York Times*, 1-31-87.

70. Quote from CIA memorandum. *TCR*, p. 208.

71. *Washington Times*, 12-3-86.

72. *Boston Globe*, 12-14-86; *Los Angeles Times*, 12-28-86; *Washington Post*, 2-12-87.

73. SSCI, p. 23.

74. SSCI, p. 32, referring to Amiram Nir, special adviser on terrorism to Prime Minister Peres.

75. *San Francisco Chronicle*, 1-31-87. Ghorbanifar made similarly false hit-team allegations in March and December 1985 in order to curry favor with the administration while pursuing his arms deals (*TCR*, p. 204).

76. *New York Times*, 1-11-87; *Tribune* (Oakland), 1-12-87. The Tower Commission wrongly dated these meetings from January 1985, but even its chronology makes clear that Israel's moves predated Ledeen's exploratory mission (*TCR*, p. 208).

77. *New York Times*, 2-1-87.

78. *TCR*, pp. 106-107. Shackley apparently passed his report first to Vernon Walters, former CIA deputy director and the roving ambassador who lined up Argentine assistance to the contras in 1981 (*TCR*, p. 521). Note that Ghorbanifar also tried to interest the United States through another alleged CIA agent, William Herrmann (*San Francisco Chronicle*, 12-29-86).

79. *New York Times*, 1-16-87.

80. *TCR*, p. 123. To further complicate the picture, Iranian sources in Europe reportedly claim that Ledeen had met Ghorbanifar in October 1984 and again in April 1985, suggesting that he was an active manipulator of Washington policy rather than a passive transmitter of Israeli suggestions *Washington Report on Middle East Affairs*, March 1987).

81. *New York Times*, 1-31-87.

82. *TCR*, pp. 135, 150, 286, 83. Casey noted in a memo that "Peres and (Defense Minister) Rabin have put their reputation on the Ghorbanifar connection" (*TCR*, p. 377).

83. Cf. *Los Angeles Times*, 11-27-86; *New York Times*, 11-22-86, 11-26-86.

84. Ibid.

85. *London Times*, 12-1-86.

86. *New York Times*, 12-23-86.

87. *Washington Post*, 12-5-86.

88. *New York Times*, 11-26-86; *Los Angeles Times*, 11-27-86.

89. *Chicago Tribune*, 8-3-86.

90. *Israeli Foreign Affairs*, June 1986.

91. *New York Times*, 11-26-86.

92. *MidEast Report*, 12-19-86.

93. *TRC*, p. 23.

94. *New York Times*, 12-11-86.

95. *Los Angeles Times*, 1-11-87.

96. *San Francisco Chronicle*, 11-21-86.

97. *New York Times*, 1-11-87, 1-17-87.

98. SSCI, p. 2.

99. *TRC*, p. 124; SSCI Report, p. 4.

100. Ibid.

101. The two reportedly had helped secure Pentagon funding for private "think-tank" studies that buttressed their case for the Israeli-brokered arms deals with Iran. (*Ta Nea*, 12-2-86; *MidEast Markets*, 12-8-86; *New York Times*, 11-27-86; *Los Angeles Times*, 12-13-86.

102. *TRC*, p. 112-14.

103. *TCR*, pp. 21, 116.

104. *TCR*, p. 22; *Los Angeles Times*, 12-28-86.

105. *TCR*, p. 118.

106. He came twice, on July 3 and August 2 (*Wall Street Journal*, 11-10-86, 11-13-86; *San Francisco Chronicle*, 11-20-86; *New York Times*, 11-22-86; *Time*, 12-22-86).

107. *San Francisco Chronicle*, 11-24-86.

108. *Los Angeles Times*, 12-28-86.

109. *Time*, 12-22-86.

110. *Wall Street Journal*, 11-13-86.

111. SSCI, p. 5; TCR, pp. 25-26.

112. SSCI, p. 5; TCR, P. 26.

113. SSCI, p. 5.

114. SSCI, p. 6, 8.

115. *Time*, 1-19-87.

116. SSCI, p. 6.

117. SSCI, pp. 6-7.

118. *New York Times*, 12-6-86; *Time*, 12-22-86.

119. SSCI, p. 7.

120. *New York Times*, 11-14-86; *San Francisco Chronicle*, 11-21-86; *TRC*, p. 151.

121. SSCI, p. 10-13. The CIA official who oversaw this operation, Duane Clarridge, had previously run the contra program. As noted above, he probably knew Ledeen from their days in Rome together in the 1970s.

122. One notorious arms operation apparently sanctioned by the Israeli government resulted in the April 1986 arrest of a former Israeli general and co-conspirators of several other nationalities, including Khashoggi's London-based lawyer. Their several schemes, taken together, would have supplied Iran with nearly $2.6 billion in U.S. arms, including sophisticated jet aircraft. The

plot leader said in one conversation taped by undercover agents that authority for the deal went "right through to Peres" (*Chicago Tribune* 4-24-86).

Significantly, too, Israeli intelligence handlers at exactly this time were using their civilian Pentagon spy, Jonathan Jay Pollard, to produce a report, based on classified U.S. secrets, on missile systems that "might be available for sale to Iran" (*Jerusalem Post,* quoted in *Baltimore Sun,* 12-27-86).

Even to this day, despite all the publicity around Irangate, the Israeli trade with Iran apparently continues to flourish:

"Each week for the past two years an Iranian agent attached to [Iran's London arms] procurement office has delivered a list of needed supplies to the military attache at the Israeli embassy in London. High-level Iranian diplomatic sources say the list is then transmitted to Tel Aviv and fed through an Israeli armed forces computer, which tracks where parts and weapons are available. The data are transmitted back to the Iranian agent in London for forwarding to Tehran. Israel is said to get 10%-to-20% commission on each contract" (*Business Week,* 12-29-86).

123. SSCI Report, 14; *Time,* 12-22-86; *London Times,* 12-1-86; *San Francisco Chronicle,* 1-12-87. Weinberger pointed out in the December 7 meeting that "attempting to keep it on a clandestine basis would leave us open to blackmail of the very most elementary kind by the people who knew about it, that is, the Israelis and also Iranians, and that any time they weren't getting what they wanted, they could in one way or another, in Mideast fashion, go public with it and cause all kinds of problems with it..." (*TCR,* p. 185).

124. *TCR,* p. 37.

125. Note that despite Ledeen's subsequent claims to have opposed arms-for-hostage deals, he is said by McFarlane to have proposed sending Tehran Phoenix air-to-air missiles, among the most lethal arms in the U.S. arsenal (*TCR,* p. 174-75). Ledeen was cut out of the official picture once U.S. officials began to suspect he was profiting on the side from the arms deals along with Schwimmer, Nimrodi and Ghorbanifar (*TCR,* pp. 237-39, 254; North memo on p. 253 notes "$50/missile to Ledeen"). Ledeen denies any financial gain. But he would stay meddling in the arms operation almost to the bitter end, at least until October 1986 (SSCI Report, p. 35).

126. SSCI, p. 15. Note that Ledeen would stay involved in the arms operation almost to the bitter end, at least until October 1986 (SSCI, p. 35).

127. *TCR,* pp. 193, 196.

128. *Tribune* (Oakland), 1-11-87; TCR, p. 38.

129. *Los Angeles Times,* 1-14-87.

130. *TCR,* pp. 37, 213-14, 202.

131. January 17, 1986 memo reprinted in *San Francisco Chronicle,* 1-10-87.

132. *TCR,* p. 38.

133. Ibid.

134. *New York Times,* 12-23-86, 12-24-86; *Los Angeles Times,* 12-20-86.

135. *TCR,* pp. 41, 43.

136. SSCI, p. 43; *Los Angeles Times*, 1-12-87; *New York Times*, 1-19-87; *TCR*, p. 53.

137. *TCR*, p. 52.

138. *San Francisco Chronicle*, 1-10-87; *Tribune* (Oakland), 1-11-87.

139. SCCI, p. 42.

140. SCCI, p. 44.

141. SCCI, p. 22

142. *TCR*, p. 257. Ghorbanifar claims Hakim tried to get him to quit the field by issuing phony instructions from President Reagan. *TCR*, p. 266.

143. *Wall Street Journal*, 12-5-86.

144. *South*, Jan. 1987, p. 22; cf. *Wall Street Journal*, 11-24-86.

145. *New York Post*, 11-29-86; cf. SSCI Report, p. 24.

146. *Guardian* 12-31-86.

147. *San Francisco Chronicle*, 1-28-87.

148. *Yedi'ot Aharonot*, 12-5-86.

149. *San Francisco Examiner*, 3-4-87; *Wall Street Journal*, 3-5-87; *New York Times*, 3-18-87.

150. *San Francisco Examiner*, 1-8-87; *New York Times*, 1-9-87; *Tribune* (Oakland), 1-11-87; SCCI, p. 22. Israeli officials were no less active on the other side of the deal. Evidence indicates that they were "helping out Ghorbanifar financially" and supplying other arms on the side to Iran (SCCI, pp. 22-23).

151. *Wall Street Journal*, 1-22-87.

152. SCCI, pp. 32-35.

153. *New York Times*, 12-7-86.

154. *New York Times*, 11-23-86.

155. *New York Times*, 1-17-87.

Footnotes to Chapter IX

1. *The Defense Monitor*, XIV (1985), no. 2.

2. Aaron Bank, *From OSS to Green Berets* (Novato, Ca: Presidio Press, 1986); John Prados, *President's Secret Wars* (NY: William Morrow, 1986), p. 89; *NACLA Report on the Americas*, July/August 1986 (on James Burnham's contribution to the doctrine of political-subversive warfare in East Europe).

3. *Nation*, 7-7-84; *Washington Post*, 3-24-85 (Green Berets in Honduras); *Miami Herald* 12-19-82 (Delta Force in Honduras).

4. *St. Louis Post Dispatch* 6-17-85; *Newsweek*, 4-22-85.

5. *The Defense Monitor*, op. cit.

6. *New York Times*, 11-26-86.

7. Michael Klare, "The New U.S. Strategic Doctrine," *Nation*, 1-4-86.

8. *New York Times*, 1-6-86.

9. The fiscal 1981 special operations budget was $440 million. The administration is asking for $2.5 billion in fiscal 1988 (Report of the Secretary of Defense Caspar W. Weinberger to the Congress, January 12, 1987, p. 296; cf *Washington Post*, 8-6-86.

10. *Armed Forces Journal International*, January 1986, p. 38; *The Defense Monitor*, op. cit.

11. Quoted in "A Plan of War for Central America," Resource Center Bulletin (Albuquerque), 1986.

12. Remarks to Association of Newspaper Editors, April 20, 1961, quoted in *The Pentagon Papers* (Gravel Edition), II (Boston: Beacon Press, 1975), 33-34. Special Forces units saw a six-fold growth under Kennedy, from 1961-63 (McClintock I, 20).

13. *New York Times*, 6-1-82; *New York Times*, 11-26-86.

14. *The Defense Monitor*, XIV, no. 2, 1985.

15. *Los Angeles Times*, 11-18-84. Lt. Col. Richard Brawn wrote of their mission, "Low-intensity conflict is a pseudonym for a war without full political support - a war without the needed political will" (*Boston Globe*, 7-10-86). An Army study in August 1986 concluded disparagingly, "As a nation, we do not understand low-intensity conflict, we respond without unity of effort; we execute our activities poorly; and we lack the ability to sustain operations"

(*New York Times*, 11-26-86). Military officers have resisted bureaucratic restructuring of special operations units "in part out of a fear that such an arrangement would make it too easy for civilian leaders to send the commandos into action," according to the *New York Times*. Many officers "believe that under the present arrangement, the cautious nature of the military serves as 'a brake' on precipitate use of special forces" (*New York Times*, 1-6-86).

16. *New York Times*, 6-8-84.

17. *The Pentagon Papers*, II, 641-3; Simpson, 145.

18. Shelby Stanton, *Green Berets at War* (SF: Presidio Press, 1985), 31.

19. Stanton, *Green Berets at War*, 37.

20. Charles Simpson, *Inside the Green Berets* (Novato, Ca: Presidio Press, 1983), p. 146. Former Air Force Colonel and CIA liaison Fletcher Prouty writes, "The important thing to understand is that the much-heralded office of SACSA had very few military responsibilities. It was almost entirely CIA oriented. Most of its dealings with the services were in areas in which the CIA was most active" (Prouty, *The Secret Team* (Englewood Cliffs: Prentice Hall, 1973), 407. The recommendation for the shift of authority to the military came from the local CIA station chief, John Richardson, to the head of the Far East Division, Desmond Firzgerald, based on a 1961 National Security Action Memorandum, which "stated in essence that whenever a secret paramilitary operation became so large and overt that the military contribution, in terms of manpower and equipment, exceeded the resources contributed by the CIA, the operation should be turned over to the Department of Defense" (Stanton, *Green Berets at War*, 51).

21. Peter Dale Scott, *The War Conspiracy* (Indianapolis: Bobbs Merrill, 1972), 54, 159-60; Charles Simpson, *Inside the Green Berets* 114; Prados, *Presidents' Secret Wars*, 248-9, 299-303.

22. James William Gibson, *The Perfect War* (Boston: Atlantic Monthly Press, 1986), 298-305; Noam Chomsky and Edward S. Herman, *The Washington Connection and Third World Fascism*, I (Boston: South End Press, 1979), 322-328.

23. *Philadelphia Inquirer*, 11-25-84.

24. As one member of the Senate Select Committee on Intelligence told an interviewer, "We are aware of the existence of the special operations units but not sufficiently informed about their activities or their connection to intelligence operations. We are trying to learn more" (*New York Times*, 6-8-84, quote from Sen. Joseph Biden, D-Del).

25. *New York Times*, 4-22-86.

26. Some of these, in Vietnam, apparently were SOG infiltrations of North Vietnam.

27. The money may have paid for Air Force personnel stationed illegally in Laos and other locations in the guise of civilian employees of Lockheed Aircraft Systems. This practice is known as "sheep dipping." (*Oklahoman*, 10-5-86). Richard Secord would certainly have been "witting" of this practice, which was prevalant at the time of his 1968 tour of duty.

28. *Miami Herald*, 2-10-83, 6-28-83; *New York Times*, 10-24-83.

29. After one probe of a special operations front, Business Security International, which supported "classified, sensitive special operations units" involved in "military and foreign intelligence missions," the Army relieved three high ranking colonels of their duties and imprisoned the former head of the Special Operations Division. Yet one of their secret Swiss bank accounts remained open after the unit was disbanded in 1983, and was apparently used by North and Secord to fund the contras in 1985. The allegations included embezzlement, drugs and prostitution. Another investigation resulted in the discipline of some 80 members of the Delta Force, a full quarter of the unit, for financial irregularities (*Washington Post*, 8-22-85; *San Francisco Chronicle*, 10-19-84; *San Jose Mercury*, 2-17-87; *New York Times*, 4-22-87).

30. *Washington Post*, 11-29-85.

31. This was accomplished under an accounting arrangement known as "Parasol-Switchback" (Simpson, 165; Prados 253).

32. Stilwell headed the Far East division of the CIA's Office of Policy Coordination, to which the NSC assigned all unconven-tional warfare responsibilities (John Prados, *Presidents' Secret Wars*, 35-36, 63). Recently he sat on the advisory committee of Americares Foundation which provides private aid to Central America. (Tom Barry and Deb Preusch, *The Central America Fact Book*, (Grove Press, 1986) p. 97).

33. Gritz commanded the Third Mobile Strike (Mike) Force in Vietnam (Simpson, 139).

34. *St Louis Post Dispatch* 6-17-85 mentions role of Delta Force as well in Dozier rescue.

35. *New York Times*, 5-11-83, 6-8-84; *San Jose Mercury*, 5-15-83; *Newsweek*, 4-22-85; *Washington Post*, 11-29-85; *San Jose Mercury*, 2-17-87. Contrary to reports of its demise, some evidence exists that ISA survived. A memo by Oliver North from June 3, 1986 said, We already have one ISA officer in Beirut..." (*Tower Report*) p. 152.

36. Simpson, op. cit., 22.

37. *Nation*, 7-7-84. "The start" goes back nearly to 1948, when the National Security Council expanded the CIA charger to include unconventional warfare activities on behalf of resistance and guerrilla groups. The Army at first resisted the CIA's seizure of UW authority, but gradually learned to demarcate its responsibilities from those of the intelligence agency (Aaron Bank, *From OSS to Green Berets*, 146ff). Cooperation was no doubt improved by the fact that both the military Special Forces and CIA reported to the White House through the same aide, C. D. Jackson (Charles Simpson, *Inside the Green Berets*, 16).

38. *Washington Post*, 9-15-84, quoting Richard C. Lawrence.

39. *Washington Post*, 11-19-85; *Newsweek*, 12-16-85.

40. Prados, 320-1; Thomas Hauser, *Missing* (NY: Avon, 1978). One military intelligence unit implicated in the coup was the Navy's Task Force 157, for which Ed Wilson was a leading operative; see "Former CIA Agent

Implicated in DP Contract Scam," *Computerworld*, 11-16-81.

41. Senate Select Committee to Study Governmental Operations with Respect to Intelligence Activities, Staff Report, "Covert Action in Chile, 1963-1973" (WDC: U.S. GPO 1975), 26.

42. Indeed, he "was notorious during a tour of duty in Guatemala, where he worked closely with right-wing death squads—so closely, in fact, that other CIA agents working in Guatemala demanded transfers elsewhere in protest" (Volkman, *Warriors of the Night*, 349).

43. Michael McClintock, *The American Connection*, v. II (London: Zed, 1985). In Volume I McClintock notes that the commander of the Special Warfare Center at Fort Bragg, Gen. William Yarborough, had recommended training "select civilian and military personnel for clandestine training" to undertake "paramilitary, sabotage and/or terrorist activities against known Communist proponents" in Colombia (23). These recommendation were put into effect elsewhere, including Vietnam where Special Forces organized irregular units for "committing terrorism against known VC (Viet Cong) personnel" and to "conduct operations to dislodge VC-controlled officials to include assassination" (24, quoting official U.S. documents).

44. *Nation*, 7-7-84.

45. *Washington Post*, 9-15-84; *Boston Globe*, 1-3-87. Richard Gadd, a figure in the private contra supply operation, may have played a role in Elephant Herd while still at the Pentagon.

46. *The Defense Monitor*, XIV (1985) no. 2; Prados, 388.

47. *Philadelphia Inquirer*, 12-16-84. The unit was the 160th Task Force.

48. Peter Maas, *Manhunt*, 26

49. Maas, 89. According to Jack Anderson, at least four of these Special Forces veterans "had been members of the ultra-secret CIA 'A Team' that went after (Che) Guevara. Each team member wore a gold ring with 'Che' engraved on the inside" (*Santa Cruz Sentinel*, 3-29-83). In all probability, these individuals knew and had worked closely with Felix Rodriguez, the contra supply specialist working out of Ilopango air force base in El Salvador.

50. Maas, 90-1; *New York Times*, 7-14-81.

51. Maas, 66-68. On Quintero, see chapter III.

52. Goulden, 189-90, 201, 243, 273ff; *New York Times*, 7-14-81 (China Lake).

53. *Newsweek*, 3-8-82.

54. Still unexplained is the fact that two counterintelligence officers at Fort Bragg told Special Forces master sergeant Luke Thompson, one of Wilson's recruits, that "We've checked this to the top and it's legal and aboveboard," referring to the claim that Wilson's operation was CIA-sanctioned (*New York Times*, 8-26-81).

55. *New York Times*, 12-9-81; MH 9-11-78.

56. Allan Nairn, "The Contras' Little List," *Progressive*, March 1987, 24.

57. See especially *Wall Street Journal*, 2-13-87.

58. The Laos war involved both the interdiction of North Vietnamese

supply lines and the training of Hmong tribesmen by Special Forces personnel to resist the military advances of the indigenous, but North Vietnamese supported, Pathet Lao communists.

59. Maas, 26-31; *San Francisco Chronicle*, 11-24-86.

60. *Washington Post*, 11-8-86; *Newsweek*, 4-22-85; Insight, 1-12-87; *San Jose Mercury*, 12-12-86.

61. *San Jose Mercury*, 2-17-87. *Nation*, 1-17-87; *New York Times*, 4-22-87.

62. *Washington Post*, 12-12-86. Secord left after refusing to fill out a personal financial disclosure form that would have revealed his deals with Albert Hakim on the Iran-contra plots (*Philadelphia Inquirer*, 12-5-86). His fellow panel member, retired Gen. LeRoy Manor, had played a key planning role with Secord in the 1980 hostage rescue mission and, before that, in the Nugan Hand Bank.

63. *Boston Globe*, 12-30-84; *Nation*, 11-2-85; *Detroit Free Press*, 2-11-86; *New Statesman* 11-2-84; John Prados, *Presidents' Secret Wars*, 270.

64. *Washington Post*, 12-10-84; *Boston Globe*, 12-30-84; *New York Times*, 10-22-86. *The Central America Fact Book*, op. cit. p. 97.

65. *San Jose Mercury*, 12-12-86.

66. *Los Angeles Times*, 7-27-86; *Newsweek*, 11-3-86.

67. *Washington Post*, 12-5-86; *Tribune* (Oakland) 12-21-86; *San Francisco Examiner*, 2-19-87.

68. *Wall Street Journal*, 2-13-87; *San Jose Mercury*, 11-2-86; Associated Press, 11-11-86; *San Jose Mercury*, 12-12-86.

69. *San Francisco Examiner*, 2-19-87.

70. *Newsweek*, 7-12-82; Prados, 364; cf. *Private Eye*, 3-11-83. On the scouting role of Green Berets in the 1980 mission, see also *New York Times*, 12-9-81.

71. *Boston Globe*, 12-30-84; *Nation*, 11-2-85; MH 2-15-86; *Nation*, 10-6-84.

72. The Son Tay raid was led by Gen. LeRoy Manor—later a figure in the Nugan Hand Bank scandal and the 1980 Iran hostage rescue mission.

73. Rebel, 11-22-83; *Washington Post*, 12-2-83; *New York Times*, 12-15-86; Prados, 364).

74. Associated Press, 11-11-86; Col. Charlie Beckwith and Donald Knox, *Delta Force*, 193.

75. *San Francisco Chronicle*, 4-11-86; *Defense Monitor*, 1985, no. 2.

76. *Armed Forces Journal International*, January 1986, p. 39.

77. *Baltimore Sun*, 4-1-85. Koch had, in fact, been a lobbyist for the Zionist Organization of America before joining the Pentagon (Claudia Wright, *Spy, Steal and Smuggle* (Belmont, MA: AAUG Press, 1986, 15).

78. SSCI report, p. 19; *TCR*, p. 246.

79. And according to Jack Anderson, Armitage was questioned by the President's Commission on Organized Crime about his close relationship with a Vietnamese refugee linked by law enforcement officials to organized crime (*Washington Post*, 1-30-87).

80. *Washington Report on Middle East Affairs*, March 1987; *Newsweek*, 12-1-86; *New York Times*, 12-14-86, 12-23-86; *Boston Globe*, 1-11-87. Armitage sat in with Koch on the Feb. 1986 logistics meeting for the Iran arms shipments.

81. *Wall Street Journal*, 12-11-86; *New York Times*, 12-14-86.

82. *Washington Times*, 12-1-86; *New York Times*, 2-1-87; *San Francisco Examiner*, 2-2-87.

83. *Washington Times*, 12-12-86; *The New Republic*, 11-24-86; *Miami Herald*, 10-14-86; *Nation*, 7-7-84.

84. *San Francisco Examiner*, 2-19-87.

85. *New York Times*, 1-15-87.

86. *San Jose Mercury*, 1-1-87; *Nation*, 1-17-87.

87. Along with Secord, he is also reported to have played some role in the Army's controversial Intelligence Support Activity (*San Jose Mercury*, 2-17-87).

88. House Armed Services Committee press release, August 5, 1985.

89. *Armed Forces Journal International*, August 1986, p. 12.

90. Section 1 (16), S.2453, "A bill to enhance the capabilities of the United States to combat terrorism and other forms of unconventional warfare;" cf. *Armed Forces Journal International*, June 1986, p. 18.

91. *Congressional Record*, May 15, 1986.

92. *Armed Forces Journal International*, January 1986, 42.

93. Conference Report to Accompany H.J. Res. 738 (WDC: U.S.GPO 1986), 128ff.

94. *U.S. News and World Report* 1-19-87.

95. *Inside the Pentagon*, 1-1-87.

Footnotes to Chapter X

1. *Washington Post*, 2-22-87, 2-24-87.
2. The *Tribune* (Oakland), 2-27-87.
3. See excerpts from press conference, *New York Times*, 2-27-87.
4. *TCR*, p. 3.
5. Ibid. p. 98.
6. *San Jose Mercury*, 10-16-86.
7. Jay Peterzell, "Legal and Constitutional Authority for Covert Operations," *First Principles*, X (Spring 1985), 1-3.
8. Ibid.
9. *New York Times*, 5-2-76.
10. *New York Times*, 5-12-76.
11. *San Francisco Chronicle*, 3-11-80. One operation not reported to Congress by Carter also involved Iran—the escape of six U.S. diplomats in Tehran who had hidden in the Canadian embassy (*Washington Post*, 3-3-80).
12. *New York Times*, 1-11-80.
13. *Washington Post*, 2-22-80.
14. *Washington Post*, 3-26-80. Perhaps the media's role in obscuring the realities involved and the public's doubt that any opinion it might have will be heard and acted upon have something to do with the public's not being eager to spend much time addressing the matter. After all, the purpose of the secrecy was, in the first place, largely preventing the public from knowing enough to have any opinion at all.
15. Jay Peterzell, "Can Congress Really Check the CIA?" *First Principles* VIII (May-June 83), 3.
16. John Ranelagh, *The Agency* (New York: Simon and Schuster, 1986), 660.
17. *Los Angeles Times*, 4-19-84.
18. *New York Times*, 5-14-84.
19. *New York Times*, 10-1-85 cf. *Congressional Quarterly Weekly*, March 7, 1987, pp. 411-13. After Oliver North misinformed the House intelligence committee about the extent of his efforts on behalf of the contras, his boss Admiral Poindexter remarked, "Well done" (*New York Times*, 2-27-87).

20. *New York Times*, 5-28-82.

21. *New York Times*, 5-14-84.

22. Jonathan Marshall, "Drugs and United States Foreign Policy," *Dealing With Drugs* (Forthcoming, Lexington Books, 1987).

23. *Washington Post*, 3-10-80.

24. Perhaps the first significant warning of the narcoterrorist threat came in 1974 from Argentina's Minister of Social Welfare, Jose Lopez Rega. Speaking on television to publicize the collaboration of his country and the United States in drug enforcement, Lopez Rega announced, "Guerrillas are the main users of drugs in Argentina. Therefore, the anti-drug campaign will automatically be an anti-guerrilla campaign as well." The deadly irony was that Lopez Rega was himself a terrorist (the organizer of the Argentine Anticommunist Alliance death squad) and on prominent cocaine trafficker. See Jonathan Marshall, "Drugs and United States Foreign Policy," op. cit. Michael Ledeen, a chief protagonist in this strategy of tension, joined the narco-terrorist bandwagon with his accusation that the Sandinistas were masterminding "a vast drug and arms-smuggling network to finance their terrorists and guerrillas, flooding our country with narcotics" (*New York Times*, 4-16-84). See chapter IV.

25. Philip Paull, "The Jerusalem Connection," unpublished ms., 1981. One of the Israelis in attendance was former military intelligence director Shlomo Gazit, who led the Israeli group that persuaded the Reagan administration in 1985 to enter the arms for hostages deal with Iran. *TCR*, p. 111.

26. *Wall Street Journal*, 7-26-79. The conference results were, in effect, written up by Robert Moss in "Terror: A Soviet Export," *New York Times Magazine*, 11-2-80. Four months later the same magazine ran another article on the identical subject by fellow conference participant Claire Sterling.

27. *Jerusalem Post*, 1-18-82.

28. *New York Times*, 4-21-81.

29. *New York Times*, 5-3-81.

30. *Washington Post*, 1-29-81.

31. Claire Sterling, "Terrorism: Tracing the International Network," *New York Times Magazine*, 3-1-81, 19).

32. Clare Sterling, *The Terror Network*, (NY: Holt, Rhinehart, and Winston, 1981), p. 2.

33. *New York Times*, 3-29-81, 10-18-81.

34. *New York Times*, 5-3-81.

35. Edward Herman and Frank Brodhead, *The Rise and Fall of the Bulgarian Connection* (NY: Sheridan Square Publications, 1986), 135-136.

36. *New York Times*, 2-9-81.

37. Blaine Harden, "Terrorism" *Washington Post Magazine*, 3-15-81 p. 16.

38. *New York Times*, 4-27-81.

39. *New York Times*, 4-24-81.

40. *Washington Post*, 2-7-81. Cf. Michael Ledeen and Arnaud de Borchgrave, "Terrorism and the KGB," *Washington Post*, 2-17-81, p. 19: "Given the crisis of the American intellligence community, our allies may not be sharing all

their information." The message was clear: Congress should cut back on its oversight to restore the confidence of allies in the CIA's ability to keep secrets.

41. Harden, op. cit., p. 21; *Washington Post*, 5-16-81. Ledeen was to share an office with Vernon Walters, whose main job seemed to be to restore good relations with the military dictatorships of Argentina, Guatemala and other countries whose murderous policies had provoked cutoffs of U.S. aid in the 1970s.

42. *Wall Street Journal*, 4-9-81.

43. *Washington Star*, 2-13-81.

44. *New York Times*, 2-19-81.

45. *New York Times*, 4-6-81. See chapter IV.

46. *Washington Post*, 2-21-81.

47. *New York Times*, 4-21-81.

48. *Baltimore Sun*, 3-13-81.

49. *Wall Street Journal*, 10-16-81.

50. *Washington Star*, 3-17-81.

51. *Miami Herald*, 3-13-81.

52. *New York Times*, 6-11-84, 9-30-84, 7-7-76; Joseph Lelyveld, "The Director," *New York Times Magazine*, 1-20-85.

53. *New Republic*, 3-7-81.

54. *Washington Post*, 9-22-81.

55. *San Jose Mercury*, 10-26-81.

56. *Corriere della sera*, 10-27-81.

57. *Newsweek*, 11-9-81.

58. More likely, the man who shot and wounded him was Chapman's unhappy Moroccan lover (*New Statesman*, 12-25-81).

59. *Tribune* (Oakland), 11-16-81.

60. *Philadelphia Bulletin*, 11-22-81.

61. *Newsweek*, 11-30-81.

62. *Miami Herald*, 12-11-81.

63. *Washington Post*, 12-8-81.

64. *Washington Post*, 12-7-81.

65. *Washington Post*, 12-8-81.

66. *Washington Post*, 12-8-81.

67. *Miami Herald*, 12-25-81.

68. *San Francisco Chronicle*, 1-31-87.

69. *Los Angeles Times*, 12-12-81. Jack Anderson added that the chief source "demanded $500,000 for his information" and "provided the names of some buddies in Beirut who would be willing to sell information on the drug traffic. The CIA recognized some of them as hustlers who had been peddling phony documents for years...Some of the informers are known to have connections with Israeli intelligence, which would have its own reasons to encourage a U.S.-Libyan rift" (*Washington Post*, 1-7-82).

70. *New York Times*, 3-10-81.

71. *New York Times*, 11-5-81.

72. *New York Times*, 12-5-81.

73. *New York Times*, 12-3-86, 2-19-87, 2-21-87; *Los Angeles Times*, 12-5-86, 2-11-87.

74. *New York Times*, 12-7-81, emphasis added.

75. *New York Times*, 6-6-84; cf *Tribune* (Oakland), 12-29-83 on the renewed enthusiasm of the military chiefs for special operations forces.

76. Senator William Cohen defended his bill (passed in late 1986) to ensure representation on the NSC and in the Pentagon of SOF advocates, as "necessary to ensure that counterterrorist and counterinsurgency operations are properly integrated into the overall framework of U.S. policy" (Congressional Record, 5-15-86). His S2453 was entitled, "A bill to enhance the capabilities of the United States to combat terrorism and other forms of unconventional warfare."

77. *Los Angeles Times*, 4-15-84; *San Francisco Examiner*, 4-22-84; *San Jose Mercury*, 2-22-87 (North).

78. Jeff McConnell, "The Counterterrorists at the Fletcher School," *Boston Review*, August 1986, p. 20.

79. *Tribune*, 6-25-84.

80. *New York Times*, 6-6-84.

81. William Casey, "International Terrorism," *Vital Speeches*, 9-15-85, p. 713.

82. *New York Times*, 6-19-85.

83. As just one example, the Tower Commission reported that "From January to March 1986, LtCol. North received fifteen encryption devices from the National Security Agency for us in transmitting classified messages in support of his counterterrorist activities. Those devices enabled LtCol. North to establish a private communication network. He used them to communicate outside of the purview of other government agencies, with members of the private contra support effort" (*TCR*, p. 462).

84. *San Jose Mercury*, 2-22-87.

85. *Wall Street Journal*, 2-20-87.

86. Ibid.; *Time* 2-2-87. Clarridge knew much about terrorism. He had planned the mining of Nicaragua's harbors with North and had approved issuance of the notorious CIA guerrilla warfare manual advocating selective assassinations of civilians as an appropriate tactic for the contras (*New York Times*, 1-21-87; *San Francisco Chronicle*, 2-9-87).

87. *San Francisco Examiner*, 2-19-87; *Wall Street Journal*, 2-20-87.

88. *San Jose Mercury*, 2-22-87.

89. *Newsweek*, 3-2-87.

90. *San Jose Mercury*, 2-22-87. North was reportedly put in charge of the Iran arms operation "with logistical help from a newly created CIA counterterrorism office. The elaborate plan kept the administration's top officials in the dark" (*Wall Street Journal*, 12-18-86).

91. *New York Times*, 1-3-87, 12-22-86, 1-27-87; *Wall Street Journal*, 3-5-85. On Koch, see chapter IX.

92. *TCR*, p. 47, 246, 266, 376.
93. *San Jose Mercury*, 3-8-87.
94. *Time*, 2-2-87.
95. *TCR*, p. 536.
96. Ibid. p. 205.
97. Ibid. p. 202-06, 240.
98. James Bamford, "Carlucci and the NSC," *New York Times Magazine* 1-18-87.
99. *Washington Times*, 2-3-87.
100. *Congressional Quarterly Weekly*, March 7, 1987, pp. 414-15.

Footnotes to Chapter XI

1. Such a sweeping hypothesis cannot be argued here. Cf. Perry Anderson, *Passages from Antiquity to Feudalism* (London: Verso, 1978), pp. 29-103 (Athens, Rome); *Lineages of the Absolutist State* (London: Verso, 1979), pp. 60-84 (Spain); Fernand Braudel, *The Mediterranean and the Mediterranean World in the Age of Philip II* (London: Collins, 1972), esp. I, 463-642 (Spain); Robert Gilpin, *U.S. Power and the Multinational Corporation: the Political Economy of Foreign Direct Investment* (New York: Basic Books, 1975) (England, United States). It is now offten forgotten that Castile was one of the first medieval kingdoms of Europe to develop a parliamentary Estates system (Anderson, *Lineages*, p. 63).

2. *Washington Post*, February 16, 1987 (see Chapter XI).

3. Although Hakim has always been presented in the press as a "private" arms dealer, we should not forget that CIA Director Casey found reason to grant him U.S. citizenship, on the CIA's quota, in 1983 (see Chapter III).

4. Predictably, the reaction of the "responsible" press to the Tower Commission report of February 1987 was to characterize it as "a depiction not of inadequate institutions but of inept stewardship" (*New York Times*, February 27, 1987). This particular bill of health for the institutional status quo came from the Times's R.W. Apple, the same man who in the midst of Watergate assured his readers that "it would not be easy in Washington to find anyone who knew [CIA Director] Dick Helms and ever doubted his word" (*The Watergate Hearings, as edited by the staff of the New York Times* [New York: Bantam, 1973], p. 57). In 1977, Helms pleaded *nolo contendere* to two misdemeanor charges of having misled the Senate Foreign Relations Committee in his testimony of February and March 1973 (Ranelagh, p. 612).

5. Nor is Congress likely, any more than during Watergate, to look at the floods of illegal foreign contributions which have helped to make

Congress what it now is (many of the more courageous critics having been exemplarily defeated by South African or South Korean funds). Cf. Chapter IV.

6. "The Talk of the Town," *The New Yorker*, February 23, 1987, p. 25. For considered thought towards a new foreign policy stance for the Democratic Party, see Sherle R. Schwenninger and Jerry W. Sanders, "The Democrats and a New Grand Strategy," *World Policy Journal* (Summer 1986, Winter 1986-87), pp. 369-418, 1-50).

7. *New York Times*, September 6, 1985; *Guardian*, October 2, 1985.

Index

About the Authors

JONATHAN MARSHALL (author of Chapters I, II, VI, VII, VIII, IX and X) is a former editor of *Inquiry*, editorial writer for the *San Jose Mercury*, and publisher of *Parapolitics/USA*. He is currently the Editorial Page Editor of the *Tribune* in Oakland, California. He has written numerous articles on U.S. foreign policy and other subjects.

PETER DALE SCOTT (author of Chapters III, IV and XI), a former Canadian diplomat, teaches English at the University of California, Berkeley. His books include: *The Politics of Escalation in Vietnam* (in collaboration); *The War Conspiriacy; The Assassinations: Dallas and Beyond* (in collaboration); and *Crime and Cover-Up*.

JANE HUNTER (author of Chapter V) is a long-time activist and the editor of the monthly *Israeli Foreign Affairs*. She is the author of *Israeli Foreign Policy: South Africa and Central America* (South End Press, 1987), as well as *Undercutting Sanctions: Israel, the U.S. and South Africa* and *No Simple Proxy: Israel in Central America*.